Union List of Geologic Field Trip Guidebooks of North America

Union List of Geologic Field Trip Guidebooks of North America

Compiled and edited by the
Geoscience Information Society
Guidebook and Ephemeral Materials Committee
Harriet E. Wallace, Chairwoman

PUBLISHED BY THE
AMERICAN GEOLOGICAL INSTITUTE
IN COOPERATION WITH THE
GEOSCIENCE INFORMATION SOCIETY

Earlier editions:

Geologic Field Trip Guidebooks of North America
A Union List Incorporating Monographic Titles

Geologic Field Trip Guidebooks of North America
A Union List Incorporating Monographic Titles

Union List of Geologic Field Trip Guidebooks of North America

Library of Congress Catalog Card Number 78-52012
International Standard Book Number 0-913312-05-3
Printed in the United States of America

American Geological Institute
5205 Leesburg Pike
Falls Church, Virginia 22041

TABLE OF CONTENTS

INTRODUCTION

One of the first projects undertaken by the Geoscience Information Society was a study to provide control of information about geologic field trip guidebooks, especially for North America. The first edition of *Geologic Field Trip Guidebooks of North America, a Union List Incorporating Monographic Titles* published in 1968 was the result of this study. In 1971 the second, revised, and expanded edition of the same title was published bringing up to date the information on guidebooks prepared for field trips held through 1970. In 1975 work was begun on a third edition in order to provide more current information. During the preparation of this volume it seemed advisable to shorten the title and to make it more precise with the result that the title of this volume is *A Union List of Geologic Field Trip Guidebooks of North America.* It incorporates and brings up to date the information in the earlier publications.

The introduction to *Geologic Field Trip Guidebooks of North America,* 1968, stated in part:

> Geologic field trip guidebooks are an important but often elusive part of the literature of geology. Frequently, the volume prepared for a field trip is out-of-print before the excursion actually takes place. Many guides are issued erratically, generally by local societies which appear and disappear, change addresses, and/or participate in joint excursions. The nature of the sponsoring organization tends to complicate distribution, collection and bibliographic control of guidebooks. The guidebooks may range from a road log consisting of a few mimeographed pages to beautifully illustrated and lavishly bound volumes with a number of articles by individual authors. It would seem that the only sure way to obtain a guidebook is to attend the field trip! Often a society itself is the only source of information on all of its publications.

Society addresses change frequently, but such changes are usually announced in *Geotimes.* The sections "Coming Up" and "Looking Back" in *Geotimes* list meetings and field conferences and for each one include the name and address of the person in charge. In addition, volume 22, number 7-8 for July-August 1977 of *Geotimes* lists all geological surveys and societies and gives the address current at that time.

The third edition continues the policy of earlier editions in restricting the coverage of guidebooks to those concerned with North American geology and the geology of the islands of Bermuda and the West Indies. For the purposes of this work, North America has been arbitrarily defined as that part of the Western Hemisphere north of the Panama Canal. The organization of the volume follows that of the previous editions. The contents contain primarily trips sponsored by a society or a survey, but a new section called "Miscellaneous" has been added to include commercial, monographic guidebooks prepared by one or more authors and depicting the geology of a small area or the geology along a highway. In all cases the primary characteristic of a guidebook for inclusion in this union list is that it must have a road log.

The new edition has been greatly revised and expanded. An attempt has been made to correct many typographical errors in the 1971 edition. For any society or survey that has had a change of name that was brought to the attention of the chairwoman, the entry is made under the current name of the organization with cross references from the previous names. Many of the societies are subsidiaries of the American Association of Petroleum Geologists, and the authority for the relationship between these organizations was their *Bulletin,* volume 58, no. 11, pt. 2, 1975, which is the annual membership issue. The relationship between organizations in this *Bulletin* issue was also used as one of the criteria for determining under which organization to place the full title of a guidebook and under which to place the "see" reference when more than one organization was involved, as so often occurs.

In order to be consistent about determining the sponsoring organization of a title for a guidebook, definite guidelines were established for new material. Priority was given to the major organization concerned in all cases.

1. If a guidebook is part of a numbered series of a state survey, bureau of mines, or a society, the title is in that series.

2. If several geological societies hold a joint field conference, and if one is a major society that has had a series of numbered field conferences, the title of the guidebook is placed under the name of the major society having the numbered series. A "see" reference is placed under the other society or societies. This choice was used primarily for the American Association of Petroleum Geologists, and the Society of Economic Paleontologists and Mineralogists, their sectional meetings, and subsidiary societies affiliated with them.

3. If several geological societies hold a joint field conference, but neither society has a numbered series of conferences, the title is placed under the name of the principle or larger organization.

4. If the title is in more than one numbered series, the title is under the names of both series.

In some cases an arbitrary decision had to be made as to the organization under which the guidebook title was included. No reference about a field conference was included under the name of a society which published a guidebook for one or more societies but which did not participate in sponsoring the field trip. One particular change was in the titles previously under the Kansas Geological Survey. None of those titles appears in the list of publications of the Kansas Geological Survey, and, therefore, they were separated and placed under the organization or group for whom the guidebook was prepared. Some titles included in the 1971 edition have been deleted, because they were not guidebooks regardless of the fact that the title included such terms as "guide," "field guide," or "guidebook." Many of the titles in the 1971 edition and many new titles submitted were checked against and information taken from the actual guidebooks in the Geology Library of the University of Illinois at Urbana-Champaign. If a particular title was not owned, the actual title page and information from the guidebook were obtained from the reporting library. No change was made unless the guidebook was seen by a member of the committee.

The authority for the symbols for libraries used in this union list is *Symbols of American Libraries,* 11th edition, 1976, Washington, D.C., Library of Congress. If a specific library was not included in this volume, a symbol was devised following the same pattern as nearly as possible, and it is shown in brackets.

The guidebooks for the Geological Society of America may be incomplete, but the Society advised that they had no record of the guidebooks prepared for field trips held in conjunction with their meetings. They also advised that guidebooks for such field trips were not to carry the Society name on the cover or title page and were not to be related to the Society meeting. It may be difficult, therefore, to provide a complete set of guidebooks of field trips held at the time of the meetings of the Geological Society of America.

Information on guidebook holdings was requested from the 327 geoscience libraries listed in the *Directory of Geoscience Libraries* published in 1974 by the Geoscience Information Society. Of these, 108 libraries responded and participated in the current edition, but 22 libraries who participated in the 1971 edition did not do so this time.

Deep appreciation is expressed to the librarians who took valuable time to submit holdings of each geoscience library. Without their efforts this volume could not have been prepared. Special gratitude is also expressed to Aphrodite Mamoulides for her efforts in obtaining the release of copyright from the former publishers. Sincere thanks are expressed to all who submitted suggestions and advice during the preparation of the volume. Thanks are also to be extended to the American Association of Petroleum Geologists for supplying information about guidebooks for field trips held in conjunction with their meetings.

The Committee has found the 1968 and 1971 editions a strong foundation upon which to build. Inconsistencies will inevitably show up in spite of the best efforts to avoid them. With the change to data bank preparation and printing by automation future revisions and editions will be easier to prepare and will appear at more frequent intervals. Please transmit your criticisms, corrections and additions to Chairperson, Guidebook and Ephemeral Materials Committee, Geoscience Information Society, c/o American Geological Institute, 5205 Leesburg Pike, Falls Church, Virginia 22041.

Harriet E. Wallace, Chairwoman
Geology Library
University of Illinois at Urbana-Champaign

Regina Brown
Orton Memorial Geology Library
Ohio State University, Columbus

Ina C. Brownridge
Library
State University of New York at Binghamton

M. Katherine L. Keener
Library
Naval Construction Battalion Center
Port Hueneme, California

Claren M. Kidd
Geology Library
University of Oklahoma, Norman

Elizabeth Loomis
Golden, Colorado

Beatrice Lukens
Earth Science Library
University of California, Berkeley

Mary W. Scott
Department of Geology
University of North Dakota,
Grand Forks

Dederick C. Ward
Geology Library
University of Colorado, Boulder

PLAN OF THE VOLUME

SAMPLES OF TITLE ENTRIES AND HOLDINGS

(2) ALABAMA ACADEMY OF SCIENCE.

1962		See Alabama. Geological Survey. (5)
1965	3rd	See Alabama Geological Society. (3)

DI-GS	1962, 65
InU	1962
NSyU	1962

(5) ALABAMA. GEOLOGICAL SURVEY. INFORMATION SERIES.

1958	No. 13	Birmingham area and celebrated coastal plain fossil locations. (102)
1960	No. 18	Selected outcrops of the Eutaw Formation and Selma Group near Montgomery, Alabama.
1962	No. 26	Selected brown iron ore deposits, Pike County, Alabama. (2)

[A-GS]	1958, 60, 62
CLU-G/G	1960, 62
CLhC	1958
CaOLU	1962
CaOWtU	1962
DI-GS	1958, 60, 62

In this volume, information on guidebooks is organized in a manner useful to geologists and librarians. Societies appear in alphabetical order, and under each organization is a chronological list of titles of individual guidebooks; first the date, then the series number, if any, and finally the title. Contrived informations is bracketed. In response to requests made by several cooperating libraries, various notes give additional information on specific titles.

Cross references

As different library holdings were sent in, it was obvious that variations in cataloging made it difficult at times to know which society was responsible for some of the guidebooks. Two types of cross references are provided. One is the standard "see" reference, sending the user to another series entry. The other reference employed is a number found in parentheses following many individual guidebook titles, referring to another participating group. (See sample entries.)

Holdings statements

At the end of the title entries for each organization is an alphabetical list of Library of Congress symbols representing libraries, followed by dates of the guidebooks which they own. When there are several guides for one year and a specific library has them all, only the date for that year is used. When only certain guides are held, then the date, followed by the month or series number, differentiates them. Occasionally other numbers have been contrived to distinguish between the holdings. If a field trip was sponsored by more than one organization, the holdings may be listed under the name of one of the organizations or under all of them, depending on the way it was reported by the libraries holding copies.

PLAN OF THE INDEX

The index is based on geographic terms derived from the titles of the trips. With some exceptions, trips are entered under state, province, or territory. The number of the reference is to the number of the sponsoring society and then the year of the trip.

As an example, guidebooks to the Rolla, Missouri, area are entered under:

Missouri

Rolla 38 - 1970(1); 41 - 1972; 181 - 1960

which leads to

(38) ASSOCIATION OF AMERICAN STATE GEOLOGISTS. GUIDEBOOKS AND ROAD LOGS.

1970	62nd	Trip 1. Guidebook to Ozark carbonate terrane, Rolla-Devils Elbow area, Missouri. Trip 2. Guide to the southeast Missouri mineral district.

and

(41) ASSOCIATION OF MISSOURI GEOLOGISTS. GUIDEBOOK TO THE ANNUAL FIELD TRIP.

1972	19th	Guidebook of the karst features and stratigraphy of the Rolla area.

and

(181) MISSOURI. GEOLOGICAL SURVEY. [MISCELLANEOUS PUBLICATION].

1960		Guidebook to the geology of the Rolla area emphasizing solution phenomena. (30)

The lists show that 38 - 1970(1) is held by two libraries, [I-GS] and OkU, which translates to the Illinois Geological Survey Library and the Geology Library of the University of Oklahoma, 41 - 1972 is held only by MoU, the Geology Library of the University of Missouri - Columbia, and 181 - 1960 is held by four libraries, IU, MoSW, NSyU, and ViBlbV.

The *Directory of Library Services* gives the addresses and loan policies of these libraries.

PARTICIPATING LIBRARIES

By Alphabetical Arrangement

Amoco Canada Petroleum Co., Ltd., Library, Calgary, Alberta	[CaACAM]
Arizona State University, Library, Science Division, Tempe, Arizona	AzTeS
Atlantic Richfield Company, Geoscience Library, Dallas, Texas	TxDaAR-T
Boise State University, Library, Boise, Idaho	IdBB
Brigham Young University, Harold B. Lee Library, Provo, Utah	UPB
Brown University, Physical Sciences Library, Providence, Rhode Island	RPB
Bryn Mawr College, Geology Library, Bryn Mawr, Pennsylvania	PBm
Calgary Public Library, Calgary, Alberta	CaAC
California Division of Mines and Geology, Library, San Francisco, California	CSfCSM
California State University, Chico, University Library, Chico, California	CChiS
Canada Institute for Scientific and Technical Information, National Research Council, Ottawa, Ontario	CaOON
Carleton University, Library, Ottawa, Ontario	CaOOCC
Chevron Oil Field Research Company, Technical Information Services Library, La Habra, California	CLhC
Colorado School of Mines, Arthur Lakes Library, Golden, Colorado	CoG
Colorado State University, The Libraries, Fort Collins, Colorado	CoFS
Columbia University, Geology Library, New York, New York	NNC
Dartmouth College, Kresge Physical Sciences Library, Hanover, New Hampshire	NhD
DeGolyer and MacNaughton Library, Dallas, Texas	TxDaDM
Earlham College, Wildman Science Library, Richmond, Indiana	InRE
Eastern New Mexico University, Library, Portales, New Mexico	NmPE
Field Museum of Natural History, Library, Chicago, Illinois	ICF
Fort Lewis College, Library, Durango, Colorado	CoDuF
Geological Survey of Alabama, Library, University of Alabama	[A-GS]
Geological Survey of Canada, Library, Ottawa, Ontario	CaOOG
Gulf Research and Development Company, Library, Pittsburgh, Pennsylvania	PPiGulf
Haileybury School of Mines, Library, Haileybury, Ontario	[CaOHaHa]
Harvard University, Geological Sciences Library, Cambridge, Massachusetts	MH-GS
Idaho State University, Library, Pocatello, Idaho	IdPI
Illinois State Geological Survey, Library, Champaign, Illinois	[I-GS]
Imperial Oil Limited, Library, Calgary, Alberta	CaACI
Indiana University, Geology Library, Bloomington, Indiana	InU
Iowa State University of Science and Technology, Library, Ames, Iowa	IaAS
Johns Hopkins University, Library, Baltimore, Maryland	MdBJ
Kentucky Geological Survey, University of Kentucky, Lexington, Kentucky	[Ky-GS]
Lakehead University, Library, Thunder Bay, Ontario	CaOPAL
Lehigh University, Mart Science and Engineering Library, Bethlehem, Pennsylvania	PBL
Library of Congress, Science and Technology Division, Washington, D.C.	DLC
Louisiana State University, Library, Baton Rouge, Louisiana	LU

McGill University, Science and Engineering Library, Montreal, Quebec	CaQMM
McMaster University, Science and Engineering Library, Hamilton, Ontario	CaOHM
Memphis State University, Herff College of Engineering Library, Memphis, Tennessee	TMM
Michigan Technological University, Library, Houghton, Michigan	MiHM
Midland County Public Library, Midland, Texas	TxMM
Milwaukee Public Museum, Reference Library, Milwaukee, Wisconsin	WM
Mississippi Geological, Economic and Topographical Survey, Library, Jackson, Mississippi	[Ms-GS]
Mobil Oil Canada, Ltd. Library, Calgary, Alberta	CaACM
Mobil Research and Development Corporation, Field Research Laboratory, Technical Information Services, Dallas, Texas	TxDaSM
Montana State University, Library, Bozeman, Montana	MtBC
National Museum of Canada, Library, Ottawa, Ontario	CaOONM
Northern Arizona University, Library, Flagstaff, Arizona	AzFU
Northwestern University, Geology Library, Evanston, Illinois	IEN
Ohio State University, Orton Memorial Library of Geology, Columbus, Ohio	OU
Oklahoma City Geological Society, Library, Oklahoma City, Oklahoma	[OkOkCGe]
Oklahoma City University, Library, Oklahoma City, Oklahoma	OkOkU
Oklahoma State University, Library, Stillwater, Oklahoma	OkS
Ontario Department of Mines Library, Toronto, Ontario	[CaOTOM]
Oregon State University, William Jasper Kerr Library, Corvallis, Oregon	OrCS
Pennsylvania Bureau of Topographic and Geological Survey, Library, Harrisburg, Pennsylvania	[P-GS]
Pennsylvania State University, Earth and Mineral Sciences Library, University Park, Pennsylvania	PSt
Princeton University, Geology Library, Princeton, New Jersey	NjP
Purdue University, Purdue Geosciences Library, West Lafayette, Indiana	InLP
Queens University, Library, Department of Geological Sciences, Kingston, Ontario	CaOKQ
Royal Ontario Museum, Library, Toronto, Ontario	CaOTRM
San Diego State University, Malcolm A. Love Library, Sciences and Engineering Library, San Diego, California	CSdS
Schlumberger Well Services, Library, Houston, Texas	TxHSW
Science Museum of Minnesota, Louis S. Headley Memorial Library, St. Paul, Minnesota	[MnSSM]
Shell Development Company, Bellaire Research Center Library, Houston, Texas	TxHSD
Smith College, Clark Science Center, Science Library, Northampton, Massachusetts	MNS
South Dakota School of Mines and Technology, Devereaux Library, Rapid City, South Dakota	SdRM
Southern Illinois University, Morris Library, Science Division, Carbondale, Illinois	ICarbS
Southern Methodist University, Science Library, Dallas, Texas	TxDaM
State University of New York at Binghamton, Science Library, Binghamton, New York	NBiSU
State University of New York, College at Oneonta, James M. Milne Library, Oneonta, New York	NOneoU
Syracuse University, Geology Branch Library, Syracuse, New York	NSyU
Texas Tech University, Library, Lubbock, Texas	TxLT
Tulsa City-County Library System, Business and Technology Dept., Tulsa, Oklahoma	OkT
United States Federal Power Commission, Library, Washington, D.C.	DFPC
United States Geological Survey, Library, Reston, Virginia	DI-GS
Universite de Montreal, Geology Library, Montreal, Quebec	CaQMU

Universite Laval, La Bibliotheque, Quebec City, Quebec	CaQQLaS
University of Alberta, Cameron Library, Edmonton, Alberta	CaAEU
University of Arizona, Science Library, Tucson, Arizona	AzU
University of British Columbia, Geological Sciences Center, Geology Reading Room, Vancouver, British Columbia	[CaBVU]
University of Calgary, Library, Calgary, Alberta	CaACU
University of California, Berkeley, Earth Sciences Library, Berkeley, California	CU-EART
University of California, Davis, Physical Sciences Library, Davis, California	[CDU]
University of California, Los Angeles, Geology-Geophysics Library, Los Angeles, California	CLU-G/G
University of Cincinnati, Geology-Geography Library, Cincinnati, Ohio	OCU
University of Colorado, Earth Science Library, Boulder, Colorado	CoU
University of Houston, Library, Houston, Texas	TxHU
University of Illinois at Chicago Circle, Science Library, Chicago, Illinois	ICIU-S
University of Illinois at Urbana-Champaign, Geology Library, Urbana, Illinois	IU
University of Iowa, Geology Library, Iowa City, Iowa	IaU
University of Kentucky, Geology Library, Lexington, Kentucky	KyU
University of Michigan, Natural Science/Natural Resources Library, Ann Arbor, Michigan	MiU
University of Minnesota, Duluth, Geology Department, Duluth, Minnesota	MnDuU
University of Minnesota, Minneapolis, Winchell Library of Geology, Minneapolis, Minnesota	MnU
University of Missouri, Columbia, Geology Library, Columbia, Missouri	MoU
University of Missouri, Rolla, Library, Rolla, Missouri	MoRM
University of Montana, Library, Missoula, Montana	MtU
University of Nebraska-Lincoln, Geology Library, Lincoln, Nebraska	NbU
University of Nevada, Las Vegas, Library, Las Vegas, Nevada	NvLN
University of Nevada, Reno, Mines Library, Reno, Nevada	NvU
University of New Brunswick, Geology Library, Fredericton, New Brunswick	CaNBFU
University of New Mexico, General Library, Albuquerque, New Mexico	NmU
University of North Carolina, Geology Library, Chapel Hill, North Carolina	NcU
University of North Dakota, Geology Branch Library, Grand Forks, North Dakota	NdU
University of Oklahoma, Geology Library, Norman, Oklahoma	OkU
University of Oregon, Science Library, Eugene, Oregon	OrU
University of Rochester, Geological Sciences Library, Rochester, New York	NRU
University of South Dakota, I. D. Weeks Library, Vermillion, South Dakota	SdU
University of Southern Colorado, Learning Resources Center Library, Pueblo, Colorado	[CoPU]
University of Tennessee, Science Library, Knoxville, Tennessee	TU
University of Texas at Austin, Geology Library, Austin, Texas	TxU
University of Texas at Dallas, Library, Richardson, Texas	TxU-Da
University of Toronto, Coleman Library, Toronto, Ontario	CaOTU
University of Utah, Science and Engineering Library, Marriott Library, Salt Lake City, Utah	UU
University of Waterloo, Engineering, Mathematics and Science Library, Waterloo, Ontario	CaOWtU
University of Western Ontario, Natural Sciences Library, London, Ontario	CaOLU
University of Wisconsin-Madison, Geology-Geophysics Library, Madison, Wisconsin	WU
University of Wisconsin-Platteville, The Karmann Library, Platteville, Wisconsin	WPlaU

University of Wyoming, Geology Library, Geology Building, Laramie, Wyoming	WyU
Virginia Polytechnic Institute and State University, Geology Library, Blacksburg, Virginia	ViBlbV
Washington State University, Science and Engineering Library, Pullman, Washington	WaPS
Washington University, Earth and Planetary Sciences Library, St. Louis, Missouri	MoSW
Wayne State University, Science Library, Detroit, Michigan	MiDW
West Texas State University, The Cornette Library, Canyon, Texas	TxCaW
Western Michigan University, Physical Sciences Library, Kalamazoo, Michigan	MiKW
Windham College, Dorothy Culbertson Marvin Memorial Library, Putney, Vermont	[VtPuW]
Yale University, Kline Science Library, New Haven, Connecticut	CtY-KS

DIRECTORY OF LIBRARY SERVICES

By Symbol Arrangement

[A-GS]

Geological Survey of Alabama
P.O. Box O
University, Ala. 35486
205-759-5721
Lends: Yes, 2 weeks.
Copying services: Photocopy ($0.10 per page); time needed depends on conditions.
Use of material on premises: Yes

AzFU

Northern Arizona University, Library
Box 6022
Flagstaff, Ariz. 86001
602-523-2171
Lends: Yes
Copying services: Photocopy, xeroxing on premises ($0.05 per page), interlibrary loan ($0.15 per page).
Use of material on premises: Yes

AzTeS

Arizona State University, Library
Science Division
Tempe, Ariz. 85281
602-965-7607
Lends: Yes
Copying services: Photocopy ($0.07 per page).
Use of material on premises: Yes

AzU

University of Arizona
Science Library
Tucson, Ariz. 85721
602-884-3706
Lends: Yes, interlibrary loan
Copying services: Photocopy, microfilm ($0.15 per page, $0.06 per exposure, $1.50 minimum for either).
Use of material on premises: Yes

CChiS

California State University, Chico
University Library
Chico, Calif. 95929
916-895-5833/5834 (Reference Dept.); 916-895-6881/6882 (Interlibrary Loan Dept.); 916-895-6501 (Circulation Dept.)
Lends: Yes
Copying services: Photocopy ($0.10 per page).
Use of material on premises: Yes

[CDU]

University of California, Davis
Physical Sciences Library
Davis, CA 95616
916-752-0348
Lends: Yes
Copying services: Photocopy ($0.10 per page), microfilm.
Use of material on premises: Yes

CLU-G/G

University of California, Los Angeles
Geology-Geophysics Library
405 Hilgard Avenue
Los Angeles, Calif. 90024
213-825-1055
Lends: Yes
Copying services: Photocopy ($0.15 per page, $5.00 minimum).
Use of material on premises: Yes

CLhC

Chevron Oil Field Research Company
Technical Information Services Library
3282 Beach Boulevard
La Habra, Calif. 90631
213-691-2241, Ext. 2500
Lends: Yes
Copying services: Photocopy, limited to 10 pages, no charge.
Use of material on premises: Yes

CSdS **San Diego State University**
Malcolm A. Love Library
Sciences and Engineering Library
San Diego, Calif. 92182
714-286-6715
Lends: Yes
Copying services: Photocopy ($0.15 per page).
Use of material on premises: Yes

CSfCSM **California Division of Mines and Geology, Library**
Ferry Building, Room 2022
San Francisco, Calif. 94111
415-557-0308
Lends: Yes
Copying services: Photocopy ($0.10 per page).
Use of material on premises: Yes

CU-EART **University of California, Berkeley**
Earth Sciences Library
230 Earth Sciences Building
Berkeley, Calif. 94720
415-642-2997
Lends: Yes
Copying services: Information available from:
Library Photographic Service
General Library
University of California, Berkeley
Berkeley, Calif. 94720
Use of material on premises: Yes

CaAC **Calgary Public Library**
616 Macleod Trail, SE
Calgary, Alberta T2G 2M2
403-268-2880
Lends: Some
Copying services: Photocopy ($0.15 per page, $1.00 minimum), microfilm ($0.25 per print, $1.00 minimum).
Use of material on premises: Yes

[CaACAM] **Amoco Canada Petroleum Co., Ltd.**
Bentall Building, Room 1024
444 7th Avenue, SW
Calgary, Alberta T2P 0Y2
403-267-0451
Lends: No
Copying services: Photocopy, no charge.
Use of material on premises: Yes

CaACI **Imperial Oil Limited, Library**
339 50th Avenue, SE
Calgary, Alberta T2G 2B3
403-259-0303
Lends: Yes, interlibrary loan only.
Copying services: Yes
Use of material on premises: With special permission only.

CaACM **Mobil Oil Canada, Ltd.**
Library, Room 2444
P.O. Box 800
Calgary, Alberta T2P 2J7
403-268-7385
Lends: Yes
Copying services: Photocopy, free up to 10 pages.
Use of material on premises: Yes

CaACU **University of Calgary, Library**
Calgary 44, Alberta T2N 1N4
403-284-5967
Lends: Yes, 2 weeks.
Copying services: Xerox ($0.10 per page).
Use of material on premises: Yes

CaAEU **University of Alberta**
Cameron Library
Edmonton, Alberta T6G 2E1
403-432-3785
Lends: Yes
Copying services: Photocopy for a fee.
Use of material on premises: Yes

[CaBVU] **University of British Columbia**
Geological Sciences Center
Geology Reading Room
Vancouver, British Columbia V6T 1W5
604-228-3766
Lends: Yes, 2 weeks.
Copying services: Photocopy for a fee.
Use of material on premises: Yes

CaNBFU **University of New Brunswick**
Geology Library
Fredericton, New Brunswick E3B 5A3
506-475-9471
Lends: Yes
Copying services: Photocopy.
Use of material on premises: Yes

CaOHM **McMaster University**
Science and Engineering Library
1280 Main Street West
Hamilton, Ontario L8S 4K1
416-525-9140, Ext. 4252
Lends: Yes
Copying services: Photocopy ($0.10 per page).
Use of material on premises: Yes

[CaOHaHa] **Haileybury School of Mines, Library**
Northern College
Haileybury, Ontario P0J 1K0
705-672-3376
Lends: Yes
Copying services: Photocopy ($0.10 per page).
Use of material on premises: Yes

CaOKQ **Queen's University**
Library, Department of Geological Sciences
Miller Hall, Bruce Wing
Kingston, Ontario K7L 3N6
613-547-2653
Lends: No
Copying services: Photocopy ($0.10 per page), microfilm can be ordered ($5.00).
Use of material on premises: Yes

CaOLU **University of Western Ontario**
Natural Sciences Library
London, Ontario N6A 5BY
519-679-2272
Lends: Yes
Copying services: Photocopy ($.10 per page, $1.00 minimum).
Use of material on premises: Yes

CaOOCC **Carleton University, Library**
Ottawa, Ontario K1S 5B6
613-213-2750
Lends: Yes
Copying services: Yes
Use of material on premises: Yes

CaOOG **Geological Survey of Canada, Library**
601 Booth Street
Ottawa, Ontario K1A 0E8
613-994-5325
Lends: Yes
Copying services: Photocopy ($0.20 per page).
Use of material on premises: Yes

CaOON **Canada Institute for Scientific and Technical Information**
National Research Council
Montreal Road
Ottawa, Ontario K1A 0S2
613-993-1600
Lends: Yes
Copying services: Photocopy and microfilm.
Use of material on premises: Yes

CaOONM **National Museum of Canada, Library**
Ottawa, Ontario K1A 0M8
613-992-8779
Lends: Yes
Copying services: Photocopy ($0.10 per page).
Use of material on premises: Yes

CaOPAL **Lakehead University, Library**
Thunder Bay, Ontario P7B 5E1
807-345-2121
Use of material on premises: Yes

[CaOTOM] **Ontario Department of Mines Library**
1603 Whitney Block, Queen's Park
Toronto, Ontario M7A 1W3
416-965-1352 or 416-965-1285
Lends: Yes
Copying services: Photocopy ($0.15 per page).
Use of material on premises: Yes

CaOTRM **Royal Ontario Museum, Library**
100 Queen's Park
Toronto, Ontario M5S 2C6
416-928-3671
Lends: Yes
Copying services: Yes
Use of material on premises: Yes

CaOTU **University of Toronto**
Coleman Library
Mining Building, Room 316
170 College Street
Toronto, Ontario M5S 1A1
416-978-3024
Lends: No
Copying services: Photocopy and microfilm.
Use of material premises: Yes

CaOWtU **University of Waterloo**
Engineering, Mathematics and Science Library
Waterloo, Ontario N2L 3G1
519-885-1211, Ext. 3261 (Reference desk)
Lends: Yes
Copying services: Photocopy ($0.05 if done by self, $0.10 if done by staff).
Use of material on premises: Yes

CaQMM **McGill University**
Physical Sciences Library
3450 University Street
Montreal, Quebec H3C 3G1
514-392-4929
Lends: No
Copying services: Photocopy and microfilm.
Use of material on premises: Yes

CaQMU **Universite de Montreal**
Geology Library, P.O. Box 6128
2900 Boulevard Edouard-Montpetit
Montreal, Quebec H3C 3J7
514-343-6831
Lends: Yes
Copying services: Yes
Use of material on premises: Yes

CaQQLaS **Universite Laval, La Bibliotheque**
Faculte des sciences
Quebec City, Quebec G1K 7P4
Lends: Yes
Copying services: No, except through la Bibliotheque generale.
Use of material on premises: Yes

CoDuF **Fort Lewis College, Library**
Durango, Colo. 81301
303-247-7342
Lends: Yes, some items preferred used on premises.
Copying services: Photocopy ($0.10 per page).
Use of material on premises: Yes

CoFS **Colorado State University**
The Libraries
Fort Collins, Colo. 80521
303-491-6626
Lends: Yes
Copying services: Photocopy ($0.15 per page with a $1.00 minimum).
Use of material on premises: Yes, unlimited

CoG **Colorado School of Mines**
Arthur Lakes Library
Golden, Colo. 80401
303-279-0300
Lends: Yes
Copying services: Photocopy ($0.20 per page out of state, $0.10 per page in state, plus $1.00 service charge).
Use of material on premises: Yes

[CoPU] **University of Southern Colorado**
Learning Resources Center Library
Pueblo, Colo. 81001
303-549-2451
Lends: Yes
Copying services: Photocopy ($0.10 per page).
Use of material on premises: Yes

CoU **University of Colorado**
Earth Science Library
204 Geology Building
Boulder, Colo. 80309
303-492-6133
Lends: Yes, through interlibrary loan, Univ. of Colo. Libraries.
Copying services: Photocopy ($0.15 per page, $1.50 minimum).
Use of material on premises: Yes

CtY-KS **Yale University, Kline Science Library**
Yale Station, P.O. Box 2161
New Haven, Conn. 06520
203-436-2480
Lends: No
Copying services: Photocopy ($0.05 per page).
Use of material on premises: Yes

DFPC **United States Federal Power Commission, Library**
825 North Capitol Street, NE, Room 8502
Washington, D.C. 20426
202-275-4303
Lends: Yes
Copying services: Photocopy ($0.10 per page).
Use of material on premises: Yes

DI-GS **United States Geological Survey, Library**
National Center - Mail Stop 950
12201 Sunrise Valley Drive
Reston, Va. 22092
703-860-6671
Lends: Yes
Copying services: Photocopy ($0.10 per page).
Use of material on premises: Yes

DLC **United States Library of Congress**
Science and Technology Division
10 First Street SE
Washington, D.C. 20540
202-426-5670
Lends: Only on interlibrary loan.
Copying services: Photocopy and microfilm.
Use of material on premises: Yes

ICF **Field Museum of Natural History, Library**
Roosevelt Road & Lake Shore Drive
Chicago, Ill. 60605
312-922-9410
Lends: Yes
Copying services: Photocopy ($0.20 per page).
Use of material on premises: Yes

ICIU-S **University of Illinois at Chicago Circle**
Science Library
P.O. Box 7565
Chicago, Ill. 60680
312-996-5395
Lends: Yes
Copying services: Photocopy ($0.05 per page), microfilm ($0.10 per page).
Use of material on premises: Yes

ICarbS **Southern Illinois University**
Morris Library, Science Division
Carbondale, Ill. 62901
618-453-2700
Lends: Yes
Copying services: Photocopy ($0.05 per page).
Use of material on premises: Yes

IEN **Northwestern University**
Locy Hall, Geology Library
Evanston, Ill. 60201
312-492-5525
Lends: Yes
Copying services: Photocopy ($0.10 per page).
Use of material on premises: Yes

[I-GS] **Illinois State Geological Survey, Library**
469 Natural Resources Building,
Champaign, Ill. 61820
217-344-1481
Lends: No
Copying services: None
Use of material on premises: Yes

IU **University of Illinois at Urbana-Champaign,**
Geology Library
223 Natural History Building
Urbana, Ill. 61801
217-333-1266
Lends: Yes
Copying services: Photocopy ($0.05 per page), microfilm ($0.10), in lieu of interlibrary loan: service charge per title ($1.50); postage ($0.30); xerographic print ($0.10 per page); microfilm 35 mm ($0.06 per exposure from original), 35 mm ($0.10 per foot from existing film); estimates per citation ($1.25).
Use of material on premises: Yes

IaAS **Iowa State University of Science and Technology, Library**
Ames, Iowa 50010
515-294-1442
Lends: Yes
Copying services: Photocopy for a fee.
Use of material on premises: Yes

IaU **University of Iowa**
Geology Library
136 Trowbridge Hall
Iowa City, Iowa 52242
319-353-4225
Lends: Yes
Copying services: Photocopy ($0.05 for geology students; $0.07 for others).
Use of material on premises: Yes

IdBB **Boise State University, Library**
Reference Department
Boise, Idaho 83725
208-385-3302
Lends: Yes
Copying services: Photocopy ($0.10 per page).
Use of material on premises: Yes

IdPI **Idaho State University, Library**
Interlibrary Loans
Pocatello, Idaho 83209
Lends: Yes
Copying services: Photocopy ($0.05 per exposure), microfilm/fiche ($0.10 per copy).
Use of material on premises: Yes

InLP **Purdue University**
Purdue Geosciences Library
West Lafayette, Ind. 47907
317-494-8360
Lends: Yes
Copying services: Photocopy ($0.05 per page).
Use of material on premises: Yes

InRE **Earlham College**
Wildman Science Library
P.O. Box E-72
Richmond, Ind. 47374
317-962-6561, Ext. 245
Lends: Yes
Copying services: Photocopy ($0.05 per page).
Use of material on premises: Yes

InU **Indiana University**
Geology Library
1005 East 10th Street, Geology 601
Bloomington, Ind. 47401
812-337-7170
Lends: Yes
Copying services: Photocopy ($0.05 per exposure), any other type of exposure ($0.10).
Use of material on premises: Yes

[Ky-GS] **Kentucky Geological Survey**
University of Kentucky
307 Mineral Industries Building
Lexington, Ky. 40506
606-257-1792
Use of material on premises: Yes

KyU **University of Kentucky**
Geology Library
100 Bowman Hall
Lexington, Ky. 40506
606-258-5730
Lends: Yes
Copying services: Photocopy ($0.10 per page), microfilm, cost varies with size.
Use of material on premises: Yes

LU **Louisiana State University, Library**
Baton Rouge, La. 70803
504-388-4364
Lends: Yes
Copying services: Photocopy ($0.10 per page), microfilm ($3.00 minimum).
Use of material on premises: Yes

MH-GS **Harvard University**
Geological Sciences Library
24 Oxford Street
Cambridge, Mass. 02138
617-495-2029
Lends: No
Copying Services: Photocopy ($0.10 per page, and $1.50 handling charge).
Use of material on premises: Yes

MNS **Smith College**
Clark Science Center, Science Library
Northampton, Mass. 01060
413-584-2700, Ext. 638
Lends: Yes
Copying services: Photocopy ($0.05 per page), microfilm ($0.10 per frame).
Use of material on premises: Yes

MdBJ **Johns Hopkins University, Library**
Singewald Reading Room
Department of Earth and Planetary Sciences
220 Latrobe Hall
Charles and 34th Streets
Baltimore, Md. 21218
301-366-3300, Ext. 824, 837
Lends: Yes, interlibrary loan.

Copying services: Photocopy for a fee.
Use of material on premises: Yes

MiDW **Wayne State University**
Science Library
Detroit, Mich. 48202
313-577-4066
Lends: Yes, $3.00 service charge per item loaned.
Copying services: Photocopy ($0.15 per page plus $2.00 service charge).
Use of material on premises: Yes

MiHM **Michigan Technological University, Library**
Houghton, Mich. 49931
906-487-2507
Lends: Yes
Copying services: Photocopy ($0.10 per page, $1.00 minimum).
Use of material on premises: Yes

MiKW **Western Michigan University**
Physical Sciences Library
Kalamazoo, Mich. 49008
616-383-4943
Lends: Yes
Copying services: Photocopy ($0.05 per page).
Use of material on premises: Yes

MiU **University of Michigan**
Natural Science/Natural Resources Library
Ann Arbor, Mich. 48104
313-764-1494
Lends: Yes
Copying services: Photocopy ($0.05 per page), microfilm at Main Library.
Use of material on premises: Yes

MnDuU **University of Minnesota, Duluth**
Geology Department
Duluth, Minn. 55812
218-726-7238
Lends: Yes
Copying services: Photocopy ($0.05 per page).
Use of material on premises: Yes

[MnSSM] **Science Museum of Minnesota**
Louis S. Headley Memorial Library
30 East 10th Street
St. Paul, Minn. 55101
612-222-6303
Lends: No
Copying services: Photocopy ($0.10 per page).
Use of material on premises: Yes

MnU **University of Minnesota, Minneapolis**
Winchell Library of Geology
Pillsbury Hall, Room 204
Minneapolis, Minn. 55455
612-373-4052
Lends: Yes for a 1 month period.
Copying services: Xerox ($0.10 per page, 1 day).
Use of material on premises: Yes

MoRM **University of Missouri-Rolla, Library**
Rolla, Mo. 65401
314-341-4227
Lends: Yes
Copying services: Photocopy ($0.10 per page), microfilm ($0.05 per page).
Use of material on premises: Yes

MoSW **Washington University**
Earth and Planetary Sciences Library
St. Louis, Mo. 63130
314-863-0100
Lends: Yes
Copying services: Photocopy ($0.10 per page), microfilm obtained through interlibrary loan only.
Use of material on premises: Yes

MoU **University of Missouri-Columbia**
Geology Library
201 Geology Building
Columbia, Mo. 65201
314-882-4860
Lends: Yes
Copying services: Photocopy ($0.10 per page).
Use of material on premises: Yes

[Ms-GS] **Mississippi Geological, Economic and Topographical Survey, Library**
2525 North West Street, P.O. Box 4915
Jackson, Miss. 39216
601-354-6228
Lends: Yes
Copying services: Photocopy ($0.10 per page).
Use of material on premises: Yes

MtBC **Montana State University, Library**
Bozeman, Mont. 59715
406-994-3171
Lends: Rarely
Copying services: Photocopy ($0.10 per page, minimum charge $1.00 via interlibrary loan).
Use of material on premises: Yes

MtU **University of Montana, Library**
Missoula, Mont. 59801
406-243-6810
Lends: Yes
Copying services: Photocopy ($0.10 per page).
Use of material on premises: Yes

NBiSU **State University of New York at Binghamton**
Science Library
Binghamton, N.Y. 13901
607-798-2000
Lends: Yes
Copying services: Photocopy ($0.05 per page).
Use of material on premises: Yes

NNC **Columbia University**
Geology Library
601 Schermerhorn Hall
New York, N.Y. 10027
212-280-4713
Lends: Yes
Copying services: Photocopy ($0.10 per page, self-service).
Use of material on premises: Yes

NOneoU **State University of New York, College at Oneonta**
James M. Milne Library
Oneonta, N.Y. 13820
607-431-2723
Lends: Yes
Copying services: Photocopy ($0.05 per page), microfilm ($0.10 per page).
Use of material on premises: Yes

NRU **University of Rochester**
Geological Sciences Library
Dewey Hall - 208
Rochester, N.Y. 14627
716-275-4487
Lends: Yes
Copying services: Photocopy ($0.05 per page).
Use of material on premises: Yes

NSyU **Syracuse University**
Geology Branch Library
300 Heroy Geology Laboratory
Syracuse, N.Y. 13210
315-423-3337
Lends: Yes
Copying services: None
Use of material on premises: Yes

NbU **University of Nebraska, Lincoln**
Geology Library
303 Morrill Hall
Lincoln, Nebr. 68806
402-472-2653
Lends: Yes, interlibrary loan only.
Copying services: Photocopy.
Use of material on premises: Yes

NcU **University of North Carolina**
Geology Library
Chapel Hill, N.C. 27514
919-933-2386
Lends: Yes
Copying services: None.
Use of material on premises: Yes

NdU — **University of North Dakota**
Geology Branch Library
Grand Forks, N. Dak. 58202
701-777-3221
Lends: Yes
Copying services: Photocopy ($0.05 per page).
Use of material on premises: Yes

NhD — **Dartmouth College**
Kresge Physical Sciences Library
Hanover, N.H. 03755
603-646-3564
Lends: Yes, interlibrary loan.
Copying services: Photocopy ($0.10 per page), microfilm ($0.10 per page).
Use of material on premises: Yes

NjP — **Princeton University**
Geology Library
Guyot Hall
Princeton, N.J. 08540
609-452-3267
Lends: Yes, with librarian's approval.
Copying services: Xerox 3100 ($0.05 per page).
Use of material on premises: Yes

NmPE — **Eastern New Mexico University, Library**
Portales, N.M. 88130
505-562-2832
Lends: Yes
Copying services: Photocopy ($0.10 per page).
Use of material on premises: Yes

NmU — **University of New Mexico**
General Library
Albuquerque, N. Mex. 87131
505-277-5961 (Reference Dept.); 505-277-5617 (Interlibrary loan Dept.)
Lends: Yes, to University personnel or through interlibrary loan.
Copying services: Photocopy ($0.10 per page), microfilm ($0.15 per page).
Use of material on premises: Yes

NvLN — **University of Nevada, Las Vegas, Library**
4505 Maryland Parkway
Las Vegas, Nev. 89154
703-739-3512
Lends: Yes
Copying services: Photocopy ($0.10 per page), microfilm ($0.10 per page).
Use of material on premises: Yes

NvU — **University of Nevada, Reno**
Mines Library
Reno, Nev. 89507
702-784-6596
Lends: Yes
Copying services: Photocopy ($0.05 per page).
Use of material on premises: Yes

OCU — **University of Cincinnati**
Geology-Geography Library
103 Old Tech Building
Cincinnati, Ohio 45221
513-475-4332
Lends: Yes
Copying services: Photocopy ($0.05 per page).
Use of material on premises: Yes

OU — **Ohio State University**
Orton Memorial Library of Geology
155 South Oval Drive,
Columbus, Ohio 43210
614-422-2428
Lends: Yes
Copying services: Photocopy ($0.15 per page plus $2.00 service charge), microfilm ($0.04 per exposure, $0.25 for reel and box plus $2.00 service charge).
Use of material on premises: Yes

[OkOkCGe] — **Oklahoma City Geological Society**
Geological Library
Cravens Building
Oklahoma City, Okla. 73102
405-235-368
Lends: No
Copying services: None
Use of material on premises: Yes

OkOkU **Oklahoma City University, Library**
2501 N. Blackwelder
Oklahoma City, Okla. 73106
405-525-5411
Lends: Yes
Copying services: Photocopy ($0.05 per page).
Use of material on premises: Yes

OkS **Oklahoma State University, Library**
Stillwater, Okla. 74074
405-372-6211, Ext. 6070 (Interlibrary Loan Dept.)
Lends: Yes
Copying services: Photocopy ($0.10 per page, plus $1.00 handling charge).
Use of material on premises: Yes

OkT **Tulsa City-County Library System**
Business and Technology Department
400 Civic Center
Tulsa, Okla. 74103
918-581-5211
Lends: Yes
Copying services: Photocopy ($0.10 per page).
Use of material on premises: Yes

OkU **University of Oklahoma**
Geology Library
830 Van Fleet Oval, Room 103
Norman, Okla. 73019
405-325-6451
Lends: Yes
Copying services: Available from University of Oklahoma interlibrary loan, photocopy ($0.15 per page), microfilm ($0.03 per page).
Use of material on premises: Yes

OrCS **Oregon State University**
William Jasper Kerr Library
Corvallis, Oreg. 97331
503-754-1592
Lends: Yes, policy determined by demand and use.
Copying services: Photocopy ($0.10 per page).
Use of material on premises: Yes

OrU **University of Oregon**
Science Library
Eugene, Oreg. 97403
503-686-3075
Lends: Yes, for 3 weeks.
Copying services: Photocopy and microfilm.
Use of material on premises: Yes

[P-GS] **Pennsylvania Bureau of Topographic and Geologic Survey, Library**
Department of Environmental Resources
916 Executive House Apts.
Harrisburg, Pa. 17120
717-787-5897
Lends: Yes
Copying services: Photocopy and microfilm for a fee.
Use of material on premises: Yes

PBL **Lehigh University**
Mart Science and Engineering Library
Bethlehem, Pa. 18015
215-691-7000
Lends: Yes, interlibrary loan.
Copying services: Photocopy for a fee.
Use of material on premises: Yes

PBm **Bryn Mawr College**
Geology Library
Bryn Mawr, Pa. 19010
215-525-1000, Ext. 256
Lends: No
Copying services: Photocopy ($0.05 per page).
Use of material on premises: Yes

PPiGulf **Gulf Research and Development Company, Library**
P.O. Drawer 2038
Pittsburgh, Pa. 15065
713-225-3141
Lends: Yes
Copying services: Photocopy and microfilm, no charge.
Use of material on premises: Yes, by appointment only.

PSt **Pennsylvania State University**
Earth and Mineral Sciences Library
105 Deike Building
University Park, Pa. 16802
814-865-9517
Lends: Yes
Copying services: Photocopy ($0.20 per page), microfilm ($0.10 per page).
Use of material on premises: Yes

RPB **Brown University**
Physical Sciences Library
Providence, R.I. 02912
401-863-2127
Lends: Yes, up to 4 weeks, interlibrary loan only.
Copying services: Photocopy ($0.15 per page, under $1.00 no charge).
Use of material on premises: Yes

SdRM **South Dakota School of Mines and Technology**
Devereaux Library
Rapid City, S. Dak. 57701
605-394-2418
Lends: Yes
Copying services: Photocopy ($0.10 per page).
Use of material on premises: Yes

SdU **University of South Dakota**
I. D. Weeks Library
Vermillion, S. Dak. 57069
605-677-5371
Lends: Yes
Copying services: Photocopy ($0.05 per page), microfilm ($0.05 per page).
Use of material on premises: Yes

TMM **Memphis State University**
Herff College of Engineering Library
Memphis, Tenn. 38152
901-454-2179
Lends: Yes
Copying services: Photocopy ($0.10 per page).
Use of material on premises: Yes

TU **University of Tennessee**
Science Library
672 Buehler Hall
Knoxville, Tenn. 37916
Lends: Yes, restricted to University-related persons.
Copying services: Photocopy for a fee.
Use of material on premises: Yes

TxCaW **West Texas State University**
The Cornette Library
West Texas Station, P.O. Box 748
Canyon, Tex. 79016
806-656-2761
Lends: Yes
Copying services: Photocopy ($0.10 per page), microfilm ($0.20 per page).
Use of material on premises: Yes

TxDaAR-T **Atlantic Richfield Company**
Geoscience Library
P.O. Box 2819
Dallas, Tex. 75221
214-651-4063
Lends: Yes
Copying services: Photocopy, no charge.
Use of material on premises: Yes

TxDaDM **DeGolyer and MacNaughton Library**
One Energy Square
Dallas, Tex. 75206
214-368-6391
Lends: Yes
Copying services: Photocopy ($0.15 per page).
Use of material on premises: Yes

TxDaM **Southern Methodist University**
Science/Engineering Library
P.O. Box 1339
Dallas, Tex. 75222
214-363-5611, Ext. 520
TWX214-899-9600 (Teletype no.)
Lends: Yes, for 3 weeks, industrial users must contact: Industrial Information Services, Southern Methodist University, Science Information Center.
Copying services: Xerox ($0.15 per page, 1 day), microfilm ($0.05 per page, $1.50 minimum; 1 week), Dennison copier ($0.10 per page, immediately)
Use of material on premises: Yes

TxDaSM **Mobil Research and Development Corporation**
Technical Information Services
Field Research Laboratory
3600 Duncanville Road
Dallas, Tex. 75211
214-331-6531
Lends: Yes, for 2 weeks, limited to material not heavily used.
Copying services: None
Use of material on premises: Yes, by appointment only.

TxHSD **Shell Development Company**
Bellaire Research Center Library
P.O. Box 481
Houston, Tex. 77001
713-667-5661
Lends: Yes
Copying services: Photocopy, no charge.
Use of material on premises: Yes

TxHSW **Schlumberger Well Services, Library**
P.O. Box 2175
5000 Gulf Freeway
Houston, Tex. 77001
713-928-2511, Ext. 510
Lends: Yes
Copying services: Photocopy.
Use of material on premises: Yes

TxHU **University of Houston, Library**
4800 Calhoun
Houston, Tex. 77004
713-749-3847
Lends: Yes
Copying services: Photocopy, interlibrary loan (academic $2.00 for first 10 pages, $0.15 per page for the balance; individual, $4.00 first 10 pages, $0.15 per page for the balance).
Use of material on premises: Yes

TxLT **Texas Tech University, Library**
P.O. Box 4079
Lubbock, Tex. 79409
806-742-2261
Lends: Some
Copying services: Photocopy ($0.07 per page).
Use of material on premises: Yes

TxMM **Midland County Public Library**
P.O. Box 1191
Midland, Tex. 79701
915-683-2708
Lends: Yes
Copying services: Photocopy ($0.10 per page).
Use of material on premises: Yes

TxU **University of Texas at Austin, The General Libraries**
Geology Library
Geology Building 302,
Austin, Tex. 78712
512-471-1257
Lends: Yes
Copying services: Photocopy, handled through Interlibrary Loan Service.
Use of material on premises: Yes

TxU-Da **University of Texas at Dallas, Library**
P.O. Box 643
Richardson, Tex. 75230
214-690-2955
Lends: Yes
Copying services: Photocopy ($0.05 per page).
Use of material on premises: Yes

UPB **Brigham Young University**
Harold B. Lee Library
Provo, Utah 84601
801-374-1211, Ext. 2905
Lends: Yes
Copying services: Photocopy (under 3 pages, no charge; over 4 pages, minimum is $1.50; increases after 15 pages).
Use of material on premises: Yes

UU **University of Utah**
Science and Engineering Library
Marriott Library
Salt Lake City, Utah 84112
Lends: Yes
Copying services: Photocopy ($0.15 per page).
Use of material on premises: Yes

ViBlbV **Virginia Polytechnic Institute and State University**
Geology Library
3040 Derring Hall
Blacksburg, Va. 24061
703-951-6101
Lends: Yes
Copying services: Photocopy ($0.05 per page).
Use of material on premises: Yes

[VtPuW] **Windham College**
Dorothy Culbertson Marvin Memorial Library
P.O. Box 205
Putney, Vt. 05346
802-387-5511, Ext. 330
Lends: Yes
Copying services: Photocopy ($0.05 per page), microfilm ($0.10 per page).
Use of material on premises: Yes

WM **Milwaukee Public Museum**
Reference Library
800 W. Wells Street
Milwaukee, Wis. 53233
414-278-2736
Lends: Yes
Copying services: Photocopy ($0.05 per page), microfilm ($0.05 per page).
Use of material on premises: Yes

WPlaU **University of Wisconsin-Platteville**
The Karrmann Library
Platteville, Wis. 53818
608-342-1688
Lends: Yes
Copying services: Photocopy ($0.05 per page).
Use of material on premises: Yes

WU **University of Wisconsin-Madison**
Geology-Geophysics Library
430 Weeks Hall
Madison, Wis. 53706
608-262-8956
Lends: Yes, if not in demand.
Copying services: Photocopy ($0.05 per page, self-service only).
Use of material on premises: Yes

WaPS **Washington State University**
Science and Engineering Library
Pullman, Wash. 99163
Lends: Yes
Copying services: Photocopy ($0.10 per page, $1.00 handling), microfilm ($0.10 per page, $1.50 handling).
Use of material on premises: Yes

WyU **University of Wyoming**
Geology Library, Geology Building
Laramie, Wyo. 82070
307-766-3374
Lends: Only through Interlibrary Loan Department, Coe Library.
Copying services: Through interlibrary loan.
Use of material on premises: Yes

UNION LIST OF GEOLOGIC FIELD TRIP

GUIDEBOOKS OF NORTH AMERICA

(1) ABILENE GEOLOGICAL SOCIETY. FIELD TRIP GUIDEBOOK. (TITLE VARIES)

1946 Whitehorse-El Reno-Clearfork groups, Abilene, Sweetwater, Rotan, Hamlin, Anson.

1948 Study of Lower Permian and Upper Pennsylvanian rocks in Brazos and Colorado River valleys of west-central Texas, particularly from Coleman Junction to Home Creek limestones, Abilene-Eastland-Colorado River.

Road log and instructions for lower Paleozoic field trip, Llano uplift, Texas.

1949 Subsurface studies and field trip (Brownwood, Ranger, and Mineral Wells districts to and from Abilene).

1950 Strawn and older rocks of Pennsylvanian and Mississippian system of Brown, San Saba, McCulloch, Mason, and Kimble counties, Texas. Cross sections prepared.

1951 Middle-Upper Permian and Cretaceous; Abilene, Sweetwater, Bronte, Paint Rock, and San Angelo.

1952 [Geological road logs of west-central Texas.]

1954 Facies study of the Strawn-Canyon series in the Brazos River area, north-central Texas.

1955 Study of the Lower Permian and Upper Pennsylvanian rocks in the Brazos and Colorado River valleys of west-central Texas, together with a preliminary report on the structural development of west-central Texas.

1957 Study of Lower Pennsylvanian and Mississippian rocks of the northeast Llano uplift. (86)

1960 See Southwestern Federation of Geological Societies. (295)

1961 A study of Pennsylvanian and Permian sedimentation in the Colorado River valley of west-central Texas.

CLU-G/G	1954, 57, 61
CLhC	1961
CSdS	1946, 50
CU-EART	1950, 52, 54, 55, 57
[CaACAM]	1949
CaACI	1954, 55, 57
CaOKQ	1954, 55, 57, 61
CoG	1950, 54, 55, 57, 61
[CoPU]	1954, 55, 61
DFPC	1961
DI-GS	1946, 48-50, 54, 55, 57, 61
ICF	1954, 55, 57, 61
IEN	1948, 49, 61
[I-GS]	1957
IU	1948, 49, 54, 55, 57, 61
IaU	1954, 55, 57
InLP	1954, 55, 59, 61
InU	1957, 61
KyU	1952, 54, 55, 57, 61
LU	1949, 50, 54, 55, 57, 61
MiDW	1954, 55, 57, 61

(1) Abilene Geological Society.

MnU	1950, 54, 55, 57, 61
MoU	1950
MtU	1954, 55, 57, 61
NNC	1950, 54, 55, 57, 61
NbU	1946, 48-50, 55, 57, 61
NcU	1952, 54, 57, 61
NjP	1961
NmPE	1954, 55, 61
NvU	1954, 55, 57
OCU	1954, 55, 61
OU	1950, 52, 54, 55, 57, 61
OkT	1949, 50, 55, 57
OkU	1946, 48, 50, 52, 54, 55, 57, 61
PSt	1954, 57
TxDaAR-T	1950, 54, 55, 57
TxDaDM	1954, 55, 57, 61
TxDaM	1954, 55, 57, 61
TxDaSM	1948, 49, 55, 57, 61
TxHSD	1948, 50, 55
TxHU	1949, 54, 55, 57, 61
TxLT	1950, 54, 55, 61
TxMM	1946, 48-50, 54, 55, 57, 61
TxU	1946, 48-51, 54, 55, 57, 61
UU	1957
ViBlbV	1954, 55, 57, 61
WU	1957

(2) ALABAMA ACADEMY OF SCIENCE.

1962		See Alabama. Geological Survey. (5)
1965	3rd	See Alabama Geological Society. (3)

DI-GS	1962, 65
InU	1962
NSyU	1962

(3) ALABAMA GEOLOGICAL SOCIETY. GUIDEBOOK FOR THE ANNUAL FIELD TRIP. (TITLE VARIES)

1964	1st	Pottsville Formation in Blount and Jefferson counties, Alabama.
	2nd	Alabama Piedmont geology.
1965	Apr.	Russellville brown iron ore district. Road log for field trip, bound with Guidebook for Second Annual Field Trip, 1964.
	3rd	Structural development of the southernmost Appalachians. (2)
1966	4th	Facies changes in the Alabama Tertiary.
1967	5th	A field guide to Mississippian sediments in northern Alabama and south-central Tennessee.
1968	6th	Facies changes in the Selma Group in central and eastern Alabama.
1969	7th	The Appalachian structural front in Alabama.
1970	8th	Geology of the Brevard fault zone and related rocks of the inner Piedmont of Alabama.
1971	9th	The Middle and Upper Ordovician of the Alabama Appalachians.
1972	10th	Recent sedimentation along the Alabama coast.
1973	11th	Talladega metamorphic front.
1974	12th	The Coosa deformed belt in the Alabama Appalachians.
1975	13th	Geologic profiles of the northern Alabama Piedmont.

[A-GS]	1964, 65(3), 66
AzTeS	1964, 66-68
[CDU]	1969
CLU-G/G	1964, 65(3), 66, 68
CLhC	1966
CSdS	1964, 65(3), 66-68, 73
CU-EART	1964, 65, 67-75
[CaBVU]	1966
CaOHM	1964, 65(3), 66-74
CaOKQ	1966
CaOOG	1964-69
CaOWtU	1969-73
CoG	1964, 65(3), 66-74
CoU	1967, 69-74
DI-GS	1964-75
DLC	1966, 71
ICIU-S	1964-69
IEN	1964, 65(3), 66-74
[I-GS]	1969
IU	1964, 65(3), 66, 67, 70-74
IaU	1964-74
InLP	1964, 65(3), 66, 67
InU	1964, 65, 67, 68, 70-74
KyU	1964-72
MH-GS	1969
MiHM	1971
MiKW	1967
MnU	1964, 65(3), 66-68
MoSW	1964, 65(3), 66, 67
MoU	1964-71
NBiSU	1965(3), 69-70
NNC	1964, 65(3)
NOneoU	1968
NSyU	1966, 71
NbU	1965
NcU	1964, 65(3), 66-71
NhD	1971
NjP	1964, 65(3), 66-74
OCU	1964, 68-70
OU	1967, 69-71
OkU	1964-73
PPiGulf	1965(3), 68
TU	1964, 65(3), 66
TxDaAR-T	1964-74
TxDaDM	1964, 65(Apr.), 66-72
TxDaM	1964, 65
TxDaSM	1964(2), 65(3), 66
TxHU	1965(lacks roadlog), 66, 67
TxLT	1970
TxMM	1965(3)
TxU	1964, 65(3), 66-74
ViBlbV	1964, 65(3), 66-74
WU	1964-75

(4) ALABAMA. GEOLOGICAL SURVEY. CIRCULAR.

1968 No. 47 Geology of the Alabama Coastal Plain; a guidebook.
1973 Circular 90. A field guide to mineral deposits in south Alabama.

AzTeS	1968, 73
CLU-G/G	1968
CU-EART	1968, 73
CoG	1968
CoU	1968, 73
DI-GS	1968, 73
ICF	1968
ICIU-S	1968
IEN	1968
IU	1968, 73
InU	1973
MNS	1968
MiHM	1968, 73
MoSW	1968
MoU	1968
NBiSU	1968
NSyU	1968, 73
NbU	1968
NcU	1968
NdU	1968
NhD	1968
NjP	1968, 73
OCU	1968, 73
OU	1968
OkT	1968
OkU	1968
OrU	1968
TMM	1968
TxDaAR-T	1968
TxU	1968
ViBlbV	1968

(5) ALABAMA. GEOLOGICAL SURVEY. INFORMATION SERIES.

1958 No. 13 Birmingham area and celebrated coastal plain fossil locations. (102)
1960 No. 18 Selected outcrops of the Eutaw Formation and Selma Group near Montgomery, Alabama.
1962 No. 26 Selected brown iron ore deposits, Pike County, Alabama. (2)

[A-GS]	1958, 60, 62
CLU-G/G	1960, 62
CLhC	1958
CaOLU	1962
CaOWtU	1962
DI-GS	1958, 60, 62
ICF	1960, 62
IEN	1958, 60, 62
[I-GS]	1960
IU	1960, 62
InU	1958, 60, 62
KyU	1960, 62

MH-GS	1968
MNS	1958, 60, 62
MiDW	1960, 62
MiHM	1960, 62
MiU	1958, 60, 62
MnU	1958, 60, 62
MoU	1962
NNC	1958
NSyU	1960, 62
NdU	1960, 62
NjP	1962
OU	1958
OkU	1960, 62
PSt	1958, 60, 62
TMM	1958, 62
TxDaAR-T	1958
TxDaDM	1958, 60
TxDaM	1958
TxU	1958, 60, 62
ViBlbV	1958, 62
WU	1960, 62

(6) ALABAMA. UNIVERSITY. GEOLOGICAL SOCIETY.

1967 See Geological Society of America. (96)

(7) ALASKA GEOLOGICAL SOCIETY. GUIDEBOOK. (TITLE VARIES)

1963 Anchorage to Sutton. (16)

1964 Sutton to Caribou Creek. (16)

Oil fields, earthquake, geology. Anchorage.

1970 Oil and gas fields in the Cook Inlet basin, Alaska.

1973 Road log and guide. Geology and hydrology for planning, Anchorage area.

AzU	1963, 64
[CDU]	1963, 70
CLU-G/G	1963, 64
CLhC	1963, 64
CSdS	1963, 64, 70
CU-EART	1963, 64, 73
[CaACAM]	1970
CaOHM	1973
CaOKQ	1964
CoG	1963, 64
CoU	1963, 64
DI-GS	1963, 64, 70, 73
IU	1963, 64, 73
MH-GS	1963, 64
MnU	1963, 64
MoSW	1963, 64
NNC	1963, 64
NdU	1964, 70
OCU	1963, 70
TxDaAR-T	1963, 64, 70, 73

TxDaDM	1963, 64
TxDaSM	1963, 64
TxLT	1963, 64
TxU	1963, 64, 67, 70
TxU-Da	1970
ViBlbV	1963, 64

(8) ALBERTA RESEARCH COUNCIL. INFORMATION SERIES.

1973 No. 65 Guide to the Athabasca oil sands area.
Road log: Fort McMurray to Fort McKay.

CaOLU	1973
CaOOG	1973
CoU	1973
MiHM	1973
NSyU	1973
NdU	1973
TxHSD	1973

ALBERTA SOCIETY OF PETROLEUM GEOLOGISTS. See CANADIAN SOCIETY OF PETROLEUM GEOLOGISTS. (61)

(9) ALBERTA. UNIVERSITY. DEPARTMENT OF GEOLOGY.

1967 Field guide for the Yellowknife field trip; a field trip held June 14-16 in conjunction with the conference, Geochronology of Precambrian stratified rocks, Edmonton, Alberta.

TxU	1967

(10) AMERICAN ASSOCIATION FOR THE ADVANCEMENT OF SCIENCE. COMMITTEE ON ARID LANDS.

1969 Guidebook of northern Mexico Sonoran Desert region. For an International Conference on Arid Lands in a Changing World. Tucson, the University of Arizona.

CLU-G/G	1969
CoG	1969
CoU	1969
DI-GS	1969
IU	1969
IaU	1969
KyU	1969
MiU	1969
MoU	1969
OU	1969
OkU	1969
PSt	1969
TxDaDM	1969
TxHSD	1969
TxLT	1969
TxMM	1969
TxU	1969

(11) AMERICAN ASSOCIATION FOR THE ADVANCEMENT OF SCIENCE. PACIFIC COAST COMMITTEE.

1915		Nature and science on the Pacific coast; a guidebook for scientific travelers in the west. IEN 1915

(12) AMERICAN ASSOCIATION OF PETROLEUM GEOLOGISTS. GUIDEBOOK FOR THE FIELD CONFERENCE HELD IN CONNECTION WITH THE ANNUAL CONVENTION. (CHECK LOCAL SPONSORING BODY AS WELL AS AAPG)

1924	9th	Palestine, [Texas].
1929		See Society of Economic Paleontologists and Mineralogists. (274)
1932	17th	Highway geology of Oklahoma. (230)
		Oklahoma City field trip.
1933		Sugarland oil field, Fort Bend County, [Texas.]
1937	22nd	Los Angeles Basin, San Joaquin Valley, Ventura County, [California].
1939	24th	Ardmore Basin field trip.
		Anadarko Basin field trip. (4, 230)
1940		1. Pre-convention field trip. [Chicago area.]
		2. Post-convention field trip at La Salle, Illinois.
1941	26th	Gulf Coast fields. (118)
1944	29th	Dallas Digest, joint annual meeting of the American Association of Petroleum Geologists, the Society of Economic Paleontologists and Mineralogists, and the Society of Exploration Geophysicists. (274, 281)
1947	32nd	[California oil fields and their geologic features]. (274, 281)
1948	33rd	Geology of central Colorado. (Also in Quarterly of the Colorado School of Mines, Vol. 43, No. 2, Apr. 1948.) (250)
		1. Denver, Boulder, Golden, Morrison
		2. Denver, Colorado Springs, Canon City.
		3. Denver, Glenwood Springs, Rifle, Leadville, South Park.
1949	34th	Southeastern Missouri and southwestern Illinois. (123)
1950	[1st]	Niagaran reefs in the Chicago area. (126)
1951	36th	Southeastern Missouri, Cape Girardeau and Gulf embayment areas.
1952	37th	Oil fields; geology (California). (274, 281)
1953	38th	Oil fields; geology. (118, 274, 281)
1954	[3rd]	Guide to the structure and Paleozoic stratigraphy along the Lincoln Fold in central western Illinois. (126)
1955		Appalachian geology; guidebook from Pittsburgh to New York City, New York. (245)
1956	4th	Niagaran reef at Thornton, Illinois. (126)
1957	42nd	Paleozoic section in the St. Louis area.
1958		A guide to the geology and oil fields of the Los Angeles and Ventura regions. (274)
1959		Geology of the Ouachita Mountains. Symposium and field trip. (32, 74, 274)
1960		Guidebooks. (145, 274)
		1. Geology of north-central part of the New Jersey coastal plain.
		2. Geology of the region between Roanoke and Winchester, Appalachian Valley of western Virginia.
		3. Lower Paleozoic carbonate rocks in Maryland and Pennsylvania.
		4. See same series, 1958, 17th. See Johns Hopkins University. (145)
1961		Pt. 1. Guide to the geology of Colorado. (96, 250)
		A-1. Geology of west-central Colorado. Mancos Shale and Mesaverde Group of Palisade area. Colorado National Monument and adjacent areas.
		A-2. Geology of south-central Colorado. Brief description of the igneous bodies of the Raton Mesa region, south-central Colorado. Permo-Pennsylvanian stratigraphy in the Sangre de Cristo Mountains, Colorado. Great sand dunes of Colorado. Geology near Orient Mine,

Sangre de Cristo Mountains.
A-3. Tectonics and economic geology of central Colorado. Kokomo mining district. Tectonic relationships of central Colorado. Structure and petrology of north end of Pikes Peak Batholith, Colorado. Pre-Cambrian rocks and structure of the Platte Canyon and Kassler quadrangles, Colorado. Gravity map of the Hartsel area, South Park, Colorado. Cripple Creek District. Geologic formations and structure of Colorado Springs area, Colorado. Placers of Summit and Park counties, Colorado.
B-1. Quaternary geology of the Front Range and adjacent plains. First day: Pleistocene geology of the eastern slope of Rocky Mountain National Park, Colorado Front Range. Second day: Surficial geology of the Kassler and Littleton quadrangles near Denver, Colorado. Quaternary sequences east of the Front Range near Denver, Colorado.
B-2. Geology of the northern Front Range-Laramie Range, Colorado and Wyoming. Summary of Cenozoic history, southern Laramie Range, Wyoming and Colorado. Laramie anorthosite. Cross-lamination and local deformation in the Casper Sandstone, southeast Wyoming. Dakota Group in northern Front Range area.
B-3. Field trip to Climax, Colorado (no road log). Geology of the Climax molybdenite deposit; a progress report.
C-1. Stratigraphy of Colorado Springs-Canon City area.
C-2. Engineering geology-distribution system of the Colorado-Big Thompson Project.
C-3. Precambrian geology of the Idaho Springs-Central City area, Colorado. Geology of the Central City-Idaho Springs area, Front Range, Colorado.
C-4. Fossil vertebrates and sedimentary rocks of the Front Range foothills, Colorado.
C-5. Geology of the Front Range foothills, Boulder-Lyons-Loveland area, Colorado.
C-6. Geology of Mountain Front west of Denver.

1962 See California. Division of Mines and Geology. (54)

1963 Stratigraphic study, Pleistocene to Middle Eocene, Houston, Texas. (118, 274, 277, 283)

1964 Geology of central Ontario, Toronto, Canada. (94, 165, 274)

1965 Molluscan fauna of Mississippi River delta, Mudlump province, Mudlump Island field trip. (In conjunction with Society of Economic Paleontologists and Mineralogists)

1966 [1] Sedimentary structures and morphology of late Paleozoic sand bodies in southern Illinois. (126)
[2] Middle Ordovician and Mississippian strata, St. Louis and St. Charles counties, Missouri. (182)

1967 52nd No. 1. Do-it-yourself road log, Los Angeles to Death Valley.
No. 2. Pliocene Seaknoll, South Mountain, Ventura County, California. (16)
No. 2. Road log for Santa Catalina Island. (16, 190, 279, 284)
No. 3. Ventura Basin stratigraphic field trip. Preface to road log for AAPG field trip to Hall Canyon and Wheeler Canyon.
No. 4. Stream injection, Wilmington Field, Los Angeles area, California. (274)
Death Valley field trip.
Underwater field trip No. 4.
Field Trip 5. North-central Los Angeles Basin and Whittier oil field. (16)
Field Trip 6. Baldwin Hills and Palos Verdes Hills, Los Angeles. (16)
Field Trip 7. Central Santa Monica Mountains stratigraphy and structure. (16)
Field Trip 8. Structural complexities, eastern Ventura Basin. (16)
Field Trip 10. Santa Catalina Island. (16)

1968 53rd [1] A guidebook to the geology of the Bluejacket-Bartlesville Sandstone, Oklahoma. (This meeting was cosponsored by the Oklahoma City Geological Society.) (230, 274)
[2] A guidebook to the geology of the western Arkhoma Basin and Ouachita Mountains, Oklahoma. (230, 274)

1969 1. A guidebook to the depositional environments and depositional history of Lower Cretaceous shallow shelf carbonate sequence, west-central Texas. (74, 274)
2. A guidebook to the Late Pennsylvanian shelf sediments, north-central Texas. (74, 274)
3. A guidebook to the stratigraphy, sedimentary structures and origin of flysch and pre-flysch

rocks, Marathon Basin, Texas. (74, 274)

1970 1. A geological guide along the highways between Drumheller-Calgary-Lake Louise. (61, 274)
2. Red Deer River badlands.

1971 1. NASA field trip. No guidebook published.
2. Recent alluvial deltaic and barrier island sediments, southeast Texas.
3. Uranium geology and mines of South Texas. (118, 308)
4. Trace-fossils as paleoecological indicators, central Texas.

1972 Energy and mineral resources of the southern Rocky Mountains. (Mountain Geologist, V. 9, No. 2-3, pt. 1)
Field Trip 1. Geology of the Denver Mountain area. (Mountain Geologist, V. 9, No. 1-2, p. 71-78)
Field Trip 2. Tertiary and Cretaceous energy resources of the southern Rocky Mountains. (Mountain Geologist, V. 9, No. 1-2)
Field Trip 3. Structure and ore deposits of central Colorado. (Mountain Geologist, V. 9, No. 1-2)
SEPM Field Trip 1. Environments of sandstone deposition, Colorado Front Range.
SEPM Field Trip 2. Carbonate and evaporite facies of the Paradox Basin.

1973 58th Trip 1. Metropolitan oil fields and their environmental impact.
Trip 2. Imperial Valley regional geology and geothermal exploration.
Trip 3. Santa Barbara Channel region revisited.
SEPM Field Trip 1. Miocene sedimentary environments and biofacies, SE Los Angeles Basin.
SEPM Field Trip 2. Sedimentary facies changes in Tertiary rocks, California transverse and Southern Coast Ranges.
SEG Field Trip 1. Seismicity of the Los Angeles Basin.

1974 (1) Geology of the Big Bend region, Texas.
(2) Stratigraphy of the Edwards Group and equivalents, eastern Edwards Plateau, Texas.
(3) Hydrogeology of the Edwards Limestone aquifer, San Antonio area, Texas.
(4) Mexico City and environs.
SEPM Field Trip 1. Precambrian and Paleozoic rocks of central mineral region, Texas.
SEPM Field Trip 2. Shallow marine sediments of Early Cretaceous (Trinity) platform in central Texas. (Louisiana State University, School of Geoscience, Miscellaneous Publication No. 74-1) (274)

1975 Trip 1. Regional geology of Arbuckle Mountains. Oklahoma.
Trip 2. Relationships in continuous deposition of clastic (deltaic) and calcareous (bank) facies of Missourian (Canyon) age, north-central Texas.
Trip 3. Edwards (Lower Cretaceous) reef complex and associated sediments in central Texas.
SEPM Field Trip 1. A guidebook to the sedimentology of Paleozoic flysch and associated deposits, Ouachita Mountains-Arkoma Basin, Oklahoma. (274)
Late Paleozoic basin facies carbonates, west Texas and New Mexico. (74)

1976 1. Field guide to Carboniferous littoral deposits in Warrior Basin. (208, 274)
2. Classic Tertiary and Quaternary localities and historic highlights of Jackson-Vicksburg-Natchez area. (208, 274)
3. Carbonate rocks and hydrogeology of Yucatan Peninsula, Mexico. (208, 274)
4. Louisiana delta plain and its salt domes with a visit to Weeks and Avery islands and Morton Salt Company Mine. (208, 274)
5. Modern Mississippi Delta; depositional environments and processes. (208)

[A-GS]	1939, 66(1)
AzFU	1955, 59, 61
CChiS	1958
[CDU]	1947, 52, 58, 70

(12) American Association of Petroleum Geologists.

CLU-G/G	1932, 37, 47, 48, 52-54, 58, 62, 66, 67(A,2,4,5,7,8,B2-4), 69, 70, 71(4), 72, 73 74(2,3)
CLhC	1952, 53, 69, 71(4), 72
CSdS	1952, 53, 55
CSfCSM	1937
CU-EART	1947, 52, 62, 66(2), 67(A2,5,7,8, B4)
CaAC	1953
[CaACAM]	1953
CaACI	1962-70
[CaBVU]	1953
CaOHM	1967, 70
CaOLU	1948, 70
CaOOG	1937, 64, 66(1)
CoG	1947, 48, 52, 53, 58, 62, 66, 67(A2,A4-8,B2,B3,B4), 68, 69(2,3), 71(2-4)
CoU	1948, 55, 57, 59, 66, 69, 71(2)
DI-GS	1947-64, 66, 68, 69, 71(2,4), 73, 74(2)
ICF	1966(2), 72
ICIU-S	1964, 69(1)
ICarbS	1966(1), 70
IEN	1941, 47, 49, 52, 54, 59, 69, 73
[I-GS]	1924, 39, 40, 49, 50(1), 53, 54(3), 55, 56(4), 57, 60(1-5), 62, 66
IU	1939(1,2), 40, 41, 49, 53, 66, 69, 72, 74(2,3)
IaU	1932, 48, 53, 55, 57-62, 64, 66, 68, 69
IdBB	1967
IdPI	1953
InLP	1964, 65, 66-68
InU	1948-50, 56, 58-60, 62, 64, 68-70, 71(2,4)
KyU	1948, 54, 55, 59-63, 66(2), 68, 69, 70, 71(3), 72, 74(1-3)
LU	1941, 49, 52, 53, 66(1)
MNS	1955, 56, 58, 60, 66, 69(1-3)
MiDW	1966
MiHM	1948, 62
MiKW	1953, 69(1,3)
MiU	1941, 52, 67(B2)
MnU	1948-69
MoSW	1948, 49, 51-53, 66(1)
MoU	1949, 52, 53, 58, 59, 62, 66(2), 68, 69, 71(3)
NBiSU	1969(1,3)
NNC	1947, 48, 52, 53, 57
NOneoU	1969(3)
NSyU	1958, 61, 66, 69, 72
NbU	1948, 53, 62, 64, 71(4)
NcU	1932, 55, 59, 61, 62, 64, 66, 68, 69, 71(2)
NdU	1947, 48, 62, 66(2), 69, 71(2,4), 72
NhD	1948, 55, 59, 62, 64, 66, 68
NjP	1939, 47-49, 52, 58, 66(2), 68, 69, 70(11), 71(3), 72, 75(1,2)
NvU	1952, 58, 64
OU	1932, 41, 48, 49, 53, 54, 56, 58-62, 65, 66, 67(A1-5,7,8,B2,4), 68-70, 72
OkT	1939, 47, 52, 53, 64
OkU	1932, 39, 41, 47-49, 52, 53, 65, 66(2), 68, 72
PPiGulf	1941, 47, 52, 53, 58
PSt	1952, 55
RPB	1956, 62
SdRM	1966, 69

TMM	1966(2)
TxDaAR-T	1937, 39, 41, 47, 48, 52, 53, 58, 64-67, 69, 70, 71(2-4), 72, 74, 75(2)
TxDaDM	1939, 41, 44, 53, 66(2), 69, 70, 72, 73(1-3)
TxDaM	1939, 47, 52, 53, 72, 73
TxDaSM	1932, 44, 48, 53, 54, 57, 58, 60, 66(2), 67, 68(1-2), 69, 72, 75(1)
TxHSD	1947, 52, 53, 65, 67(2), 68, 74(3)
TxHU	1941, 48, 51-53, 58, 64, 66(2)
TxLT	1939, 41, 47, 52, 53, 66(2)
TxMM	1933, 39, 41, 47, 52, 53, 58, 66
TxU	1924, 37, 39, 49, 52, 53, 58, 63, 64, 66, 68-72
TxU-Da	1932, 41, 47, 52, 53, 56, 60, 61, 73
ViBlbV	1953, 58, 64, 66(2)
WU	1966(1), 72
WyU	1947

(13) AMERICAN ASSOCIATION OF PETROLEUM GEOLOGISTS. REGIONAL MEETING. (TITLE VARIES)

1937 Southwestern Pennsylvania, West Virginia, western Virginia, western Maryland. [midyear meeting.]

1938 Field trips, midyear meeting, El Paso, Texas. (338)
No. 1. Alamogordo trip.
No. 2. Glass Mountains-Marathon Basin trip.
No. 3. Carlsbad; oil field trip.
No. 4. Malone Mountain-Green Valley trip.
No. 5. Silver City trip.

1947 See South Texas Geological Society. (290)
1948 See Pittsburgh Geological Society. (245)
1950 See Canadian Society of Petroleum Geologists. (61)
1951 See South Texas Geological Society. (290)
1958 See North Texas Geological Society. (220)
1959 See Gulf Coast Association of Geological Societies. (114)
1960 See Southwestern Federation of Geological Societies. (295)
1965 See Gulf Coast Association of Geological Societies. (114)

[I-GS]	1948
IU	1947
KyU	1959, 60, 65
OCU	1937
OU	1948, 58-60, 65
TxMM	1938
TxU	1938

(14) AMERICAN ASSOCIATION OF PETROLEUM GEOLOGISTS. EASTERN SECTION. FIELD TRIP GUIDEBOOK.

1956 One-day field trip in the New York City area.
1972 1st No. 1. Geology of Silurian rocks, northwestern Ohio. (226)
No. 2. Pennsylvanian deltas in Ohio and northern West Virginia.

CLU-G/G	1972(1)
CU-EART	1956
CaOKQ	1972(1)
CoG	1956, 72
DI-GS	1956
ICF	1972(1)
ICarbS	1972(2)

(14) American Association of Petroleum Geologists. Eastern Section. Field Trip Guidebook.

IU	1972(2)
InU	1956
KyU	1972
MNS	1956
MoSW	1972(1)
NcU	1974
NjP	1972(1)
OU	1972(1)
OkU	1956
TxDaAR-T	1972
ViBlbV	1972(1)

(15) AMERICAN ASSOCIATION OF PETROLEUM GEOLOGISTS. MID-CONTINENT SECTION. GUIDEBOOK FOR THE FIELD TRIP HELD AT THE ANNUAL MEETING.

1955 Regional stratigraphy and structure of the Arbuckle Mountain region.
1957 See Tulsa Geological Society. (314)
1959 See Kansas Geological Society. (147)
1961 Palo Duro Canyon State Park.

DI-GS	1959
NcU	1959
OU	1957
TxLT	1955
TxU	1961

(16) AMERICAN ASSOCIATION OF PETROLEUM GEOLOGISTS. PACIFIC SECTION. GUIDEBOOK FOR THE FIELD TRIP HELD AT THE ANNUAL MEETING.

1944 Type locality of Sycamore Canyon Formation, Whittier Hills, Los Angeles County, California. (279)
1947 Gaviota Pass-Refugio Pass areas, Santa Barbara County, California. (279)
1950 North Mt. Diablo monocline, Contra Costa County, California. (279)
1951 May Cuyama District, California. (256, 279)
1953 Santa Ana Mountains, California. (279)
1954 San Marcos Pass to Jalama Creek. (279)
1955 Devils Den-McLure Valley area. (256, 279)
1956 May Huasna Basin, San Luis Obispo County, California. (256, 279)
1958 Imperial Valley, California. (279)
1960 Type Panoche-Panoche Hills area, Fresno County, California. (256, 279)
1961 1. Geology and paleontology of the southern border of San Joaquin Valley, Kern County, California. (256, 279, 284)
June Rincon Island-Casitas-Ventura Avenue field areas.
1962 See Society of Economic Paleontologists and Mineralogists. Pacific Section. (279)
See California. Division of Mines and Geology. (54)
1963 Geology of Salinas Valley; Production, stratigraphy, structure and the San Andreas Fault. (279)
See Alaska Geological Society. (7)
1964 See Society of Economic Paleontologists and Mineralogists. Pacific Section. (279)
1965 1. Western Santa Ynez Mountains, Santa Barbara, California. (279)
[1] Geology of southeastern San Joaquin Valley, California; Kern River to Grapevine Canyon. (279)
[2] Placerita-Soledad-Vasquez rocks area, Soledad Basin, Los Angeles County, California. (279)

1966		1. Santa Susana Mountains. (279)
		2. A tour of the coastal oilfields of the Los Angeles Basin in and adjacent to San Pedro Bay, California. (279)
1967		1. Geology of the Big Mountain oil field and the nearby area, including notes on the trip from Piru to Big Mountain, Ventura County, California. (279)
		2. Gabilan Range and adjacent San Andreas Fault. (279)
1968		1. Tehachapi Mountain crossing of the California aqueduct, Kern and Los Angeles counties, southern California.(279)
		2. Field trip guide to Santa Rosa Island. October. (279)
		3. Geology and oil fields, the west side, southern San Joaquin Valley. (279)
1969		[1] Geology of the northern Channel Islands and southern California borderlands. (AAPG/SEPM. Pacific Section. Special Publication.) (279)
	Mar.	Geology and oilfields of coastal areas, Ventura and Los Angeles Basins, California. (279, 284)
	Oct.	Geologic setting of upper Miocene gypsum and phosphate deposits, upper Sespe Creek and Pine Mountain, Ventura County, California. (279)
		[2] Geology of the central part of the Fillmore Quadrangle, Ventura County, California.
1970	Mar.	Geologic guide book. Southeastern rim of the Los Angeles Basin, Orange County, California; Newport Lagoon-San Joaquin Hills-Santa Ana Mountains.
	June	Ventura Avenue & San Miguelito oil fields.
	Fall	Pacific slope geology of northern Baja California and adjacent Alta California. (279, 284)
1971		Summary field trip guide, San Andreas Fault-San Francisco Peninsula.
		San Fernando earthquake field trip, road log.
1972		[1] Central Santa Ynez Mountains, Santa Barbara County, California.
		[2] Geology and oil fields, west side, central San Joaquin Valley. (279, 284)
1973		No. 1. Metropolitan oil fields and their environmental impact.
		No. 2. Imperial Valley regional geology and geothermal exploration.
		No. 3. Santa Barbara Channel region revisited.
		[4] Spring field trip. Traverse of Castaic-Ridge basins and basement complex north of Valencia, California, with tour of west branch, California aqueduct system, Antelope Valley to Castaic.
		[5] Miocene sedimentary environments and biofacies, southeastern Los Angeles Basin.
1974	49th	A guidebook to the geology of peninsular California prepared for the annual meeting of AAPG-SEPM-SEG
	Oct.	The Paleogene of the Panoche Creek-Cantua Creek area, central California.
1975		A tour of the oil fields of the Whittier fault zone, Los Angeles Basin, California.

AzTeS	1947, 51, 54, 56-74
[CDU]	1944, 47, 50, 51, 53, 54(2), 55, 56, 58, 61, 62, 63, 65-68, 69(2), 70, 71, 72(2), 73(1-3), 74(49th)
CLU-G/G	1961, 65-68, 69(Mar.), 70, 71(Feb.), 72(2), 74(49th), 75
CLhC	1963, 65(1,Apr.), 66(2), 67, 68(3), 69(1,2), 72(2), 73(2)
CSdS	1947, 50, 54, 58, 66(2), 67(2), 68-70, 72, 73, 74(49th)
CSfCSM	1963, 65, 66(2), 67(2), 68(1,3), 69(Mar.,Oct.), 70(Mar.), 72(2), 73(1,2,4)
CU-EART	1947, 50, 54, 58, 60, 61(June), 62-66, 67(2), 68(2,3), 69(1,2,Mar.), 70, 71(Feb.), 72(2), 73(1-4), 75
CaACU	1967
[CaBVU]	1967
CaOHM	1965, 73(2), 75
CaOKQ	1965(1), 67-69
CaOLU	1963, 65, 66(1), 67, 68
CaOWtU	1970
CoFS	1965(1), 66(2), 67, 68(3), 69(1,2,Mar.)

(16) American Association of Petroleum Geologists. Pacific Section.

CoG	1960, 65(1), 66, 67, 68-70
CoU	1968-70
DI-GS	1965, 66, 67(2), 68, 70, 71-73(1-4), 75
DLC	1967(2)
ICF	1968
IU	1947, 54, 58, 61, 63, 64, 65(2), 66, 67, 68-72, 73(1-3), 74(49th), 75
IaU	1963, 64, 65(1), 66-68, 69(1,Mar.,Oct.), 70(Mar.,Fall), 71, 72, 73(1-4), 74(49th)
IdBB	1962, 64, 65(1), 67(2), 68, 70, 71
IdPI	1963
InU	1954, 68(3), 69, 70(Fall)
KyU	1965(1), 66(2), 67, 70(Fall), 72(2)
MH-GS	1970(Fall)
MNS	1958
MiU	1961(June), 67(1), 69(Mar.), 70(June,Fall)
MnU	1950-59, 61-69
MoSW	1965(1), 68(3)
MoU	1965(1), 66(2), 67, 68(1,3), 69(Mar.)
NOneoU	1967(2), 68(3), 69(1), 70
NRU	1970(Mar.,Fall)
NSyU	1958, 72(2)
NcU	1964, 65, 67(2), 71(Feb.)
NjP	1958, 65(1), 66, 67, 68, 69(1,Mar.), 70(Fall)
OCU	1965-68, 69(1,Mar.),70,71(Feb.)
OU	1947, 55, 56, 61(1), 62-68, 69(Mar.), 70, 71(Feb.), 72
OkU	1963, 65(1), 66(2), 67(2), 68, 69(Mar.)
OrU	1965(2)
PPiGulf	1966(1), 68(2), 69(Mar.), 70(Mar.,Fall), 72
PSt	1970(M)
TxDaAR-T	1965(2), 66-70, 71(Feb.), 72, 73(1-4), 74(49th), 75
TxDaDM	1947, 60, 61(June), 64, 65(2), 66, 67, 68, 69(1,2,Mar.), 70, 71(Feb.), 72(2), 73(4)
TxDaM	1960, 66
TxDaSM	1950, 62, 64, 65, 67(1), 68(2), 69(Mar.), 70(Mar.,Fall), 72(2), 73(1-4)
TxHSD	1963, 65(1), 66(2), 67(2), 68(1), 69(Mar.,Oct.)
TxMM	1956(1), 66(2), 67, 68(3), 69(Mar.)
TxU	1963, 65(1), 66, 67(spring), 68, 69, 70, 71(Feb.), 72, 74(49th)
TxU-Da	1965, 67(2), 68, 69, 70(Mar.,June), 72, 73(1-4)
ViBlbV	1965(1), 67(2), 68, 70(Fall)
WyU	1965-68

(17) AMERICAN ASSOCIATION OF PETROLEUM GEOLOGISTS. ROCKY MOUNTAIN SECTION. GUIDEBOOK FOR THE ANNUAL MEETING AND FIELD TRIP.

1964	Durango-Silverton. (88)
1967	[Casper Mountain and Alcova] Road log.
1974	Parkman Delta in central Wyoming.
	Upper Cretaceous field trip log.
	Pratt Ranch First Frontier Sandstone outcrop.
	Geology and geochemistry of the Highland uranium deposit.
	Dave Johnston coal strip mine road log. (Wyoming Geological Association. Earth Science Bulletin. Vol. 6:4.)
1975	Field trips to central New Mexico.

[A-GS]	1964
CLU-G/G	1964, 74
CLhC	1964
CU-EART	1964, 67
CoDuF	1964
CoG	1964
DI-GS	1964
ICIU-S	1964
ICarbS	1964
IU	1964
IaU	1964
KyU	1964
MiDW	1964
MnU	1964
NBiSU	1964
NNC	1964
NcU	1964
NdU	1975
OU	1964
OkU	1964
PBL	1964
TxDaAR-T	1964
TxDaDM	1964
TxDaM	1964
TxDaSM	1964
TxHSD	1964
TxHU	1964
TxLT	1964
TxMM	1964
TxU	1964, 67

(18) AMERICAN ASSOCIATION OF STRATIGRAPHIC PALYNOLOGISTS. FIELD TRIP GUIDEBOOK.

1968	1st	Lower Mississippi Valley, Baton Rouge to Vicksburg.
1969	2nd	Field trip to the Allegheny Front and Appalachian Plateau of central Pennsylvania.
		Sedimentation in the Carboniferous of western Pennsylvania.
1971	4th	[1] Geology along Arizona Highways 77 and 87 between Tucson, Holbrook, and Phoenix. Field guidebook from Tucson, Arizona to the Petrified Forest National Park and the Meteor Crater.
		[2] Lehner early man-mammoth site.
1972	5th	Field guide to geology of the Cape Cod National Seashore.
1973	6th	Field guidebook for Sequoia and Kings Canyon national parks.
		Guidebook [to] coastal area geology at Torrey Pines State Preserve, and La Jolla, San Diego County, California.

CLU-G/G	1969
CLhC	1969
CSdS	1969
CaOLU	1968
CaOOG	1968, 73
DI-GS	1968, 71-73
ICarbS	1969
IU	1971
IaU	1969, 72, 73

(18) American Association of Stratigraphic Palynologists.

InU	1972
KyU	1969, 71
MH-GS	1972
MoSW	1969
MoU	1972
NRU	1972
NcU	1972
NdU	1972
NhD	1972
NjP	1969, 72
OU	1968, 69
OkU	1968
PSt	1969
TxDaAR-T	1965, 68, 69, 71-73
TxDaDM	1969
TxDaSM	1969, 71
TxU	1968, 69, 73(2)

(19) AMERICAN CRYSTALLOGRAPHIC ASSOCIATION.

1965 Gatlinburg, Tennessee-southern Appalachians. (172)

CoG	1965
DI-GS	1965
IEN	1965
IU	1965
IaU	1965
NBiSU	1965
NNC	1965
NOneoU	1965
NcU	1965
NdU	1965
NhD	1965
NjP	1965
NmPE	1965
OkU	1965
PBL	1965
PBm	1965
TMM	1965
TxDaDM	1965
ViBlbV	1965

(20) AMERICAN GEOGRAPHICAL ASSOCIATION OF NEW YORK.

1912 Guidebook for the transcontinental excursion.

CoG	1912
DI-GS	1912
IaU	1912

(21) AMERICAN GEOLOGICAL INSTITUTE. INTERNATIONAL FIELD INSTITUTE. GUIDEBOOK. (TITLE VARIES)

1970 Guidebook to the Caribbean Island-arc system.

CLU-G/G	1970
CaOHM	1970

CaOKQ	1970
CaOWtU	1970
DI-GS	1970
IU	1970
InLP	1970
MH-GS	1970
MoRM	1970
NBiSU	1970
NRU	1970
NcU	1970
NhD	1970
PSt	1970

AMERICAN INSTITUTE OF BIOLOGICAL SCIENCES. See BOTANICAL SOCIETY OF AMERICA. PALEOBOTANICAL SECTION. (49)

(22) AMERICAN INSTITUTE OF MINING AND METALLURGICAL ENGINEERS. SOUTHWESTERN NEW MEXICO SECTION.

1949 No. 3. Geology and ore deposits of Silver City region, New Mexico. (96, 338)

DI-GS	1949
NhD	1949

(23) AMERICAN INSTITUTE OF MINING, METALLURGICAL AND PETROLEUM ENGINEERS. INDUSTRIAL MINERALS DIVISION.

1950 Guidebook of field trip in the Arbuckle Mountains.
1952 Industrial sand deposits of the Indiana dunes.

IU	1950
OU	1952
OkU	1950
TxLT	1950
TxU	1950

(24) AMERICAN INSTITUTE OF MINING, METALLURGICAL AND PETROLEUM ENGINEERS. SOUTHERN CALIFORNIA PETROLEUM SECTION.

1956 Ventura Avenue and San Miguelito fields.

OCU	1956
OU	1956

(25) AMERICAN INSTITUTE OF MINING, METALLURGICAL AND PETROLEUM ENGINEERS. SOUTHWEST MINERAL INDUSTRY CONFERENCE.

1965 Field trip guidebook; A.I.M.E. Southwest Mineral Industry Conference.

(26) AMERICAN MUSEUM OF NATURAL HISTORY.

1968 Geology of New York City and environs.
A. Geologic features in Fort Tryon and Indwood Hill Parks.
B. The geology seen on a cross-Bronx to Manhattan field trip.
C. The geology of the northern Palisade and Watchung ridges.
D. Geologic features in the northern part of the New Jersey lowland.
E. Some geologic features on Staten Island (Borough of Richmond), New York City.

F. The Precambrian and Paleozoic geology of the Hudson Highlands and vicinity.
G. The geology seen on a trip to the Delaware Water Gap.
H. Some geologic features seen in the southern part of the Connecticut Valley lowland.

CChiS	1968
[CDU]	1968
CSdS	1968
CU-EART	1968
CaAEU	1968
CaOOG	1968
CoG	1968
DI-GS	1968
ICF	1968
InU	1968
MiHM	1968
NBiSU	1953, 55, 57, 59, 63, 70
NSyU	1968
NbU	1968
NcU	1968
NdU	1968
NhD	1968
NjP	1968
OU	1968
OrU	1968
PBL	1968
TMM	1968
ViBlbV	1968

(27) AMERICAN PETROLEUM INSTITUTE.

1948 Spring meeting, Eastern District, White Sulphur Springs, West Virginia, log of field trip.

InU	1948
OkU	1948

(28) AMERICAN PETROLEUM INSTITUTE. NORTHERN CALIFORNIA CHAPTER. DIVISION OF PRODUCTION.

1972 Field trip to the Geysers geothermal field, Lake and Sonoma counties.

[CDU]	1970
TxHSD	1970

(29) AMERICAN QUATERNARY ASSOCIATION.

1972 2nd Field Trip No. 1. Windley's Key Quarry (Key Largo Limestone-late Pleistocene).
Field Trip No. 2. Holocene sedimentation in the Everglades and saline tidal lands.

1976 San Francisco Peaks; a guidebook to the geology. Second edition, 1976. First edition, 1970.
(92)

[I-GS]	1972
IU	1976

AMERICAN STATE GEOLOGISTS. See ASSOCIATION OF AMERICAN STATE GEOLOGISTS. (38)

(30) ANNUAL MIDWEST GROUNDWATER CONFERENCE.

1960 5th See Missouri. Geological Survey. (181)

(31) APPALACHIAN GEOLOGICAL SOCIETY. GUIDEBOOK; FIELD TRIP.

1949	Log of field trip; Morgantown, West Virginia to Terra Alta gas field, Salt Lick Creek.
1952	Development of new gas fields in eastern West Virginia and western Maryland; West Virginia field trip log book.
1953	Elkins, West Virginia to Clifton Forge, Virginia to White Sulphur Springs, West Virginia. (339)
1955	Harrisonburg area, Virginia. (339)
1957	Blackwater Falls State Park, West Virginia to mouth of Seneca, West Virginia. (339)
	Some stratigraphic and structural features of the Middlesboro Basin. (104)
1958	See Johns Hopkins University. (145)
1959	Cacapon State Park, Berkeley Springs, West Virginia. (245)
1961	Blackwater Falls State Park, West Virginia. (245, 339)
1963	Tectonics and Cambrian-Ordovician stratigraphy in the central Appalachians of Pennsylvania. (245)
1964	The Great Valley in West Virginia. (245, 339)
1970	Silurian stratigraphy, central Appalachian Basin.
1972	See American Association of Petroleum Geologists. Eastern Section. Field Trip Guidebook. (14)

CLU-G/G	1952, 53, 55, 57, 61, 63, 64, 70
CLhC	1970
CU-EART	1955
CaOKQ	1963, 70
CaOOG	1953, 63
CoG	1955, 59, 61, 70
CoU	1970
DI-GS	1953, 55, 57, 59, 63, 70
ICF	1959, 61
ICarbS	1955
IEN	1970
IU	1959, 61, 64
IaU	1958, 70
InLP	1957, 61, 64
InU	1949, 53, 63, 68
KyU	1955, 70, 72
MH-GS	1970
MnU	1955, 57, 59, 63, 64
MoSW	1953
MoU	1970
NBiSU	1953, 57
NNC	1952, 53, 61, 63
NSyU	1970
NbU	1959, 61
NcU	1955, 63, 70
NjP	1963
OCU	1964
OU	1949, 52, 53, 55, 59, 70
OkT	1955
OkU	1948, 49, 52, 53, 55, 57, 59, 61, 63
PBm	1963

PPiGulf	1952, 53, 55, 57, 70
PSt	1963
RPB	1953
TMM	1955
TxDaAR-T	1955, 59, 70
TxDaDM	1952, 53, 55, 59, 61, 63, 64, 68, 70
TxDaM	1959, 61
TxDaSM	1970
TxHSD	1970
TxHU	1959
TxMM	1953, 63
TxU	1955, 59, 61, 63, 64
ViBlbV	1955, 59, 64

(32) ARDMORE GEOLOGICAL SOCIETY. FIELD CONFERENCE GUIDEBOOK.

1936	Mar.	Pennsylvanian of the Ardmore Basin.
	Apr. 4	Pre-Pennsylvanian of the Ardmore area.
		Ardmore to the Wichita Mountains, Oklahoma.
	May 5	The Pennsylvanian System of the Ardmore Basin.
		Ouachita Mountain field conference, southeastern Oklahoma.
	June	Ardmore to the Ouachita Mountains, Oklahoma.
	Dec.	Study of the Pennsylvanian outcrops of Palo Pinto, Parker, Eastland, Brown and Coleman counties, Texas.
1937	Mar.	The Hoxbar and upper Deese formations south of Ardmore.
	Apr.	Study of Lower Pennsylvanian, Mississippian, and Ordovician formations north and west sides of the Llano Uplift, central Texas.
	May	Structure of the Criner Hills.
1938		The Lower Pennsylvanian of the Berwyn and Baum areas.
1940	11th	Washita Valley fault system and adjacent structures.
1942	13th	[No title available.]
1946		A structural and stratigraphic consideration of the Arbuckle Mountains and the Criner Hills.
1948		A study of Pennsylvanian formations, Ardmore area, Oklahoma.
1950	14th	Study of structure and stratigraphy in the Arbuckle Mountains and related structures in Carter, Murray and Johnston counties, Oklahoma.
1952	15th	Ouachita Mountains in Johnston and Atoka counties, Oklahoma. (Paleozoic structures and stratigraphy.)
1954	16th	Southern part of the Oklahoma Coal Basin.
1955	17th	See Oklahoma. Geological Survey. (232)
1956	18th	Ouachita Mountains, southeastern Oklahoma.
1957	19th	Criner Hills field conference, Lake Murray area, southern Oklahoma.
1959		See American Association of Petroleum Geologists. (12)
1963		Basement rocks and structural evolution of southern Oklahoma.
1966		Pennsylvanian of the Ardmore Basin, southern Oklahoma.
1969		Geology of the Arbuckle Mountains along Interstate 35, Carter and Murray counties, Oklahoma.

[A-GS]	1950
AzFU	1954-56, 66
CLU-G/G	1948, 50, 52, 54-57, 59, 66, 69
CLhC	1966, 69
CU-EART	1936(Mar.,Apr. 18,June,Dec.), 37, 38, 54, 66, 69
CaAC	1956
[CaBVU]	1957, 63

CaOHM	1966, 69
CoG	1940, 48, 50, 56, 57, 63, 66, 69, 70
[CoPU]	1969
CoU	1963
DFPC	1959
DI-GS	1936(May,Dec.), 37(Mar.), 48, 50, 54, 56, 59, 63, 66
ICF	1950, 54, 56, 57
ICIU-S	1956
IEN	1940, 48
[I-GS]	1940
IU	1948, 50, 54-57, 59, 63, 66
IaU	1957, 59, 63, 66, 69
IdPI	1957
InLP	1963, 69
InU	1950, 53, 56, 57, 59, 63
KyU	1954, 55, 59, 66, 69
MnU	1936(1), 54-57, 59, 63, 66
MoSW	1963, 69
MoU	1963, 66
NNC	1940, 48, 50, 54, 56, 57, 63
NSyU	1955, 63
NbU	1950, 56, 57, 63
NcU	1955, 59, 63, 66
NdU	1963
NhD	1955, 59
NmPE	1966, 69
OCU	1952, 63
OU	1948, 50, 52, 54, 55, 57, 59, 63
OkOkU	1957, 63
OkT	1936(Mar.,Apr. 4), 37(Mar.), 38, 48, 50, 54, 56, 57, 63
OkU	1936(Mar.,Apr. 4,18,June), 37, 38, 40, 46, 48, 50, 52, 54, 56, 57, 60, 63, 66, 67, 69
PBL	1956
PSt	1963
TMM	1966, 69
TxDaAR-T	1940, 48, 50, 52, 54, 56, 57, 63, 66, 69
TxDaDM	1950, 54, 56, 57, 63, 69
TxDaM	1940, 42, 46, 50, 52, 54, 56, 57, 63, 66
TxDaSM	1948, 52, 56, 57, 63, 66, 69
TxHSD	1936, 57, 66, 69
TxHU	1948, 50, 52, 54, 56, 63, 66, 69
TxLT	1936(Apr. 18), 46, 50, 54, 56, 57
TxMM	1936(Apr. 4,Dec.), 37(Apr.), 38, 40, 46, 48, 50-54, 56, 57, 63, 66
TxU	1936(Mar.,Apr. 4,18,May 5,June), 37, 38, 48, 50, 52, 54, 56, 57, 63, 66, 69
UU	1946, 56
ViBlbV	1950, 56
WU	1948, 56, 57, 63
WyU	1963

(33) ARIZONA. BUREAU OF MINES. BULLETIN.

1965	174	Guidebook 1. Highways of Arizona. U. S. Highway 666.
1967	176	Guidebook 2. Highways of Arizona. Arizona Highways 77 and 177.
1971	183	Guidebook 3. Highways of Arizona. Arizona Highways 85, 86 and 386.
	184	Guidebook 4. Highways of Arizona. Arizona Highways 87, 88 and 188.

AzTeS	1965, 67
CLU-G/G	1965, 67
CSdS	1965, 67
CaOKQ	1965, 67
CoG	1965, 67
CoU	1965, 67, 71
DI-GS	1965, 67, 71
ICF	1965, 67, 71
IEN	1965, 67, 71
IU	1965, 67, 71
IaU	1965, 67, 71
InU	1965, 67, 71
KyU	1965, 67, 71
MH-GS	1967
MiHM	1965, 67, 71
MoSW	1965, 67, 71
MoU	1965, 67
NSyU	1967
NbU	1965, 67
NdU	1965, 67, 71
NhD	1965, 67, 71
NjP	1965, 71
NvLN	1965, 67
OCU	1965, 67, 71
OU	1965, 67
OkT	1965, 67, 71
OkU	1965, 67
OrU	1965, 67
PBL	1965, 67
PSt	1965, 67
TxDaAR-T	1971
TxU	1965, 67, 71

(34) ARIZONA GEOLOGICAL SOCIETY. SOUTHERN ARIZONA GUIDEBOOK. (TITLE VARIES)

1952	1st	Southern Arizona. (97, 279)
		Trip 1. Ground water problems of Queen Creek area. (97)
		Trip 2. Paleozoic and Cretaceous stratigraphy of the Tucson Mountains. (97)
		Trip 3. Santa Catalina Mountains metamorphic area. (97)
		Trip 4. Economic geology; Ajo porphyry copper. (97)
		Trip 5. Stratigraphy, structure, and economic geology typical of southern Arizona. (97)
1958		See New Mexico Geological Society. (207)
1959	2nd	Nos. 1-6(Combined with the 2nd annual Arizona Geological Society Digest.) See Geological Society of America. Cordilleran Section. (97)
1966		Road log for southern Santa Rita Mountains, Santa Cruz and Pima counties, Arizona. (U. S. Geological Survey Reports-Open File Series, No. 827.)
1968	3rd	Field Trips 1-6. See Geological Society of America. Cordilleran Section. (97)

AzFU	1952, 59, 68
AzTeS	1952, 58, 59, 68
[CDU]	1968
CLU-G/G	1959, 68
CLhC	1952, 59, 68
CSdS	1952, 68
CSfCSM	1959
CU-EART	1959, 68
CaACU	1968
[CaBVU]	1959
CaOHM	1968
CaOKQ	1968
CaOLU	1959, 68
CaOOG	1959, 68
CoDuF	1968
CoG	1952, 59, 68
CoU	1952, 59, 68
DI-GS	1952, 58, 59, 66, 68
ICF	1968
ICarbS	1959
IEN	1959, 68
IU	1952, 59, 68
IaU	1958, 59, 68
IdPI	1968
InRE	1968
InU	1952, 59, 68
KyU	1959, 68
LU	1959
MH-GS	1959, 68
MNS	1952, 59
MiDW	1952, 59, 68
MiHM	1968
MiU	1968
[MnSSM]	1968
MnU	1952, 58, 59, 66
MoSW	1952, 59, 68
NBiSU	1968
NNC	1952, 59
NRU	1959, 68
NSyU	1959, 68
NbU	1968
NcU	1952, 68
NdU	1959, 68
NhD	1968
NjP	1952, 68
NmPE	1968
NvLN	1952, 68
NvU	1952, 59, 68
OCU	1952, 59, 68
OU	1959, 68
OkT	1959, 68
OkU	1952

(34) Arizona Geological Society.

OrU	1952, 59, 68
PBL	1959
PBm	1959
PSt	1958, 59, 68
RPB	1959, 68
TMM	1968
TxDaAR-T	1952, 59, 68
TxDaDM	1952, 59, 68
TxDaM	1959
TxDaSM	1952, 59
TxHSD	1959, 68
TxLT	1959, 68
TxMM	1952, 59, 68
TxU	1952, 59, 68
UU	1952, 59
ViBlbV	1959
WU	1952, 68

(35) ARKANSAS. GEOLOGICAL COMMISSION. GUIDEBOOK. (TITLE VARIES)

1956 Northwest Arkansas and Magnet Cove. (147)

1963 Southeastern Arkansas Valley. The Ouachita and Frontal Ouachita Mountains, Arkansas.

1967 Central Arkansas economic geology and petrology. (96)

1973 (1) Geology of the Ouachita Mountains, Arkansas.
(2) Geological field trip excursion on Lake Ouachita.
(3) Lower and Middle Ordovician strata of northeastern Arkansas and generalized log of route from Little Rock to Batesville, Arkansas.

CLU-G/G	1967
CU-EART	1967
CaAEU	1967
DI-GS	1967
ICarbS	1973
IEN	1973
IU	1967
InU	1967
KyU	1967, 73
MnU	1963, 67
MoSW	1967
MoU	1967
NBiSU	1967
NdU	1967
NjP	1967
OU	1956
PSt	1967
RPB	1967
TMM	1967
TxDaAR-T	1967

(36) ARKANSAS. RESOURCES AND DEVELOPMENT COMMISSION. DIVISION OF GEOLOGY.

1951 Guidebook to the Paleozoic rocks of northwest Arkansas. (Reprint of Shreveport Geological Society, annual field trip, 1951, 18th). (259)

CLU-G/G	1951
CoU	1951
ICarbS	1951
IEN	1951
[I-GS]	1951
IU	1951
InLP	1951
InU	1951
KyU	1951
MoU	1951
NSyU	1951
NdU	1951
OU	1951
OkT	1951
PPiGulf	1951
TxHU	1951
TxLT	1951
TxU-Da	1951

(37) ASOCIACION MEXICANA DE GEOLOGOS PETROLEROS.

1961		See Southwestern Federation of Geological Societies. (295)

(38) ASSOCIATION OF AMERICAN STATE GEOLOGISTS. GUIDEBOOKS AND ROAD LOGS.

1927		Program and itinerary of field excursion in northern Illinois.
1946	40th	Field conference, Black Hills of South Dakota and Wyoming.
1948		Alabama meeting.
1952	44th	A summary of the geology of Florida and a guidebook to the Cenozoic exposures of a portion of the state.
1953		Hartford, Connecticut. Trip A-B. (Bibliography separate).
		Geologic log for Ventura Basin field trip, Los Angeles to Wheeler Springs and return via coast route. (Mineral Information Service, Vol. 6, No. 2, Feb. 1953, Supplement.)
1955		Southeastern New Mexico-Socorro to Carlsbad, Carlsbad Caverns, potash mining district. (Published by New Mexico Bureau of Mines and Mineral Resources, New Mexico Institute of Mining and Technology, Socorro.)
1956		Selected features of Kentucky geology.
1957		Keweenaw copper range, Marquette iron range; Houghton, Michigan.
1958		See Texas. University. Bureau of Economic Geology. (308)
1959		Kansas field conference. Geological understanding of cyclic sedimentation represented by Pennsylvanian and Permian rocks of northern midcontinent region.
1960		Guidebook, southeastern Pennsylvania.
1961		Guidebook to the geology of the Coeur D'Alene mining district. (120)
1963		Centennial field trip: Appalachian Mountains of West Virginia. (339)
1964		Ardmore Basin.
1966		See Indiana. Geological Survey. (128)
1967	59th	Centennial guidebook to the geology of southeastern Nebraska. (198)
1968		Geology of the Alabama Coastal Plain.
1970	62nd	Trip 1. Guidebook to Ozark carbonate terrane, Rolla-Devils Elbow area, Missouri.
		Trip 2. Guide to the southeast Missouri mineral district.
1973		Geologic log for Ventura Basin field trip, Los Angeles to Wheeler Springs and return via coast route. (Mineral Information Service, Vol. 6, No. 2, Feb. 1953, Supplement.)

(38) Association of American State Geologists.

[A-GS]	1966
CLU-G/G	1963, 66
CLhC	1958, 59
CU-EART	1966
DI-GS	1953(A-B), 56-59, 63, 66, 67, 75
ICarbS	1966
[I-GS]	1927, 46, 48, 52, 56-58, 66-68, 70(1)
IU	1957, 59, 63, 66
IaU	1958-61, 66, 68
InLP	1963
InU	1946, 52
KyU	1953, 56, 58
MNS	1961, 66
MiDW	1966
MiHM	1953, 66-69, 71 66
MnU	1946, 48, 53, 56, 58, 59, 61, 63, 66, 67
MoU	1956
[Ms-GS]	1952
NNC	1956, 59, 63, 66
NSyU	1958, 61
NbU	1953, 58, 66, 67
NcU	1958
NdU	1948, 53, 56, 57, 59, 63, 66, 68
NhD	1961, 66
NjP	1956, 66
OCU	1966
OU	1953, 55-57, 61, 66, 68
OkT	1959
OkU	1946, 53, 55-57, 59, 60, 63, 67, 68, 70, 73
PSt	1958, 63
RPB	1961
TMM	1956
TxDaAR-T	1959, 66
TxDaM	1953(Feb.), 56, 66
TxDaSM	1956
TxU	1953(Feb.), 56, 59, 63, 64
UU	1953, 66
ViBlbV	1956, 66

(39) ASSOCIATION OF EARTH SCIENCE EDITORS.

1973 Ottawa region.

CaOOG 1973

(40) ASSOCIATION OF ENGINEERING GEOLOGISTS. GUIDEBOOK.

1966 Engineering geology in southern California. (Special publication. Reprinted 1969.)

1968 Field trips 1-5 in various areas of Washington State prepared for 1968 national meeting in Seattle.

Geologic exploration of the Guayanes River multipurpose dam, Puerto Rico.

1969 Engineering geology in southern California.

Field Trip 1. California state water project.

Field Trip 2A and 2B. Hayward and Calaveras fault zones.

	Field Trip 3. San Francisco peninsula-Stanford linear accelerator.
	Field Trip 4. Bay areal rapid transit system.
	Field Trip 5. San Francisco peninsular trip for planners and public officials.
	Field Trip 6. The San Francisco Bay and delta model.
1970	Field Trip No. 1, Pt. 1. Engineering geology of the Raystown Dam.
	Field Trip No. 1, Pt. 2. Pennsylvania glass sand corporation plant, Berkeley Springs, West Virginia.
	Field Trip No. 2. Engineering geology in northeastern Pennsylvania and New Jersey.
	Field Trip No. 5. Historical engineering geology of the Chesapeake and Ohio canal. (96)
	(6) Engineering geology in Puerto Rico.
1971	Field Trip No. 1. Columbia Gorge by boat.
	Field Trip No. 2. Oregon coast.
	(3) Mount Hood Loop.
	(4) Portland metropolitan area.
1972 •	Field Trip No. 1. Proposed salt mine repository for radioactive wastes.
	Field Trip No. 2. Underground mines in northeast Kansas.
	Field Trip No. 3. Two-tier occupancy of space-surface and subsurface in the Kansas City area.
	Field Trip No. 4. Highway construction in the Kansas City area.
	Field Trip No. 5. Engineering geology and utilization of underground space in the Kansas City area.
1973	Studies on the geology and geologic hazards of the Greater San Diego area, California.

AzFU	1969
AzTeS	1968, 69
CLU-G/G	1970(1,2,5,6), 73
CSfCSM	1968, 73
CaOOG	1968, 69
CoU	1968
DI-GS	1968, 69
InLP	1968, 69, 71(1,2,4), 72
InU	1968
KyU	1969, 70(1,2,5,6), 71(2,3,4), 73
MNS	1969
MoU	1969
NSyU	1973
NcU	1969
NjP	1968, 73
OCU	1968, 70(1,2), 71(1,2,4), 72
PSt	1971
TMM	1969
TxHSD	1968
TxU	1971
ViBlbV	1968, 69, 70(2,6), 71, 72

(41) ASSOCIATION OF MISSOURI GEOLOGISTS. GUIDEBOOK TO THE ANNUAL FIELD TRIP.

1954	1st	Southeast Missouri lead belt area, sponsored by the St. Joseph Lead Company.
1955	2nd	See Missouri Geological Survey. Report of Investigations. (182)
1956	3rd	Central Missouri.
1957	4th	Eastern Kansas, from Kansas City to Manhattan, Kansas via the Turnpike, U. S. Highway 40 and Kansas Highway 13.
1958	5th	Mexico to Cave Hill.
1959	6th	[Basal relations of the Mississippian in central Missouri.]

(41) Association of Missouri Geologists.

1960	7th	Middle Mississippian and Pennsylvanian stratigraphy of St. Louis and St. Louis County, Missouri.
1961	8th	See Missouri Geological Survey. Report of Investigations. (182)
1962	9th	Geology in the vicinity of Cape Girardeau, Missouri, including Crowleys Ridge.
1963	10th	Geology in the vicinity of Joplin, Missouri, including the Westside-Webber Mine, Oklahoma.
1964	11th	Cryptovolcanic structures of south-central Missouri.
1965	12th	No guidebook published.
1966	13th	Engineering geology of Kaysinger Bluff and Stockton dams, west-central Missouri.
1967	14th	Middle Devonian of central Missouri.
1968	15th	Guidebook to Pleistocene and Pennsylvanian formations in the St. Joseph area, Missouri.
1969	16th	Bonne Terre, Missouri.
1970	17th	Guidebook to the highway geology of Missouri, Route 79 TR, Hannibal to Clarksville.
1971	18th	Guidebook to the geology and utilization of underground space in the Kansas City area, Missouri.
1972	19th	Guidebook of the karst features and stratigraphy of the Rolla area.
1973	20th	Engineering and environmental geology of the Springfield urban area.
1974	21st	Geology of east-central Missouri with emphasis on Pennsylvanian fire clay and Pleistocene deposition.
1975	22nd	Pennsylvanian-Pleistocene channel fill and Quaternary geomorphology near Warrensburg, Missouri.

[A-GS]	1955
CLU-G/G	1955, 61
CLhC	1955
CoG	1967, 68
CoU	1955, 63, 67
DI-GS	1954-56, 58-64, 66-71, 73
ICF	1955
ICIU-S	1962
ICarbS	1955, 74
[I-GS]	1955, 62, 63, 68
IU	1955, 57, 58, 60-63, 66, 67, 71, 73-75
IaU	1961
InLP	1963
InRE	1955
InU	1955, 66-69, 71
KyU	1955, 61, 67-70
MNS	1955, 61
MiKW	1962
MnU	1955, 61-63, 66-68
MoSW	1954, 62, 63, 66, 67, 71, 73
MoU	1955, 59, 62, 63, 66-73
NNC	1962, 63
NRU	1955, 61-63
NbU	1955
NcU	1961
NhD	1955, 61-63
OCU	1955, 58, 67-71
OU	1962
OkT	1955
OkU	1954-56
PSt	1966
RPB	1961

SdRM	1955, 61
TMM	1967
TxDaAR-T	1955, 67, 68, 70
TxDaDM	1955, 59-64, 66-70
TxDaM	1955
TxHSD	1955, 63
TxHU	1955
TxLT	1955
TxU	1954-60, 62-64, 66-71
ViBlbV	1955

(42) ASSOCIATION QUEBECOISE POUR L'ETUDE DU QUATERNAIRE.

1976 Stratigraphie du Wisconsinien dans la region de Trois Rivieres-Shawinigan.

(43) ATLANTIC COASTAL PLAIN GEOLOGICAL ASSOCIATION. GUIDEBOOK FOR THE ANNUAL FIELD CONFERENCE.

1960	1st	Stratigraphic problems of the latest Cretaceous and earliest Tertiary sediments in New Jersey.
1961	2nd	Some remarks pertaining to geology of Atlantic Coastal Plain of New Jersey, Delaware, and Maryland. Non-marine Cretaceous sediments.
1962	3rd	The coastal plain of Virginia north of the James River. (Also issued as Information Circular 6, Virginia Division of Mineral Resources.) (330)
1963	4th	Geology of northeastern North Carolina.
1964	5th	The Cretaceous formations along the Cape Fear River, North Carolina.
1965	6th	Terrace sediment complexes in central South Carolina.
1966	7th	See Georgia. Geological Survey. (112)
1967	8th	Delaware guidebook.
1968	9th	See Maryland. Geological Survey. (160)
1969	10th	See College of William and Mary. (65)
1970	11th	Part 1. Geology of the outer coastal plain, southeastern Virginia, Chesapeake-Norfolk-Virginia Beach.
		Part 2. Geology of the upland gravels near Midlothian, Virginia.
1971	12th	Neogene stratigraphy of the lower coastal plain of the Carolinas.
		Guide to the geology of Delaware's coastal environments. (96)
1972	13th	The geology of the coastal plain from the sounds near New Bern to the Piedmont of Wake County.
1973	14th	A guide to the geology of Delaware coastal environments.
1974	15th	Environmental geology and stratigraphy of Richmond, Virginia area. (332)
1975		Plio-Pleistocene faunas of the central Carolina coastal plain.

[A-GS]	1962
CLU-G/G	1962, 65, 68
CU-EART	1962, 63, 65-72
CoG	1962, 65-71
CoU	1962
DI-GS	1960-68
ICF	1966
ICIU-S	1962, 65-72
[I-GS]	1962, 72
IU	1961-67, 76
IaU	1962, 66
InLP	1965

InU	1961, 62, 65-71
KyU	1962, 65-72, 74
MiHM	1962
MiU	1965-67
MnU	1961, 62, 65-69
NSyU	1962
NbU	1962
NcU	1960-71
NdU	1962
NhD	1966
NjP	1960-72
NvU	1962
OCU	1962, 64, 65, 67, 71
OU	1966, 68, 71
OkU	1962
PBL	1970
PPiGulf	1968
PSt	1962, 65-74
RPB	1962
TxDaAR-T	1963, 66, 68, 70-72, 74
TxDaDM	1960-68
TxDaM	1962
TxHSD	1971
TxHU	1965, 66
TxU	1960-65, 68, 70, 71
ViBlbV	1960, 61, 71

(44) AUGUSTANA COLLEGE, ROCK ISLAND, ILLINOIS. DEPARTMENT OF GEOLOGY. GUIDEBOOK FOR THE ANNUAL SPRING FIELD TRIP.

1953		St. Francois Mountains and mineral district, southeastern Missouri.
1954		Ouachita Mountains magnet cove, Bauxite, Arkansas.
1970	41st	Upper Peninsula Michigan.

IaU	1970
TxU	1953, 54

(45) BASIN AND RANGE GEOLOGY FIELD CONFERENCE.

1965	1st	Guidebook.
1969	2nd	Guidebook.

[CDU]	1969
CLU-G/G	1969
CU-EART	1965, 69
DI-GS	1965, 69
IdBB	1969
InLP	1969
KyU	1969
NdU	1969
NvU	1965, 69
TxHSD	1965

(46) BAYLOR UNIVERSITY, WACO, TEXAS. BAYLOR GEOLOGICAL SOCIETY. FIELD CONFERENCE GUIDEBOOK.

1958	1st	Mid-Cretaceous geology of central Texas.
1959	2nd	Layman's guide to the geology of central Texas.
1960	5th	Cretaceous stratigraphy of the Grand and Black prairies, east-central Texas. (294)
1961		Central Texas field trip.
1962	Feb.	Upper Cretaceous and lower Tertiary rocks in east-central Texas.
	Mar.	Precambrian rocks of the Wichita Mountains, Oklahoma.
1963	Apr.	Geology of the Pennsylvanian-Permian-Cretaceous sequences of central west Texas.
	Nov.	See Texas. University. Geological Society. (310)
1964		Shale environments of the mid-Cretaceous section, central Texas.
	Dec.	Geology and the city of Waco, a guide to urban problems, field trip conducted by the Baylor Geol. Soc. for Texas Academy and National Association of Geology Teachers.
1966		Precambrian and Paleozoic rocks of the eastern part of the Llano Uplift, central Texas.
1967		Valley of the giants.
1968		The Hog Creek watershed.
		2. The Waco region
1969		1. The Bosque watershed.
		2. Mound Valley.
1970		1. The middle Bosque Basin.
		2. Field conference guide. "Lampasas Cut Plain."
		3. Field conference guide.
1971		The Walnut Prairie field conference guidebook.
1972		Urban geology, guidebook for field trip I-35 growth corridor, central Texas.
1973		1. "Valley of the Giants" around the Paluxy River basin.
		2. "Geology in the city," urban geology of the I-35 growth corridor, central Texas.
1974		1. "The Black and Grand prairies."
		2. "Whitney Reservoir."

CChiS	1960
CLU-G/G	1958, 63, 64, 66-69
CLhC	1958
CaAC	1970(3)
CoU	1968
DI-GS	1958, 60, 62(1,2), 63(2), 64-68, 70, 71-74
ICF	1960
IEN	1958
IU	1958, 60, 62-64, 66, 68, 69, 70-74
IaU	1962, 70(3)
KyU	1961, 72
LU	1958, 60
MNS	1958
MnU	1958, 60, 62(Feb.)
NNC	1958, 60, 62(Mar.)
NSyU	1972
NjP	1968
OU	1960
OkT	1960, 62
OkU	1958, 60, 62
PSt	1960
TxDaAR-T	1958, 60, 62(Feb.), 64(1)
TxDaDM	1958, 60, 62, 64(1)
TxDaM	1958-60
TxDaSM	1958, 60

TxHSD	1962(Mar.)
TxHU	1958, 60-64, 68, 70
TxLT	1960, 64
TxMM	1958, 60, 70(3)
TxU	1958, 60, 61, 62(Mar.), 63, 64, 67-69
TxU-Da	1959, 60
UU	1958
WU	1960, 62(Feb.)

(47) BAYLOR UNIVERSITY, WACO, TEXAS. BAYLOR GEOLOGICAL SOCIETY. POPULAR GEOLOGY. NON-TECHNICAL FIELD CONFERENCE.

1960	4th	Popular geology of central Texas; west-central McLennan County.
1961	5th	Bosque County. Popular geology of central Texas, Bosque County.
	6th	Popular geology of central Texas, northwestern McLennan County.
1962	7th	Southwestern McLennan County and eastern Correll County.
1963	8th	Hill country.

CLU-G/G	1963
DI-GS	1961(5,6), 62(7), 63(8)
IU	1961(spring, fall), 62(spring), 63
IaU	1961-63
MnU	1961, 63
NNC	1961(fall)
OCU	1963
OU	1960
OkU	1961, 62
PBL	1962
TxDaDM	1961, 63
TxHU	1961(5,7), 63
TxLT	1963
TxMM	1961
TxU	1961-63
TxU-Da	1963

(48) BERMUDA BIOLOGICAL STATION FOR RESEARCH. SPECIAL PUBLICATION.

1970 No. 4 Field guide to Bermuda geology.

NSyU	1970

BILLINGS GEOLOGICAL SOCIETY. See MONTANA GEOLOGICAL SOCIETY. (186)

(49) BOTANICAL SOCIETY OF AMERICA. PALEOBOTANICAL SECTION.

1970 Eocene plant localities of western Kentucky and Tennessee.

TxDaSM	1970
TxU	1970

(50) BRIGHAM YOUNG UNIVERSITY, PROVO, UTAH. DEPARTMENT OF GEOLOGY. GEOLOGY STUDIES.

1968 15th No. 1, Pt. 2. Guide to the geology of the Wasatch Mountain Front, between Provo Canyon and Y Mountain, northeast of Provo, Utah.

No. 2, Pt. 3. Guide to the geology and scenery of Spanish Forks Canyon along U. S. highways 50 and 6 through the southern Wasatch Mountains, Utah.

No. 3, Pt. 4. Bonneville; an ice-age lake. (With road log.)

		No. 4, Pt. 5. Guidebook to the Colorado River; Part 1, Lee's Ferry to Phantom Ranch in Grand Canyon National Park.
1969	16th	No. 5, Pt. 1. Guidebook to the Colorado River; Part 2, Phantom Ranch in Grand Canyon National Park to Lake Mead, Arizona-Nevada.
1971	18th	No. 6, Pt. 2. Guidebook to the Colorado River; Part 3, Moab to Hite, Utah, through Canyonlands National Park.
1973	20th	No. 7, Pt. 2. Geologic road logs of western Utah and eastern Nevada.
		No. 8. [Not a guidebook].
1974	21st	No. 9, Pt. 2. Geologic guide to the northwestern Colorado Plateau.
1975		Field guide and road log to the western Book Cliffs, Castle Valley, and parts of the Wasatch Plateau. (96)

AzFU	1968(4)
CaACI	1968(2,3)
CaOOG	1968, 69(5)
CaOWtU	1968, 73, 74
CoU	1968, 69(5), 71-74
DI-GS	1973, 74
ICF	1968, 69, 71, 73, 74
ICIU-S	1968, 69, 71-75
IEN	1968, 69, 71, 74
[I-GS]	1973, 74
IU	1968-75
IaU	1968, 69(5), 73, 74
IdBB	1968(4)
IdPI	1968(2-4), 69-74
InRE	1969, 71, 73
InU	1968(4), 71, 74
KyU	1968(4), 75
MiHM	1968, 69, 73
MoSW	1968, 69
NBiSU	1968-74
NcU	1968, 69
NdU	1968-74
NhD	1968, 69
NjP	1968, 69(5), 71-74
NvU	1968(4), 69
OCU	1968-74
OU	1968-74
OkU	1968-74
OrU	1968-71, 74, 75
PBL	1968-73
TMM	1968(4)
TxMM	1968(4)
TxU	1968
TxU-Da	1968(4), 69
UPB	1971-74
ViBlbV	1968-74

(51) BRIGHAM YOUNG UNIVERSITY, PROVO, UTAH. DEPARTMENT OF GEOLOGY. GUIDEBOOK FOR THE GEOLOGY FIELD TRIP.

1957 Provo to Bryce Canyon and Zion national parks, Utah.
1959 Provo to Bryce Canyon and Zion national parks.

[CaBVU] 1959
DI-GS 1957, 59
TxDaSM 1957
TxMM 1959

(52) BRITISH COLUMBIA. UNIVERSITY. DEPARTMENT OF GEOLOGY. GUIDEBOOK FOR GEOLOGICAL FIELD TRIPS.

1962 San Juan Island, Washington.
1965 San Juan Island, Washington.
1968 No. 6. Guidebook for geologic field trips in southwestern British Columbia; a revision of a guidebook prepared by the Geological Discussion Club in March, 1960. (95)
No. 7. Mineralogical Association of Canada field trip to the southern interior of British Columbia. (171)

[CaBVU] 1965
CaOOG 1968
DI-GS 1968(6,7)
InU 1968
NNC 1968
NbU 1962, 68(6)
TxU 1962

(53) CALIFORNIA ASSOCIATION OF ENGINEERING GEOLOGISTS. SACRAMENTO SECTION.

1959 East side San Joaquin Valley field trip.
1962 Dixie Valley and Sand Springs Range, Nevada. (107, 201)

CSfCSM 1959

(54) CALIFORNIA. DIVISION OF MINES AND GEOLOGY. BULLETIN.

1948 No. 141 Geologic guidebook along Highway 49-Sierran gold belt-the Mother Lode country.
1951 No. 154 Geologic guidebook of the San Francisco Bay counties.
1952 No. 169 1st National Conference on clays. (193)
1954 No. 170 Geology of southern California. (96)
1962 No. 181 Geologic guide to the gas and oil fields of northern California. (AAPG/SEPM and Pacific Sections of AAPG/SEPM/SEG annual meetings.) (12, 16, 274, 279, 284)
Field Trip 1. Sacramento Valley.
Field Trip 2. San Francisco to Monterey.
Field Trip 3. Point Reyes peninsula and San Andreas Fault zone.
Field Trip 4. San Francisco peninsula.
Field Trip 5. North flank of Mount Diablo.
No. 182 Field Trip 6. Geologic guide to the Merced Canyon and Yosemite Valley, California, with road logs from Hayward through Yosemite Valley via Tracy, Patterson, Turlock, and Merced Falls. (16, 274, 279, 284)
1966 No. 190 Field trips. (96)
No. 1. Point Reyes peninsula and San Andreas Fault zone.
No. 2. San Francisco peninsula.
No. 3. San Andreas Fault from San Francisco to Hollister.
No. 4. Hydrogeology field trip. East Bay area and northern Santa Clara Valley.

No. 5. Sacramento Valley and northern coast ranges.
No. 6. Yosemite Valley and Sierra Nevada batholith.
No. 7. Mineralogy of the Laytonville Quarry, Mendocino County, California.
No. 11. Special supplement; a walker's guide to the geology of San Francisco. (Vol. 19)

[A-GS]	1948, 51
AzFU	1951, 54, 62
AzTeS	1954
[CDU]	1948-66
CLU-G/G	1948, 51, 54-66
CLhC	1948, 51, 54, 62, 66
CSdS	1948-54, 62(4,6), 66
CU-EART	1948-66
[CaBVU]	1948, 51, 54, 62(181,182), 66
CaOWtU	1961(180-186,190-191)
CaOHM	1951, 54, 62
CaOKQ	1948-54, 62(4,6), 66
CaOON	1949(1942,1952)
CaQQLaS	1948, 51, 52, 54, 62(181,182), 66
CoG	1948, 51, 54, 62(1-5,6), 66
CoU	1948, 51, 52, 54, 62, 66
DFPC	1951
DI-GS	1948, 51, 54, 62(181,182), 66(190)
ICF	1948-66
ICarbS	1951
IEN	1948-54, 62(4,6), 66
[I-GS]	1962(6)
IU	1948, 51, 62, 66
IaU	1948, 51, 54, 62(181,182), 66
IdBB	1954
IdPI	1948, 51, 62
InU	1948-66
KyU	1948, 51, 54, 62(181,182), 66(1-7)
LU	1948-66
MH-GS	1951, 66
MiDW	1948-66
MiHM	1948-54, 62(4,6), 66
MnU	1948, 51, 54, 62, 66
MoSW	1948-66
MoU	1948-62
NBiSU	1948-66
NSyU	1948-66
NbU	1948-66
NcU	1948-66
NdU	1948-66
NhD	1948, 51, 54, 62(181), 66
NjP	1950-62, 65-67
OCU	1948-66
OU	1948-66
OkT	1948, 51, 54-66
OkU	1948, 51, 54-66
OrU	1948-66
PSt	1948, 51, 52, 54, 62(181,182), 66

RPB	1948, 51, 52, 54, 62, 66
TxDaAR-T	1951, 54, 62(181,182), 66
TxDaDM	1948, 51, 54, 62, 66
TxDaM	1948, 51, 62, 66
TxDaSM	1951, 54-66
TxHU	1948, 51, 54, 62, 66
TxMM	1948, 51, 54, 62(181,182), 66
TxU	1954, 66
TxU-Da	1954
ViBlbV	1948-66
WU	1948, 51, 54-66

(55) CALIFORNIA. DIVISION OF MINES AND GEOLOGY. SPECIAL REPORT.

1975 No. 118 San Andreas Fault in southern California; a guide to San Andreas Fault from Mexico to Carrizo Plain. 1975, No. 1. (97)

CU-EART	1975
IU	1975
KyU	1975

(56) CALIFORNIA. STATE UNIVERSITY, CHICO. GEOLOGY DEPARTMENT. FIELD TRIPS.

1959-68 Northern California. (Note: one plus ephemeral sheet for each trip.)

CChiS	1959-68
DI-GS	1959-68

(57) CALIFORNIA. UNIVERSITY, SAN DIEGO. GEOLOGY DEPARTMENT. GUIDEBOOK FOR FIELD TRIPS.

1961 San Diego County. (97)

[CDU]	1961
CSdS	1961
DI-GS	1961
IU	1961
NNC	1961
TxDaDM	1961
TxU	1961

(58) CANADA. GEOLOGICAL SURVEY. GUIDEBOOK.

1913 See International Geological Congress. (136)

(59) CANADIAN INSTITUTE OF MINING AND METALLURGY.

1967 C.I.M.M. Centennial field excursion; northwestern Quebec and northern Ontario.

[CaOHaHa]	1967
CaOOG	1967
DI-GS	1967
IU	1967
InU	1967
MiHM	1967
NBiSU	1967
NOneoU	1967
NjP	1967
TxU	1967

(60) CANADIAN SOCIETY OF EXPLORATION GEOPHYSICISTS.

1975		See Canadian Society of Petroleum Geologists. (61)

(61) CANADIAN SOCIETY OF PETROLEUM GEOLOGISTS. GUIDEBOOK FOR THE ANNUAL FIELD CONFERENCE.

1950		No. 1. Banff area. (94, 282)
		No. 2. Banff Formation, Lac des Arc Fault, Palliser Formation, etc., along Banff-Calgary Highway. (13, 94, 282)
1952	2nd	Kananaskis Valley. (Also contains additional information on Highwood Valley east to Calgary via Turner Valley oil field.)
1953	3rd	Calgary and Crowsnest Pass, southern Alberta.
1954	4th	Banff-Golden-Radium; southern Canadian Rocky Mountains.
1955	5th	Jasper National Park.
1956	6th	Bow Valley, Alberta.
1957	7th	Waterton, Alberta.
1958	8th	Nordegg, Alberta.
1959	9th	Drumheller-Moose Mountain, Alberta.
1960	10th	Map 1 geological. Rocky Mountains, Banff to Golden; structure and stratigraphy.
		Map 2 geological. Banff-Minnewanka-Canmore area. (Maps only for these field trips were published.)
1961	11th	Turner Valley-Savannah Creek, Kananaskis.
1962	12th	Coleman-Cranbrook-Radium. (Also in Journal of the Alberta Society of Petroleum Geologists, Vol. 10, No. 7, July-Aug., 1962.)
1963	13th	Ghost River area.
1964	14th	Flathead Valley, southeast British Columbia. (Bulletin of Canadian Petroleum Geology, Vol. 12, Special Issue, Aug. 1964.)
1965	15th	Cypress Hills Plateau, Alberta and Saskatchewan.
1967		See International Symposium on the Devonian System. (138)
1968	16th	Canadian Rockies-Bow Valley to North Saskatchewan River.
1970		See American Association of Petroleum Geologists. (12)
1971		A guide to the geology of the Eastern Cordillera along the Trans-Canada Highway between Calgary, Alberta, and Revelstoke, British Columbia.
1974		Geology of the Banff area; a student's guide
1975		Structural geology of the foothills between Savanna Creek and Panther River, S.W. Alberta, Canada. (60)

AzFU	1955
[CDU]	1963, 64
CLU-G/G	1953-59, 62, 63-65, 68-71
CLhC	1954-59, 62-64
CSdS	1953, 54
CSfCSM	1970
CU-EART	1953-59, 61-69, 71
CaAC	1953-59, 61, 64, 65, 68-71 (circulate only 1954-56, 58, 62, 64)
[CaACAM]	1954-59, 61-71, 75
CaACI	1950, 52-59, 61-68, 70
CaACM	1950, 53-59, 61-65, 67, 70, 71
CaACU	1953-59
CaAEU	1954-56, 61-65
[CaBVU]	1953-59, 61, 62, 65
CaNBFU	1954
CaOHM	1953

(61) Canadian Society of Petroleum Geologists.

CaOKQ	1953-59, 61-65, 67
CaOLU	1953-59, 62, 63
CaOOCC	1954-60
CaOOG	1952-70
CaOPAL	1955, 56, 59
CaOTRM	1954
CaOWtU	1954-59, 64
CaQMU	1954-59, 61-64
CoG	1953-59, 62-65, 68, 70
[CoPU]	1956, 68, 70
CoU	1953-59, 61-65, 67
DI-GS	1953-59, 62-65, 68, 70, 74
ICF	1955-59, 61
IEN	1954-59, 62-64
[I-GS]	1954-59
IU	1954-59, 61-68, 71
IaU	1950, 54-59, 61-65
IdBB	1956, 57, 62, 68
IdPI	1959
InLP	1954-59, 63, 64
InU	1954-59, 62, 65
KyU	1954, 56, 59, 62, 64-65, 68, 70, 71
LU	1950-59
MH-GS	1954
MNS	1954-56
MiDW	1965
MiHM	1967
NNC	1953-59, 62-65, 67
NSyU	1954-59, 62-64, 69
NbU	1955-59, 62, 63
NcU	1954-59, 61-70
NdU	1954, 56, 61, 62, 64, 67
NhD	1954-59, 62-65, 68
NjP	1950, 54-64
NvU	1954-59, 61
OU	1954-59, 61, 63, 65, 67-71
OkT	1950, 53-56, 58-59
OkU	1953-59, 61, 64
OrU	1956-59, 62-64
PSt	1954-59, 62, 64-65
RPB	1964
SdRM	1954-59, 62, 64, 65
TU	1954-59, 62
TxDaAR-T	1950, 53-59, 62, 64, 65, 67, 70, 71, 75
TxDaDM	1953-59, 61, 64, 68
TxDaM	1953-59, 62-65
TxDaSM	1953-59, 64, 65, 71
TxHSD	1950, 53-55, 59, 64
TxHU	1953-59, 62-65, 67, 75
TxLT	1953, 55
TxMM	1953-59, 62, 64, 65, 67
TxU	1950, 52-65, 67, 70
TxU-Da	1953-59, 62, 63
UU	1955-59, 61, 64

ViBlbV	1956, 68
WU	1954-59, 64, 65

(62) CARIBBEAN GEOLOGICAL CONFERENCE. FIELD GUIDE.

1959	2nd	Roadlog and guide for a geologic field trip through central and western Puerto Rico.
1968		Field guide to the geology of the Virgin Islands.
		1. Guide to the geology of St. Thomas and St. John, Virgin Islands.
		2. Field guide to the geology of St. Croix, U.S. Virgin Islands.

CLU-G/G	1959
IU	1968
TxDaAR-T	1968

(63) CAROLINA GEOLOGICAL SOCIETY. GUIDEBOOK OF EXCURSIONS.

1952		The Great Smoky Mountains.
1955		The coastal plains of North Carolina.
1957		Guidebook for the South Carolina coastal plain field trip. (287)
1958		Lake Murray, South Carolina, and surrounding area.
1959		Geology of the Albemarle and Denton quadrangles, North Carolina; stratigraphy and structure in the Carolina volcanic-sedimentary group.
1960		Road log of the Grandfather Mountain area, North Carolina.
1961		Carolina slate belt...fall line stratigraphy...Columbia, S.C. and Charlotte belt in Newberry County. (South Carolina. Division of Geology. Geologic Notes, Vol. 5, No. 5, Sept.-Oct. 1961.)
1962		Road log of the geology of Moore County, North Carolina.
1963		Geology of Pickens and Oconee counties, South Carolina. (South Carolina. Division of Geology. Geologic Notes, Vol. 7, No. 5, Sept.-Oct. 1963.)
1964		South Carolina coastal plain.
1965		Geology of York County, South Carolina. (South Carolina. Division of Geology. Geologic Notes, Vol. 9, No. 2, Sept. 1965.)
1966		Excursion in Cabarrus County, North Carolina.
1967		Mount Rogers area, Virginia, North Carolina, Tennessee.
1968		Stratigraphy, structure and petrology of the Piedmont in central South Carolina. (South Carolina. Division of Geology. Geologic Notes, Vol. 12, No. 4, Oct. 1968.)
1969		A guide to the geology of northwestern South Carolina (Geologic Notes, Vol. 13, No. 4.)
1970		Stratigraphy, sedimentology and economic geology of Dan River basin, N.C.
1971		Stratigraphy and structure of the Murphy Belt, North Carolina.
1972		The geology of the coastal plain from the sounds near New Bern to the Piedmont of Wake County.
1973	53rd	Granitic plutons of the central and eastern Piedmont of South Carolina.
1974		Geology of the Piedmont and coastal plain near Pageland, South Carolina and Wadesboro, North Carolina.

CLU-G/G	1957, 61, 63, 65, 68, 69
CoG	1957
CoU	1957, 61, 63, 65, 68, 69
DI-GS	1952, 55, 57-67
[I-GS]	1972
IU	1953, 57, 64, 65, 67-73
IaU	1957, 65, 68, 69
InU	1961, 63, 66-69
KyU	1952, 57, 61, 63-73
MH-GS	1952, 67

(63) Carolina Geological Society.

MnU	1957, 61, 63-68
NNC	1952, 57
NbU	1961
NcU	1955, 58-60, 62, 64, 66, 67, 70, 71
NdU	1968, 69
NjP	1959, 60, 62, 64, 66-69, 72
OCU	1952, 53, 66
OU	1957, 61, 63, 65, 68, 69
OkU	1957, 60
PSt	1957
TxDaAR-T	1959, 61, 63, 65-74
TxDaDM	1963-65, 68, 69
TxDaM	1957
TxDaSM	1955
TxU	1959, 61, 63, 65, 68

(64) COAST GEOLOGICAL SOCIETY. GUIDEBOOK.

1965 1st Western Santa Ynez Mountains, Santa Barbara County, California. (16)

[CDU]	1965
CLU-G/G	1965
CLhC	1965
CSfCSM	1965
CU-EART	1965
DI-GS	1965
IdBB	1965
MnU	1965
MoU	1965
OCU	1965
OU	1965
PPiGulf	1965
TxDaDM	1965
TxDaSM	1965
TxU	1965
TxU-Da	1965

(65) COLLEGE OF WILLIAM AND MARY. DEPARTMENT OF GEOLOGY. GUIDEBOOK.

1969 1 Guidebook to the geology of the York-James peninsula and south bank of the James River. (43, 332)

ICIU-S	1969
InU	1969
KyU	1969
NcU	1969
NjP	1969
OCU	1969
PSt	1969
TxU	1969

(66) COLUMBIA UNIVERSITY, NEW YORK GANDER CONFERENCE. (TITLE VARIES)

1967

Geology along the North Atlantic.
Field Trip No. 1. St. John's area.
Field Trip No. 2. St. John's-Random Island-Gander.
Field Trip No. 3. Gander-Carmanville-Change Islands.
Field Trip No. 4. Gander-Boyds Cove-New World Island.
Field Trip No. 5. Gander-Baie Verte.
Field Trip No. 6. Deer Lake-Bonne Bay-St. Anthony.
Field Trip No. 7. Corner Brook-Humber Arm Stephenville-Port au Port Peninsula.

CaOWtU 1967
DLC 1967
MnDuU 1967

(67) COMMONWEALTH MINING AND METALLURGICAL CONGRESS. 6TH BANFF, ALBERTA.

1957

1. Field conference; a study of the stratigraphy and structure of the Canadian Rockies, as exposed in the Banff-Lake Louise area, Alberta, Canada.
[2] Geology and mineral deposits of the Sudbury area, Ontario.

CaOKQ 1957
CaOLU 1957
InU 1957
OkT 1957
PBL 1957

(68) CONFERENCE ON GEOLOGIC PROBLEMS OF THE SAN ANDREAS FAULT SYSTEM, STANFORD UNIVERSITY. PALO ALTO, CALIFORNIA.

1967

Self-guiding field trip map.

[CDU] 1967
CLU-G/G 1967
CSdS 1967
CU-EART 1967
CaOOG 1967
CoG 1967
ICF 1967
ICIU-S 1967
IU 1967 (no map)
InU 1967
KyU 1967
MoU 1967
NSyU 1967
NbU 1967
NcU 1967
NdU 1967
NhD 1967
PBL 1967
TMM 1967
TxU 1967
WU 1967

(69) CONFERENCE ON THE HISTORY OF GEOLOGY, UNIVERSITY OF NEVADA, RENO.

1964 — Sierran trip; Reno, Steamboat Springs, Carson City, Glenbrook, Bijou, Emerald Bay, Tahoe City, Truckee, Reno.
Basin and Range trip; Reno, Fallon, Fairview Peak, Fallon, Virginia City, Reno. (202)

CU-EART	1964
CoU	1964
DI-GS	1964
IU	1964
NhD	1964

(70) CONNECTICUT. STATE GEOLOGICAL AND NATURAL HISTORY SURVEY. GUIDEBOOK.

1965 1st — Post-glacial stratigraphy and morphology of coastal Connecticut. (Originally issued as Geological Society of America. Annual meeting. Guidebook for the field trips, 1963, No. 5.) (96)

1968 2nd — Guidebook for field trips in Connecticut. (204)
Trip A-1. Post-glacial geology of the Connecticut shoreline.
Trip B-1. Two-till problem in Naugatuck-Torrington area, western Connecticut.
Trip B-2. Periglacial features and pre-Wisconsin weathered rock in the Oxford-Waterbury-Thomaston area, western Connecticut.
Trip B-3. Hydrogeology of southwestern Connecticut.
Trip B-4. Engineering geology as applied to highway construction.
Trip C-1. Sedimentology of Triassic rocks in the lower Connecticut Valley.
Trip C-2. General geology of the Triassic rocks of central and southern Connecticut.
Trip C-3. Geology of Dinosaur Park, Rocky Hill, Connecticut.
Trip C-4. Stratigraphy and structure of the Triassic strata of the Gaillard Graben, south-central Connecticut. (For full text see 1970, 3rd.)
Trip C-5. Late Triassic volcanism in the Connecticut Valley and related structure.
Bedrock geology of western Connecticut.
Trip D-1. Progressive metamorphism of pelitic, carbonate, and basic rocks in south-central Connecticut.
Trip D-2. Multiple folding in western Connecticut; a reinterpretation of structure in the Naugatuck-New Haven-Westport area.
Trip D-4. Metamorphic geology of the Collinsville area.
Trip D-5. The bedrock geology of the Waterbury and Thomaston quadrangles.
Trip D-6. Geology of the Glenville area, southwesternmost Connecticut and southeastern New York.
Trip E-1. Animal-sediment relationships and early sediment diagenesis in Long Island Sound.
Bedrock geology of eastern Connecticut.
Trip F-1. The Honey Hill and Lake Char faults.
Trip F-3. Stratigraphy and structure of the metamorphic rocks of the Stony Creek antiform (a "folded fold") and related structural features, southwestern side of the Killingworth Dome.
Trip F-4. A structural and stratigraphic cross-section traverse across eastern Connecticut.
Trip F-5. The Brimfield(?) and Paxton(?) formations in northeastern Connecticut.
Trip F-6. Mineral deposits of the central Connecticut pegmatite district.

1970 3rd — Stratigraphy and structure of the Triassic strata of the Gaillard Graben, south-central Connecticut.

[A-GS]	1965
CLU-G/G	1965, 70
CU-EART	1968
CaOLU	1965, 68

CoG	1965, 68
CoU	1965, 68, 70
DI-GS	1965, 68, 70
ICF	1965-70
ICIU-S	1965-70
ICarbS	1965, 68, 70
IEN	1965
[I-GS]	1965-70
IU	1965, 70
IaU	1965, 68, 70
InLP	1965-70
InU	1965-70
KyU	1965, 68, 70
MH-GS	1970
MNS	1968
MiDW	1965, 70
MiHM	1965-70
MiKW	1965, 68
MnU	1965, 68, 70
MoSW	1965
MoU	1965-70
NBiSU	1965-70
NRU	1965, 68
NSyU	1965-70
NbU	1970
NcU	1965, 68
NdU	1965, 68
NhD	1965-70
NjP	1965, 70
NvU	1965-70
OCU	1968, 70
OU	1965-70
OrU	1965, 68, 70
PPiGulf	1968, 70
PSt	1965, 68, 70
RPB	1965, 68
TxDaM	1965
TxU	1965, 68, 70
WU	1965-70

(71) CORNELL UNIVERSITY. DEPARTMENT OF GEOLOGY. GUIDEBOOK.

1959	See New York State Geological Association. (210)

(72) CORPUS CHRISTI GEOLOGICAL SOCIETY. ANNUAL FIELD TRIP.

1948	Field trip.
1949	Three Rivers, Cotulla, Artesia Wells, Carrizo Springs, Eagle Pass, Del Rio.
1950	Corpus Christi to Laredo to Rio Grande City.
1951	A trip to six selected salt dome structures in southwest Texas.
1952	Northeastern Mexico; Reynosa to Monterrey, Mexico; Cortinas and Huasteca canyons.
1953	Quaternary (Beaumont) to Cretaceous (Fredericksburg).
1954	Quaternary (Beaumont) to Eocene (Mt. Selman).

(72) Corpus Christi Geological Society.

1955		Cretaceous of Austin, Texas area.
1956		Route Corpus Christi, Laredo, Monterrey [Mexico].
1957		South Texas domes.
1958		Sedimentology of south Texas. (114)
1959		Geology of the upper Rio Grande Embayment and a portion of the Edwards Escarpment, Corpus Christi to Del Rio.
1960		Geology of the Chittim Arch and the area north to the Pecos River.
1961		Geology of the Pleistocene-Jurassic of northeastern Mexico, Nuevo Laredo to Monterrey to Reynosa, Mexico.
1962		Sedimentology of south Texas; Corpus Christi to Brownsville.
1963		Geology of Peregrina Canyon and Sierra de El Abra. Corpus Christi to Cds. Valles and Victoria, Mexico.
1964		See Gulf Coast Association of Geological Societies. (114)
1965		Upper Cretaceous asphalt deposits of the Rio Grande Embayment.
1966		Geology of the Austin-Llano area, central Texas. (Supplement to Texas. University. Bureau of Economic Geology. Guidebook, 1963, 5th. Houston Geological Society. Guidebook, 1962, 1st.) (118, 308)
1968		South Texas uranium.
1970	spring	Hidalgo Canyon and La Popa Valley, Nuevo Leon, Mexico. Tertiary-Mesozoic; structure-stratigraphy. Corpus Christi, Nuevo Laredo, Sabinas Hidalgo, Monterrey, China, Reynosa.
1972		See Gulf Coast Association of Geological Societies. (114)
1975		Triple energy field trip, Duval, Webb, and Zapata counties, Texas; uranium, coal, gas.

AzFU	1950, 61-63, 65, 68, 70
CLU-G/G	1949-63, 65, 68, 70
CLhC	1951-54, 57-59, 61-63, 65
CU-EART	1952, 55, 56, 61-63, 65, 68, 70
[CaBVU]	1958, 63
CaOHM	1961, 65, 68, 70
CaOKQ	1950, 62, 63, 65, 66
CoG	1950-53, 55-63, 65, 68, 70
CoU	1961-63, 65, 68
DFPC	1954
DI-GS	1950, 66, 68
ICF	1950, 58, 61-63, 65
IEN	1960
IU	1950, 57-63, 65, 68, 70
IaU	1958, 63, 64
InLP	1963, 65, 66, 68, 70
InU	1950-52, 54, 57, 58, 60-65, 68
KyU	1950, 51, 56, 57, 61-63, 65, 66, 68, 70
LU	1949-63, 65, 68, 70
MiU	1950, 56-58, 61-63, 65, 66
MnU	1950, 51, 56(supp.), 57-66, 68
MoSW	1950, 61-63, 65
MoU	1950, 61-63, 65, 68
NNC	1950-58, 61, 63
NbU	1950, 61, 62
NcU	1950, 58, 63-65
NdU	1950
NjP	1958, 63, 65
OCU	1958, 65, 68, 70

OU	1950, 52, 53, 55, 58-63, 65, 68, 70
OkT	1950, 51, 57, 59-61, 63
OkU	1948-50, 52-55, 58-60, 63, 66
PPiGulf	1958
TxDaAR-T	1950-54, 56-59, 61-63, 65, 66, 68, 70
TxDaDM	1950, 51, 53, 56-63, 65, 68, 70, 72
TxHSD	1950, 58, 60, 61-63, 65
TxHU	1950, 51, 53-63, 65, 68
TxLT	1954, 61, 63, 68
TxMM	1950, 51, 57-61, 63, 65, 68, 70
TxU	1950-63, 68, 70
UU	1958
ViBlbV	1957, 58, 65, 66, 68, 70
WU	1958

(73) CUBA. SECRETARIA DE AGRICULTURA, COMERCIO Y TRABAJO.

1938 Field guide to geological excursion in Cuba.

CaACU	1938
DI-GS	1938

(74) DALLAS GEOLOGICAL SOCIETY. FIELD GUIDE.

1955 The Washita Group in the valley of the Trinity River, Texas. (Southern Methodist University, Fondren Science Series, No. 5.)

1959 See American Association of Petroleum Geologists. (12)

1969 See American Association of Petroleum Geologists. (12)

1975 See American Association of Petroleum Geologists. (12)

AzFU	1959
AzTeS	1969
AzU	1969
CLU-G/G	1955, 59, 69, 75
CU-EART	1959
[CaACAM]	1969(3)
CaACI	1969
CaOHM	1959, 69
CaOKQ	1959, 69
CaOOG	1969
CoG	1955, 59, 69
CoU	1955, 59, 69
DI-GS	1955, 59, 69
ICF	1959
ICIU-S	1969
ICarbS	1959
IEN	1955, 59, 69
IU	1959, 69(3)
IaU	1959, 69
IdBB	1959, 69
IdPI	1959
InLP	1969
InU	1959, 75
KyU	1959, 69
LU	1959

MH-GS	1959
MNS	1959
MiHM	1969
MiKW	1969
MnU	1959, 69
MoSW	1959, 69
NBiSU	1969
NRU	1969
NSyU	1969
NbU	1969
NcU	1959, 69
NdU	1959, 69
NhD	1959
NjP	1959, 69
OCU	1959, 69
OU	1959, 69
OkT	1959
OkU	1959, 69
OrU	1959
PPiGulf	1959, 69
TMM	1959, 69
TU	1959
TxDaAR-T	1955, 59, 69, 75
TxDaDM	1955, 59, 69
TxDaM	1955
TxHSD	1959, 69
TxHU	1955
TxLT	1955, 59, 69
TxMM	1959, 65, 69
TxU	1955, 59, 69
TxU-Da	1955, 69
ViBlbV	1959
WU	1959

(75) DESK AND DERRICK CLUB, DALLAS CHAPTER. GUIDEBOOK FOR THE FIELD TRIP.

1951 [East Texas oil fields.]
TxDaSM 1951

(76) EARLHAM COLLEGE, RICHMOND, INDIANA. GEOLOGY SENIOR SEMINAR.

1973 spring Ohio and Pennsylvania geology.
InRE 1973

(77) EAST TEXAS GEOLOGICAL SOCIETY. FIELD TRIP.

1939 Claiborne field trip, Tyler, Texas to Natchitoches, Louisiana.

1945 [Pecan Gap, Wolfe City and Annona formations in East Texas.]

1951 The Woodbine and adjacent strata of the Waco area of central Texas. (Southern Methodist University, Fondren Science Series, No. 4.)

1959 The Edwards Formation of central Texas. (Guide book to accompany Symposium on Edwards Limestone in central Texas; Texas University. Bureau of Economic Geology. Publication 5905.)

1960 Claiborne-Wilcox Eocene, Smith and Cherokee counties, Texas.

CU-EART	1951
CoG	1945, 60
CoU	1951
DI-GS	1945, 60
IEN	1945, 51, 59, 60
IU	1951
IaU	1951
InU	1951, 59
KyU	1945
LU	1951
MoSW	1951
NNC	1945
NSyU	1951
NcU	1951
OkT	1951
OkU	1939, 45
PSt	1951
RPB	1951, 59
TxDaAR-T	1951, 59
TxDaDM	1951
TxDaM	1945
TxDaSM	1945, 51
TxHSD	1945, 51
TxHU	1945, 51
TxLT	1945
TxMM	1951
TxU	1945, 59, 60
TxU-Da	1951, 59, 60

(78) EAST TEXAS STATE UNIVERSITY. GEOLOGICAL SOCIETY.

1972 Paleozoic geology of the Arbuckle Mountains, Oklahoma.
OkU 1972

(79) EASTERN NEVADA GEOLOGICAL SOCIETY.

1960 See Intermountain Association of (Petroleum) Geologists. (133)

(80) EDMONTON GEOLOGICAL SOCIETY FIELD TRIP GUIDEBOOK.

1959	1st	Cadomin area.
1960	2nd	Rock Lake.
1961	3rd	Jasper.
1962	4th	Peace River.
1963	5th	Sunwapta Pass area.
1964	6th	Medicine and Maligne lakes, Jasper Park.
1965	7th	David Thompson Highway, from near Nordegg to Banff-Jasper Highway.
1966	8th	Cadomin, Alberta.
1967		No field trip held.
1969		Edmonton, Jasper, Ft. Nelson, Watson Lake, Pine Pt. (lead-zinc), Ft. McMurry, Tersands, Edmonton.
1970		Peace River, Pine Pass, Yellowhead, Field Conference.

CaAC	1961-64, 66, 69
[CaACAM]	1960-64, 66, 69, 70
CaACI	1959-66, 69, 70
CaACM	1959-64
CaACU	1959-61
[CaBVU]	1961-63
CaOHM	1962-64, 66, 69
CaOKQ	1962-64, 66, 69, 70
CaOLU	1962-64, 66, 69
CaOOG	1959-64
CoG	1962-64, 66
DI-GS	1959-66
ICF	1962-64
IU	1959, 61-64, 66
IaU	1964
MiU	1962-66, 69, 70
MnU	1962-64, 66
NNC	1962-64
NhD	1962-66, 69, 70
NjP	1962-64
OU	1963, 66, 69
OkU	1962-64, 66
TxDaAR-T	1962, 64, 70
TxDaDM	1961-64, 66, 69
TxDaM	1962, 64, 66
TxDaSM	1961
TxHSD	1960, 63
TxU	1959-66, 69, 70
ViBlbV	1966, 69, 70

(81) EL PASO GEOLOGICAL SOCIETY. GUIDEBOOK.

1967		Precambrian rocks of the Franklin Mountains, Texas.
1968		General geology of the Franklin Mountains, Texas.
1969	3rd	Ordovician symposium. (280)
1970	4th	Cenozoic stratigraphy of the Rio Grande Valley area, Dona Ana County, New Mexico.
1971	5th	A glimpse of some of the geology and mineral resources of the Sierra Blanca-Van Horn area, Hudspeth and Culberson counties, Texas.
1972	6th	The stratigraphy and structure of the Sierra de Juarez, Chihuahua, Mexico.
1973	7th	The geology of south-central Dona Ana County, New Mexico.
1974	8th	Geology of the Florida Mountains, Luna County, New Mexico.
1975	9th	Exploration from the mountains to the basin.

AzU	1972
CLU-G/G	1969-74
CU-EART	1972
[CaBVU]	1969
CaOOG	1969
CoG	1967-73
CoU	1969
DI-GS	1967-69
IU	1970, 71
IaU	1967-69
InLP	1969

InU	1967
KyU	1970-74
MH-GS	1969
MnU	1968, 69
MoSW	1969
MoU	1969
NmPE	1970-74
OCU	1967-74
TxDaAR-T	1967-74
TxDaSM	1967-72
TxHSD	1972
TxMM	1967-75
TxU	1967-72

(82) FAULT FINDERS GEOLOGICAL SOCIETY.

1949		See Texas. University. Geological Society. (310)

(83) FIELD CONFERENCE OF PENNSYLVANIA GEOLOGISTS. ANNUAL MEETING. GUIDEBOOK.

1931		Guidebook for the first field conference of Pennsylvania geologists.
1932	2nd	Around and near the "Forks of the Delaware" and various sundry gaps.
1933		Guidebook for the third field conference of Pennsylvania geologists.
1934		Guidebook for the fourth field conference of Pennsylvania geologists.
1935	5th	In the Philadelphia area of southeastern Pennsylvania.
1936	6th	Geological inspection of anthracite field.
1937		Bradford district trip.
1938		Guidebook, Virginia.
1939		Guidebook for the ninth field conference of Pennsylvania geologists.
1940		Guidebook for the tenth field conference of Pennsylvania geologists.
1941	11th	Allegheny Front Trip; Blue Knob, East Freedom, Hollidaysburg, Williamsburg area, Pennsylvania.
1946	12th	From the Cambrian to the Silurian near State College and Tyrone.
1947	13th	Bethlehem, Pennsylvania; local geology.
1948	14th	Harrisburg, Pennsylvania. Excursions.
		No. 1. Smith Mountain.
		No. 2. Pennsylvania Turnpike.
		No. 3. Cornwall Mines.
		No. 4. Susquehanna-Juaniata rivers.
		Supplement: Silurian sediments and relationships at Susquehanna Gap in Blue or Kittatinny Mountain, five miles north of Harrisburg, Pennsylvania. (Revised and reissued in 1957-58.)
1949	15th	Trip 1. Old Mines and Mine Ridge anticline.
		Trip 2. Martic overthrust.
		Trip 3. Appalachian drainage and Pleistocene terraces.
1950	16th	Pittsburgh-Pennsylvania field excursions.
		Trip 1. Aliquippa Plant, Jones and Loughlin Steel Company.
		Trip 2. Glacian "foreland" of northwest Pennsylvania.
		Trip 3. Chestnut Ridge anticline.
1951	17th	Geology of Philadelphia area.
1952	18th	Sussex County, New Jersey. Pleistocene geology-dikes of petrologic interest.
1953	19th	Easton, Pennsylvania field trip and guidebook with summary of regional geology and sections on Paleozoic rocks and Precambrian geology.
1954	20th	Cambro-Ordovician limestones. Martinsburg Formation.

(83) Field Conference of Pennsylvania Geologists.

1955	21st	[Geology of central Pennsylvania].
		No. 1. Stratigraphy of Ordovician limestones and dolomites of Nittany Valley from Bellefonte to Pleasant Gap.
		No. 2. Stratigraphy and structure of ridge and valley from University Park to Tyrone, Mt. Union and Lewiston.
		No. 3. Structure and stratigraphy of Pennsylvanian sediments of the plateau area near Philipsburg and Clearfield.
1956	22nd	Trenton, New Jersey.
1958	23rd	Guidebooks to the geology of Maryland.
		No. 4,5. geology of South Mountain and Appalachians in Maryland. (145)
1959	24th	Glacial geology of Crawford and Erie counties, Pennsylvania. Bedrock and oil geology of northwestern Pennsylvania and the great Oildorado. Erosion channel in Penn Dixie limestone mine.
1960	25th	Some tectonic and structural problems of the Appalachian piedmont along the Susquehanna River.
1961	26th	Structure and stratigraphy of the Reading Hills and Lehigh Valley, in Northampton and Lehigh counties, Pennsylvania.
1962	27th	Stratigraphy, structure, and economic geology of southern Somerset County and adjacent parts of Bedford and Fayette counties, Pennsylvania.
1963	28th	Stratigraphy and structure of Upper and Middle Devonian rocks in northeastern Pennsylvania.
1964	29th	Cyclic sedimentation in the Carboniferous of western Pennsylvania.
1965	30th	Stratigraphy of the Pennsylvanian and Permian rocks of Washington, Mercer, and Lawrence counties, Pennsylvania.
1966	21st	Revised edition of the 21st meeting held in 1955.
		Trip 1. Stratigraphy of Ordovician limestones and dolomites of Nittany Valley from Bellefonte to Pleasant Gap.
		Trip 2. Stratigraphy and structure of Ridge and Valley area from University Park to Tyrone, Mt. Union and Lewistown appendices, 1966.
		Trip 1, Appendix No. F1. Erosional benches along Bald Eagle Mountain in the area from Waddle Gap to Milesburg Gap, Pennsylvania.
		Trip 2, Appendix No. S1. Subsurface faults in the vicinity of Birmingham and Jacksonville, Pennsylvania.
		Appendix No. S2. Comparison of geologic, magnetic and gravimetric features in parts of central Pennsylvania.
	31st	Comparative tectonics and stratigraphy of the Cumberland and Lebanon valleys.
1967	32nd	Geology in the region of the Delaware to Lehigh water gaps.
1968	33rd	Geology of mineral deposits in south-central Pennsylvania.
1969	34th	The Pocono Formation in northeastern Pennsylvania.
1970	35th	New interpretations of eastern Piedmont geology of Maryland or granite and gabbro or graywacke and greenstone.
1971	36th	Upper Devonian sedimentation in Susquehanna County
		Hydrology, glacial geology and environmental geology of the Wyoming-Lackawanna Country.
1972	37th	Stratigraphy, sedimentology, and structure of Silurian and Devonian rocks along the Allegheny Front in Bedford County, Pa., Allegheny County, Maryland, and Mineral and Grant counties, West Virginia.
1973	38th	Structure and Silurian-Devonian stratigraphy of the valley and ridge province, central Pennsylvania.
1974		Geology of the Piedmont of southeastern Pennsylvania.
1975		The late Wisconsinan drift border in northeastern Pennsylvania

[A-GS] 1938
CLU-G/G 1946, 49, 55, 59, 60, 62-66

CLhC	1955
CU-EART	1963, 64, 66, 67
CaOKQ	1955, 59, 60, 62-69
CoG	1938, 48, 49, 54
DFPC	1959
DI-GS	1932, 35, 47-56, 58-69, 71-75
ICF	1946
ICarbS	1938, 55, 66(Rev. 21)
IEN	1955
IU	1946, 55, 59-76
IaU	1955, 58, 60, 66
InRE	1970
InU	1949, 55, 59, 60, 62-65, 66(31), 67, 68
KyU	1938, 58, 66, 70-74
MH-GS	1949, 51, 53, 74
MNS	1948, 49
MiU	1962-69
MnDuU	1960
MnU	1949, 55, 56, 58-60, 62-68
MoSW	1949, 71
NNC	1935, 38, 49, 52, 55, 56, 60, 62, 63
NRU	1959, 62, 64-73
NcU	1938, 64, 66-69, 71-73
NdU	1938
NhD	1953, 58
NjP	1935, 37, 38, 55, 56, 60, 62-68
OCU	1965
OU	1960, 62-69
PBL	1936, 61, 64
PBm	1934, 35, 46-52, 54-56, 60, 62, 66-72, 74
[P-GS]	1931-75
PSt	1946, 48, 55, 59, 60, 62-73
RPB	1959-67
TxDaAR-T	1963, 67, 69-74
TxDaDM	1938, 55, 59, 60, 62-69
TxU	1935, 46, 48(sup), 50, 55, 59, 60, 62-65, 67, 68, 70
ViBlbV	1938, 60

(84) FLINTSTONE ROCK CLUB.

1964 1st Okmulgee, Oklahoma.

OkU	1964

(85) FORT SMITH GEOLOGICAL SOCIETY. GUIDEBOOK, REGIONAL FIELD CONFERENCE.

1959	1st	Western portion of Arkansas Valley basin.
1961		See Tulsa Geological Society. (314)
1963	2nd	Southeastern Arkansas Valley and the Ouachita and frontal Ouachita Mountains, Arkansas.

CU-EART	1959, 63
CoG	1959, 61
DI-GS	1959, 61
ICF	1963
IU	1963

(85) Fort Smith Geological Society.

IaU	1959, 61
InLP	1963
InU	1959, 61
KyU	1963
MnU	1959, 61, 63
MoU	1959
NNC	1963
NcU	1963
NjP	1961, 63
[OkOkCGe]	1959
OkT	1959
OkU	1959, 63
PPiGulf	1959
TMM	1963
TxDaAR-T	1959, 63
TxDaDM	1959, 61, 63
TxDaM	1959, 63
TxDaSM	1959, 63
TxHSD	1959, 63
TxHU	1963
TxU	1959, 63

(86) FORT WORTH GEOLOGICAL SOCIETY.

1939	fall	See West Texas Geological Society. (338)
1957		See Abilene Geological Society. (1)
1969		Arbuckle Mountains field trip.

CoG	1969
DI-GS	1939, 57
IaU	1957
InU	1957
KyU	1957
MnU	1957
NcU	1957
[OkOkCGe]	1969
OkU	1969
TxDaAR-T	1969
TxU	1939, 57, 69

(87) FORUM ON GEOLOGY OF INDUSTRIAL MINERALS. FIELD TRIP.

1968	4th	Burnet County. (308)
1973	9th	1. A geologic excursion to fluorspar mines in Hardin and Pope counties, Illinois. Illinois-Kentucky mining district and adjacent upper Mississippi Embayment. (126)
		2. Geologic guide to a portion of the fluorspar mining district in Livingston and Crittenden counties, Kentucky.
1974	10th	Field trip. Sequential land use of some pits and quarries along the Scioto River.

AzTeS	1973(2)
CLU-G/G	1968, 73
CaOOG	1973(2)
ICF	1973(1)
[I-GS]	1973
IU	1973, 74

IaU	1966-68, 72, 73(1)
KyU	1971, 73
NU	1973(2)
NjP	1973
OU	1971, 73(2)
OkU	1973(2)
TxDaDM	1973(1)
WU	1973(2)

(88) FOUR CORNERS GEOLOGICAL SOCIETY. GUIDEBOOK FOR THE FIELD CONFERENCE.

1952		Geological symposium of the Four Corners region.
1955	1st	Geology of parts of Paradox, Black Mesa, and San Juan basins.
1957	2nd	Geology of southwestern San Juan Basin.
1960	3rd	Geology of Paradox Basin fold and fault belt.
1963	4th	Shelf carbonates of the Paradox Basin.
1964		See American Association of Petroleum Geologists. Rocky Mountain Section. (17)
1969	5th	Geology and natural history of the Grand Canyon region; the Powell Centennial. River expedition 1969. Including separate river log. Lee's Ferry to Phantom Ranch and geologic color map of eastern Grand Canyon (Colorado River).
1971	6th	1. Geology; Canyonlands National Park, Utah. 2. Geology; Cataract Canyon, Utah.
1972		Cretaceous and Tertiary rocks of the southern Colorado Plateau. Road log: Durango to Farmington via Cortez, Shiprock, Biclabito dome, and Big Gap reservoir with selected side trips.
1973	7th	Geology of the canyons of the San Juan River.
1974	4th	River runners' guide to the canyons of the Green and Colorado rivers, with emphasis on geologic features.
1975	8th	Canyonlands country.

AzFU	1957, 60, 69, 71
AzTeS	1952, 57-64, 73
AzU	1971, 73
CChiS	1955
[CDU]	1957, 63, 69, 71
CLU-G/G	1955, 57, 60, 63, 69, 71, 72
CLhC	1955-63, 71
CSfCSM	1955
CU-EART	1955-63, 69-73
CaACI	1957, 64
CaACU	1955, 57, 60
CaAEU	1963
[CaBVU]	1955, 60
CaOHM	1957-64
CaOKQ	1957, 60, 63
CaOLU	1969
CaOOG	1955, 57, 60, 63, 64, 69
CoDuF	1955, 57
CoG	1955, 57, 60, 63, 64, 69, 71
[CoPU]	1957, 63, 71
CoU	1955, 57, 60, 63, 69, 71
DFPC	1957
DI-GS	1955, 57, 60, 63, 64, 69, 71, 73
DLC	1969

(88) Four Corners Geological Society.

ICF	1957, 60, 63, 69
ICIU-S	1957, 60, 64-71, 73
IEN	1955-69
IU	1955, 57, 60, 63, 69, 71, 73
IaU	1955, 57, 60, 63, 64, 69, 71
IdBB	1952, 64
InLP	1957-63, 69
InU	1957-63, 69, 71
KyU	1955, 57, 60, 63, 64, 69
LU	1955-64, 69, 71
MH-GS	1957-63, 69
MNS	1971
MiU	1969, 71
MnU	1955, 57, 60, 63
MoSW	1955, 60
MoU	1955-63
MtBC	1960
NBiSU	1957-63, 71, 73
NNC	1955, 57, 60, 63
NOneoU	1971
NSyU	1957-63, 69, 71
NbU	1955-63, 69-73
NcU	1957-69
NdU	1957, 60, 63, 69, 71
NhD	1955-63
NjP	1957, 60, 69, 71
NmPE	1957, 60, 64, 69
NmU	1957
NvU	1955-63
OCU	1957, 63, 69, 71
OU	1952-63, 71
[OkOkCGe]	1957
OkT	1957, 60, 63, 69
OkU	1952-63, 69, 71, 75
OrU	1957-63, 69, 71, 73, 75
PPiGulf	1955, 60
PSt	1955, 57, 60
RPB	1955
TMM	1969
TU	1957, 60, 63
TxDaAR-T	1955, 57, 60, 63, 69, 73, 74
TxDaDM	1955, 57, 60, 63, 69, 71
TxDaM	1957, 60, 63
TxDaSM	1952, 57-63, 69, 72
TxHSD	1955-63, 69, 73
TxHU	1955-63, 69, 71
TxLT	1955-60
TxMM	1955, 57, 60, 63, 69, 73
TxU	1952, 55, 57, 60, 63, 64, 69, 71
TxU-Da	1957, 63, 69
UU	1952-63, 69
ViBlbV	1957-63, 69
WU	1955-63, 71, 73

(89) FRIENDS OF THE PLEISTOCENE. EASTERN GROUP. FIELD CONFERENCE GUIDEBOOK.

1935	2nd	New England Pleistocene geologists' conference; suggested program.
1937	4th	Hanover-Mt. Washington, New Hampshire.
1939	6th	Annual invasion; announcement only.
1940	7th	No formal guidebook. (See Geological Society of America. Bulletin. Vol. 53, Aug. 1942.)
1941	8th	Glacial features of the Catskills.
1947	10th	Finger lakes.
1948	11th	Toronto-Barrie, Ontario.
1950	13th	Ithaca, New York.
1952	15th	Columbus, Ohio.
1953	16th	Glacial geology field meeting. Ayer, Massachusetts Quadrangle and adjacent areas.
1954	17th	Wellsboro, Elmira, Towanda region, Pennsylvania-New York.
1955	18th	Malone, New York area.
1956	19th	Drummondville region, Quebec, Canada.
1959	22nd	London, Ontario.
1960	23rd	Dunkirk, New York. Glacial geology of Cattaraugus County, New York.
1961	24th	Late Pleistocene stratigraphy and history of southwestern Maine.
1962	25th	The Charlestown Moraine and the retreat of the last ice sheet in southern Rhode Island.
1963	26th	Riviere-du-Loup, Quebec, Canada.
1964	27th	The Pleistocene geology of Martha's Vineyard.
	28th	Long Island.
1966	29th	Annual reunion. Chesapeake, Va.
1967	30th	Annual reunion.
1970	33rd	1. Glen House, Chandler Ridge, top of Mt. Washington. 2. Pinkham Notch, Dolly Copp Road.

CLU-G/G	1952
[CaBVU]	1959
CaOOG	1959
DI-GS	1935, 37, 39-41, 47-50, 52-56, 59-64, 66, 67
[I-GS]	1952, 59, 63
IU	1948, 52, 59-61, 64
IaU	1952
InU	1952, 59
MiHM	1940
MnU	1959, 61, 62
NNC	1959, 61
NSyU	1940, 60
NbU	1940
NdU	1940
OCU	1959
OU	1954
OkU	1952
TxDaSM	1952
TxU	1961, 63, 70

(90) FRIENDS OF THE PLEISTOCENE. MIDWEST GROUP. ANNUAL FIELD CONFERENCE. GUIDEBOOK. (TITLE VARIES)

1950	1st	Wisconsin Pleistocene.
1951	2nd	Southeastern Minnesota.
1952	3rd	Tazewell drift, western Illinois and eastern Iowa.
1953	4th	Northeastern Wisconsin.

(90) Friends of the Pleistocene. Midwest Group.

1954	5th	Central Minnesota.
1955	6th	Review of the relationships of the Pleistocene stratigraphy, geomorphology and soils in Pottawattamie, Cass, and Adair counties, southwestern Iowa.
1956	7th	The northwestern part of the southern peninsula of Michigan.
1957	8th	Field guide and road log for study of Kansan, Illinoian and early Tazewell tills, loesses and associated faunas in south-central Indiana.
1958	9th	East-central North Dakota. (217)
1959	10th	Glacial geology of west-central Wisconsin.
1960	11th	Eastern South Dakota.
1961	12th	Edmonton, Alberta, Canada. (289)
1962	13th	Evidence for "early Wisconsin" in central and southwest Ohio.
1963	14th	Loess stratigraphy, Wisconsinan classification and accretion-gleys in central western Illinois. (126)
1964	15th	Eastern Minnesota. Wisconsin glaciation of Minnesota. (175)
1965	16th	Iowan problem.
1966	17th	Evidence of multiple glaciation in the glacial-periglacial area of eastern Nebraska.
1967	18th	Glacial geology of the Missouri Coteau and adjacent areas. (217)
1969	19th	Saskatchewan and Alberta; a reappraisal of the pre-late Ferry paleosol.
1971	20th	Pleistocene stratigraphy of Missouri River valley along the Kansas-Missouri border.
1972	21st	Pleistocene stratigraphy of east-central Illinois. (126)
1973	22nd	The Valderan problem; Lake Michigan Basin.
1975	23rd	Quaternary paleoenvironmental history of the western Missouri Ozarks.
1976	24th	Stratigraphy and faunal sequence, Meade County, Kansas. (149)

[A-GS]	1963
CLU-G/G	1958, 67, 72
CU-EART	1958, 64, 66, 67, 72
CaOLU	1958
CaOOG	1958, 60, 63, 67
CoU	1966, 67, 71, 72
DI-GS	1950-67
ICF	1972
ICarbS	1963
[I-GS]	1952-60, 62-66, 72
IU	1951, 52, 55-60, 62, 64-67, 71-73, 75
IaU	1952, 55, 57, 58, 64, 65, 67, 72
InU	1957-59, 63, 67
KyU	1958, 66, 71, 72
LU	1963
MH-GS	1963, 72
MNS	1963, 64, 67
MiDW	1963, 67, 72
MiHM	1967
MiKW	1966
MiU	1956, 58
MnU	1954, 55, 57-59, 63, 64, 66, 67, 69
MoSW	1964, 66
NNC	1959-63
NSyU	1958, 63, 67
NbU	1967
NcU	1958, 67
NdU	1954, 57-61, 63, 67, 71-73
NhD	1967

NjP	1972
OCU	1957, 63, 67, 72
OU	1951, 56, 57, 60, 63, 67, 72
TxDaAR-T	1966, 67, 71-73
TxDaDM	1960, 71, 72
TxDaM	1963, 67
TxDaSM	1963
TxU	1959, 62-64, 67, 69
ViBlbV	1967, 72
WU	1953, 56, 59, 62-64, 66, 67, 75, 76

(91) FRIENDS OF THE PLEISTOCENE. PACIFIC COAST GROUP. GUIDEBOOK.

1966	1st	Glaciomarine environments and the Fraser glaciation in northwest Washington.
1967		Pleistocene geology and palynology, Searles Valley, California.
1969		No title, text or itinerary. It consists of copies of several preliminary USGS topographic maps, profiles, and other data. Contains Sugar House Quadrangle, Salt Lake County, Utah, and Fort Douglas Quadrangle, Utah.
1971		Glacial and Pleistocene history of the Mammoth Lakes; Sierra County, California; a geologic handbook.
1972		Progress report on the USGS Quaternary studies in the San Francisco Bay area.

CChiS	1971(Sept.)
CLU-G/G	1966, 67, 71(Sept.)
CU-EART	1966
CaOOG	1966, 67, 69
DI-GS	1967, 71, 72
IU	1966, 69
KyU	1971(Sept.)
MnU	1969
NbU	1969(maps)
NdU	1971(Sept.)
TxDaAR-T	1971
TxU	1967

(92) FRIENDS OF THE PLEISTOCENE. ROCKY MOUNTAIN GROUP. FIELD TRIP GUIDEBOOK.

1952	1st	Estes Park, Colorado.
1953	2nd	Twin Lakes area, Colorado.
1958	4th	Jackson Hole area, Wyoming.
	5th	Not issued.
1960	6th	Little Valley, Promontory Point, Utah, and Little Cottonwood-Draper area, near Salt Lake City, Utah.
1961	7th	Recent geologic history of Bear Lake Valley, Utah-Idaho.
1962	8th	Twin Falls, Glenns Ferry and Bruneau, Idaho to study Pleistocene history of Snake River canyon. (Road log)
1963		Madison River and Yellowstone River from Hayden Valley to Pine Creek, Montana.
1964	10th	Quaternary geology of the Duncan-Virden-Safford area, New Mexico, Arizona. (USGS Geological Map I-442 used as tour guide.)
1965	10th	Upper Gila River region, New Mexico, Arizona.
1966	11th	Landscape evolution and soil genesis in the Rio Grande region, southern New Mexico.
1967		No formal guidebook.
1968	13th	San Pedro Valley, Arizona.
1969	14th	Pleistocene lake deposits, Jordan Valley.

(92) Friends of the Pleistocene. Rocky Mountain Group.

1970	15th	Guidebook to the geology of the San Francisco Peaks, Arizona.
1971	16th	Guidebook to the Quaternary geology of the east-central Sierra Nevada.
1972		Canon City, Colorado, to Wetmore, Westcliffe, Texas Creek and return.
1974		Hebgen Lake area to Bozeman, Montana via Hwy. 191. Itinerary and road log. Excursion to Schmitt site, Three Forks, Montana.
1976		Road log and field guide to the southern Alberta Caper.

AzTeS	1971
AzU	1971
[CDU]	1971
CLU-G/G	1955, 64(map), 69-71
CLhC	1971
CSdS	1971
CaOHM	1971
CaOOG	1971
CoDuF	1969(2)
CoG	1971
CoU	1969(2), 71
DI-GS	1952, 53, 58, 60, 62, 63, 65-68, 70, 71
ICarbS	1971
IEN	1971
[I-GS]	1966
IU	1966, 69-72, 74, 76
InU	1960
KyU	1970, 71, 74
MH-GS	1971
MnU	1952-60, 62, 63, 68(handout--no guidebook), 69
MoSW	1971
MoU	1971
NNC	1960, 61, 71
NRU	1971
NbU	1964(map), 69
NcU	1971
NdU	1971
NjP	1971
NmPE	1971
OU	1971
OkU	1971
OrU	1971
TxDaAR-T	1968, 69(2), 70, 71, 74
TxDaDM	1960, 61
TxDaSM	1971
TxU	1960, 62, 64, 66, 68, 71
UU	1971

(93) GARDEN CITY, NEW YORK, ADELPHI UNIVERSITY, DEPARTMENT OF BIOLOGY.

1972	Field conference on Tertiary biostratigraphy of southern and western Wyoming.

MiU	1972
OU	1972

(94) GEOLOGICAL ASSOCIATION OF CANADA. GUIDEBOOK FOR THE ANNUAL MEETING.

1950 See Canadian Society of Petroleum Geologists. (61)

1953 66th Toronto. (96)
No. 1. Petrology of the nepheline and corundum rocks, Bancroft area, eastern Ontario.
No. 2. Mineral occurrences of Wilberforce, Bancroft and Craigmont-Lake Clear areas of southeastern Ontario.
No. 3. Glacial geology of the Toronto Orangeville area, Ontario.
No. 4,5. Geology of part of the Niagara peninsula of Ontario.
No. 6. Sir Adam Beck-Niagara generating station No. 2, Niagara Falls, Ontario; a resume of the engineering geology.
No. 7. Geology and mineral deposits, Sudbury area, Ontario.
No. 8. Geology and mineral deposits of the Kirkland-Larder mining district, Ontario.
No. 9. The Porcupine mining district, Ontario.
No. 10. Geology and mineral deposits of northwestern Quebec.

1963 16th [Southern Quebec] field trips; region around Montreal. (171)
No. 1. Oka Complex.
No. 2. Pleistocene geology, St. Lawrence lowland north of Montreal.
No. 3. Laurentian area north of Montreal.
No. 4. Grenville mineralization, Glen Almond, Quebec.
No. 5. Ordovician stratigraphy, St. Lawrence lowland north of Montreal.
No. 6. Mount Royal.
No. 7. Pleistocene geology between Montreal and Covey Hill.
No. 8. Mounts St. Hilaire and Johnson.
No. 9. Western edge of Appalachians in southern Quebec.
No. 10. Breccia localities.

1964 See American Association of Petroleum Geologists. (12)

1966 19th Geology of parts of the Atlantic provinces. (171)
Trip 1. Southwestern New Brunswick.
Trip 2. Bathurst-Dalhousie area, New Brunswick.
Trip 3. Zeolites, Nova Scotia.
Trip 4. Surficial geology, north shore of Minas Basin.
Trip 5. Halifax to Bay of Fundy, Nova Scotia.
Trip 6. Walton area, Nova Scotia.
Trip 7. Cape Breton Island, Nova Scotia.
Trip 8. Corner Brook area, Newfoundland.

1967 20th Geology of parts of eastern Ontario and western Quebec. (171)
Trip 1. Sudbury, Cobalt and Bancroft areas, Ontario.
Trip 2. Nepheline rocks, Bancroft areas, Ontario.
Trip 3. Paleozoic stratigraphy, Kingston area, Ontario.
Trip 4. The Grenville Province (12-day field trip).
Trip 5. Surficial geology east and west of Kingston.
Trip 6. Grenville structure, stratigraphy, and metamorphism, southeastern Ontario.
Trip 7. Alkaline rocks, Oda and St. Hilaire, Province of Quebec.
Trip 8. Tectonic intrusions, Shawinigan region, Province of Quebec.

1969 June Guidebook for the geology of Monteregian Hills. (171)
No. 1. Flysch sediments in parts of the Cambro-Ordovician sequence of the Quebec Appalachians.
No. 4. Geologic evolution of the Grenville Province in the Shawinigan area.
No. 5. Quaternary geology of the Lac St. Jean and Seguenay River areas.
No. 6A. Diatreme breccia pipes and dykes and the related alnoite, kimberlite and carbonatite intrusions occurring in the Montreal and Oka areas, Quebec.
No. 6B, Pt. 1. Geology of Mount Rougemont.

Pt. 2. Geology of Mount Johnson.
No. 6C. Geology of Brome and Shefford Mountains.
No. 7. Structural geology of the Sherbrooke area.
No. 8A. Stratigraphy of the St. Lawrence Lowlands (Covey Hill). The Cambrian sandstones of the St. Lawrence Lowlands.
No. 9. Mineralogy at Mont St. Hilaire.

1970 23rd Field Trip No. 1. Geology of the Moak-Setting Lakes area, Manitoba (Manitoba nickel belt). (171)
Field Trip No. 2. Comparative geology and mineral deposits of the Flin Flon-Snow Lake and Lynn Lake-Fox Lake areas.
Field Trip No. 4. Geology of the Bisset-Lac du Bonnet area, Manitoba.
Field Trip No. 5. Lower Paleozoic of the interlake area, Manitoba.
Field Trip No. 6. Paleozoic and Mesozoic of the Dawson Bay area and Manitoba escarpment, Manitoba.
Field Trip No. 7. Surficial geology and Pleistocene stratigraphy of an area between the Red and Winnipeg rivers.

1971 Sudbury.

1973 Trip C. Quaternary geology and its application to engineering practice in the Saskatoon-Regina-Watrous area, Saskatchewan.

1974 A-1. A cross-section of the Newfoundland Appalachians.
A-2. The regional setting and structure of the west Newfoundland ophiolites.
A-4. Aspects of the Pleistocene geology of the eastern Avalon peninsula.
A-5. Environmental geology of a rural area near St. John's. Conception Bay south.
B-2. The regional setting and structure of the west Newfoundland ophiolites.
B-3. Ore deposits and their setting in the central mobile belt of northeast Newfoundland.
B-3a. Advocate asbestos mine.
B-3b. Ore deposits and their tectonic setting in the central Paleozoic mobile belt of northern Newfoundland.
B-3c. The consolidated rambler deposits.
B-3d. Geology of Tilt Cove.
B-3e. Volcanogenic copper deposits in probable ophiolitic rocks, Springdale peninsula.
B-3f;B-3g. Geology of the Pilleys Island area.
B-3h. Geology, geochemistry and ore deposits of the Buchans area.
B-3i. Geology of the Betts Cove area.
B-4. Fossils and sedimentology of the Paleozoic strata of Port au Port Peninsula.
B-5. Igneous rocks of the Avalon Platform.
B-6. Late Precambrian and Cambrian sedimentary sequences of southeastern Newfoundland.
B-7. Polydeformed metamorphic belts on the southeastern and northwestern margins of the Newfoundland central mobile belt.
B-8. Applications of refraction seismology and resistivity surveys in environmental and engineering geology.
B-9. St. Lawrence, Canada's only fluorspar producing area.
B-10. Geology and mineralization of the Newfoundland Carboniferous.
B-11. The Cape Ray fault; a possible cryptic suture in S.W. Newfoundland.
S-1. Aerial field trip over eastern Avalon Platform.
S-2. The pyrophyllite mine south of Foxtrap, Conception Bay.

1975 Waterloo '75
Part A. Precambrian geology. (98, 171)
Granitoid rocks of the Madoc-Bancroft-Haliburton area of the Grenville Province.
Grenville gneisses in the Madawaska highlands (eastern Ontario).
Precambrian economic geology of the Timmins area.
Mineralogy and economic geology of the Cobalt silver deposits.
Part B. Phanerozoic geology. (98, 171)

Ordovician to Devonian stratigraphy and conodont biostratigraphy of southern Ontario.
Quaternary stratigraphy of the Toronto area.
Late Quaternary stratigraphy of the Waterloo-Lake Huron area, southwestern Ontario.
Part C. Environmental geology. (98, 171)
Industrial minerals of the Paris-Hamilton district, Ontario.
Engineering geology of the Niagara peninsula.
Environmental geology, Kitchener-Guelph area. (98)

[CDU]	1963
CLU-G/G	1966, 67
CU-EART	1963, 66, 67, 69
[CaACAM]	1966
CaACI	1966, 67
CaACM	1966, 67, 69
[CaBVU]	1967, 69(1,4,5,7,8a)
CaOHM	1963, 66, 74
CaOKQ	1963, 67, 69, 70(4,5,7)
CaOLU	1963, 67
CaOOG	1963, 66, 67, 69(1,4,5,6A-C,7,8A,9), 1974(A2,4,5,B2-6,8,10), 75
CaOONM	1967, 70(4-7)
[CaOTOM]	1963, 67, 71, 74(A-1,A-3)
CoU	1967, 69
DI-GS	1963, 66, 67, 69
ICF	1969(4-5,7-8A), 70(4-7)
ICarbS	1963, 67
[I-GS]	1953(3-5)
IU	1963, 66, 67, 69(4,5,7,8A), 70(4-7), 75
IaU	1950, 63, 64, 67
InLP	1953(1,4,5,7,9,10), 63, 67
InRE	1963
InU	1953, 64, 66, 67
KyU	1963, 67, 70(4-7), 75
MH-GS	1963, 67
MNS	1953, 67
MiDW	1963
MiHM	1963, 67
MnU	1964, 66, 67
MoSW	1967, 69(1)
MoU	1963
MtBC	1963
NBiSU	1963, 67
NNC	1963
NOneoU	1967
NRU	1963, 67
NSyU	1953, 63
NcU	1963, 64, 67
NdU	1963, 67, 69(1,4,5,7,8A), 70, 73(C)
NhD	1953, 67, 70(4-7)
NjP	1963, 66, 67, 75
NvU	1963
OCU	1963, 67
OU	1963, 67, 70(1,4-7), 75
PBm	1975

PSt	1963, 67, 69
RPB	1967
TxDaAR-T	1967, 69(1,4,5,7,8A), 70(1,2), 75
TxDaDM	1966, 67, 69(4,5,7,8a)
TxDaSM	1969(1)
TxHU	1966
TxU	1963, 66, 67, 69(June), 70(1,2)
WU	1963

(95) GEOLOGICAL DISCUSSION CLUB, VANCOUVER, BRITISH COLUMBIA.

1960 Guidebook for geological field trips in southwestern British Columbia. (97)

1968 Report No. 6. Southwestern British Columbia (rev. ed.). Issued as British Columbia. University. Department of Geology. (52)

CLU-G/G	1960
CSfCSM	1960
CU-EART	1960
[CaACAM]	1960
[CaBVU]	1960, 68
CaOOG	1960
CoG	1960
DI-GS	1960, 68
ICF	1960
IU	1960
InU	1968
MnU	1960
NNC	1960
NjP	1960
OrU	1960
TxDaDM	1960
TxU	1960

(96) GEOLOGICAL SOCIETY OF AMERICA. ANNUAL MEETING. GUIDEBOOK FOR FIELD TRIPS. (TITLE VARIES)

1931		Log of G.S.A. field trip in Arbuckle Mountains from Ada to Springer, Oklahoma.
1932	44th	Field Trip No. 3. Ardmore Basin and western Arbuckle Mountains.
1940	53rd	Austin, Texas.
		Trip 1, 2. Cretaceous in the vicinity of Austin.
		Trip 3. Fault-line oil fields.
		Trip 4. Pre-Cambrian of the Llano region.
		Trip 5. Paleozoic of the Llano region.
		Trip 6. Lower Tertiary of the Colorado River.
		Trip 7. Oil fields of south Texas.
		Trip 8. Pennsylvanian, Permian, and Triassic of northwestern Texas.
		Trip 9. Meteor Crater of Ector County.
		Trip 10. Paleozoic of the Marathon region.
		Trip 11. Vertebrate fossils and artifacts, Bee County.
1948	61st	New York.
		Excursion No. 1. Franklin Mine, Franklin, New Jersey.
		Excursion No. 2. Pleistocene and Tertiary geology, Staten Island and eastern New Jersey.
		Excursion No. 3. Petrology and flow structure of the Cortlandt norite, and granitization phenomena at Bear Mountain.
		Excursion No. 4. Engineering geology in and near New York.

Excursion No. 5. Squier laboratory, Fort Monmouth, New Jersey.
Excursion No. 6. American Museum of Natural History, New York.
Excursion No. 7. Bell Telephone laboratory, Murray Hill, New Jersey (for American citizens only).
Excursion No. 8. Glacial and ground-water geology on Long Island.
Excursion No. 9. Detailed geology of the Palisades diabase.
Excursion No. 10. Dutchess County, New York.
Excursion No. 11. Zeolite minerals and geology of the Watchung basalt sheets.
Excursion No. 12. Engineering geology of the New York City aqueducts.

1950 Washington, D.C. Guidebooks to the geology of Maryland. (145)
1. Geology of the South Mountain anticlinorium.
2. Geology of Bear Island, Potomac River.
3. The coastal plain geology of southern Maryland.

1951 [1]A Detroit. Devonian rocks of southeastern Michigan and northwestern Ohio.
[2]B Study of Pleistocene features of the Huron-Saginaw ice lobes in Michigan.

1952 65th Boston. Guidebook for field trips in New England.
Field Trip No. 1. Geology of the Appalachian highlands of east-central New York, southern Vermont, and southern New Hampshire.
Field Trip No. 2. Outstanding pegmatites of Maine and New Hampshire.
Field Trip No. 3. Geology of the "Chelmsford Granite" area.
Field Trip No. 4. Glacial geology in the Buzzards Bay region and western Cape Cod.

1953 66th Toronto. (94)
No. 1. Petrology of the nepheline and corundum rocks, Bancroft area, eastern Ontario.
No. 2. Mineral occurrences of Wilberforce, Bancroft and Craigmont-Lake Clear areas of southeastern Ontario.
No. 3. Glacial geology of the Toronto Orangeville area, Ontario.
No. 4,5. Geology of part of the Niagara peninsula of Ontario.
No. 6. Sir Adam Beck-Niagara generating station No. 2, Niagara Falls, Ontario; a resume of the engineering geology.
No. 7. Geology and mineral deposits, Sudbury area, Ontario.
No. 8. Geology and mineral deposits of the Kirkland-Larder mining district, Ontario.
No. 9. The Porcupine mining district, Ontario.
No. 10. Geology and mineral deposits of northwestern Quebec.

1954 67th Los Angeles. (54)

1955 68th New Orleans. Guides to southeastern geology. With supplemental field guide covering physiography and geology along U. S. Highway 90 from New Orleans to Lafayette.
No. 1. Appalachian; an outline of the geology in the segment in Tennessee, North Carolina and South Carolina. The Kings Mountain area. Geomorphology. Outline of the geology of the Great Smoky Mountains area.
No. 2. Type localities (Mississippi and Alabama).
No. 3. Alabama (coastal plain and west-central).
No. 4. Louisiana (northwestern and southern).
No. 5. South Louisiana salt domes.
Addenda to field trips:
Appalachian, inner piedmont belt. Guide to the geology of the Spruce Pine district, North Carolina.

1956 69th Minneapolis.
No. 1. Precambrian of northeastern Minnesota.
No. 2. Lower Paleozoic of the upper Mississippi Valley.
No. 3. Glacial geology, eastern Minnesota.

1957 Atlantic City.
No. 1. Cretaceous and Cenozoic of New Jersey coastal plain.
No. 2. Triassic formations in the Delaware Valley.
No. 3. Precambrian of New Jersey highlands.

		No. 4. Delaware Valley Paleozoics.
		No. 5. Crystalline rocks of Philadelphia area.
		No. 6. Cretaceous and Tertiary geology of New Jersey, Delaware, and Maryland.
		No. 7. General geology of the folded Appalachian Mountains of Pennsylvania.
1958	71st	St. Louis.
		No. 1. Southeast Missouri lead belt.
		No. 2. Problems of Pleistocene geology in the greater St. Louis area.
		No. 3. Mississippian rocks of western Illinois.
		No. 4. Onondaga Cave.
		No. 5. Pennsylvanian (Desmoinesian of Missouri). (182)
1959	72nd	Pittsburgh.
		No. 1. Structure and stratigraphy in central Pennsylvania and the anthracite region.
		No. 2. The Pennsylvanian of western Pennsylvania.
		No. 3. Monongahela series, Pennsylvanian system, and Washington and Green series, Permian system, of the Appalachian Basin.
		No. 4. Mineral deposits of eastern Pennsylvania.
		No. 5. Glacial geology of northwestern Pennsylvania.
		No. 6. Engineering geology of the Pittsburgh area.
1960	73rd	Denver.
		Pt. 1. Guide to the geology of Colorado. (250)
		A-1. Geology of west-central Colorado. Mancos Shale and Mesaverde Group of Palisade area. Colorado National Monument and adjacent areas.
		A-2. Geology of south-central Colorado. Brief description of the igneous bodies of the Raton Mesa region, south-central Colorado. Permo-Pennsylvanian stratigraphy in the Sangre de Cristo Mountains, Colorado. Great sand dunes of Colorado. Geology near Orient Mine, Sangre de Cristo Mountains.
		A-3. Tectonics and economic geology of central Colorado. Kokomo mining district. Tectonic relationships of central Colorado. Structure and petrology of north end of Pikes Peak Batholith, Colorado. Pre-Cambrian rocks and structure of the Platte Canyon and Kassler quadrangles, Colorado. Gravity map of the Hartsel area, South Park, Colorado. Cripple Creek District. Geologic formations and structure of Colorado Springs area, Colorado. Placers of Summit and Park counties, Colorado.
		B-1. Quaternary geology of the Front Range and adjacent plains. First day: Pleistocene geology of the eastern slope of Rocky Mountain National Park, Colorado Front Range. Second day: Surficial geology of the Kassler and Littleton quadrangles near Denver, Colorado. Quaternary sequences east of the Front Range near Denver, Colorado.
		B-2. Geology of the northern Front Range-Laramie Range, Colorado and Wyoming. Summary of Cenozoic history, southern Laramie Range, Wyoming and Colorado. Laramie anorthosite. Cross-lamination and local deformation in the Casper Sandstone, southeast Wyoming. Dakota Group in northern Front Range area.
		B-3. Field trip to Climax, Colorado (no road log). Geology of the Climax molybdenite deposit; a progress report.
		C-1. Stratigraphy of Colorado Springs-Canon City area.
		C-2. Engineering geology-distribution system of the Colorado-Big Thompson Project.
		C-3. Precambrian geology of the Idaho Springs-Central City area, Colorado. Geology of the Central City-Idaho Springs area, Front Range, Colorado.
		C-4. Fossil vertebrates and sedimentary rocks of the Front Range foothills, Colorado.
		C-5. Geology of the Front Range foothills, Boulder-Lyons-Loveland area, Colorado.
		C-6. Geology of Mountain Front west of Denver.
1961	74th	Cincinnati.
		No. 1. Grand Appalachian field excursion with a description of the Pennsylvanian rocks along the West Virginia Turnpike. (334)
		No. 2. Geology from Chicago to Cincinnati.
		No. 3. Pleistocene geology of the Cincinnati region (Kentucky, Ohio, and Indiana).

No. 4. Pennsylvanian geology of eastern Ohio.
No. 5. Engineering geology of flood control and navigation structures in the Ohio River Valley.
No. 6. A guide to the hydrogeology of the Mill Creek and Miami River valleys, Ohio.
No. 7. Sunday all-day field excursion in the Cincinnati region.
No. 8. Examination of Ordovician through Devonian stratigraphy and the Serpent Mound chaotic structure area.
No. 9. Field excursion to the Falls of the Ohio.
No. 10. Geology of the St. Francois Mountain area.

1962 75th Houston. Geology of the Gulf Coast and central Texas.
No. 1. Geology of Llano region and Austin area. (308)
No. 2. Tertiary and uppermost Cretaceous of the Brazos River valley, southeastern Texas.
No. 3. Recent and Pleistocene geology of southeast Texas.
No. 4. Tertiary stratigraphy and uranium mines of the southeast Texas Coastal Plain, Houston to San Antonio, via Goliad.
No. 5. Active faults, subsidence and foundation problems in the Houston, Texas area.
No. 6. Palestine and Grand Saline salt domes, eastern Texas.
No. 7. Sulphur mine at Boling Dome.
No. 8. Fresh water from sea water...magnesium from sea water.
No. 9. Coastal Louisiana swamps and marshlands.
No. 10. Tertiary formations between Austin and Houston, with special emphasis on the Miocene and Pliocene.
No. 11. Hydrogeology of the Edwards and associated limestones.
No. 12. Engineering geology of Canyon Dam, Guadalupe River, Comal County, Texas.

1963 76th New York City.
No. 1. Stratigraphy, facies changes and paleoecology of the Lower Devonian Helderberg limestones and the Middle Devonian Onondaga limestones.
No. 2. Stratigraphy, structure, and petrology of Rhode Island and southeastern Connecticut.
No. 3. Stratigraphy, structure, sedimentation and paleontology of the southern Taconic region, eastern New York.
No. 4. Geology of the southern part of the eastern Pennsylvania anthracite region.
No. 5. Postglacial stratigraphy and morphology of coastal Connecticut.
No. 6. Atlantic Cement Company at Ravena, New York. (not published)
No. 7. Hydrologic problems of central Long Island. (not published)
No. 8. Engineering geology of urban area. (not published)

1964 77th Miami Beach.
No. 1. South Florida carbonate sediments.
No. 2. Carbonate sediments, Great Bahama Bank.
No. 3. Living and fossil reef types of south Florida.
No. 4. Geology and hydrology of southeastern Florida.
No. 5. [Not held]
No. 6. The geology and geochemistry of the Bone Valley Formation and its phosphate deposits, west-central Florida.
No. 7. Littoral marine life of southern Florida.
No. 8. [Not held]
No. 9. Guidebook for field trip in Puerto Rico.
No. 10. Environments of coal formation in southern Florida. See also 1968. (163)

1965 78th Kansas city.
No. 1. Pennsylvanian marine banks in southeastern Kansas.
No. 2. Upper Cretaceous stratigraphy, paleontology, and paleoecology of western Kansas.
No. 3. Upper Pennsylvanian cyclothems in the Kansas River valley.
No. 4. Cryptoexplosive structures in Missouri. (182)
No. 5. Geology of the Kansas City Group at Kansas City. (182)
No. 6. Pennsylvanian fossil plants from Kansas coal balls.

		No. 7. Hydrogeology of the lower Kansas River valley.
		No. 8. Engineering geology of Kaysinger Bluff and Stockton dams, west-central Missouri.
1966	79th	San Francisco. Special supplement; a walker's guide to the geology of San Francisco. (Mineral Information Service, Vol. 19, No. 11.)
		No. 190. Field trips. (54)
		No. 1. Point Reyes peninsula and San Andreas Fault zone.
		No. 2. San Francisco peninsula.
		No. 3. San Andreas Fault from San Francisco to Hollister.
		No. 4. Hydrogeology field trip East Bay area and northern Santa Clara Valley.
		No. 5. Sacramento Valley and northern coast ranges.
		No. 6. Yosemite Valley and Sierra Nevada batholith.
		No. 7. Mineralogy of the Laytonville quarry, Mendocino County, California.
		Central Utah coals. (321)
1967	80th	New Orleans.
		No. 1. Geology of the coastal plain of Alabama.
		[No. 2.] Lower Mississippi alluvial valley and terrace.
		[No. 3.] Central Arkansas; economic geology and petrology. (43)
		[No. 4.] Cancelled. (Arkansas-Louisiana coastal plain)
		[No. 5.] Carboniferous detrital rocks in northern Alabama.
		[No. 6.] Five Islands salt domes and the Mississippi deltaic plane.
		No. 7. Peninsula of Yucatan. (2nd ed.) (208)
		[No. 8.] Guatemala. (Instituto Geografico Nacional Guatemala. Bulletin No. 4)
		Local Excursion A. Aerial tour of Mississippi River deltaic plain.
		Local Excursion B. New Orleans and vicinity.
1968		Mexico City, D.F.
		No. 1. Sabinas coal region guidebook. Geology of the Sabinas coal basin, Coahuila.
		No. 2. Geology of the northern part of the valley of Mexico and of the Pachuca-Real del Monte mining district.
		No. 3. General geology of the Sierra Madre Oriental between Tulancingo and Poza Rica.
		No. 4. General, ground water and engineering geology of the metropolitan area of Mexico City and immediate (sic) surroundings.
		No. 5. General geology of the Morelos Basin and adjacent areas.
		No. 6. Geology and utilization of geothermic energy at Pathe, State of Hidalgo.
		No. 7. Paleozoology of the marine Upper Jurassic in the Petlalcingo area, State of Puebla, and paleobotany of the continental Middle Jurassic of the Tezoatlan area, State of Oaxaca.
		No. 8. Volcanology and geomorphology of the southeast corner of Mexico Basin, west side of Ixtacihuatl and north side of Popocatepetl volcanoes, Mexico.
		No. 9. General geology of south-central Mexico, between Mexico City and Acapulco.
1969		Atlantic City.
		Pre-convention. Some Appalachian coals and carbonates; models of ancient shallow-water deposition.
		Geology of selected areas in New Jersey and eastern Pennsylvania and guidebooks of excursions.
		No. 1A. Precambrian and lower Paleozoic geology of the Delaware Valley, New Jersey-Pennsylvania.
		No. 1B. Geology of the Valley and Ridge province between Delaware water gap and Lehigh gap, Pennsylvania.
		Structural control of wind gaps and water gaps and of stream capture in the Stroudsburg area, Pennsylvania, and New Jersey.
		No. 1C. Sedimentology of some Mississippian and Pleistocene deposits of northeastern Pennsylvania.
		No. 2. Shelf and deltaic paleoenvironments in the Cretaceous-Tertiary formations of the New Jersey coastal plain.

No. 3. Quaternary geology of part of northern New Jersey and the Trenton area.
No. 4. Late Triassic Newark Group, north-central New Jersey and adjacent New York and Pennsylvania.
No. 5. Engineering geology of the Yards Creek hydro-electric pumped storage project.
Geology of Tocks Island area and its engineering significance.
No. 6. Ilmenite deposits of the New Jersey coastal plain.

1970 Milwaukee.
No. 1. Cambrian-Ordovician geology of western Wisconsin. (346)
No. 2. Geology of the Baraboo district, Wisconsin. (Wisconsin Geological and Natural History Survey Information Circular 14) (346)
No. 3. The Mississippian and Devonian of Iowa. (Published by the Iowa Geological Survey.) (141)
No. 4. Pleistocene geology of southern Wisconsin. (346)
No. 5. Marquette iron range, Michigan. (Published by the Wisconsin Geological and Natural History Survey.)
No. 6. Hydrogeology of the Rock-Fox River basin of southeastern Wisconsin. (346)
No. 7. Upper Mississippi Valley base metal district. (346)
No. 8. Depositional environments in parts of the Carbondale Formation; western and northern Illinois, Francis Creek shale and associated strata and Mazon Creek biota. (126)
No. 9. Glacial geology of Two Creeks forest bed, Valderan type locality, and northern Kettle Moraine State Forest. (346)

1971 Washington, D.C.
1. A guide to the geology of Delaware's coastal environments. (University of Delaware. College of Marine Studies. Publication 2GL039) (43)
2. Guidebook to contrast in style of deformation of the southern and central Appalachians of Virginia. (334)
3. New interpretations of the eastern Piedmont geology of Maryland, or granite and gabbro or graywacke and greenstone. (160)
4. The Piedmont crystalline rocks at Bear Island, Potomac River, Maryland. (160)
5. Environmental history of Maryland Miocene. (160)
6. Environmental geology in the Pittsburgh area.
7. Historical engineering geology of the Chesapeake and Ohio Canal. (40)
8. Alkalic complex and related rocks of the central Shenandoah Valley (Virginia), Devonian Tioga tuff, and Eocene felsites.
(1) Field trip to igneous rocks of Augusta, Rockingham, Highland and Bath counties, Virginia. (330)
(2) Geologic setting of Triassic-Jurassic-Eocene dike swarm in west-central Virginia, and adjacent parts of West Virginia.
9. Depositional environments of eastern Kentucky coals.
10. Slope stability and denudational processes; central Appalachians.
11. Hydrogeology and geochemistry of folded and faulted carbonate rocks of the central Appalachian type and related land use problems.
12. No guidebook.

1972 Minneapolis.
1. Field trip guidebook for lower Precambrian volcanic-sedimentary rocks of the Vermilion district, northeastern Minnesota. (No. 2.) (176)
2. Field trip guidebook for Precambrian North Shore Volcanic Group, northeastern Minnesota. (No. 3.) (176)
3. Field trip guidebook for Paleozoic and Mesozoic rocks of southeastern Minnesota. (No. 4.) (176)
4. Field trip guidebook for Precambrian migmatitic terrane of the Minnesota River valley. (No. 5.) (176)
5. Field trip guidebook for Precambrian geology of northwestern Cook County, Minnesota. (No. 6.) (176)

6. Field trip guidebook for geomorphology and Quaternary stratigraphy of western Minnesota and eastern South Dakota. (No. 7.) (176)
7. Field trip guidebook for hydrogeology of the Twin Cities artesian basin. (No. 8.) (176)
8. Depositional environments of the lignite-bearing strata in western North Dakota. (217, 218)

1973
1. The Edwards reef complex and associated sedimentation in central Texas. (308)
6. Igneous geology of the Wichita Mountains and economic geology of Permian rocks in southwest Oklahoma. (Published by Oklahoma Geological Survey.)
7. Environmental geologic atlas of the Texas coastal zone, Galveston-Houston area. (Published by University of Texas Bureau of Economic Geology, 1972.)
8. Pennsylvanian depositional systems in north-central Texas. A guide for interpreting terrigenous clastic facies in a cratonic basin. (308)
10. Lignite geology, mining, and reclamation at Big Brown Steam Plant near Fairfield, Texas.
11. Mineral resources of east Texas. (Texas. Univ. Bureau of Economic Geology Guidebook 9, "Field excursion, East Texas: Clay glauconite, ironstone deposits", 1969, supplemented by a new road log.)

1974 Miami Beach.

[A] Field guide to selected Jamaican geological localities. (144)

No. 1. Guidebook to the geology and ecology of some marine and terrestrial environments.
No. 2. Field seminar on water and carbonate rocks of the Yucatan Peninsula, Mexico. (208)
No. 3. Modern Bahaman platform environments.
No. 4. Field trip cancelled; no guidebook published.
No. 5. Sabellariid reef, beach erosion and environmental problems of the Barrier Island-Lagoon system of the lower east Florida coast.
No. 6. The comparative study of the Okefenokee Swamp and the Everglades-Mangrove swamp-marsh complex of southern Florida.
No. 7, 8. No guidebook. (Used "Land from the sea;" the geologic story of south Florida.)
No. 9. Field trip cancelled; no guidebook published.
No. 10. Same guidebook as 1974, No. 3.
No. 12. Field guide to some carbonate rock environments, Florida Keys and western Bahamas.

1975 Salt Lake City.

A. Field guide and road log to the western Brook Cliffs, Castle Valley, and parts of the Wasatch Plateau. (50)

[A-GS]	1955, 57, 58
AzTeS	1956-62, 64, 65, 66(1), 69
CChiS	1969
[CDU]	1955, 56, 61, 66(2,3), 69, 70
CLU-G/G	1940, 48, 50, 52, 53(1-5,7-10), 55-62, 63(1-5), 64(1-4,6,10), 65(1-4,6,7), 66(B), 67(1,3,5-10,B), 69(preconv.), 70, 71(1-5,7), 72, 73(1,8,10), 74([A],1,2,5,6,11,12)
CLhC	1950, 55-59, 61, 62, 64(1-3), 65(1,2)
CSdS	1950, 53, 55, 56, 59, 61, 62, 67
CSfCSM	1954, 57-59, 61, 62
CU-EART	1948, 53(4,5), 55-60, 61(2-9), 62, 64(1-3,6,7,10), 67(1,2,5-8, A,B), 68, 69, 70(1,3-7,9), 72, 73(1,8,10), 74(1)
CaAC	1957-59, 61, 71(3)
CaACI	1959, 60, 64(1-3,6,7,9,10)
CaACM	1956(1-3), 57(1-7), 59(1-6), 61(1-9)
CaAEU	1957-59, 61(2-9), 62, 63(3), 64(1-3,6,7,10), 65(1-7), 67(1-3), 69
[CaBVU]	1953, 58, 59, 61(1-9), 64(1-3), 65(1-5), 69
CaOHM	1953(1-3,7-10), 55, 57(1,2), 59, 61, 62, 63(3-5), 64(2,3), 67(1,5), 69, 71(2-4)

CaOKQ	1940, 50, 53(1-5,7-10), 55-59, 61, 69
CaOLU	1948, 53, 55-57, 59-62, 64(10), 70(8)
CaOOG	1940, 53, 55-59, 61, 63(4), 64(1-3), 65(8), 67(B), 68, 69, 70(5), 71(1,A)
CaOONM	1953(1-9)
CaOWtU	1967(1)
CoDuF	1957
CoFS	1956, 57, 60, 61, 65, 69
CoG	1940, 48, 53(1,3-5,9), 55(1-5), 57(1-5), 58, 59, 61(1-9), 62, 63(1-3), 64(1,2,6,10), 65(4,5), 67(1,5,7), 69, 70(1,2,4,6,7,9), 71(2,6,7,10)
CoU	1940, 53(1,6,8), 55-59, 61, 62, 63(3-5), 64(1-3,6,7,10), 65(1-8), 67(1-3,5-8,A,B), 68, 69, 70(1,2,4-9), 71(2,6,7,9,11), 72, 73(1), 74(3,11)
DI-GS	1940, 48-60, 61(1-9), 62, 63(1-5), 64, 65(1,2,4,5,7,8), 66, 67(1-3,5-8,A,B), 68-72, 73(4-6), 74
DLC	1967(7), 71(9)
ICF	1951, 55-59, 61, 62, 64(1-3,6,7), 65(4,5), 69, 70(1,2,4,6-9), 75(A)
ICIU-S	1948, 55, 59, 61, 62, 69
ICarbS	1955-59, 61(1), 62, 69, 70(1,2,4,6-9), 71(1)
IEN	1948, 49, 52, 53(1-5,7-10), 54-60, 61(1-9), 62, 63(3,4), 64(1-3,6,9,10), 65, 66, 69-72, 73(1,5,6,8,10), 74(1,2,6,7)
[I-GS]	1940, 48, 50, 51(B), 52, 53(3,4,5), 55-60, 61(1-9), 62, 63(1,4), 64(1,2,6,7,9,10), 65(3,4-6), 67(2), 70(6,8), 71(3-5,11), 72(11), 73(1,8)
IU	1931, 32, 40, 48, 52, 53, 55-63, 64(1-3,6,7,10), 65(1-5), 67-75
IaAS	1940, 56-60
IaU	1940(1-10), 49, 50, 55-60, 61(1-9), 62, 63(1-5), 64(1-3,6,7,9,10), 65(1-3,6,7), 66, 67(1-3,58,A,B), 69, 70, 71(1-4,6,7,9-11)
InLP	1955-57, 59-61, 63(3,4), 70(1-7,9), 71(6)
InRE	1956-59, 61, 65(3), 70(1), 71(7)
InU	1948-53(1-5,7-9), 54-57, 58(5), 59-62, 63(4,5), 64(1-3,6,7,10), 65, 66(B), 67(1,3,5,7), 69, 70(1,2,5-9), 71(10), 74(2)
IdBB	1956, 59, 61(1-9)
IdPI	1964(3), 70(8), 75(2;Pt.1)
KyU	1949-51, 54-62, 63(3-5), 64(1-3,6,7,9,10), 65(1,4,5), 67(1,3,5,7,8), 69, 70, 71(1-7,9-11), 72(1-7), 73(1,5-8,10,11), 74(1,3,5-7,11,12)
LU	1955-63, 69
MH-GS	1952, 53(1,3,7), 55, 56(1), 57-59, 61, 62, 63(3), 64(1,2,10), 68(9), 69, 71(6), 72(8)
MNS	1950, 53(1-5,7,8,10), 55, 57-61, 70(1,2,4,6-8), 71(1)
MdBJ	1950, 53, 55-61
MiDW	1952, 53, 55-59, 61, 63, 65(1-7), 67, 69
MiHM	1952, 53, 55-59, 61(2-9), 62, 63(3), 65(1-3,6-8), 69, 70(1,2,5-9), 72(1-7)
MiKW	1951, 56, 57, 59, 61
MiU	1955-57, 59, 61, 63, 72(2,4-7)
MnDuU	1948, 53(2), 56(1), 58, 70(1,2,4-7,9)
MnU	1940, 48, 50, 51(1,2), 52(1-4), 53(1-5,7-10), 55-59, 61(1,2), 62, 63(1-5), 64(1-3,6,7,9,10), 65, 67
MoRM	1955-62
MoSW	1940, 48, 51, 53(7), 55, 57-59, 61-63(4), 65(2-7), 67(1-3,5-8,A,B), 70, 71(1,2,6,7,9,10), 73(5,6)
MoU	1948, 50, 53(1-5,7-10), 55-62, 63(3,4), 64(3,10), 65(1-3), 66, 67(1,5), 69, 70(1,2,4,6-9)
MtBC	1958-61, 65(1,2), 68
MtU	1958, 59, 61
NBiSU	1951, 53(10), 55(1-5), 56(1-3), 57, 59, 61(2-9), 62, 63(3,4), 64(1,6,9,10), 65(1-4), 67(1,5,6,A,B), 69, 71(1)

NNC	1940, 48, 51, 53, 55-59, 61-63(5), 64(1-3), 65(1-7)
NOneoU	1958, 60, 63(3), 69
NRU	1953(1-7), 56, 61, 62, 69
NSyU	1940, 53(1), 54, 56, 57, 58(5), 59, 60, 61(2-9), 62, 63(5), 64(1), 65(1-7), 66, 67(A), 69, 70(3,10), 73(1)
NbU	1953-60, 61(1-9), 62, 65(1-7), 66
NcU	1950, 54, 55(1-5), 56-62, 63(5), 64(1,3,6,7), 65(4-6), 66(A), 67(1-3,5,7), 69, 70(5,8)
NdU	1955-59, 61, 62, 63(3-5), 64(1-3,6,7), 65(1-7), 67(1,3,7,8,8A,8B), 69, 70(1,2,4,6-9), 71(1-7,10), 72, 74(1-3,10,11)
NhD	1948, 50(3), 51, 53-59, 61(1), 62, 64(3,6), 65(4,5), 66, 67(7), 69(preconv.), 71(1), 75(A)
NjP	1940, 51-53, 55-62, 63(4,5), 64(1-3,6,10), 65, 67(1,5,7), 68(7), 69, 70(1,2,4,6-9), 71(1,3,5,6), 73(5,6,14,15), 75(A)
NmPE	1957-59, 61, 69
NvLN	1969
NvU	1955-57, 59, 61, 67(5,7), 70(5)
OCU	1940, 48, 53, 55-59, 61(1-9), 62, 64(1-3,6,7,9,10), 65(1-7), 67(3,7,8), 69, 70(2,8), 71(1-5,8,9), 72(8), 75(2,11)
OU	1948-52, 53(1-5,10), 55(1-5), 56-60, 61(1-9), 62, 63(5), 64(1-3,6,7,9,10), 65(1-7), 69, 70(2,4,6-9), 71(3)
OkT	1955, 57-59, 61-63(3), 65(4,5)
OkU	1931, 32(3), 48, 51, 53, 56-59, 61, 62, 64(1-4,6,7,9,10), 65(1-3,5-7), 67(1,3,7), 69, 70(2,4,6-9), 71(3)
OrU	1948, 55-60, 61(1-9)
PBL	1955, 57-59, 69, 70(1,2,5-7,9)
PBm	1948, 55-59, 61, 69, 73(3-7, 10)
PPiGulf	1940, 56(1,2), 57-59, 62, 71(1,4)
PSt	1948, 52, 53(6), 55, 57-59, 61(1-9), 62, 63(3-5), 64(9,10), 65(1-7), 66, 67(2,3,6,7), 69, 70, 71(1-4,6,7,9), 72(1-7), 73(11), 74(1-3,5)
RPB	1951-59, 61(1-9), 63(2-5), 64(4,10), 65(1-7), 66, 67(1,3,5-8,A,B), 69
SdRM	1950, 56-62, 65
SdU	1958, 60, 61
TMM	1959, 61, 67(5), 69, 73(5)
TU	1958, 59, 61, 65(1-7)
TxDaAR-T	1940, 55-59, 61, 62, 63(3,5), 64(1-3,6,7,10), 65(1-7), 67(1,3,5,7), 69-72, 73(6-8,10,11), 74(2,3,6,10)
TxDaDM	1940, 48, 53(1-5,9), 55-59, 61, 62, 64(1), 65(2,4,8), 67(1,2,6-8,B), 69(preconv.), 70(1,4,6,7,9), 71(9), 72(8), 73(1,8)
TxDaM	1940, 55-59, 61, 62, 63(3,4), 64, 65(4,5), 67(7)
TxDaSM	1956-59, 61, 62, 67(1,2,5,7), 69, 71, 73(5,6)
TxHSD	1948, 55, 58, 59, 62, 63(3,4), 64(1-3,6,7,9,10), 65(1,3-5), 67(3), 69, 70(3,5), 71(1), 73(5,6), 74([A],11)
TxHU	1940, 55-62, 63(3-5), 65(1-5), 67(7), 69
TxLT	1953(1-5,7-10), 57-59, 61, 62(1), 65(4,5), 69
TxMM	1940, 53(1-5,7-10), 55-59, 62, 64(1-3,6,7,9), 65(1-7)
TxU	1940, 48, 52, 53, 55-59, 61-71
TxU-Da	1955, 57, 58, 60, 64(1-3), 67(B)
UU	1957-59, 70(B), 73(1)
ViBlbV	1955, 57-59, 61(1-9), 62, 65(4,5), 69, 70(8), 74(2,5,6,12)
[VtPuW]	1955, 61
WU	1951, 53, 55-57, 59, 61, 62, 63(2,4,5), 64(2,10), 65(1-7), 67(1,5-8,A,B), 69, 70(1,2,4-8), 72(8), 73(5), 75(3,11,A,B)
WaPS	1971

WyU	1950, 56-59, 61	

(97) GEOLOGICAL SOCIETY OF AMERICA. CORDILLERAN SECTION. GUIDEBOOK FOR THE ANNUAL MEETING.

1952		Guidebook for field trip excursions in southern Arizona. (34)
		Trip 1. Ground water problems of Queen Creek area
		Trip 2. Paleozoic and Cretaceous stratigraphy of the Tucson Mountains.
		Trip 3. Santa Catalina Mountains metamorphic area.
		Trip 4. Economic geology; Ajo porphyry copper.
		Trip 5. Stratigraphy, structure, and economic geology typical of southern Arizona.
1955		Trip 1. Petrology; Sonoma-Petaluma area.
		Trip 2. Stratigraphy; Oakland-Mt. Diablo area.
1958		Columbia River Gorge: Portland to The Dalles; Eugene to Coos Bay field trip; Willamette Valley field trip.
1959	55th	Southern Arizona guidebook II. (34)
		1. Structure and ore deposits of the east Sierrita area, Arizona. (34)
		2. Stratigraphy of the Waterman and Silver Bell Mountains. (34)
		3. Geology of the Santa Catalina Mountains. (34)
		4. Chaotic breccias in the Tucson Mountains. (34)
		5. General geology of southeastern Arizona. (34)
		6. Volcanic craters of the Pinacate Mountains, Sonora, Mexico. (34)
1960		See Geological Discussion Club, Vancouver, British Columbia. (95)
		A field trip to illustrate geology of coast mountains, North Vancouver, British Columbia. (95)
		Engineering geology, North Vancouver. (95)
		Field trip; Vancouver to Kamloops and return. (95)
1961	57th	See California. University, San Diego. (57)
1963	59th	Alameda and Contra Costa counties, California.
1964	60th	No. 1. Tertiary stratigraphy of the Port Angeles, Lake Crescent, Olympic Peninsula area.
		No. 2. A geologic trip guide along the northern Olympic Peninsula highways.
1965		No. 1. Mercury, jadeite, and asbestos regions near Panoche Pass, California.
		No. 2. The alluvial fans of western Fresno County, California.
		No. 3. Geology of the Sierran foothills in eastern Fresno and Madera counties, California.
		Engineering geology of the San Luis project.
1966	62nd	Guidebook for field trip excursions in northern Nevada.
1967	63rd	No. 1. The South Mountain area, Ventura County, California.
		No. 2. The central Santa Ynez Mountains, Santa Barbara County, California.
		No. 3. The San Luis Obispo-Nipomo area, San Luis Obispo County, California.
1968		No. 3. Southern Arizona guidebook III. (34)
		Field Trip 1. Volcanic geology, southwestern New Mexico and southeastern Arizona. (34)
		Field Trip 2. Mesozoic stratigraphy and Laramide tectonics of part of the Santa Rita and Empire Mountains, southeast of Tucson, Arizona. (34)
		Field Trip 3. Engineering geology, Tucson and Benson areas. (34)
		Field Trip 4. Structure and ore deposits of the Pima mining district. (34)
		Field Trip 5. Stratigraphic and volcanic geology, Tucson Mountains. (34)
		Field Trip 6. Quaternary geology of the San Pedro River valley. (34)
1969	65th	A. Geology of the Newport area, Oregon. (Ore Bin, Feb., Mar. 1969)
		No. 1. Road log, northern Klamath Mountains field trip.
		No. 2. Andesite conference guidebook. Eugene and Bend, Oregon (Oregon. State Department of Geology and Mineral Industries, Bulletin 62).
1970		Field Trip No. 1. Central California coast ranges.
		Field Trip No. 4. Geology of the Diablo Canyon nuclear power plant site, San Luis Obispo County, California.
		Field Trip No. 5. Hayward-Hollister field trip. Active slippage of the Calaveras, Hayward and

San Andreas faults.

1971 Geological excursions in southern California. (California. University. Riverside Campus Museum Contributions, No. 1.)

Field Trip No. 1. Clark Mountain thrust complex in the Cordillera of southeastern California.

Field Trip No. 2. Structural geology and tectonics of the Salton Trough, southern California.

Field Trip No. 3. Vertebrate paleontology of the northern Mojave Desert, southern California.

Field Trip No. 4. Geology of the northern peninsular ranges, southern California.

Field Trip No. 5. Contact metamorphic minerals at Crestmore quarry, Riverside, California.

Field Trip No. 6. Geological engineering problems posed by the San Jacinto fault.

Field Trip No. 7. The San Andreas Fault between San Bernardino and Palmdale, California.

Field Trip No. 8. Stratigraphy and structure of the area between Oceanside and San Diego, California.

Field Trip No. 9. Non-marine turbidites and the San Andreas Fault, San Bernardino Mountains, California.

1972 68th Road guide to points of geologic interest in the Hawaiian Islands.

1973 Geologic field trips in northern Oregon and southern Washington. (Oregon. State Department of Geology and Mineral Resources. Bulletin No. 77.) (236, 294)

Trip 1. Cretaceous and Cenozoic stratigraphy of north-central Oregon.

Trip 2. Volcanoes and intrusive rocks of the central part of the Oregon Coast Range.

Trip 3. Cenozoic stratigraphy of northwestern Oregon and adjacent southwestern Washington. (236)

Trip 4. Columbia River gorge; basalt stratigraphy, ancient lava dams and landslide dams. (236)

Trip 5. Urban environmental geology and planning, Portland, Oregon.

Trip 6. Stratigraphy and structure of Yakima basalt in Pasco Basin, Washington.

Trip 7. Geological field trip guide, Mt. St. Helen's lava tubes.

1974 70th Field Trip No. 1. Guidebook: Death Valley region, California and Nevada.

Field Trip No. 3. Guidebook to the geology of four Tertiary volcanic centers in central Nevada. A road log and trip guide to the collapse calderas at Northumberland Canyon in the Toquima Range and at Black Mountain in Pahute Mesa and to the precious-metal mining districts of Tonopah and Goldfield. (Nevada Bureau of Mines and Geology. Report 19.) (202)

Austin-Northumberland caldera-Carver station.

Carver station-Tonopah district.

Goldfield district.

Black Mountain volcanic center.

Field Trip No. 4. Interbasin ground-water flow in southern Nevada. (Nevada Bureau of Mines and Geology. Report 20.) (202)

1975 71st No. 1. San Andreas Fault in southern California, a guide to San Andreas Fault from Mexico to Carrizo Plain. (55)

No. 2. Peninsular ranges.

No. 3. Eocene sedimentation and paleocurrents San Nicolas Island, California.

No. 4, Pt. 1. Guidebook to the Quaternary geology along the western flank of the Truckee Meadows, Washoe County, Nevada. (Nevada Bureau of Mines and Geology. Report 22.) (202)

No. 5. Preliminary report and geologic guide to the Jurassic ophiolite near Point Sal, southern California coast.

A field guide to Cenozoic deformation along the Sierra Nevada Province and Basin and Range boundary. (In: California Division of Mines and Geology. California Geology. Vol. 28, No. 5, May 1975.)

1976 72nd Field Guide No. 1. Guide to field trip between Pasco and Pullman, Washington; emphasizing stratigraphy, vent areas, and intracanyon flows of Yakima basalt.

Field Guide No. 2. Channeled scablands of southeastern Washington; a roadlog via Spokane, Coulee City, Vantage, Washtucna, Lewiston and Pullman.

Field Guide No. 3. Hydrology and engineering geology of the Columbia Basin.
Field Guide No. 4. The Idaho batholith and related subduction complex.
Field Guide No. 5. Geologic guide to Hells Canyon, Snake River.

[CDU]	1971
CLU-G/G	1961, 67, 69(1), 70(1,5), 71, 73, 74(1,3,4), 75
CLhC	1974(1)
CSdS	1961, 71, 73
CSfCSM	1955, 58, 61, 63, 65(2), 71
CU-EART	1955(1), 58, 60, 61, 65-67, 69(A), 71, 73
CaACM	1973
CaOKQ	1964
CaOOG	1970(1,3,5)
CaOONM	1973
CoG	1970(3)
CoU	1969(65,3), 73, 74(1,3), 75(4, Pt.1)
DI-GS	1952, 55, 59-69, 70(1,4,5), 71, 74(1,3,4)
DLC	1973
[I-GS]	1955, 60, 74(3,4)
IU	1952, 55, 59, 60, 63, 67, 68, 70-74, 76
IaU	1959, 75
InRE	1974(1)
InU	1953, 55, 59, 60, 68, 69, 74, 75
KyU	1959, 68, 70(1,4,5), 71, 75(1,2)
MH-GS	1958
MnDuU	1973
MNS	1959
MiKW	1974(1)
MiU	1974(3,4)
MnU	1952, 59, 60, 63, 67(1,2), 68
MoSW	1973
MoU	1968
NNC	1955
NSyU	1959, 68(3), 74(1)
NcU	1952, 68(3)
NdU	1969(2), 71, 73, 74
NhD	1961, 66, 71
NjP	1952, 69(2), 71, 73, 74(3)
NvU	1958, 66, 71, 74(1,3,4), 75(4 Pt. 1)
OCU	1967(1,3), 74(1)
OU	1969(A), 71
OkS	1971
OkU	1974(1)
PSt	1971(1), 74(1)
RPB	1959, 68
TxDaAR-T	1967(3), 69, 70(1,4,5), 71-73
TxDaDM	1955, 67(1-3), 69, 74(3), 75
TxDaSM	1971, 74(1)
TxHSD	1966, 74(1), 75(3,5)
TxMM	1968
TxU	1961, 68, 69, 70(1,4,5)
ViBlbV	1974(1), 76(2)
WU	1973, 74(3)

(98) GEOLOGICAL SOCIETY OF AMERICA. NORTH CENTRAL SECTION. FIELD TRIP GUIDEBOOK.

1967 1st
No. 1. Karst geomorphology of south-central Indiana.
No. 2. Silurian and Devonian stratigraphy of southeastern Indiana.
No. 3. Pleistocene stratigraphy of west-central Indiana.
No. 4. Nonmetallic mineral resources of southwestern Indiana.

1968 2nd
No. 1. Niagaran bioherms in the vicinity of Iowa City (Linn and Cedar counties).
No. 2. Geology of U. S. Gypsum Company's Sperry mine. (103)
No. 3. Mississippian (Osage and Kinderhook) stratigraphy and Mississippian-Devonian boundary problems in southeastern Iowa.
No. 4. Middle River traverse of Iowa (Pennsylvanian stratigraphy). (143)
No. 5. A review of Pleistocene Lake Calvin.
No. 6. Conodont successions.

1969 3rd
No. 1. Devonian outcrops in Columbus, Ohio and vicinity.
No. 2. Till stratigraphy from Columbus southwest to Highland County, Ohio.
No. 3. Ordovician conodont localities, southwestern Ohio.
No. 4. Mississippian strata of the Granville-Newark area, Ohio.

1970 4th
No. 1. Devonian strata of Alpena and Presque Isle counties, Michigan. (165)
No. 2. Glacial history of the Glacial Grand Valley. (165)
No. 3. Precambrian of the Marquette area, Michigan. (165)

1971
No. 1. Guidebook to the late Pliocene and early Pleistocene of Nebraska.
No. 2. Guidebook for field trip on urban geology in eastern Nebraska.
No. 3. Guidebook to selected Pleistocene paleosols in eastern Nebraska.
No. 4. Guidebook to the geology along portions of the lower Platte River valley and Weeping Water valley of eastern Nebraska.

1972
No. 2. Geology for land-use planning, McHenry County, Illinois.
No. 3. Pennsylvanian conodont assemblages from La Salle County, northern Illinois. (126)
No. 4. Pleistocene geology between DeKalb and Danville, Illinois.

1973
Special. Canadian-Ordovician field trip.
No. 1. Field trip not held; therefore no guidebook published. (41)
No. 2. Pleistocene and engineering geology of north-central Missouri.
No. 3. Fletcher Mine trip.
No. 4. Barite deposits of the Central Mineral district.
No. 5. Central Missouri fire clay deposits.

1974
No. [1,2,3.] Selected field trips in northeastern Ohio.
Field Trip 1. General geology of the International Salt Company Cleveland mine, Cleveland, Ohio.
Field Trip 2. Sedimentary environments of the Lower Pennsylvanian Sharon Conglomerate.
Field Trip 3. Engineering and Pleistocene geology of the lower Cuyahoga River valley.
Field Trip 4. Natural and manmade features affecting the Ohio shore of Lake Erie.
Field Trip 5. Pennsylvanian conodont localities in northeastern Ohio. (225, 240)
Field Trip 6. Energy resources Canton-Cadiz area field trip.

1975 9th
Waterloo '75.
Part A. Precambrian geology.
Trip 1. Granitoid rocks of the Madoc-Bancroft-Haliburton area of the Greenville province.
Trip 2. Greenville gneisses in the Madawaska highlands, eastern Ontario.
Trip 3. Precambrian economic geology of the Cobalt silver deposits.
Trip 12. Mineral and economic geology of the Cobalt silver deposits.
Part B. Phanerozoic geology.
Trip 4,5. Ordovician to Devonian stratigraphy and conodont biostratigraphy of southern Ontario.
Trip 6. Quaternary stratigraphy of the Toronto area.
Trip 7. Late Quaternary stratigraphy of the Waterloo-Lake Huron area, southwestern

Ontario.
Part C. Environmental geology. (94, 171)
Trip 8. Industrial minerals of the Paris-Hamilton district, Ontario.
Trip 9. Engineering geology of the Niagara peninsula.
Trip 10. Environmental geology Kitchener-Guelph area.
Trip 11. No guidebook.

1976 No. 1. Geology of the Kentland structural anomaly, northwestern Indiana.
No. 2. Field trip guidebook to coastal and environmental geology of southeastern Lake Michigan.
No. 3. Guidebook to the Indiana portion of a field trip on Silurian reefs, interreef facies, and faunal zones of northern Indiana and northeastern Illinois.
No. 4. Guidebook for a field trip on some aspects of the glacial geology in the Kalamazoo area.

CLU-G/G	1972(3), 74(1-3)
CU-EART	1967, 74(2,3)
CaOLU	1970
* CaOOG	1967, 70(1)
CoG	1967, 73(2,4,5)
DI-GS	1967-71, 72(2,4), 73, 74
ICF	1973(3)
ICarbS	1972(3)
[I-GS]	1969, 72(1-3)
IU	1967-76
IaU	1968-70, 72(3), 74
InU	1967, 68(4), 69
KyU	1969-71, 73(2-5), 74(1-3), 75
MnDuU	1969
MiHM	1967
MiU	1969
MnU	1967, 69
MoSW	1967
MoU	1967, 68(4), 69, 70, 74(1-3)
NNC	1970
NcU	1975
NdU	1968, 71, 73(2)
NjP	1950, 52, 57, 58, 67-70, 72(3), 74(1-3), 75
NvU	1968
OCU	1972, 74(1-5)
OU	1969, 72(3), 75
OkU	1967, 69, 74(2,3)
PBm	1975
PPiGulf	1969
TxDaAR-T	1967, 70, 71, 72(3,4), 75
TxDaDM	1968, 70, 72, 74(1-3,5)
TxDaSM	1970
TxU	1967-71, 72(3)

(99) GEOLOGICAL SOCIETY OF AMERICA. NORTHEASTERN SECTION. GUIDEBOOK FOR FIELD TRIPS.

1973 Field Trip No. 1. Field guide to the Friedensville Mine of the New Jersey Zinc Company.
1974 Field Trip No. 2. No guidebook.

IU	1973

(100) GEOLOGICAL SOCIETY OF AMERICA. ROCKY MOUNTAIN SECTION. GUIDEBOOK FOR FIELD TRIPS.

1951	4th	[No title. Prepared by the members of the geological staffs of the South Dakota School of Mines and the Homestake Mining Company.]
1952	5th	Geology and hydrothermal alteration of the Bingham Copper Mine.
1953	6th	Guidebook of field excursions, Butte, Montana.
		Trip 1. Stratigraphy and structure in the Three Forks area.
		Trip 2. Underground trip to mines of the Anaconda Company.
		Trip 3. Dewey-Divide contact of the Boulder batholith.
		Trip 4. Petrology and ore deposits in the northern part of the Boulder batholith.
		Trip 5. Structure and stratigraphy in the Phillipsburg-Drummond area.
1957	10th	Northern central Utah and southeastern Idaho.
1958	11th	Precambrian field trip, Front Range. Sedimentary field trip, Golden to Deer Creek, Colorado.
1959	12th	[No title. Held at Montana State University, Missoula, Montana.]
		Field Trip 1. Stratigraphy of the Belt series.
		Field Trip 2. Drummond-Helmville-Ovando area with emphasis on post-Precambrian geology.
		Field Trip 3. Glacial geology of the Flathead Valley and environs.
		Field Trip 4. Northern Bitterroot Range and Idaho batholith border facies.
1960	13th	Rapid City to Bell Fourche, South Dakota via Sturgis, Deadwood, and Spearfish.
1962	15th	Geology of the southern Wasatch Mountains and vicinity, Utah; a symposium.
1965	18th	Resume of the geology of the Laramie anorthosite mass and road log.
		Field Trip No. 1. The anorthosites of the Laramie Range.
		Field Trip No. 2. Diatremes containing lower Paleozoic rocks in southern Wyoming and northern Colorado.
		Field Trip No. 3. Itinerary, cement plant field trip.
		Field Trip No. 4. Tertiary of the Gangplank area; trip from Fort Collins, to Wellington, Cheyenne, Granite Canyon and return via State Highway 14, U. S. Highways 87 and 30 and local roads.
		Field Trip No. 5. Sandstone members of the Pierre Shale in the Fort Collins, Colorado area.
		Field Trip No. 6. Big Thompson Canyon and vicinity.
1966	[19th]	The Nevada test site. (Geological Society of America, Memoir 110).
		Road log; Cedar City, Utah to Las Vegas, Nevada via Caliente, Nevada.
		Central Utah coals.
		Tintic mining district.
		Willard thrust.
		Great Salt Lake and Antelope Island.
		Geology of Bingham mining district.
1967		Precambrian basement rocks of the Colorado Front Range.
1968		No. 1. Butte mines.
		No. 2. Cretaceous rocks of the western Crazy Mountains Basin and vicinity, Montana.
		No. 3. Boulder batholith.
		No. 4. Stillwater igneous complex.
		No. 5. Geomorphology and Cenozoic history of the Yellowstone Valley, south of Livingstone, Montana.
		No. 6. Igneous and hydrothermal geology of Yellowstone National Park.
1969		Guidebook of northern Utah. (321)
1970	23rd	No. 1. Road log, Rapid City to Homestake Mine via Interstate 90. Road log, Rapid City to Homestake Mine via Central Hills. The Homestake Mine.
		Field Trip No. 2. Road log, Precambrian metasediments and pegmatites of the Black Hills.
		Field Trip No. 3. Road log, Tertiary stratigraphy of the northern part of the Big Badlands.
		Field Trip No. 4. Road log, Paleozoic and Mesozoic stratigraphy of the Rapid City area.
		Field Trip No. 5. Road log, engineering geology of the Rapid City area.
1971	24th	No. 1. Coal, oil, gas and industrial mineral deposits of the interior plains, foothills and Rocky

Mountains of Alberta and British Columbia.
No. 1a. Cascade and Crowsnest coal basins.
No. 1b. A guide to the geology of the Eastern Cordillera along the Trans-Canada Highway between Calgary, Alberta and Revelstoke, British Columbia.
No. 2a. Geological guide along the Trans-Canada Highway from Calgary to Banff.
No. 3. Geologic guidebook to the Canadian Cordillera between Calgary and Revelstoke.
No. 4. A guide to the Pleistocene geology.
No. 5,6. A guide to the geology betweeen Calgary and Banff.

1972 [25th] No. 1. Depositional environment of the Green River Formation, Wyoming.
No. 2. Mining in the Hanna coal field.
No. 3. Field trip guide and road log to northern Laramie anorthosite complex.
No. 4. Late Paleozoic rocks of the southern Laramie Basin.

1973 26th No. 1. Geomorphology, palynology, and paleomagnetic record of glacial Lake Devlin, Front Range.
No. 2. Virginia Dale ring-dike complex.
No. 3. No guidebook published.
No. 4. Nature of the early Tertiary intrusives between Golden and Lyons, Colorado, and their relation to the structural development of the Front Range.
No. 5. Lyons sandstone.
No. 6. Urban geology of the Boulder area, Colorado.
No. 7. Tundra environment on Niwot Ridge, Colorado Front Range.
No. 8. Petrologic, tectonic, and geomorphic history of central Colorado.
No. 9. Dakota group.
No. 10. Environmental geology for planning Windsor study area: Fort Collins, Loveland, and Greeley.

1974 27th Geology of northern Arizona with notes on archaeology and paleoclimate; Part 1, Regional studies, Part 2, Area studies and field guides.
[No. 1.] Kaibab trail guide to the southern part of Grand Canyon, northern Arizona.
[No. 2.] Geologic resume and field guide, north-central Arizona.
[No. 3.] Field guide to the geology of the San Francisco volcanic field, Arizona.
[No. 4.] Field guide to the geology of the San Francisco Mountain, northern Arizona.
[No. 5.] Field guide for southeast Verde Valley, northern Hackberry Mountain area, north-central Arizona.
[No. 6.] Field guide for Hopi buttes and Navajo buttes area, Arizona.
[No. 7.] Field guide for the Black Mesa-Little Colorado River area, northeastern Arizona.
[No. 8.] Economic geology and field guide for the Jerome district, Arizona.

1975 28th No. 1. Engineering geology approaches to highway construction in central Idaho; Boise, Idaho to Whitebird Hill, Idaho.
No. 2. No guidebook.
No. 3. Geologic field guide to the Quaternary volcanics on the south-central Snake River plain, Idaho. (122)
No. 4. Field trip guide to the Idaho-Wyoming thrust fault zone.
No. 5. Rock alteration and slope failure, Middle Fork of the Payette River.
No. 6. The evaluation of geologic processes in the Boise foothills that may be hazardous to urban development. (A report prepared for the Ada Council of Governments, May 1973.)
No. 7. The later Tertiary stratigraphy and paleobotany of the Weiser area, Idaho.
No. 8. The geology and scenery of the Snake River on the Idaho-Oregon border from Brownlee Dam to Hells Canyon Dam. (Idaho Bureau of Mines and Geology, Moscow, Idaho. Information Circular 28.) (121)

AzFU	1966, 67, 69, 74
AzU	1969
[CDU]	1974

CLU-G/G	1953, 58, 69, 70, 74
CSfCSM	1957, 59
CU-EART	1956, 59, 65, 67-69
[CaACAM]	1971(3)
CaOHM	1969
CaOOG	1969, 72(2), 73(1,2,4,6,7)
CoG	1967, 69, 70, 71(3,4), 72(1-4)
CoU	1951, 57, 69, 70, 71(1,4-6), 72(1-4), 73, 75(3,7,8)
DI-GS	1951, 52, 57-60, 62, 66, 70, 71, 72(1,3,4), 73(1,2,4,6-8,10), 74, 75
ICIU-S	1962
IU	1959, 65-67, 70-72, 73(1,2,4-8), 75
IdBB	1975(1,3-8)
IdPI	1969, 75(3,7,8)
InU	1951, 59, 69, 70
KyU	1966, 68-72, 73(1,2,4-10), 74, 75
MH-GS	1958, 74
MnU	1968-70
MoSW	1973(1,2,4,6-8), 75(3,7,8)
MoU	1966, 68(4), 69
MtU	1970
NBiSU	1973(1,2,4,6,7)
NNC	1959
NbU	1968, 69
NcU	1966
NdU	1967, 69, 70, 74, 75(3,7,8)
NjP	1959, 69
NvU	1969
OCU	1970, 74
OU	1970, 73(1,2,4,6,7)
OkU	1975(3)
SdU	1970
TxDaAR-T	1969, 70, 71(3,5,6), 72(1,3), 73(1,2,4,5,7-9), 74, 75(3-5)
TxDaDM	1959, 60, 69
TxDaSM	1959, 72(1,4), 74
TxU	1966, 69, 70, 71(1,3), 72
TxU-Da	1960
WU	1974, 75(3,4,6,7,8)
WyU	1957, 59

(101) GEOLOGICAL SOCIETY OF AMERICA. SOUTH CENTRAL SECTION. FIELD TRIP GUIDEBOOK FOR THE ANNUAL MEETING.

1967	1st	The structure and igneous rocks of the Wichita Mountains, Oklahoma.
1968	2nd	Stratigraphy of the Woodbine Formation, Tarrant County, Texas.
1969	3rd	Pleistocene geology of Doniphan County, Kansas.
1970	4th	Outcrops of the Claiborne Group (middle Eocene) in the Brazos Valley, southeast Texas.
1971		Mesozoic and Cenozoic geology of the Lubbock, Texas region.
1972	6th	Stratigraphy and depositional environments of the Crouse Limestone (Permian) in north-central Kansas.
1973	7th	No. 1. Ouachita Mountains; a guidebook to the geology of the Ouachita Mountains, Arkansas.
		No. 2. Lake Ouachita; geological field trip excursion.
		No. 3. Guidebook to Lower and Middle Ordovician strata of northeastern Arkansas and

		generalized log of route from Little Rock to Batesville, Arkansas.
1974		No. 1. Environmental geology of metropolitan Tulsa.
		No. 2. Distribution of algae and corals in Upper Pennsylvanian-Missourian rocks in northeastern Oklahoma.
		No. 3. Guidebook to the depositional environments of selected Pennsylvanian sandstones and carbonates of Oklahoma.
1975	9th	Field Trip No. 1. Precambrian rocks of the southeastern Llano region, central Texas. Geologic description and road log.
		Field Trip No. 2. Utilization of land resources in the Austin area.
		Field Trip No. 3. Geology of the Llano region and Austin area.
		Stratigraphy of the Austin chalk in the vicinity of Pilot Knob.
1976		Field Trip No. 2. Plutonic igneous geology of the Wichita magmatic province, Oklahoma.

[CDU]	1967-70
CLU-G/G	1967, 69, 70, 74(1,3)
CU-EART	1967
CaOHM	1967, 68
CaOLU	1967
CaOOG	1971, 74(3)
CoU	1967
DI-GS	1967-72, 74, 75(1,2,4)
IEN	1967-72, 73(3), 74(2)
IU	1967, 68, 70-75, 76(2)
IaU	1967-72, 74(2)
IdBB	1967
IdPI	1967, 68
InLP	1969-72
InU	1967, 68
KyU	1967-73, 75
MH-GS	1967, 68
MnU	1967-70
MoSW	1973(2)
MoU	1973(2), 74(3)
NBiSU	1967, 68, 70-72
NSyU	1967, 68
NbU	1968
NcU	1967, 68
NdU	1967, 68
NhD	1967, 71, 72
NjP	1967-72
OCU	1968-72
OU	1967, 68, 70
OkU	1967-71, 74(2,3), 76(2)
PBm	1967
RPB	1967, 68
SdRM	1967, 68
TMM	1967
TxDaAR-T	1967-73, 74(2,3)
TxDaDM	1967-72
TxDaSM	1969, 70, 73(1,3)
TxHSD	1974(3)
TxLT	1968
TxU	1967-70
ViBlbV	1975(1,2,4)

(102) GEOLOGICAL SOCIETY OF AMERICA. SOUTHEASTERN SECTION. GUIDEBOOK...FIELD TRIP.

1953 Central Tennessee phosphate district.
1954 Coastal plain and Piedmont.
1955 Coastal plain field trip.
1956 Panhandle Florida.
1957 No. 1. Morgantown, West Virginia to Greer, West Virginia. (341)
No. 2. Morgantown, West Virginia to the Humphrey coal preparation plant. (341)
1958 See Alabama. Geological Survey. (5)
1959 Piedmont field trip featuring metamorphic facies in the Raleigh area, North Carolina. Coastal plain field trip featuring basal Cretaceous sediments of the Fayetteville area, North Carolina.
1960 No. 1. Physiographic and stratigraphic profile in Kentucky, Lexington to the Mammoth Cave region. (104)
No. 2. Geology of the central Bluegrass area. (104)
1961 Geology of the Mascot-Jefferson City zinc district, Tennessee. (300)
Structural geology along the eastern Cumberland escarpment, Tennessee. (300)
1962 No. 1. The Georgia marble district. (112)
No. 2. Stone Mountain-Lithonia district. (112)
No. 3. Ocoee metasediments, north-central Georgia, southeast Tennessee. (112)
1963 Tectonics of the southern Appalachians.
Geological excursions in southwestern Virginia. (334)
1964 No. 1. Jackson-Vicksburg type sections.
No. 2. Geology of central Louisiana.
No. 3. Flood plain and terrace geomorphology; Baton Rouge fault zone.
No. 4. Five Islands and Mississippi deltaic plain.
1965 No. 1. Geologic structures in northern Sequatchie Valley and adjacent portion of the Cumberland Plateau of Tennessee.
No. 2. Selected features of the Wells Creek basin cryptoexplosion structure
No. 3. Ordovician of central Tennessee.
1966 No. 1. Pleistocene and Holocene sediments, Sapelo Island, Georgia. (Georgia. University. Marine Institute, Sapelo Island, Ga. Contribution 105.)
No. 2. Extrusive volcanics and associated dike swarms in central east Georgia.
No. 3. Stratigraphy and economic geology of the coastal plain of the central Savannah River area, Georgia.
1967 No. 1. Sedimentation and coastal features of the Alligator Point area and the area between the Fenholloway and Steinhatchee rivers.
No. 2. Paleontology of a part of west Florida.
No. 3. Attapulgite; economic geology.
1968 No. 1. Sedimentation in Onslow Bay.
No. 2. Geology of the Sauratown Mountain anticlinorium and vicinity, North Carolina. (Southeastern Geology, Special publication No. 1, 1968).
1969 No. 1. Paleocene stratigraphy of South Carolina and the question of Tertiary volcanism. (Geologic notes of the South Carolina Division of Geology, Vol. 13, No. 1, spring 1969 and Southeastern Geology, Vol. 4, No. 4, May 1963.)
No. 2. Geology of the slate belt in central South Carolina.
No. 3. Geology of the Charlotte belt in central South Carolina. (South Carolina, Division of Geology, Geologic notes, Vol. 12, No. 4, Oct. 1968 guidebook for field trips No. 2 and 3)
A field guide to the Allegheny deltaic deposits in the upper Ohio Valley, with a commentary on deltaic aspects of Carboniferous rocks in the northern Appalachian plateau.
1970 No. 1. Geologic features of southeastern Kentucky.
No. 2. Lithology and fauna of the Lexington Limestone (Ordovician) of central Kentucky.
No. 3. Borden Formation (Mississippian) in southeast-central Kentucky.

		No. 4. Paleozoic section on east flank of Cincinnati arch along Interstate 64, Lexington to Olive Hill, Kentucky. (104)
		Pt. 1. Lexington eastward to valley of Licking River.
		Pt. 2. Valley of Licking River eastward to Olive Hill interchange.
1971		Guidebook to Appalachian tectonics and sulfide mineralization of southwestern Virginia. (334)
		Field Trip No. 1. Sulfide mineralization, southwestern Virginia.
		Field Trip No. 2. Geology of the Blue Ridge in southwestern Virginia and adjacent North Carolina.
		Field Trip No. 3. Appalachian structural and topographic front between Narrows and Beckley, Virginia and West Virginia.
		Field Trip No. 4. Appalachian overthrust belt, Montgomery County, southwestern Virginia.
1972		Guidebook for field trips. (300)
	21st	Field Trip No. 1. Meta-Paleozoic rocks, Chilton County, Alabama.
		Field Trip No. 2. Upper Cretaceous series in central Alabama.
		Field Trip No. 3. Southern Appalachian Valley and Ridge province; structures and stratigraphy.
		Field Trip No. 4. Limestone hydrology and environmental geology. (3, 300)
		Carboniferous depositional environments in the Cumberland plateau of southern Tennessee and northern Alabama. Pre-Meeting field trip. (300)
1973		Geology of Knox County, Tennessee. (299)
		Field Trip No. 1,2. Stratigraphy and depositional environments in the Valley and Ridge at Knoxville.
		Field Trip No. 3. Mineral resources of Knox County, Tennessee.
1974	23rd	Field guide to some carbonate rock environments.
		See Georgia. Geological Survey. (112)
1975		Field trips in west Tennessee. (300)
		Field Trip No. 1. Fossiliferous Silurian, Devonian, and Cretaceous formations in the vicinity of the Tennessee River.
		Field Trip No. 2. Environmental geology of Memphis, Tennessee.
		Field Trip No. 3. Geology of Reelfoot Lake and vicinity.
		Field Trip No. 4. The northeastern part of west Tennessee.
		Field Trip No. 5. Paleocene and Eocene localities in southwest Tennessee.

[A-GS]	1960, 62, 65(1)
CLU-G/G	1960(2), 61, 63, 68-71
CSdS	1964(1)
CU-EART	1961, 62, 64-66, 72, 73, 75
[CaBVU]	1961
CaOHM	1972
CaOKQ	1960(2), 65, 66(3)
CaOOG	1960, 68(1), 69, 71, 73
CaOWtU	1964, 72(1,2)
CoG	1960, 62, 65, 66, 71, 72
CoU	1956, 57, 61, 65, 66, 68, 71, 73
DI-GS	1953-66, 68, 69(1), 70-72, 75
DLC	1973
ICF	1960(2), 61, 62, 71, 72, 75
[I-GS]	1956, 72, 73, 75
IU	1959-62, 64, 65, 66(1), 67-75
IaU	1961, 64, 66(1,3), 68, 69, 72, 75
InLP	1965, 67, 70
InU	1953, 60, 61, 62(1,2), 63, 66(2,3), 68(2), 69, 70, 75
KyU	1952, 57, 59-65, 66(2,3), 67, 68, 70-75

MH-GS	1959
MNS	1958, 61
MiDW	1962
MiHM	1961, 68, 69(4), 71, 75
MiKW	1964, 70
MiU	1968, 72
MnU	1960, 62-64, 65(1), 66
MoSW	1961, 63, 66(1), 68(2), 70, 74, 75
MoU	1960, 62(2), 63, 71
NNC	1960-63
NSyU	1961, 69, 72, 73
NbU	1961
NcU	1955, 59, 61, 63, 64, 65(1), 66(1), 67, 68(1,2), 74
NdU	1961, 62, 69(1,3), 72(preconv.), 73, 75
NhD	1961, 68(2), 71, 72
NjP	1960, 63, 65(1), 66, 68-70, 72
NvU	1962
OCU	1953, 56, 57, 60-62, 63(2), 65, 66(2,3), 68(2), 69, 70-73, 75
OU	1956, 57, 60, 61, 66(3), 68, 69(1,3), 70, 72
OkU	1960-65, 66(1,3), 69(preconv.), 70, 72
PSt	1958, 61, 62, 66, 68
RPB	1961
TMM	1960, 65, 68, 73
TxDaAR-T	1960, 62, 63, 66, 67(3), 68, 71-73, 74(1,2), 75
TxDaDM	1960(2), 61, 62, 64, 65, 66(1), 70, 72, 73
TxDaM	1960, 66(1,3)
TxDaSM	1961, 66(1)
TxHSD	1965
TxHU	1961, 62, 68
TxMM	1965(1)
TxU	1957, 58, 60, 62-71
ViBlbV	1952, 60(1), 61-63, 68
[VtPuW]	1968, 72
WU	1961, 62, 74, 75
WaPS	1971

(103) GEOLOGICAL SOCIETY OF IOWA. FIELD TRIPS. GUIDEBOOK.

1962	May	Skvor-Hartl area, southeast Linn County, Iowa.
	July	Maquoketa of northeast Iowa.
1963	May	Silurian bioherms of eastern Iowa. (312)
	July	Upper Devonian in Mason City and Garner areas. (312)
1964		Southwestern Iowa.
1965		Pre-Cedar Valley, post-Maquoketa sediments.
1967		Field Trip 2. Emphasis on industry; plant tours, Concrete Materials Division of Martin Marietta Corporation, Cedar Rapids and tour of quarries.
	June 2	United States Gypsum Company mine, Sperry, Iowa. (98)
	June 3	Osage and Kinderhook series, Des Moines County, Iowa.
	fall	Middle River traverse.
1968	March	Field trip; Middle River traverse.
	June	Field trip (Mississippian: Maynes Creek, Chapin, Prospect Hill, McCraney; Devonian: Encligh River, Maple Mill, Aplington, Sheffield, Lime Creek). See Geological Society of America. North Central Section. (98)
1970		Field trip to Red Rock Dam (map only).
1972		Revision of galena stratigraphy.

CLU-G/G	1964
DI-GS	1962-65, 67, 68
IU	1963, 64, 67(June,fall), 68
IaU	1962-65, 67, 68, 70(map), 72
InU	1968
MnU	1963(July), 65
NNC	1964
TxDaAR-T	1963, 67
TxDaDM	1967(1)
TxU	1962(May), 63(July), 65, 68

(104) GEOLOGICAL SOCIETY OF KENTUCKY. GUIDEBOOK FOR THE FIELD TRIP. (TITLE VARIES)

1941	Itinerary of field conference held April 25-26, 1941, starting at Litchfield, Kentucky.
1942	Pennsylvanian stratigraphy of Laurel, Clay, and Perry counties, southeastern Kentucky.
1950	Southwestern Virginia.
1952	Chester field excursion; outcrop of the Chester formations of Crawford and Perry counties, Indiana, and Breckinridge County, Kentucky.
	Since 1952 these guidebooks have been prepared in cooperation with the Kentucky Geological Survey. Series IX.
1953	Some Pennsylvanian sections in Morgan, Magoffin, and Breathitt counties, Kentucky.
1954	Geology of the Mammoth Cave region; Barren, Edmonson, and Hart counties, Kentucky.
1955	Exposures of producing formations of northeastern Kentucky.
1956	Selected geologic features of southwestern Kentucky.
1957	Some stratigraphic and structural features of the Middlesboro Basin. (31)
1958	Sedimentation and stratigraphy of Silurian and Devonian rocks in the Louisville area, Kentucky.
1959	Stratigraphy of Nelson County and adjacent areas.
1960	See Geological Society of America. Southeastern Section. (102)
1961	Geologic features of the Cumberland Gap area, Kentucky, Tennessee, and Virginia.
1962	Selected features of the Kentucky fluorspar district and the Barkley dam site.
1963	Geologic features of the Mississippian plateau, south-central Kentucky.
1964	Geologic features of the Mississippian plateau in the Mammoth Cave and Elizabethtown areas, Kentucky.
1965	No. 1. Lithostratigraphy of the Ordovician Lexington Limestone and the Clays Ferry Formation of the central Bluegrass area near Lexington, Kentucky.
	No. 2. Excursion to the cryptoexplosive structure near Versailles, Kentucky.
1966	Geologic features of selected Pennsylvanian and Mississippian channel deposits along the eastern rim of the western Kentucky coal basin.
1967	Some aspects of the stratigraphy of the Pine Mountain front near Elkhorn City, Kentucky with notes on pertinent structural features.
1968	Geologic aspects of the Maysville-Portsmouth region, southern Ohio and northeastern Kentucky. (226)
1969	Middle and Upper Pennsylvanian strata in Hopkins and Webster counties, Kentucky.
1970	No. 1. Geologic features of southeastern Kentucky.
	No. 2. Lithology and fauna of the Lexington limestone (Ordovician) of central Kentucky.
	No. 3. Borden Formation (Mississippian) in southeast-central Kentucky.
	No. 4. See Geological Society of America. Southeastern Section. (102)
1971	Carboniferous depositional environments in northeastern Kentucky.
1972	Geology of the Jackson Purchase region, Kentucky.
1973	Depositional environments of eastern Kentucky coals.
	Pt. 2. Depositional environments of Pennsylvanian rocks along the Mountain Parkway and Kentucky Highway 15, Wolfe County to Knott County, Kentucky.

1974 Late Cenozoic geologic features of the middle Ohio River valley.

1975 Selected structural features and associated dolostone occurrences in the vicinity of the Kentucky River fault system.

AzTeS	1952, 55-59, 61-67, 69, 74
CLU-G/G	1952-57, 59-69, 71, 72, 74
CU-EART	1974
CaOKQ	1952, 55, 58, 59, 65
CaOLU	1954, 61, 62
CaOOG	1952-59, 61, 62
CoG	1957-59, 61, 62, 66, 67
DI-GS	1952-69, 71, 72, 74
DLC	1968
ICF	1952, 54, 56-59, 61-64
IEN	1950
[I-GS]	1957, 58, 64, 67, 69, 71, 74
IU	1941, 52-59, 61-65
IaU	1964, 67, 74
InLP	1952-68
InU	1952-55, 57-59, 61, 62, 65, 67-69, 71, 72, 74
KyU	1942, 50, 52-74
LU	1952, 53
MiDW	1955, 56, 61, 63, 64, 66, 67, 71, 72
MnU	1952-68
MoSW	1954, 67, 74
MoU	1952, 55, 57-59, 61-66
NBiSU	1971, 74
NNC	1950, 52-59, 61-66
NbU	1954, 55, 58, 59, 61, 62
NcU	1952-56, 59, 61-69
NdU	1964, 73-75
NjP	1952, 55-59, 61-70, 75
NvU	1974, 75
OCU	1955, 59, 61-68
OU	1953-59, 61-69, 72-75
[OkOkCGe]	1954, 55
OkU	1942, 46, 52-59, 61-69, 73
PBL	1952-55
PSt	1955
RPB	1954
TMM	1952, 55-57, 59, 61-66, 68, 69
TxDaAR-T	1958, 59, 69, 71, 72, 74
TxDaDM	1952-59, 61-69, 71, 72, 74
TxDaM	1952-59, 61-66
TxDaSM	1954-56, 64
TxHSD	1968
TxLT	1968
TxMM	1942
TxU	1952, 54-59, 61-68
ViBlbV	1950, 52, 54-59

(105) GEOLOGICAL SOCIETY OF NEW JERSEY.

1959 Stokes forest.

DI-GS	1959
NjP	1959
TxU	1959

(106) GEOLOGICAL SOCIETY OF PUERTO RICO.

1966 Field trip on Puerto Rico. [No guidebook published]

1968 Karst field trip; stratigraphy and geomorphology.

TxU	1968

(107) GEOLOGICAL SOCIETY OF SACRAMENTO. ANNUAL FIELD TRIP GUIDEBOOK.

1955 [Itinerary of the spring field trip.]

1956 Indian Valley region, Plumas County, California.

1957 The Cretaceous and associated formations of the Redding area, Shasta County, California.

1958 East side Sacramento Valley-Mother Lode area, California.

1959 Coast Ranges; Livermore Valley to Hollister area.

1960 Northwestern California; a traverse of the Klamath uplift, northern Coast Ranges, and Eel River basin.

1961 East-central Sacramento Valley: Marysville (Sutter) Butte, Chico Creek, and Oroville.

1962 U. S. Highway 40; Sacramento to Reno, Dixie Valley and Sand Springs range, Nevada. (53, 201)

1963 Central portion of Great Valley of California, San Juan Bautista to Yosemite Valley.

1964 Mount Diablo.

1965 La Porte to the summit of the Grizzly Mountains, Plumas County, California.

1966 East-central front of the Sierra Nevada.

1967 Quaternary geology of northern Sacramento County, California.

1968 Geological studies in the Lake Tahoe area, California and Nevada.

1969 Geologic guide to the Lassen Peak, Burney Falls and Lake Shasta area, California.

1970 Geologic guide to the Death Valley area, California.

1971 Geologic guide to the northern Coast Ranges, Point Reyes region, California.

1972 Geologic guide to the northern Coast Ranges: Lake, Mendocino and Sonoma counties, California.

1973 Environmental geology; a field trip to eastern Sacramento County and western El Dorado County.

1974 Geologic guide to the southern Klamath Mountains.

1975 Stanislaus River guide, Camp Nine to Melones.

AzFU	1970-73
AzTeS	1972, 73
AzU	1968, 69, 72, 73
CChiS	1956, 58, 62, 63, 65-67, 69-73
[CDU]	1956, 57, 63-73
CLU-G/G	1956-61, 63, 65-73
CLhC	1963, 65, 68, 70-72
CSfCSM	1956-74
CU-EART	1955-75
[CaBVU]	1968-70
CaOHM	1967, 68
CaOLU	1958, 68
CaOOG	1963

CoG	1959, 60, 62, 65-73
CoU	1963, 65-67
DI-GS	1956, 58-70, 72-74
ICF	1959, 60
ICIU-S	1965, 67-74
IU	1956-62, 65-75
IaU	1965-73
IdBB	1968, 70
InLP	1965, 67, 68
InU	1969, 70
KyU	1962, 65, 67-71
MH-GS	1968-70
MiDW	1968, 69
MiHM	1968
MiKW	1962, 63
MiU	1965-73
MnU	1959-63, 65-70
MoSW	1963, 65-67
MoU	1964, 65, 68-73
NNC	1955, 58-63
NSyU	1970
NbU	1955, 58, 62-75
NcU	1969, 72
NdU	1967, 68, 71
NhD	1962-74
NjP	1965, 67-74
NvU	1974, 75
OCU	1963, 64, 66-73
OU	1958-60, 63, 65-72
OkU	1956, 58, 63, 65-68, 71-75
OrU	1968-75
PBL	1952-55
PBm	1968, 69
PSt	1968, 69
SdRM	1963, 65-67
TMM	1968-70
TxDaAR-T	1968, 70-72, 74
TxDaDM	1958-61, 65, 67, 68, 70, 71, 73, 74
TxDaM	1960, 65
TxDaSM	1962
TxLT	1968-73
TxU	1956-70
UU	1963, 65, 67, 68, 70
ViBlbV	1959, 60, 62, 63, 66, 68, 69

(108) GEOLOGICAL SOCIETY OF THE OREGON COUNTRY.

1964	Geological trip log through the eastern foothills of the Oregon Coast Range between Vernonia and banks on the Vernonia, South Park and Sunset Steam Railroad.
1965	No. 1. Geological guidebook for central Oregon.
	No. 2. The Columbia River Gorge; geological notes from Cascade Locks to Bingen.
1966	No. 1. President's campout. [Second edition, 1968]
	Our central Oregon "Moon Country".

	Field Trip No. 1. Salem to Bend via the North Santiam Highway.
	Field Trip No. 2. Bend to Todd Lake via North Century Drive.
	Field Trip No. 3. Bend to Newberry Mountain and then to Todd Lake via Highway 97 and South Century Drive area.
	Field Trip No. 4. Bend to McKenzie Pass area and on to Clear Lake Highway.
1967	Columbia River Gorge and "Grand Canyon" of the Deschutes River. (5th revised edition)
	Field Trip No. 1. Columbia River section.
	Field Trip No. 2. Deschutes River section.
1968	No. 2. Deschutes Canyon field trip.
1969	Geological trips in the Mitchell-John Day area.
	Field Trip No. 1. To Dayville and the South Fork of the John Day River.
	Field Trip No. 2. To Ochoco Summit area and cuts to the east as far as the Eocene-Cretaceous contact.
	Field Trip No. 3. To Mitchell Mesozoic rock and fossil areas.
	Field Trip No. 4. To Twickenham area and the Painted Hills.
1970	No. 1. A glimpse in the Quaternary and Tertiary of central Oregon (Maupin to Smith Rock State Park and Cove Park).
	No. 2. Condon's first island; geological trips in the Siskiyous and along the Rogue.
	Field Trip No. 1. Dow Rogue River to old Benton Mine.
	Field Trip No. 2. Up Illinois River as far as the Waldo-Takilma gold mining area.
	Field Trip No. 3. Up the Applegate River via Jacksonville.
	Field Trip No. 4. Up through Medford area to Mt. Ashland area.
1971	Condon's second island; a guidebook issue.
1972	Geological trips in Wallowa County.
	Field Trip No. 1. Elgin to Wallowa Lake.
	Field Trip No. 2. Wallowa Lake to Mount Howard.
	Field Trip No. 3. Lostine Valley.
	Field Trip No. 4. Wallowa Lake to Hat Point.
	Field Trip No. 5. Joseph to Black Marble Quarry.
	Field Trip No. 6. Joseha Imnaha Loop.
n.d.	Trip log for field trip to Warm Springs Reservation.

CLU-G/G 1971
IU 1964, 65, 67-7?

(109) GEOLOGICAL SOCIETY OF U.C.L.A. ANNUAL SPRING FIELD TRIP.

1971	Field guide to Papoose Flat in the Inyo Mountains, eastern California.
1972	Field guide to the peninsular ranges of southern California.
1973	Field guide to the San Gabriel anorthosite of southern California.

CLU-G/G 1971-73

(110) GEOLOGY CLUB OF PUERTO RICO. BULLETIN.

1959	No. 1. Road log and guide for a geologic field trip through central and western Puerto Rico.

CLU-G/G 1959
DI-GS 1959
ICF 1959
IU 1959

GEORGIA. DEPARTMENT OF MINES, MINING AND GEOLOGY. See GEORGIA. GEOLOGICAL SURVEY. (112)

GEORGIA. DEPARTMENT OF NATURAL RESOURCES. EARTH AND WATER DIVISION. GEOLOGICAL SURVEY. See GEORGIA. GEOLOGICAL SURVEY. (112)

(111) GEORGIA GEOLOGICAL SOCIETY. ANNUAL FIELD TRIP.

1966		See Georgia. Geological Survey. (112)
1967	2nd	The geology of the Barnesville area and the Towaliga fault, Lamar County, Georgia. (112)
1968	3rd	Late Tertiary stratigraphy of eastern Georgia. (112)
1969	4th	A guide to the stratigraphy of the Chicamauga supergroup in its type area. (112)
1970	5th	Stratigraphic and structural features between the Cartersville and Brevard fault zones.
1971	6th	Norite intrusives in western Jasper County and eastern Monroe County, Georgia.
		Lithostratigraphy and biostratigraphy of the north-central Georgia coastal plain.
		The mining methods utilized by Freeport Kaolin Company at their mines near Gordon, Georgia.
		Stratigraphy and paleontology of Huber Kaolin Company, Pit 22.
1972	7th	Sedimentary environments in the Paleozoic rocks of northwest Georgia. (112)
1973	8th	The Neogene of the Georgia coast.
1974	9th	The Lake Chatuge sill outlining the Brasstown antiform. (112)
		An introduction to the Blue Ridge tectonic history of northeast Georgia. (112)

CLU-G/G	1966
CU-EART	1966-68, 70-72
CaOHM	1973
CaOLU	1973
CoG	1967
CaOOG	1973
DI-GS	1966-68, 72, 73, 74(12)
DLC	1973
ICF	1966-69
IU	1966, 67
IaU	1973
InLP	1967
KyU	1966-69, 72, 73
MH-GS	1968
MiDW	1967, 68, 70, 72
MnU	1966-68
NOneoU	1973
NRU	1973
NSyU	1973
NcU	1966-68, 70
NdU	1966
NhD	1973
NjP	1966-73
NvU	1966
OCU	1966, 67
OU	1973
PSt	1966, 72
TMM	1970
TxDaAR-T	1966, 67, 72-74
TxDaDM	1966-68
TxDaM	1966
TxDaSM	1973
TxHU	1966-68, 72, 74
TxU	1966-70
ViBlbV	1966, 67, 73
WU	1966, 70

(112) GEORGIA. GEOLOGICAL SURVEY. GUIDEBOOK.

1962	1st	The Georgia marble district. (102)
	2nd	Stone Mountain-Lithonia district. (102)
	3rd	Ocoee metasediments, north-central Georgia, southeast Tennessee. (102)
1966	4th	The Cartersville fault problem. (43, 111)
1967	5th	Geology of the Miocene and Pliocene series in the north Florida-south Georgia area. (291)
		The geology of the Barnesville area and the Towaliga fault, Lamar County, Georgia. (111)
1968	7th	Late Tertiary stratigraphy of eastern Georgia. (111)
1969	8th	A guide to the stratigraphy of the Chickamauga supergroup in its type area. (111)
1972	11th	Sedimentary environments in the Paleozoic rocks of northwest Georgia. (111)
1974	12th	Brevard fault zone in western Georgia and eastern Alabama. (102)
		Tertiary stratigraphy of the central Georgia coastal plain. (102)
	13th	The Lake Chatuge sill outlining the Brasstown antiform. (111)
	13-A	An introduction to the Blue Ridge tectonic history of northeast Georgia. (111)
	14th	Field conference on kaolin and fuller's earth. (273)
1975	15th	A guide to selected Upper Cretaceous and lower Tertiary outcrops in the lower Chattahoochee River valley of Georgia.

DI-GS	1962
ICF	1967-69
IU	1962-67, 69, 74(12), 75
InU	1962(1,2), 66
KyU	1962-69, 74(13-A,14)
MiDW	1966, 69
MoSW	1974, 75
NBiSU	1962, 66, 69-72
NcU	1962-68
NjP	1962, 66, 67
PSt	1962, 66, 72
TxDaAR-T	1974
WU	1974(13)

GEORGIA. UNIVERSITY. MARINE INSTITUTE, SAPELO ISLAND, GEORGIA, CONTRIBUTION. See GEOLOGICAL SOCIETY OF AMERICA. SOUTHEASTERN SECTION. (102)

(113) GRAND JUNCTION GEOLOGICAL SOCIETY.

1961	Guidebook to western San Juan Mountains.

TxDaDM	1961

(114) GULF COAST ASSOCIATION OF GEOLOGICAL SOCIETIES. ANNUAL MEETING. GUIDEBOOK FOR THE FIELD TRIPS.

1956	6th	[No. 1.] Lower Claiborne. (277)
		[No. 2.] Lower Cretaceous. (277)
1958	8th	Sedimentology of south Texas. (72)
1959	9th	Recent sediments of the north-central Gulf Coastal Plain. (13, 277)
1960	10th	Cenozoic field trips. (277)
		[No. 1.] Recent sedimentation on Horn Island, Mississippi.
		[No. 2.] Stratigraphy of the Quaternary and upper Tertiary of the Pascagoula Valley, Mississippi.
1961	11th	Southern Edwards plateau. (290)
1962	12th	Little Stave Creek, Salt Mountain, Jackson, Alabama. (277)

1964	14th	Depositional environments, south-central Texas coast. (72)
1965	15th	Deltaic coastal plain. (13, 118)
1966	16th	No. 1. Lafayette-Atchafalaya-Five Islands flight.
		No. 2. Belle Island salt dome trip.
1967	17th	San Antonio, Uvalde, Carrizo Springs, Laredo, Freer, Encinal, Pearsall, San Antonio, Texas.
1968	18th	A field guide to Cretaceous and Tertiary exposures in west-central Alabama.
1969	19th	See Society of Economic Paleontologists and Mineralogists. (274)
1970		Guidebook to north-central Louisiana salt domes.
1971	21st	The southern shelf of British Honduras. (277)
1972		Padre Island national seashore field guide. (72)
1973	23rd	A field guide to the Moffatt Mound near Lake Belton, Bell County, Texas.
		Northeastern coast of Yucatan.
		Recent sediments of southeastern Texas.
		Trace fossils. [This is a textbook and not a guidebook.]
1974		See Society of Economic Paleontologists and Mineralogists. Gulf Coast Section. (277)
		Lafayette-Atchafalaya-Five Islands Flight.
1975	25th	Field Trip No. 1. Thomasville field sour gas plant, Rankin County, Mississippi.
		Field Trip No. 2. U. S. Army Engineers waterways experiment station, Corps of Engineers, Vicksburg, Mississippi.
		Field Trip No. 3. Tertiary localities of east-central Mississippi.

[A-GS]	1962
[CDU]	1958-61, 64-66, 72
CLU-G/G	1958-62, 64-67, 71, 72
CLhC	1959, 60, 64
CSdS	1959, 61, 64, 65
CU-EART	1956, 58-62, 64-69
[CaBVU]	1958
CaOHM	1958-61, 64, 65, 67-69
CaOKQ	1959, 60-62
CaOOG	1959-61, 64, 65, 68
CoG	1956, 59-62, 64-66, 68
CoU	1958-60, 64-66
DI-GS	1956, 58-62, 64-69
ICF	1959-62
ICIU-S	1959, 61, 64-66, 72
IEN	1958-62, 72
[I-GS]	1958
IU	1956, 59-61, 64-66, 69, 72, 74
IaU	1958-62, 64-69, 72
InU	1956(1), 58, 64, 66, 68, 69, 71
KyU	1956, 59, 61, 62, 65-68, 71
LU	1956, 59-62, 64, 65
MH-GS	1969
MNS	1956
MiDW	1964-66
MiU	1959-62, 64-68, 72
MnU	1956, 58-62, 64-66, 68, 69
MoSW	1959, 62, 64-66, 69
MoU	1959, 61, 64-67
[Ms-GS]	1958, 60, 75
MtU	1958-61, 64, 65
NBiSU	1971, 72

NNC	1956, 59-62, 64, 65
NOneoU	1964
NcU	1958-66, 68, 69
NdU	1959, 60, 62, 64-66, 72
NjP	1958-62, 64-69
OCU	1956, 59-62, 64-69, 72
OU	1959-62, 64-66, 72
OrCS	1961
OrU	1960
PBL	1959, 61, 64, 65
PPiGulf	1959-62
PSt	1958-62, 64-66, 72
TMM	1959-62, 64-66
TxDaAR-T	1956, 59-62, 64-69, 71-74
TxDaDM	1956, 59-62, 64-66, 68, 71, 72
TxDaM	1956, 59-62, 64-66
TxDaSM	1956, 61, 64, 65, 72
TxHSD	1956, 59, 61, 64, 65, 67, 70
TxHU	1956, 58-62, 64-66, 72
TxMM	1956, 59, 61, 64, 65, 72
TxU	1956, 59-62, 64-68, 71
TxU-Da	1951, 61
ViBlbV	1956, 72
WU	1959

(115) HARDIN SIMMONS UNIVERSITY. GEOLOGICAL SOCIETY. FIELD CONFERENCE. GUIDEBOOK.

1963 See Southwestern Association of Student Geological Societies. (294)

(116) HIGHWAY GEOLOGICAL SYMPOSIUM. PROCEEDINGS. ANNUAL.

1967	18th	Field trip guidebook for 18th annual highway geology symposium, vicinity of Lafayette, Indiana.
1969	20th	Annual field trip near East St. Louis, Illinois.
1970	21st	Geo-engineering in northeastern Kansas; greater Kansas City area.
1971	22nd	Highway geology in the Arbuckle Mountains and Ardmore area, southern Oklahoma. (232)

CLU-G/G	1968
CU-EART	1964, 66-68, 70
CaOOG	1967, 70
[I-GS]	1969
IU	1969-71
InU	1968, 70
MoU	1968
NdU	1968
NhD	1968
NjP	1968
OU	1968
OkU	1971
TxDaDM	1968
TxU	1970

(117) HOBBS GEOLOGICAL SOCIETY. GUIDEBOOK.

1962 See West Texas Geological Society. (338)
1968 See New Mexico Geological Society. (207)
The San Andres Limestone, a reservoir for oil and water in New Mexico; a symposium.

CLU-G/G 1968
[CaBVU] 1962
ICF 1962
IaU 1962
InU 1962
KyU 1962
MoU 1962
NhD 1962
NmPE 1968
TxU 1968

(118) HOUSTON GEOLOGICAL SOCIETY. GUIDEBOOK.

1938 Road log of the Jackson-Claiborne field trip of the Houston Geological Society.
1941 26th See American Association of Petroleum Geologists. (12)
1952 Geologic strip maps: U. S. Highway 77, Texas-Oklahoma state line to Dallas; U. S. Highway 75, Dallas to Galveston.
1953 38th See American Association of Petroleum Geologists. (12)
1958 See Society of Economic Paleontologists and Mineralogists. Gulf Coast Section. (277)
1959 No. 1. Boling Field, Fort Bend and Wharton counties, Texas.
No. 2. Lower Tertiary and Upper Cretaceous of Brazos River valley, Texas. (277)
No. 3. Geologic strip maps: U. S. Highway 80, Texas-New Mexico state line to Van Horn; U. S. Highway 90, Van Horn to Texas-Louisiana state line.
1960 See Society of Economic Paleontologists and Mineralogists. Gulf Coast Section. (277)
1962 No. 1. Geology of the Austin-Llano area, central Texas. (For supplement see: Corpus Christi Geological Society. Annual field trip, 1966; also same as: Texas. University. Bureau of Economic Geology. Guidebook, 1963, 5th.) (72, 308)
1963 See American Association of Petroleum Geologists. (12)
Guidebook to the geology of El Rancho, Cima, Hays and Comal counties, Texas.
1964 Houston and vicinity geological field trip for earth science teachers secondary schools.
1965 See Gulf Coast Association of Geological Societies. (114)
1968 Environments of deposition, Wilcox Group, Texas Gulf Coast.
1969 Holocene geology of the Galveston Bay area. (Project of the Delta Study Group of the Houston Geological Society.) Title: Galveston Bay Geology.
1971 Uranium geology and mines, south Texas. (12, 308)

[A-GS] 1962
CChiS 1969
[CDU] 1969
CLU-G/G 1952, 58-62, 68, 69
CLhC 1962
CSdS 1962
CU-EART 1952, 59(2,3), 68
CaACU 1962
CaOHM 1968
CaOKQ 1959, 62, 68
CaOLU 1962
CoG 1962, 68
DI-GS 1953, 58-61, 62(1), 63, 65

ICarbS	1961
IEN	1941, 62, 69
[I-GS]	1962
IU	1959, 68
IaU	1953, 58-62, 65, 68
InU	1957, 58, 59(May), 60, 62, 69
KyU	1958, 59, 61-63, 65, 68, 71
MiKW	1958, 60
MiU	1959, 60, 63
MNS	1958, 60
MnU	1958-60, 62, 63
MoSW	1959
NNC	1959
NSyU	1958, 62, 69
NbU	1969
NcU	1957, 60-62, 65, 69
NdU	1969
NjP	1971
OkU	1963, 68
PBL	1969
TMM	1969
TxDaAR-T	1968
TxDaDM	1959
TxDaSM	1968
TxHSD	1938, 52, 59(3), 68
TxHU	1961, 62, 64, 65, 69
TxU	1959, 62, 68
TxU-Da	1941, 58
ViBlbV	1962, 68
WU	1962

(119) HOUSTON, TEXAS. UNIVERSITY. DEPARTMENT OF GEOLOGY. FIELD TRIP.

[n.d.]	Physical geology trip to central Texas.
1965	Historical geology field trip.
1966,67,70	Big Bend field trip.
1970	Houston to Uvalde, via U. S. 90A and 90 to Big Bend region.

CLU-G/G	[n.d.], 1965-67
IU	[n.d.] 1965-67
TxHU	1965, 70

(120) IDAHO. BUREAU OF MINES AND GEOLOGY. BULLETIN.

1961 No. 16 Guidebook to the geology of the Coeur d'Alene mining district. (38)

CLU-G/G	1961
CU-EART	1961
[CaBVU]	1961
CaOKQ	1961
CaOLU	1961
CoG	1961
CoU	1961
DI-GS	1961
ICF	1961

(120) Idaho. Bureau of Mines and Geology.

IEN	1961
[I-GS]	1961
IU	1961
IaU	1961
IdBB	1961
IdPI	1961
InU	1961
LU	1961
MNS	1961
MiDW	1961
MnU	1961
MoSW	1961
NSyU	1961
NbU	1961
NdU	1961
NhD	1961
NvU	1961
OU	1961
OkT	1961
OkU	1961
OrU	1961
PBL	1961
PSt	1961
RPB	1961
SdRM	1961
TxDaM	1961
TxHU	1961
TxMM	1961
TxU	1961
WU	1961

(121) IDAHO. BUREAU OF MINES AND GEOLOGY. INFORMATION CIRCULAR.

1975 Field Trip No. 7. The later Tertiary stratigraphy and paleobotany of the Weiser area, Idaho. (100)

Field Trip No. 8. The geology and scenery of the Snake River on the Idaho-Oregon border from Brownlee Dam to Hells Canyon Dam. (100)

NdU	1975
IU	1975

(122) IDAHO. BUREAU OF MINES AND GEOLOGY. PAMPHLET.

1963 No. 130 Geology along U. S. Highway 93 in Idaho.

1975 No. 160 Geologic field guide to the Quaternary volcanics of the south-central Snake River Plain, Idaho. (100)

CoG	1963
IU	1963, 75
IdBB	1963
NdU	1975

(123) ILLINOIS GEOLOGICAL SOCIETY. GUIDEBOOK OF THE FIELD CONFERENCE.

1938 Field conference on Chester Series and Ste. Genevieve Formation.
1939 Urbana, Illinois to Madison, Wisconsin.
1946 Field conference on Chester stratigraphy.
1949 Southeastern Missouri and southwestern Illinois. (12)
1953 Basis of subdivision of Wisconsin glacial stage in northeastern Illinois. (128)
1956 Southern Illinois, lower Chester rocks of southwestern Illinois.
1957 Ordovician, Silurian, Devonian and Mississippian rocks of western Illinois.
1959 Extreme southeastern Illinois.
1965 Mineral resources of southeast Missouri.
1968 Geology and petroleum production of the Illinois Basin; a symposium. (130)
1973 Guidebook to the Cambro-Ordovician rocks of eastern Ozarks.

CLU-G/G	1957
CoG	1956, 57, 59, 65
ICF	1956-65, 73
ICarbS	1953, 65
IEN	1946, 59
[I-GS]	1938, 46, 56, 57
IU	1946, 53, 58, 59
InU	1946, 49, 56, 57, 68
MiHM	1959
MnU	1956, 57, 59, 65
NjP	1965
OCU	1973
OU	1957
OkU	1946, 56, 57
OkT	1956, 57, 59
TxDaAR-T	1956, 57, 59
TxDaSM	1956, 57, 59, 65

(124) ILLINOIS STATE ACADEMY OF SCIENCE.

1961 Charleston area.
1964 Bloomington area.

Most of the guidebooks for geologic field trips held by this organization are included as issues of the series: Illinois. State Geological Survey. Guide Leaflet. (125)

IU	1961, 64
NNC	1961, 64

(125) ILLINOIS. STATE GEOLOGICAL SURVEY. GEOLOGICAL SCIENCE FIELD TRIP. GUIDE LEAFLET.

The Illinois State Geological Survey maintains a supply of the latest revision of each Guide Leaflet. Occasionally, specific titles will be withdrawn from the series and others added. Those titles showing no date of publication were published before 1960. The Survey suggests that the desired leaflet(s) be requested by current title as listed below:

Alto Pass, 1965 -- Alton -- Amboy, 1962 -- Anna-Jonesboro -- Apple River Canyon.

Barrington-Fox Lake -- Barry, 1968 -- Beardstown, 1965 -- Belvidere, 1963 -- Bloomington, 1964 -- Bloomington-Normal -- Bourbonnais, 1967 -- Breese, 1974 -- Byron, 1966.

Cairo -- Canton -- Carbondale -- Carlinville -- Carlock, 1972 -- Carrier Mills, 1965 -- Carrollton, 1975, 76 -- Casey -- Cave in Rock -- Champaign-Urbana -- Charleston, 1961 -- Chester, 1964 -- Chicago Heights -- Colchester, 1964.

Dallas City -- Danville, 1972 -- De Kalb-Byron -- Des Plaines -- Dixon, 1967, 68 -- Downers

Grove -- Dupo, 1963.
Edinburgh, 1964 -- Eldorado -- Elgin -- Elizabeth -- Elizabethtown-Cave in Rock, 1967 -- Equality, 1969 -- Eureka.
Fairbury -- Fairfield -- Farmington, 1963 -- Freeport, 1966, 70 -- Fulton.
Galena, 1965, 71 -- Galesburg -- Georgetown, 1961 -- Golconda, 1962 -- Grafton, 1960 -- Grand Tower -- Greenup -- Greenville, 1962.
Hamilton, 1961 -- Hamilton-Warsaw, 1970, 71 -- Hardin -- Harrisburg, 1960 -- Havanna, 1969 -- Homer -- Hoopeston.
Jacksonville -- Joliet -- Jonesboro, 1964.
Kankakee -- Kewanee -- Knoxville, 1973.
LaSalle, 1971, 72 -- Lake region-Crystal Lake -- Lawrenceville -- Lena, 1961.
Macomb -- Makanda, 1971 -- Marion, 1963 -- Marseilles-Ottawa -- Marshall -- Metropolis, 1975 -- Milan, 1974, 75 -- Milan-Rock Island, 1960 -- Millstadt -- Millstadt-Dupo, 1970 -- Moline -- Monmouth -- Monticello-Mahomett, 1969 -- Morris, 1961 -- Morrison, 1964 -- Mt. Carroll, 1969, 70 -- Mt. Sterling, 1971 -- Murphysboro.
Naperville -- Nashville -- Neoga, 1962 -- Newton -- North Shore.
Oakwood, 1967 -- Olney -- Oregon.
Palos Park -- Pana, 1960 -- Paris, 1966 -- Pecatonica -- Pekin -- Peoria, 1962 -- Pere Marquette -- Petersburg, 1967 -- Pinckneyville -- Pine Hills -- Pittsfield, 1962 -- Potomac-Danville, 1972 -- Pontiac, 1963 -- Pontiac-Streator -- Port Byron -- Princeton, 1968, 69 -- Princeville.
Quincy, 1966.
Red Bud, 1972 -- Rochelle, 1964 -- Rockford, 1974 -- Robinson, 1973 -- Rockton, 1973, 74 -- Rock Island-Moline -- Rosiclare, 1960.
Salem, 1960 -- St. Anne-Momence, 1975, 76 -- Saint Elmo, 1968 -- Savanna, 1963 -- Shawneetown -- Shelbyville, 1965 -- Sparta, 1961 -- Springfield -- Starved Rock, 1962 -- Steeleville, 1966 -- Stockton, 1972, 73.
Thebes, 1968.
Valmeyer, 1961 -- Vienna, 1966.
Warsaw -- Waterloo -- Watseka -- Waukegan -- West Chicago -- Wheaton, 1962 -- Wilmington -- Winchester, 1970 -- Woodstock, 1960 -- Wyoming.
Yorkville, 1965.

CSdS	most
DI-GS	most
ICarbS	some
IEN	most
[I-GS]	all
IU	most
InU	some
MiHM	1948 to date
NjP	1959
OU	some
OkU	most

(126) ILLINOIS. STATE GEOLOGICAL SURVEY. GUIDEBOOK SERIES. (TITLE VARIES)

1950	[1st]	Niagaran reefs in the Chicago area. (12, 274)
1952	[2nd]	Central northern Illinois. (312)
1954	[3rd]	Guide to the structure and Paleozoic stratigraphy along the Lincoln fold in central western Illinois. (12)
1956	4th	Niagaran reef at Thornton, Illinois. (12, 274)
1963	5th	Loess stratigraphy, Wisconsinan classification and accretion-gleys in central western Illinois. (90)

[1964]	6th	Western Illinois. (312)
1966	7th	Sedimentary structures and morphology of late Paleozoic sand bodies in southern Illinois. (12)
1970	8th	Depositional environments in parts of the Carbondale Formation, western and northern Illinois, Francis Creek Shale and associated strata and Mazon Creek biota. (96)
1972	9th	Pleistocene stratigraphy of east-central Illinois. (90)
	10th	Pennsylvanian conodont assemblages from LaSalle County, northern Illinois. (98, 240)
1973	11th	A geologic excursion to fluorspar mines in Hardin and Pope counties, Illinois; Illinois-Kentucky mining district and adjacent upper Mississippi embayment. (87)

CLU-G/G	1954, 63-70, 72, 73
CU-EART	1966, 70, 72(10), 73
CaACI	1950
[CaBVU]	1956, 66
CaOHM	1966, 70, 72, 73
CaOKQ	1966, 72, 73
CaOLU	1970
CaOOG	1950, 73
CoFS	1956-66
CoG	1966, 72, 73
CoU	1966-72
DI-GS	1972(9)
ICF	1972, 73
ICarbS	1954, 56, 63, 64, 66, 72
IEN	1954-73
[I-GS]	1950-73
IU	1950-52, 54-73
IaU	1966, 72, 73
IdBB	1966-73
InLP	1952, 54-72
InU	1950, 63, 64, 70, 72, 73
KyU	1954, 70, 73
LU	1956-73
MH-GS	1966
MNS	1956-73
MiDW	1970-73
MiHM	1972, 73
MiKW	1970-73
MnU	1952, 54, 56, 63, 66
MoSW	1964-70
MoU	1954, 66-73
NBiSU	1966-73
NSyU	1963-73
NbU	1956, 63, 64, 66, 70-73
NcU	1966-73
NdU	1963, 72(10), 73
NhD	1970-73
NjP	1966, 70-73
NvU	1966-73
OCU	1973
OU	1973
OkT	1970-73
OkU	1963-70

PBL	1971-73
PBm	1966-73
PSt	1973
RPB	1956, 63, 64, 66
TMM	1970-73
TxDaAR-T	1966, 70, 72
TxHU	1954, 56, 66, 70-73
TxLT	1950, 66-73
TxU	1963, 64, 66, 70, 72
UU	1963, 66, 72, 73
ViBlbV	1966, 72(10), 73
WU	1956, 70-73

(127) INDIANA ACADEMY OF SCIENCE. GUIDEBOOK FOR GEOLOGIC FIELD TRIP.

1959		Guide to some geological features of McCormick's Creek State Park and vicinity.
	spring	Some features of karst topography in Indiana.
1965		Glacial geology and soils of the area around Lake Maxinkuckee.

IU	1965
InU	1959, 62, 65
MoSW	1962
TxU	1962

INDIANA GEOLOGICAL SOCIETY. See INDIANA. GEOLOGICAL SURVEY. (128)

(128) INDIANA. GEOLOGICAL SURVEY. FIELD CONFERENCE GUIDEBOOKS.

1947	1st	Silurian and Devonian formations of southeastern Indiana.
1948	2nd	Upper and Middle Mississippian formations of southern Indiana.
1949	3rd	Silurian formations and reef structures of northern Indiana. (129)
1950	4th	Stratigraphy along the Mississippian-Pennsylvanian unconformity of western Indiana. (129)
1951	5th	Pennsylvanian geology and mineral resources of west-central Indiana. (129)
1953	6th	Ordovician stratigraphy and the physiography of part of southeastern Indiana.
	June	See Illinois Geological Society. (123)
1954	7th	Salem limestone and associated formations in south-central Indiana.
1955	8th	Sedimentation and stratigraphy of the Devonian rocks of southeastern Indiana.
1957	9th	Rocks associated with the Mississippian-Pennsylvanian unconformity of southeastern Indiana.
1961	10th	Stratigraphy of the Silurian rocks of northern Indiana.
1965	11th	Geomorphology and groundwater hydrology of the Mitchell plain and Crawford upland in southern Indiana.
1966	12th	Excursions in Indiana (38)
1972	13th	A field guide to the Mt. Carmel fault of southern Indiana. (130)
1973		(1) Guidebook to an environmental field trip of the Terre Haute-Brazil, Indiana area.
		(4) Guidebook to the geology of some Ice Age features and bedrock formations in the Fort Wayne, Indiana area.
		(5a) Guidebook to the geology of the New Albany-Jeffersonville area of southern Indiana.
		(5b) Road log and stop description.

[A-GS]	1947-51, 53-55, 57, 61, 65
CLU-G/G	1947-51, 53-55, 57, 61, 65, 72
CLhC	1953-55, 57
CU-EART	1947-66
CaOKQ	1947-72
CaOLU	1947, 49, 53, 55, 61

CaOOG	1947-51, 53-55, 57, 61, 65
CoG	1947-51, 53(6), 54-65, 72
CoU	1954
DI-GS	1947, 67, 72
DLC	1972
ICF	1947-51, 53(6), 54, 55, 61, 65, 72
ICarbS	1947-51, 54, 55, 57, 61-65
ICIU-S	1966, 72
IEN	1947-51, 53(5), 54-65, 72
[I-GS]	1947-51, 53(6), 54-72
IU	1947-51, 53, 55, 57, 61, 65, 72
IaU	1947-51, 53-55, 57, 61, 65-67
InLP	1947-72
InRE	1947, 48, 50, 51, 53(6), 54-66, 72
InU	1947-51, 53(6), 54-72
KyU	1947-51, 53-57, 61, 65, 66, 72, 73(1,4,5a,5b)
LU	1947-51, 53-55, 57, 61, 65, 66, 72
MH-GS	1954
MnDuU	1972
MNS	1947-51, 53, 55-66
MiDW	1947-51, 53-55, 57, 61, 65, 72
MiHM	1947-51, 55-72
MiKW	1947-51, 57-72
MiU	1947-72
MnU	1947-51, 53-55, 57, 61, 65, 66
MoSW	1947-51, 53-55, 57, 61, 65, 66
MoU	1947-51, 53-57
NNC	1947-51, 53, 54, 57, 61, 65
NSyU	1949-65
NbU	1947-51, 53(6), 54-66
NdU	1947-51, 53(6), 54-65, 72
NhD	1949-51, 53(6), 54-72
NjP	1948-51, 53-55, 57, 61, 65, 66, 72
NvU	1947-65, 72
OCU	1947-51, 53(6), 54-65, 72, 73
OU	1947-51, 53(6), 54-72
OkT	1948-51, 53-55, 57, 61
OkU	1947-72
PSt	1947-66
RPB	1948-66
TU	1948-51, 53-55, 57
TxDaAR-T	1947-51, 53-55, 57, 61, 65
TxDaDM	1947-51, 53-55, 57, 61, 65
TxDaM	1948-51, 53-55, 57, 61
TxHU	1947-66, 72
TxLT	1948, 50, 54, 57, 61
TxU	1947-51, 53-55, 57, 61, 65, 66, 72
TxU-Da	1955
UU	1947-65, 72
ViBlbV	1947-51, 53(6), 54, 72
WM	1951, 54
WU	1947-51, 53(6), 54-72

(129) INDIANA. UNIVERSITY. DEPARTMENT OF GEOLOGY.

1949	Silurian formations and reef structures of northern Indiana. (128)
1950	Stratigraphy along the Mississippian-Pennsylvanian unconformity of western Indiana. (128)
1951	Pennsylvanian geology and mineral resources of west-central Indiana. (128)
1962	Guidebook. Bloomington, Indiana to Indiana geologic field station, Cardwell, Montana. Prepared for course, Geology G429, Field Geology in the Rocky Mountains.
1966	A survey of Indiana geology with road logs for two field trips. (268)
1968	Appalachian field trip.
	Road logs and geological descriptions of the Black Hills and the Rocky Mountains; prepared for the course Geology G429, Field Geology in the Rocky Mountains.
1969	Regional geologic field trip to the Ozarks and Ouachitas, G420.
1970	G420 regional geology field trip to the Lake Superior region.
1973	Field conference on Borden Group and overlying limestone units, south-central Indiana. (276)

CLhC	1966
CSdS	1949-51
CU-EART	1966
IaU	1962, 66
InU	1962, 68-70, 73
MnDuU	1968
MoSW	1966
NBiSU	1949, 50, 66
NcU	1962, 66
NjP	1966
OCU	1968, 69
OU	1966
PSt	1966

(130) INDIANA-KENTUCKY GEOLOGICAL SOCIETY. GUIDEBOOK GEOLOGY. (TITLE VARIES) FALL FIELD TRIP. (TITLE VARIES)

1940	Itinerary; outcrop of the Chester series of southern Indiana.
1968	Geology and petroleum of the Illinois basin; a symposium. (123)
1972	A field guide to the Mt. Carmel fault of southern Indiana. (128)
1973	Geologic features of the Rough Creek fault, Grayson and Ohio counties, Kentucky.

CLU-G/G	1973
CU-EART	1972
ICF	1972
[I-GS]	1940, 72, 73
IU	1973
IaU	1972
InU	1968, 73
KyU	1968, 73
NvU	1973
OCU	1973
OkU	1973
WU	1973

(131) INSTITUTE ON LAKE SUPERIOR GEOLOGY. (TITLE VARIES)

1964	10th	Field trip, Marquette iron-mining district and Republic trough.
1965	11th	St. Paul, Minnesota.
1966	12th	Includes areal description and guidebooks: Ontario.

		[1] Sault Ste. Marie area.
		[2] Geology and mineral deposits of the Manitouwadge Lake area.
		[3] Relationship of mineralization to the Precambrian stratigraphy, Blind River area, Ontario.
		[4] Sudbury nickel irruptive tour.
1967	13th	Field trip to the Grenville of southeastern Ontario.
1968	14th	The Duluth complex, near Ely, Minnesota.
1969	15th	Central Wisconsin volcanic belt.
1970	16th	A. Proterozoic formations in the Thunder Bay area.
		B. Sturgeon River metavolcanics-metasedimentary formations in the Beardmore-Geraldton area.
		C. The Port Coldwell alkalic complex.
		D. Atikokan. (exact title not known)
1971	17th	A. The north shore volcanic group (Keweenawan).
		B. Guide to the Precambrian rocks of northwestern Cook County as exposed along the Gunflint trail.
		C. Mesabi range magnetite taconite.
		D. Geology of the Vermilion metavolcanic sedimentary belt, northeastern Minnesota.
1972	18th	A. Penokean orogeny in the central and western Gogebic region, Michigan and Wisconsin.
		B. Guide to Penokean deformational style and regional metamorphism of the western Marquette range, Michigan.
1973	19th	1. Guidebook to the Precambrian geology of northeastern and north-central Wisconsin.
		2. Guidebook to the geology and mineral deposits of the central part of Jackson County and part of Clark County, Wisconsin.
		3. Guidebook to the upper Mississippi Valley base-metal district. (Reprint with slight modification of Wisc. Geological and Natural History Survey Information Circular No. 16.)
1974	20th	Field Trip No. 1. Middle Keweenawan rocks of the Batchawana-Mamainse Point area.
		Field Trip No. 3. Precambrian igneous rocks of the north shore of Lake Huron region.
		Field Trip No. 4. Stratigraphy and sedimentation of the Huronian supergroup.
		Field Trip No. 5. The Michipicoten greenstone belt.
1975		Field Trip No. 1. Glacial geology. Cancelled, no guidebook.
		Field Trip No. 2. Greenstone.
		Field Trip No. 3. The Jacobsville Sandstone; evidence for a lower-middle Keweenawan age.
		Field Trip No. 4. Marquette iron range.
		Field Trip No. 5,6. The Empire mine and mill, Palmer, Michigan.
1976	22nd	A. Minnesota River valley. No guidebook.
		B. Engineering geology, Pleistocene geology and geomorphology in the Twin City area.

CLU-G/G	1969
CU-EART	1967
CaOHM	1970
CaOLU	1956, 66
CaOOG	1969
CaOONM	1967-73, 75
CaOWtU	1972
CoU	1969
DI-GS	1966, 70-75
IU	1968-76
IaU	1967, 69, 71
InLP	1965, 67, 69, 72, 73
InU	1961, 64, 70
KyU	1969-73
MNS	1964, 67, 69, 70, 73
MiHM	1964-76

MiU	1967
MnU	1965, 69
NSyU	1969
NjP	1959, 62-70
OCU	1966, 70
OU	1964, 69, 71
OkOkU	1969
PBm	1969
TxU	1965-69
WU	1966, 69-75

(132) INTERAMERICAN MICROPALEONTOLOGICAL COLLOQUIUM. FIELD TRIP GUIDEBOOK.

1970 1st Texas. (Summary of Upper Cretaceous stratigraphy; the Gulf of Mexico province.)

CLU-G/G	1970
CLhC	1970
MoSW	1970
PPiGulf	1970
TxDaAR-T	1970
TxHSD	1970
TxU	1970

(133) INTERMOUNTAIN ASSOCIATION OF (PETROLEUM) GEOLOGISTS. GUIDEBOOK FOR THE ANNUAL FIELD CONFERENCE.

1950	1st	See Utah Geological Society. (326)
1951	2nd	See Utah Geological Society. (326)
1952	3rd	See Utah Geological Society. (326)
1953	4th	Geology of northern Utah and southeastern Idaho.
1954	5th	Geology of portions of the high plateaus and adjacent canyon lands, central and south-central Utah.
1955	6th	Geology of northwest Colorado. (250)
1956	7th	Geology and economic deposits of east-central Utah.
1957	8th	Geology of Uinta Basin.
1958	9th	Geology of the Paradox Basin.
1959	10th	Geology of the Wasatch and Uinta Mountains, transition area.
1960	11th	Geology of east-central Nevada. (79)
1963	12th	Geology of southwestern Utah.
1964	13th	Geology and mineral resources of the Uinta Basin; Utah's hydrocarbon storehouse.
1965		Geology and resources of south-central Utah; resources for power. (326)
1967	15th	Anatomy of the western phosphate field; a guide to geologic occurrence, exploration methods, mining engineering, recovery technology. Supplement to guidebook: Descriptive geology along the 1967 field conference route.
1969	16th	Geologic guidebook of the Uinta Mountains, Utah's maverick range. (326)

AzFU	1953, 55-60, 63, 67, 69
AzTeS	1954, 56-64, 67, 69
AzU	1969
CChiS	1958, 59, 63, 64, 67, 69
[CDU]	1964-69
CLU-G/G	1953-60, 63, 64, 67, 69
CLhC	1953-69
CSdS	1953, 55-64
CU-EART	1953-69

CaAC	1958
[CaACAM]	1967
CaACI	1956, 58
CaACU	1950-60
[CaBVU]	1953, 57-59, 63, 64, 67
CaOHM	1956, 58-64, 67
CaOKQ	1958-60, 63-65, 67
CaOOG	1953-64, 69
CoDuF	1955, 57, 58
CoFS	1956-60, 63, 64, 67, 69
CoG	1953-60, 63, 64, 67, 69
CoU	1951, 53-60, 63-67, 69
DFPC	1957, 58, 63, 64
DI-GS	1950-60, 63, 65, 67
ICF	1953-63
ICIU-S	1958, 59, 63-69
ICarbS	1953-55, 58-60, 63, 64, 67, 69
IEN	1950-69
[I-GS]	1960
IU	1953-60, 63, 64, 67, 69
IaU	1950-60, 63-65, 67, 69
IdBB	1953, 55, 56, 58, 59, 63, 64, 67
IdPI	1953, 58-60
InLP	1953-64, 67, 69
InU	1950-53, 55-69
KyU	1950-60, 63-65, 67, 69
LU	1953-64, 67, 69
MH-GS	1963
MNS	1952, 53, 55-58, 65
MiDW	1953, 55-60, 63, 64, 67, 69
MiHM	1967
MiKW	1958-60, 63, 67, 69
MiU	1953, 54, 56-69
MnDuU	1969
[MnSSM]	1960
MnU	1950-60, 63-65, 67, 69
MoSW	1950-60, 63, 64, 67
MoU	1955
MtBC	1953, 59
NBiSU	1953, 56, 58-67
NNC	1953, 55-64
NOneoU	1958, 59, 63, 64
NRU	1953, 56-60
NSyU	1951-63, 65
NbU	1951-60, 63-69
NcU	1951-69
NdU	1953, 54, 56, 58-60, 63, 67, 69
NhD	1950-69
NmU	1960
NvU	1953-60, 64, 67, 69
OCU	1958, 59, 63, 64, 67, 69
OU	1953-56, 58-65
[OkOkCGe]	1955
OkT	1953-60, 63, 67

OkU	1950, 52-69
OrU	1953-69
PPiGulf	1953, 54, 56-60, 64
PSt	1953-64, 67-69
RPB	1950-69
SdRM	1956-59
TMM	1963
TU	1956-60, 63, 64
TxDaAR-T	1953-60, 63, 64, 67, 69
TxDaDM	1953-60, 63, 64, 67, 69
TxDaM	1953, 55-60, 63, 64
TxDaSM	1953, 55-60, 63, 64, 67
TxHSD	1953, 55-64
TxHU	1951-69
TxLT	1951, 53-69
TxMM	1953-60, 63, 64, 67
TxU	1953-60, 63, 64, 67
TxU-Da	1953-55, 58
UU	1953, 58-60
ViBlbV	1953, 56-64, 69
WU	1953-69
WyU	1953, 55-67

(134) INTERNATIONAL ASSOCIATION FOR QUATERNARY RESEARCH. CONGRESS. GUIDEBOOKS FOR FIELD CONFERENCE.

1965 7th
A. New England-New York State.
B-1. Central Atlantic coastal plain.
B-3. Mississippi delta and central Gulf Coast. (eleven guidebooks)
C. Upper Mississippi valley.
D. Central Great Plains.
E. Northern and middle Rocky Mountains.
F. Central and south-central Alaska.
G. Great Lakes-Ohio River valley.
H. Southwestern arid lands.
I. Northern Great Basin and California.
J. Pacific northwest.
K. Boulder area, Colorado.

AzTeS	1965
CLU-G/G	1965
CaAEU	1965
[CaBVU]	1965
CaOKQ	1965(A-J)
CaOLU	1965
CaOONM	1965(A,B-1,B-3,C - J)
CaOWtU	1965(A-J)
CoFS	1965
CoG	1965
CoU	1965
DI-GS	1965([K])
IU	1965
IaU	1965
IdBB	1965(C,E)

InLP	1965
InU	1965
LU	1965(C)
MiHM	1965(C)
MiKW	1965(A-J)
MnU	1965
NbU	1965
NcU	1965(A-J)
NdU	1965
NjP	1965
OU	1965(B-1 thru K)
OrU	1965(A,B-1,C-K) B-3)
RPB	1965
TxDaAR-T	1965
TxDaDM	1965(H)
TxDaSM	1965
TxHU	1965
TxU	1965
UU	1965(A-C,E-G,I-K)
ViBlbV	1965
WU	1965
WaPS	1965(E,H-J)

INTERNATIONAL CONFERENCE ON ARIDS LANDS. **See AMERICAN ASSOCIATION FOR THE ADVANCEMENT OF SCIENCE. (10)**

(135) INTERNATIONAL CONFERENCE ON THE PERMIAN AND TRIASSIC SYSTEM.

1971 Guidebook: Permian and Triassic exposures of western North America; Calgary, Alberta to El Paso, Texas.

NvU 1971

INTERNATIONAL FIELD INSTITUTE FOR COLLEGE AND UNIVERSITY GEOLOGY TEACHERS. **See AMERICAN GEOLOGICAL INSTITUTE. (21)**

(136) INTERNATIONAL GEOLOGICAL CONGRESS. GUIDE DES EXCURSIONS. (TITLE VARIES)

1891	5th	Excursion A. Geology of Washington and vicinity.
		Excursion B. Geological guidebook of the Rocky Mountain excursion.
		Excursion C. Excursion to Lake Superior, Pre-Cambrian geology of the Lake Superior region.
1897	7th	St. Petersburg, guide to excursions; 34 parts, outside North America.
1900	8th	Paris, guide des excursions; 41 parts, outside North America.
1903	9th	Vienna; 43 parts, outside North America.
1906	10th	Excursions avant le Congres.
		1. De Mexico a Jalapa.
		2. Excursions a Chavarrillo, Santa Maria Tatetla, Veracruz et Orizaba.
		3. De Esperanza a Mexico.
		4. De Mexico a Tehuacan.
		5. L'archaique du Canon de Tomellin.
		6. Les ruines de Mitla.
		7. Excursion de Tehuacan a Zopotitlan et San Juan Raya.
		8. De Mexico a Patzcuaro et Uruapam.
		9. Le Xinantecatl ou Volcan Nevado de Toluca.

10. Phenomenes postparoxysmiques du San Andres.
11. Le Jorullo.
12. Les Geysers d'Ixtlan.
13. Le Volcan de Colima.
14. Les crateres d'explosion de Valle de Santiago.
15. Etude de la Sierra de Guanajuato.
16. Geologie des environs de Zacatecas.
17. Etude miniere du District de Zacatecas.
18. Le Mineral de Mapimi.
19. Excursion aux mines de Soufre de la Sierra de Banderas.
20. Excursion au Cerro de Muleros.
21. Esquisse geologique et petrographique des environs de Parral.
22. Etude miniere de la "Veta Colorada" de Minas Nueva a Hidalgo del Parral.
23. Excursions dans les environs de Parras, Coah.
24. Geologie de la Sierra de Concepcion del Oro.
25. Le Mineral d'Aranzazu.
26. Geologie de la Sierra de Mazapil et Santa Rosa.
27. Les gisements carboniferes de Coahuila.
28. Les gisements carboniferes de Coahuila.
29. Excursions dans les environs de Monterrey et Saltillo.
30. De San Luis Potosi a Tampico.
31. Excursion a l'Isthme de Tehuantepec.

1910 11th Stockholm; 40 parts, outside North America.

1913 12th Guidebooks of excursions in Canada. (Canada. Geological Survey.)
1. Excursion in eastern Quebec and the Maritime Provinces.
2. Excursions in the eastern townships of Quebec and the eastern part of Ontario.
3. Excursions in the neighborhood of Montreal and Ottawa.
4. Excursions in southwestern Ontario.
5. Excursions in the western peninsula of Ontario and Manitoulin Island.
6. Excursions in vicinity of Toronto and to Muskoka and Madoc. (English edition issued by Ontario Bureau of Mines.)
7. Excursions to Sudbury, Cobalt, and Porcupine. (English edition issued by Ontario Bureau of Mines.)
8. Toronto to Victoria and return, via Canadian Pacific and Canadian Northern railways.
9. Toronto to Victoria and return, via Canadian Pacific and Grand Trunk Pacific and National transcontinental railways.
10. Excursions in northern British Columbia and Yukon Territory and along the north Pacific coast.

1922 13th Brussels; 23 parts, outside North America.

1926 14th Madrid; 20 parts, outside North America.

1929 15th Pretoria; 23 parts, outside North America.

1933 16th Washington, D.C.
1. Eastern New York and western New England.
2. Mining districts of the eastern states.
3. Southern Appalachian region.
4. The Paleozoic stratigraphy of New York.
5. Chesapeake Bay region.
6. Oklahoma and Texas.
7. Geomorphology of the central Appalachians.
8. Mineral deposits of New Jersey and eastern Pennsylvania.
9. New York City and vicinity.
9a. The Catskill region.
10. Southern Pennsylvania and Maryland.
11. Northern Virginia.

12. Southern Maryland.
13. Western Texas and Carlsbad Caverns.
14. Ore deposits of the southwest.
15. Southern California.
16. Middle California and western Nevada.
17. The Salt Lake region.
18. Colorado Plateau region.
19. Colorado.
20. Pennsylvanian of the northern mid-continent region.
21. Central Oregon.
22. The channeled scabland.
23. The Butte mining district, Montana.
24. [Yellowstone-Beartooth-Big Horn region.]
25. The Black Hills.
26. Glacial geology of the central states.
27. Lake Superior region.
28. An outline of the structural geology of the United States.
29. Stratigraphic nomenclature in the United States.
30. The Baltimore and Ohio Railroad.

1956 20th Mexico City.

Excursion A-1. Geologia minera del noroeste de Mexico. Depositos de cobre de cananea, Sonora y de cobre y manganeso de El Boleo y Lucifer, Baja California.

Excursion A-2. Geologia a lo largo de la Carretera Panamericana entre Cuidad Juarez, Chih. y Mexico, D. F. Distritos Mineros de Santa Eulalia, Naica, Parral, San Francisco del Oro y Santa Barbara, Chih. Yacimiento de Fierro del Cerro do Mercado en Durango, Dgo. Distritos Mineros de Sombrerete, San Marin, Fresnillo y Zacatecas, Zac. y Guanajuato, Gto.

Excursion A-3. Geologia a lo largo de la carretera entre Mexico, D.F. Pachuca y Zimapan, Hgo. Distritos Mineros de Pachuca Real del Monte y de Zimapan, Hgo.

Excursion A-4. Geologia a lo largo de la carretera entre Mexico, D.F. y Taxco, Gro. Distrito Minero de Taxco. Visita a un yacimiento de Fluorita en rocas del Terciario Inferior.

Excursion A-5. See Excursion A-2.

Excursion A-6. Geologia a lo largo de la Carretera Panamericana entre Mexico, D.F. y Tehuantepec, Oax. Distritos Mineros de Natividad y Pluma Hidalgo, Oax., y visita a monumentos precoloniales de Oaxaca.

Excursion A-7. Geologia general de la parte sur de la Peninsula de Baja California. Depositos continentales y volcanicos del Cenozoico superior y marinos del inferior, asi como sedimentos marinos del Cretacico superior. Caracteristicas fisiograficas y efectos de Intemperismo en la region desertica.

Excursion A-8. Estratigrafia de las formaciones Paleozoicas y Mesozoicas de Altar-Caborca, Estado de Sonora.

Excursion A-9. Geologia a lo largo de la carretera entre Mexico, D.F. y Acapulco, Gro., via Taxco, Gro. y Chilpancingo, Gro. Geologia de los alrededores de Acapulco, Gro. Los yacimientos de dolomita de El Ocotito, Gro.

Excursion A-10. Geologia entre Mexico, D.F. y Huauchinango, Pue. Campos petroleros de Poza Rica, Ver. y la Nueve Faja de Oro, Ver.

Excursion A-11. Estratigrafia del Mesozoico y tectonica del sur del estado de Puebla; Presa de Valsequillo, Sifon de Huexotitlanapa y problemas hidrologicos de Puebla.

Excursion A-12. Estratigrafia y paleontologia del Mesozoico de la Cuenca sedimentaria de Oaxaca y Guerrero, especialmente del Jurasico Inferior y Medio.

Excursion A-13. Estratigrafia Mesozoica y tectonica de la Sierra de Chihuahua; Permico de Placer de Guadalupe, Chih.; geohidrologia de la region lagunera; estratigrafia Mesozoica y Tectonica de la Sierra Madre Oriental entre Mapimi, Dgo. y Monterrey, N.L.

Excursion A-14. Estratigrafia del Cenozoico y del Mesozoico a lo largo de la carretera entre

Reynosa, Tamps. y Mexico, D.F. Tectonica de la Sierra Madre Oriental. Volcanismo en el Valle de Mexico. (English edition: Stratigraphy of the Tertiary and Mesozoic along the highway between Reynosa, Tampa, and Mexico, D.F. Tectonics of the Sierra Madre Oriental. Volcanic and continental sedimentary rocks in the Valley of Mexico.)

Excursion A-15. Volcanismo Terciario y Reciente del Eje Volcanico de Mexico. Formaciones andesiticas de las Sierras de Las Cruces y Ozumatian. Formaciones basalticas de las Sierras de Zitacuaro, Morelia, Paracho, y alrededores del Paricutin. Fenomenos post-paroxismales de la Sierra de San Andres y el Lago de Cuitzeo y estructura e historia del nuevo Volcan Paricutin.

Excursion A-16. Geologia a lo largo de la carretera entre Mexico, D.F. y Guadalajara, Jal., via Morelia, Mich. y entre Guadalajara, Jal. y Mexico, D.F., via Leon, Gto. Condiciones geohidrologicas de los Valles de Atemajac y Tesistan y de las zonas adyacentes a la ciudad de Guadalajara.

Excursion C-1. See Excursion A-3.

Excursion C-2. See Excursion A-4.

Excursion C-3. Geologia a lo largo de la carretera entre Mexico, D.F., y Saltillo, Coah. Distritos mineros de Guanajuato, Gto. y Avalos-Concepcion del Oro-Mazapil, Zac. Minas de carbon de Monclava y Nueva Rosita, Coah.

Excursion C-4. See Excursion A-1.

Excursion C-5. Estudio de la estratigrafia del Mesozoico y de la tectonica de la Sierra Madre Oriental entre Monterrey, N.L. y Torreon, Coah. Estudio de la cuenca carbonifera de Sabinas, Coah. Visita a las Grutas de Garcia. Morfologia tipica de bolson y observacion del tipo de pliegues en la Sierra de Parras. (For partial translation, see Southwestern Association of Student Geological Societies, 1964, 5th).

Excursion C-6. See Excursion A-14.

Excursion C-7. Geologia general de la Sierra Madre Oriental entre Mexico, D.F., y Cordoba, Ver. Depositos continentales y volcanicos del Cenozoico Superior y sedimentos marinos del Mesozoico y Cenozoico. Campos petroleros de la Cuenca de Veracruz. Obras hidraulicas del Rio Papaloapan. Campos petroleros y azufreros del Istmo de Tehuantepec. Geomorfologia de la Peninsula de Yucatan. Visitas a las zonas arqueologicas Mayas.

Excursion C-8. Estratigrafia y paleontologia del Jurasico Inferior y Medio. Marino de la region central de la Sierra Madre Oriental.

Excursion C-9. Volcanes, rocas volcanicas, sedimentos lacustres y aluviales del Pleistoceno y Plioceno; rocas clasticas y volcanicas Terciarias; yeso y caliza no marinos del Terciario Inferior; calizas y lutitas del Cretacico Superior y calizas y dolomitas del Cretacico Inferior, en el sur de la cuenca de Mexico y en el Edo. de Morelos.

Excursion C-10. Estratigrafia Mesozoica y tectonica de la Sierra Madre Oriental entre Zimapan, Hgo., y Cuidad Valles, S.L.P. Rocas igneas y sedimentarias del Cenozoico. Geologia petrolera. Plantas de refinacion y produccion de Poza Rica, Ver.

Excursion C-11. Estratigrafia del Cenozoico continental de las sierras del sur y la costa del Golfo de Mexico entre Coatzacoalcos, Ver., y Veracruz. Vulcanologia del Pleistoceno. Geologia general y paleontologia vertebrada.

Excursion C-12. See Excursion A-9.

Excursion C-13. See Excursion A-10.

Excursion C-14. Espeleologia y fenomenos carsticos de las grutas de Cacahuamilpa, Mor.; estratigrafia y geologia superficial.

Excursion C-15A. Geologia del Mesozoico y estratigrafia del Permica del Estado de Chiapas. Geologia sedimentaria y petrolera: campos del Istmo de Tehuantepec. Domos salinos con yacimientos de azufre y su explotacion por el metodo Frasch.

Excursion C-15B. Geologia a lo largo de la carretera entre Tuxtla Gutierrez, Chih. y Mexico, D.F., y visita a monumentos precoloniales de Oaxaca, Oax.

Excursion C-16. Visita a las localidades tipo de las formaciones del Eoceno, Oligoceno y Mioceno de la cuenca sedimentaria de Tampico-Misantla, en la llanura costera del Golfo de Mexico, entre Poza Rica, Ver., Tampico, Tamps. y Ciudad Valles, S.L.P.

1960 21st Copenhaven; 5 sets (40 numbers), outside North America.
Iceland; 1, outside North America.
Norway; 17 parts, outside North America.
Sweden; 12 parts, outside North America.
Finland; 4 parts, outside North America.
Denmark; 6 parts, outside North America.

1964 22nd New Delhi; 18 parts, outside North America.

1968 23rd Prague; 50 guidebooks, outside North America.

1972 24th Field excursions, Montreal.
Excursion X01-A01. Structural style of the southern Canadian Cordillera.
Excursion A02. Quaternary geology of the southern Canadian Cordillera.
Excursion A03-C03. Geology of the southern Canadian Cordillera.
Excursion A04-C04. Plutonic and associated rocks of the Coast Mountains of British Columbia.
Excursion A05-C05. Geology of Vancouver area of British Columbia.
Excursion A06-C06. Mineral deposits along the Pacific coast of Canada.
Excursion A07. Not published.
Excursion A08-C08. Engineering geology of the southern Cordillera of British Columbia.
Excursion A09-C09. Copper and molybdenum deposits of the western Cordillera.
Excursion A10. Stratigraphy and structure Rocky Mountains and foothills of west-central Alberta and northeastern British Columbia.
Excursion A11. Quaternary geology and geomorphology, southern and central Yukon (northern Canada).
Excursion A12. Volcanic rocks of the northern Canadian Cordillera.
Excursion A13. Not published.
Excursion A14. Lower and middle Paleozoic sediments and paleontology of Royal Creek and Peel River, Yukon, and Powell Creek, Northwest Territories.
Excursion A15-C15. The Canadian Rockies and tectonic evolution of the southeastern Canadian Cordillera.
Excursion A16. The Permian of the southeastern Cordillera.
Excursion A19. Cambrian and Ordovician biostratigraphy of the southern Canadian Rocky Mountains.
Excursion A20. The Cretaceous and Jurassic of the foothills of the Rocky Mountains of Alberta.
Excursion A21. Vertebrate paleontology, Cretaceous to Recent, Interior plains, Canada.
Excursion A24-C24. Major lead-zinc deposits of western Canada.
Excursion A25-C25. Coal, oil, gas, and industrial mineral deposits of the Interior plains, foothills and Rocky Mountains of Alberta and British Columbia.
Excursion A26. Hydrogeology of the Rocky Mountains and Interior plains.
Excursion A27. Archean and Proterozoic geology of the Yellowknife and Great Bear areas, Northwest Territories.
Excursion A28. Archean and Proterozoic sedimentary and volcanic rocks of the Yellowknife-Great Slave Lake area, Northwest Territories.
Excursion A29. Muskox intrusion and Coppermine River lavas, Northwest Territories, Canada.
Excursion A30. Quaternary geology and geomorphology, Mackenzie delta to Hudson Bay.
Excursion A31-C31. Geology and mineral deposits of the Flin Flon, Lynn Lake and Thompson areas, Manitoba, and the Churchill-Superior front of the western Precambrian shield.
Excursion A32a-A32b. Precambrian geology of the Lake Athabasca area, Saskatchewan and Baker Lake area, Northwest Territories.
Excursion A33-C33. Archean geology and metallogenesis of the western part of the Canadian Shield.
Excursion A35-C35. The geology of the Canadian Shield between Winnipeg and Montreal.

Excursion A36-C36. Precambrian geology of the southern Canadian Shield with emphasis on the lower Proterozoic (Huronian) of the north shore of Lake Huron.
Excursion A37-C37. Not published.
Excursion A39-39b-C39. Precambrian geology and mineral deposits of the Timagami, Cobalt, Kirkland Lake and Timmins region, Ontario.
Excursion A40-C40. Precambrian volcanism of the Noranda, Kirkland Lake, Timmins, Michipicoten, and Mamainse Point areas, Quebec and Ontario.
Excursion A41-C41. Precambrian geology and mineral deposits of the Noranda-Val d'Or and Matagami-Chibougamau greenstone belts, Quebec.
Excursion A42. Quaternary stratigraphy and geomorphology of the eastern Great Lakes region of southern Ontario.
Excursion A43. The Great Lakes of Canada; Quaternary geology and limnology.
Excursion A44-C44. Quaternary geology and geomorphology, southern Quebec.
Excursion A45-C45. Stratigraphy and paleontology of the Paleozoic rocks of southern Ontario.
Excursion A46-C46. The Grenville province of the Precambrian in Quebec.
Excursion A47-C47. Classic mineral collecting localities in Ontario and Quebec.
Excursion A48. Hydrogeology of representative areas of the southern part of Ontario.
Excursion C-50. Not published.
Excursion A51a. Engineering geology in Quebec-Labrador region, eastern Canada.
Excursion A53-C53. Alkalic rock complexes and carbonatites of Ontario and part of Quebec.
Excursion A54. Igneous rock of central Labrador, with emphasis on anorthositic and related intrusions.
Excursion A55. Iron ranges of Labrador and northern Quebec.
Excursion A56-C56. Appalachian structure and stratigraphy, Quebec.
Excursion A57-C57. Appalachian stratigraphy and structure of the Maritime Provinces.
Excursion A58-C58. Mineral deposits of southern Quebec and New Brunswick.
Excursion A59. Vertebrate paleontology of eastern Canada.
Excursion A60. Stratigraphy and economic geology of Carboniferous basins in the Maritime Provinces.
Excursion A61-C61. Quaternary geology, geomorphology and hydrogeology of the Atlantic provinces; Quaternary deposits and events.
Excursion A62-C62. A cross-section through the Appalachian orogen in Newfoundland.
Excursion A63-C63. Appalachian geotectonic elements of the Atlantic provinces and southern Quebec.
Excursion A64-C64. Not published.
Excursion A65. Some astroblemes, craters and cryptovolcanic structures in Ontario and Quebec.
Excursion A66. The Canadian Arctic Islands and the Mackenzie region.
Excursion A68. Eastern Canadian Cordillera and Arctic Islands; an aerial reconnaissance.
Excursion B01. Petrology and structure of the Morin anorthosite; 20 parts.
Excursion B02. Stratigraphy and tectonics of the Precambrian of the Grenville province in the Saint Paulin-Saint Boniface de Shawinigan area.
Excursion B03. Stratigraphy of the Montreal area.
Excursion B04. Pleistocene deposits northeast of Montreal.
Excursion B05. Structural geology of the Sherbrooke area.
Excursion B06. A crypto-explosion structure at Charlevoix and the St. Urbain anorthosite.
Excursion B07. Base metal deposits of southeastern Quebec.
Excursion B08. Asbestos deposits of southern Quebec.
Excursion B09. Quebec Iron and Titanium Corporation ore deposit at Lac Tio, Quebec.
Excursion B10. Monteregian Hills; diatremes, kimberlite, lamprophyres and intrusive breccias west of Montreal.
Excursion B11. The Monteregian Hills; ultra-alkaline rocks and the Oka carbonatite complex.
Excursion B12. Geology of Mount Royal.

Excursion B13. The geology of the Brome and Shefford igneous complexes.
Excursion B14. Monteregian Hills; Mounts Johnson and Rougemont.
Excursion B15. The Monteregian Hills; mineralogy of Mount St. Hilaire.
Excursion B16. Not published.
Excursion B17. Quarries in the Montreal area.
Excursion B18. Engineering geology of Montreal.
Excursion B19. Geology of the environs of Quebec City.
Excursion B20. Engineering geology in the Quebec city area.
Excursion B21. Appalachian tectonics in the eastern townships of Quebec.
Excursion B22. Not published.
Excursion B23-B27. Geology of the national capital area.
Excursion C17. Lower Carboniferous stratigraphy and sedimentology of the southern Canadian Rocky Mountains.
Excursion C18. Devonian stratigraphy and facies of the southern Rocky Mountains of Canada, and the adjacent plains.
Excursion C22. Quaternary geology and geomorphology between Winnipeg and the Rocky Mountains.
Excursion C23. Industrial and non-metallic minerals of Manitoba and Saskatchewan (Central Plains).
Excursion C34. The Precambrian rocks of the Atikokan-Thunder Bay-Marathon area.
Excursion C38. General geology of the Sudbury-Elliot Lake region.
Excursion C49. Visits to deposits of industrial minerals and building materials in Quebec and Ontario.
Excursion C51b. Engineering geology of eastern Canada-southern Ontario.
Excursion C52. Stratigraphy and structure of the St. Lawrence lowland of Quebec.
Excursion C67. Uranium deposits of Canada.

AzTeS	1956, 72
[CDU]	1891, 1913
CLU-G/G	1891(A), 1906, 13, 33, 56, 72
CLhC	1972(A02)
CSdS	1913, 33
CU-EART	1906(1,2,4-15,17-31), 13, 33, 56(A-1 thru A-7,A-9, A-16,C-5 thru C-8,C15A,C15B), 72(A01 thru A06,A08 thru A68,B01 thru B21)
CaAC	1972(A02,A04-C04, A05-C05,A10,A12,A53-C53,A55,B13,B14,C49)
[CaACAM]	1972(X01-A01 thru A68)
CaACI	1913(1,8-10)
CaACM	1913(8,9), 72(X01-A01 thru A68)
CaACU	1913(1-8,10), 33
CaAEU	1913(1-6,8-10), 33
[CaBVU]	1891(B), 1913, 33, 56(A-1 thru A-7,A-9 thru A-16,C-1 thru C-9, C-12,C-13,C-15,C-16)
[CaOHaHa]	1972(A39-39b-C39)
CaOHM	1913, 72
CaOKQ	1891, 1913, 33, 56(A-1 thru A-4,A-7,A-11 thru A-16,C-8,C-9,C-15B,C-16)
CaOLU	1891, 1913, 33, 56, 72
CaOOG	1894-1937, 56-58
CaOONM	1972
[CaOTOM]	1972(X01-A01 thru A68)
CoG	1933, 56, 72
CoU	1913, 33, 56(C-9), 72
DI-GS	1891, 1906, 13, 33, 56
DLC	1972

ICF	1913(1-5,8-10), 33(1-8,10-27,29,30)
ICarbS	1913(1-6,8-10), 33, 72(A01 thru A63,C67,B01 thru B06,B08 thru B27)
IEN	1913, 33, 72
IU	1891, 1913, 33, 56, 72
IaU	1906, 13, 33, 56
InRE	1933(3,4,6,10,13,17,19-21,23,24,28)
InU	1906, 13(1-6,8-10), 33, 56(A-1,A-16,C-4,C-9Eng.)
KyU	1891, 1906, 13, 33, 56, 72
LU	1906, 13(1-5,9,10)
MH-GS	1906, 13, 33(1-15,17-23,25-30), 72
MNS	1913, 33(1-29), 56(A-1 thru A-5,A-7,A-9 thru A-16,C-8,C-15A,C-15B,C-16), 72(A01-A16,A19-A68, B01-B27)
MiDW	1913(1-5,8-10), 33(1-8,9a-30)
MiHM	1891, 1913, 33, 56(A-1 thru A-7,A-10 thru A-16,C-5,C-8,C-9,C-15A,C-15B,C-16), 72
MiKW	1913, 33(2,3,10,12,26)
MnU	1913(1-5,8-10), 56(lack A-8,C-3,C-5,C-7,C-10,C-14)
MoSW	1891, 1906, 33, 56
MoU	1913, 33, 56(A-1 thru A-7,A-9 thru A-16,C-5 thru C-9,C-15A,C-15B, C-16), 72
MtBC	1972
NBiSU	1933(3,5,6,8,11-22,26,29,30)
NNC	1906, 13, 33, 56
NOneoU	1972(X01-A01 thru A06-C06,A08-C08 thru A12-C12,A14-C14 thru A36-C36,A38-C38 thru A49-C49,A51-C51 thru A68,B01,B02,B05,B06,B08-B15,B19,B21, B23-B27)
NRU	1972
NSyU	1913, 33, 56(A-1 thru A-16,C-1,C-2,C-4,C-5,C-8,C-15A,C-15B,C-16), 72
NbU	1933, 56, 72
NdU	1913, 33(5,10-12,17,20-22,25,26,30), 56(A-1 thru A-4,A-6,A-7,A-9 thru A-16,C-1,C-2,C-4 thru C-6,C-8,C-12,C-13,C-15A,C15B,C-16), 72
NhD	1906, 13, 56
NjP	1891, 1906, 13, 33, 56, 72(X01-A01 thru A68)
NvLN	1972
NvU	1933, 56
OCU	1891, 1913, 33, 72(X01-A01 thru A68)
OU	1906, 13, 33, 56(A-1 thru C-2,C05,C-8,C-9,C-15A thru C-16), 72(X01-A01 thru A68)
OkU	1913, 33, 56, 72(Series A)
OrU	1906, 13(1-10), 33, 56(A-3,C-1,C-9), 60, 68
PBL	1913, 33, 56
PBm	1972
PPiGulf	1933
PSt	1913, 33, 56(A-1 thru A-7,A-9 thru A-16,C-1 thru C-9,C-12,C-13,C-15A, C-15B,C-16), 72
RPB	1891, 1906, 13, 33, 56(lacks A-8,C-3,C-10,C-14)
TMM	1933
TU	1933, 56(1-5,7,13)
TxDaAR-T	1913(1-5,8-10), 72(X01-A08,A03-C03 thru A05-C05, A10-C10, A14-C14 thru A16-C16,C17,C18,A19-C19,A20-C20,A25-C25,A26-C26,C52,A56-C56, A60-C60,A62-C62,A63-C63,A66-C66,A68-C68)
TxDaDM	1933(1-30), 56(A-1 thru A-7,C-1 thru C-8, C-12,C-13)
TxDaM	1891, 1906, 13, 33, 56

TxDaSM	1956(A-1 thru A-3, A-5, A-11 thru A-16, C-1,C-4,C-5,C-6,C-8,C-15A, C-15B,C-16), 72
TxHSD	1933 (2,6-12,14,16,17,20-28,30), 56(A-1 thru A-16,C-5,C-8,C-15A,C-15B,C-16), 72
TxHU	1913(2-4), 56(A-1 thru A-4,A-7,A-9 thru A-16,C-5,C-7,C-9,C-15A,C-15B, C-16)
TxLT	1906(1-30), 13, 33, 56(C-9)
TxMM	1913(1,10), 33
TxU	1891, 1906, 13, 33, 56(A-14,C-6)
UU	1933, 56
ViBlbV	1913, 33, 56, 72
WU	1891, 1906, 33, 56, 72
WyU	1913(1-6,8-10)

(137) INTERNATIONAL MINERALOGICAL ASSOCIATION. CONGRESS.

1962 3rd Washington, D.C., northern field excursion and southern field excursion. A visitor's guide to the geology of the National Capitol area. (2 separate guidebooks)

CaOLU	1962
CoG	1962
ICIU-S	1962
IEN	1962
IU	1962
LU	1962 (southern guidebook only)
MnDuU	1962
NBiSU	1962(southern)
NOneoU	1962
NcU	1962(southern)
NdU	1962
NhD	1962
NjP	1962
OkU	1962
PBL	1962
PBm	1962
TMM	1962
TxDaSM	1962
TxLT	1962
TxU	1962
ViBlbV	1962(southern)

(138) INTERNATIONAL SYMPOSIUM ON THE DEVONIAN SYSTEM. CALGARY.

1967 Guidebook for Canadian Cordillera field trip. (61)

CLU-G/G	1967(reprint 1969)
CaACI	1967
CaAEU	1967
CaOLU	1967
CoU	1967
DI-GS	1967
IdBB	1967
NcU	1967
NdU	1967
TxDaAR-T	1967
TxHSD	1967
TxU	1967

(139) INTERNATIONAL UNION OF GEODESY AND GEOPHYSICS.

1963 Guidebook for seismological study tour.
CLU-G/G 1963
CSfCSM 1963
CU-EART 1963

(140) IOWA GEOLOGICAL SOCIETY.

1941 Southeast Missouri guidebook.
1964 Southwestern Iowa field trip; outcrops Pennsylvanian system, Shawn group, near Thurman, Iowa.
1965 Pre-Cedar Valley post-Maquoketa sediments, northeast Iowa.
CLU-G/G 1964
[I-GS] 1965
MnDuU 1941

(141) IOWA. GEOLOGICAL SURVEY.

1935 See Kansas Geological Society. (147)
1970 No. 3 See Geological Society of America. (96)

(142) IOWA. GEOLOGICAL SURVEY. EDUCATIONAL SERIES.

1967 No. 1. Fossils and rocks of eastern Iowa.
Field Trip No. 1. Cambrian and Ordovician, northeastern Iowa.
Field Trip No. 2. Ordovician and Silurian, northeastern and east-central Iowa.
Field Trip No. 3. Silurian and Devonian, east-central Iowa.
Field Trip No. 4. Middle Devonian, east-central Iowa.
Field Trip No. 5. Upper Devonian, north-central Iowa.
Field Trip No. 6. Lower Mississippian (Kinderhook), north-central Iowa.
Field Trip No. 7. Mississippian, north-central Iowa.
Field Trip No. 8. Mississippian, southeastern and south-central Iowa.
Field Trip No. 9. Mississippian, southeastern Iowa.
IU 1967
OkT 1967
TxLT 1967

(143) IOWA. UNIVERSITY. DEPARTMENT OF GEOLOGY.

1961 Lake Superior region petrology-economic geology field trip.
1962 Central and northeast Wisconsin petrology-economic geology field trip.
1963 Southeast Missouri and south Illinois stratigraphy-economic geology, Precambrian.
1964 Missouri-Illinois-Arkansas-Oklahoma.
1968 No. 4 See Geological Society of America. North Central Section. (98)
spring The Grand Canyon.
1970 Big Bend area, Texas, Gomez field trip.
1971 spring The southern Appalachians.
1972 spring Florida.
1973 spring The Grand Canyon and vicinity; a guidebook by participants.
1974 Big Bend field trip.
IaU 1961-64, 70
TxU 1968

(144) JAMAICA. MINES AND GEOLOGY DIVISION. SPECIAL PUBLICATION.

1974 No. 1 See Geological Society of America. (96)

(145) JOHNS HOPKINS UNIVERSITY. DEPARTMENT OF GEOLOGY. STUDIES IN GEOLOGY.

1950 16th Guidebooks to the geology of Maryland. (96)
No. 1. Geology of the South Mountain anticlinorium.
No. 2. Geology of Bear Island, Potomac River.
No. 3. The coastal plain geology of southern Maryland.
1958 17th Guidebooks to the geology of Maryland.
No. 4,5. Structural geology of South Mountain and Appalachians in Maryland. (83)
1960 18th Guidebooks. (12, 274)
No. 1. Geology of north-central part of the New Jersey coastal plain. (12)
No. 2. Geology of the region between Roanoke and Winchester, Appalachian Valley of western Virginia. (12)
No. 3. Lower Paleozoic carbonate rocks in Maryland and Pennsylvania. (12)
No. 4. See same series, 1958, 17th. (12)

CLU-G/G	1950, 58, 60
CLhC	1950
CSdS	1950
CU-EART	1950, 58, 60
CaOHM	1958, 60
CaOKQ	1950, 58
CaOLU	1971, 73
CaOOG	1958-60
CaQMM	1950
CoG	1950, 58, 60
CoU	1950
DI-GS	1950, 58, 60
ICF	1950, 58, 60
ICarbS	1950, 58, 60
IEN	1950, 58, 60
[I-GS]	1950, 60
IU	1950, 58, 60
IaU	1950, 58, 60
InRE	1958
InU	1950, 58, 60
KyU	1950, 58, 60
MdBJ	1950, 58, 60
MiDW	1950
MiHM	1950
MNS	1950, 58, 60
MnU	1950, 58
MoSW	1950, 58
MoU	1950, 58, 60
NBiSU	1950, 58
NNC	1950
NRU	1958
NSyU	1960
NbU	1950, 58, 60
NhD	1950, 58, 60
NjP	1950, 60

(145) Johns Hopkins University.

OCU	1950-60
OU	1950, 60
OkU	1950, 58
TxDaAR-T	1960
TxDaDM	1958, 60(1-3)
TxDaM	1950, 58, 60
TxHU	1950, 58, 60
TxLT	1950
TxU	1950, 58, 60
TxU-Da	1960
ViBlbV	1950, 60
WU	1950, 58, 60

(146) KANSAS ACADEMY OF SCIENCE.

1951	83rd	Geology and botany field trips in vicinity of Lawrence, Kansas.
1953		Guidebook for geology section field trip; Tuttle Creek damsite.

[I-GS]	1951, 53
NjP	1951
TxLT	1951

(147) KANSAS GEOLOGICAL SOCIETY. GUIDEBOOK...ANNUAL FIELD CONFERENCE.

1927	1st	Iowa field trip.
1928	2nd	Ozark Mountains of Missouri and Arkansas.
1929	3rd	Black Hills of South Dakota and Front Range of Rocky Mountains in Wyoming and northern Colorado.
1930	4th	Mountains of south-central Colorado, north-central and northeastern New Mexico and the Texas Panhandle.
1931	5th	Wichita, Arbuckle, and Ouachita Mountains of Oklahoma and the Ouachita Mountains of Arkansas, with geologic cross sections.
1932	6th	Carboniferous rocks of eastern Kansas and Nebraska, and western Missouri.
1933	7th	Older Paleozoic rocks of Missouri, Arkansas and Oklahoma.
1934	8th	Southwestern Kansas and the adjacent parts of Colorado, New Mexico, Oklahoma and Texas.
1935	9th	Paleozoic rocks of upper Mississippi Valley, Iowa City, Iowa to Duluth, Minnesota. (141, 175, 345)
1936	10th	Pennsylvanian and Permian rocks of northeastern Kansas and northwestern Missouri.
1937	11th	Southeastern Kansas and northeastern Oklahoma.
1938	12th	Along the Front Range of the Rocky Mountains, Colorado. (250)
1939	13th	Southwestern Illinois, southeastern Missouri. (123)
1940	14th	Western South Dakota, eastern Wyoming; Black Hills, Hartville uplift, and Laramie Range.
1941	15th	Central and northeastern Missouri and adjoining area in Illinois.
1946	Mar.	Permian and Pennsylvanian rocks, Winfield to Sedan, Kansas.
	June	Permian rocks, Augusta to Elmdale, Kansas.
1947	June	Southeastern Kansas-Sedan to Iola.
1949	Apr.	Permian and Pennsylvanian rocks, Winfield to Sedan.
	June	Pennsylvanian field conference. Pennsylvanian rocks in Kansas, lower Kansas River valley.
	Oct.	Western Shawnee and eastern Wabaunsee counties, Kansas.
1951	Nov.	Lyon County, Kansas.
1952	16th	West-central Missouri. (182)
1954	17th	Southeastern and south-central Missouri. (182)
1955	18th	Southwestern Kansas.

1956	19th	New Virgilian sections along the Kansas Turnpike, east-central Kansas.
	20th	Northwest Arkansas and Magnet Cove. (35)
1957	21st	Eastern Kansas, from Kansas City to Manhattan, Kansas via the Kansas Turnpike, U. S. Highway 40, and Kansas Highway 13.
1958	22nd	South-central Colorado.
1959	23rd	Northeastern Kansas; Pennsylvanian and Permian cyclic deposits. (15)
	24th	South-central Kansas. (15)
1960	25th	Northeastern Oklahoma.
1961	26th	Northeastern Missouri and west-central Illinois. (41, 182)
1962	27th	Geoeconomics of the Pennsylvanian marine banks in southeast Kansas.
1964	28th	Northeastern Oklahoma. (232)
1966	29th	Flysch facies and structure of the Ouachita Mountains.
1969	30th	Excursion to the Kansas Geological Survey and core party at Lawrence, Kansas.
1975	31st	Upper Pennsylvanian limestone facies in southeastern Kansas.

[A-GS]	1952, 61
AzFU	1960
AzTeS	1951-54, 56(19), 57, 59(24), 61-64, 66
AzU	1969
CChiS	1958
[CDU]	1966
CLU-G/G	1930(cross-sections only), 31, 38, 41, 46, 47, 49(June,Oct.), 51, 52, 54, 56(19), 57, 58, 59(24), 61, 62, 64, 66
CLhC	1961, 62
CSdS	1931, 52
CU-EART	1932, 35, 41, 49, 52-58, 59(24), 60-64, 66, 69, 75
[CaACAM]	1935, 39, 40
CaAEU	1932
[CaBVU]	
CaOHM	1954, 56, 57, 59(24), 61, 62, 66, 69
CaOKQ	1927-29, 32-35, 54, 57, 58, 61, 69
CaOLU	1951, 56(19), 57, 59(24), 61, 62, 66, 69
CaOOG	1935, 40-54, 61
CoFS	1958
CoG	1930-41, 49, 51, 52, 56-61, 64, 66, 69
CoU	1930, 35, 38, 40, 52, 54-56, 58-62, 64, 66, 69
DFPC	1954, 60, 61
DI-GS	1927-66
ICF	1936, 40, 41, 52, 57, 58, 59(24), 60, 61, 66
ICarbS	1935, 37, 39, 40, 49(Oct.), 61, 62
IEN	1931-33, 35, 38-41, 52, 56-58, 60-64, 66, 69, 75
[I-GS]	1928, 31-33, 35-40, 49(Oct.), 52, 57-61, 66
IU	1932, 35-41, 49, 52, 54, 56-62, 64, 66, 75
IaU	1927-41, 52, 54-62, 64, 66
InLP	1954, 57-66
InRE	1935, 61
InU	1929, 35-41, 49(Oct.), 51-54, 56(19), 57, 58, 59(24), 60-64, 66, 69
KyU	1932-41, 46, 47, 49, 52, 54-62, 64-66, 69
LU	1930, 35, 36, 38, 40, 52, 55-62, 64-69
MNS	1929, 32, 34-41, 58, 61
MiDW	1928-41, 49(June,Oct.), 51, 52, 56(19), 57, 58, 59(24), 61, 62, 64
MiHM	1935, 39-41, 49
MiKW	1961

MiU	1927-64, 66, 69, 75
[MnSSM]	1952, 54
MnU	1929-36, 40-52, 54, 56-64, 66
MoSW	1933, 35, 36, 38-41, 49(June,Oct.), 51, 52, 55, 57, 61, 62, 64, 66
MoU	1930-32, 34-52, 56, 57, 59, 61-64, 66
MtU	1940, 52, 54, 56-62
NNC	1927, 29-32, 34-41, 49(June,Oct.), 51, 52, 55-62, 64, 66
NRU	1929, 37, 41, 52, 54, 56-58, 59(23), 61-64, 69
NSyU	1935, 52, 54, 61, 69
NbU	1932, 35-41, 54, 55, 56(19,20), 57, 58, 59(24), 60-62, 64, 66, 69
NcU	1932, 34-41, 49, 51, 54, 56-58, 59(24), 61-66
NdU	1929, 39, 52, 56(20), 58, 61, 62
NhD	1932-41, 52-64, 66, 69
NjP	1929, 31, 32, 34-41, 49, 52-62, 64, 66, 69
OCU	1929-35, 39, 41, 52, 56, 61
OU	1930, 32-41, 49-52, 55-64, 66
[OkOkCGe]	1937, 49, 51
OkT	1928-41, 52, 55, 56(20), 57, 58, 59(24), 61, 62
OkU	1927-58, 60-69
OrCS	1935, 61-64, 66, 69
OrU	1961-62
PBL	1935-38, 52, 54, 61
PPiGulf	1935, 39-41, 49, 52, 61
PSt	1935
RPB	1935, 41
SdRM	1929-31, 34-41, 52, 54, 55, 61
TMM	1952
TxDaAR-T	1929-38, 40, 41, 46, 49(June,Oct.), 51, 52, 55-62, 65, 66
TxDaDM	1941, 51, 52, 56-62, 64, 66, 69
TxDaM	1929, 30, 32, 35-41, 49(Oct.), 51, 52, 56(19), 57-62, 64
TxDaSM	1932, 41, 49, 51, 52, 54-58, 60, 61
TxHSD	1930, 32, 35, 37, 41, 49(Oct.), 51, 52, 57, 59-64, 66
TxHU	1930, 31, 35, 36, 38-41, 52, 56(20), 57-64, 66, 69
TxLT	1930, 31, 35-37, 41, 49, 51-55, 61
TxMM	1929-33, 36-41, 51, 52, 58, 64, 66
TxU	1929-41, 46, 47, 49, 51, 52, 55-62, 64, 66, 69
TxU-Da	1930, 32, 33, 35, 36, 40, 52, 58, 61, 66
UU	1952, 58, 61
ViBlbV	1935, 52, 59, 61
WPlaU	1935, 54, 58
WU	1932, 35-41, 49, 52, 55-64, 66, 69, 75

(148) KANSAS STATE COLLEGE OF PITTSBURG. NATIONAL SCIENCE FOUNDATION CLASS.

1960 — Pittsburg, Bourbon, Crawford and Cherokee counties. [Kansas]
IU 1960

(149) KANSAS. STATE GEOLOGICAL SURVEY. FIELD TRIP GUIDE.

1960 May — Geologic field trip in south Osage Cuesta region; vicinity of Neodesha, Wilson and Montgomery counties, Kansas. (For science students, Neodesha High School.)

July — A geologic tour in the Turkey Creek camp of south-central Kansas. (For Girl Scouts of Turkey Creek camp.)

1976 — See Friends of the Pleistocene. Midwest Group. (90)

IU 1960

(150) KANSAS STATE TEACHERS COLLEGE, EMPORIA, KANSAS. SCIENCE TEACHERS INSTITUTE.

1957 Flint Hills of Lyon, Chase, Morris and Wabaunsee counties, Kansas.
1960 4th Flint Hills-Osage Cuestas of Lyon, Chase, Butler, Greenwood, Wilson, Woodson and Allen counties, Kansas.
1961 5th Flint Hills of Lyon, Chase, Morris, and Wabaunsee counties, Kansas.
1962 6th Flint Hills of Lyon, Chase, Morris and Wabaunsee counties, Kansas.
CaOLU 1957
IU 1957-62
OU 1957

(151) KANSAS STATE UNIVERSITY. UNIVERSITY FOR MAN.

1976 Land of the post rock.
IU 1976

(152) KANSAS. UNIVERSITY. SCIENCE AND MATHEMATICS CAMPUS.

1957 Geologic field conference in northeastern Kansas between Lawrence and Wyandotte County Park.
1961 Same as 1957.
IU 1961
OU 1957

(153) KEY GEOLOGISTS REGIONAL CONFERENCE.

1963 Geology of DeGray damsite; field trip. (Arkansas)
TxHU 1963

(154) LAFAYETTE GEOLOGICAL SOCIETY. LAFAYETTE, LOUISIANA. FIELD TRIP.

1959 Tertiary of west-central Louisiana.
1961 Tertiary of central Louisiana and Mississippi.
1962 Tertiary of central Louisiana.
1964 Tertiary of central Louisiana and east Texas.
1965 Tertiary of Mississippi.
1968 Tertiary of central Louisiana.
CU-EART 1968
CoG 1968
IU 1965
TxDaAR-T 1968
TxHSD 1968
TxHU 1962
TxMM 1968
TxU 1959, 61, 62, 64, 65

LAMAR STATE COLLEGE OF TECHNOLOGY. DEPARTMENT OF GEOLOGY. **See TEXAS. LAMAR STATE COLLEGE OF TECHNOLOGY, BEAUMONT. (304)**

(155) LIBERAL GEOLOGICAL SOCIETY. ANNUAL BOY SCOUT GEOLOGY FIELD TRIP.

1961 Cimarron River valley, Black Mesa area.
1967 Meade County field trip.
1968 9th Boy Scout field trip, Black Mesa area of Cimarron County, Oklahoma and Union County, northern Missouri.

IU 1961, 67, 68
TxDaAR-T 1967
TxDaDM 1967

(156) LONG BEACH, CALIFORNIA. DEPARTMENT OF OIL PROPERTIES.

1967 Field trip...to Long Beach unit, offshore operations; Wilmington oil field data.

TxU 1967

(157) LOS ANGELES BASIN GEOLOGICAL SOCIETY.

1971 San Fernando earthquake field trip. Road log.

CU-EART 1971
OCU 1971
OU 1971
TxDaAR-T 1971
TxDaDM 1971

(158) LOUISIANA. STATE UNIVERSITY. SCHOOL OF GEOSCIENCE. GUIDEBOOK.

1973 Guidebook to Paleozoic Ozark shelf of northern Arkansas. (259)

CLU-G/G 1973
OkU 1973

(159) LUBBOCK GEOLOGICAL SOCIETY.

1956 See West Texas Geological Society. (338)

(160) MARYLAND. GEOLOGICAL SURVEY. GUIDEBOOK.

1968 1st Coastal plain geology of southern Maryland. (Prepared for the 9th annual field conference of the Atlantic Coastal Plains Geological Association, 1968). (43)
1971 2nd Field Trip No. 3. New interpretations of the eastern Piedmont geology of Maryland or granite and gabbro or graywacke and greenstone. (96)
4th Field Trip No. 4. The Piedmont crystalline rocks at Bear Island, Potomac River, Maryland. (96)
3rd Field Trip No. 5. Environmental history of Maryland Miocene. (96)

CLU-G/G 1968, 71
CU-EART 1968, 71
CaOOG 1968
CoG 1968
ICIU-S 1968
[I-GS] 1971
IU 1971
InU 1968
KyU 1968, 71
MiHM 1968
MiKW 1968, 71

MnU 1968
MoSW 1968, 71
NBiSU 1971
NOneoU 1971(4)
NRU 1971(3)
NcU 1968, 71(4)
NjP 1968, 71(2,3)
OCU 1968
OU 1968
OkU 1968, 71
PSt 1968
TxDaAR-T 1968, 71
TxU 1968, 71

(161) MASSACHUSETTS. UNIVERSITY. COASTAL RESEARCH GROUP.

1969 1st Field trip guidebook; coastal environments of northeastern Massachusetts and New Hampshire. (275)

CLU-G/G 1969
CLhC 1969
CaOOG 1969
CoU 1969
ICarbS 1969
IU 1969
InU 1969
KyU 1969
MH-GS 1969
MiU 1969
MoSW 1969
NBiSU 1969
NcU 1969
NdU 1969
NhD 1969
NjP 1969
OCU 1969
OkU 1969
TxDaAR-T 1969
TxDaSM 1969
TxHSD 1969
TxU 1969

(162) METEORITICAL SOCIETY. ANNUAL MEETING. FIELD TRIP GUIDEBOOK.

1974 Guidebook to the geology of Meteor Crater, Arizona.

CLU-G/G 1974
DI-GS 1974

(163) MIAMI GEOLOGICAL SOCIETY. ANNUAL FIELD TRIP.

1967 1st Field guidebook on geology and ecology of Everglades National Park.

1968 2nd Late Cenozoic stratigraphy of southern Florida; a reappraisal, with additional notes on Sunoco-Felda and Sunniland oil fields. See also 1964, No. 10. (96)

1969 Field guide to some carbonate rock environments; Florida Keys and western Bahamas.

	3rd	Late Pleistocene geology in an urban area.
1970	4th	Sedimentary environments and carbonate rocks of Bimini, Bahamas.
1971		Field guide to some carbonate rocks environments, Florida Keys and western Bahamas. Revised edition.

CLU-G/G	1968, 69, 71
CU-EART	1968, 69
CaOKQ	1969, 70
CoG	1968, 69
CoU	1968-70
DI-GS	1968
ICarbS	1971
IU	1968
IaU	1968, 69(3)
IdBB	1970
InU	1968, 69
KyU	1969, 70
LU	1968
MH-GS	1968, 69
MNS	1968
MoU	1968
NBiSU	1968
NbU	1971
NcU	1968, 70
NdU	1968, 69
OCU	1968-70
OU	1968-70
OkU	1968-70
TMM	1969
TxDaAR-T	1968, 69, 71
TxDaDM	1968, 69
TxDaSM	1968
TxHSD	1968
TxU	1967-69
ViBlbV	1969
WU	1968-70

(164) MICHIGAN ACADEMY OF SCIENCE, ARTS, AND LETTERS. SECTION OF GEOLOGY AND MINERALOGY. ANNUAL GEOLOGICAL EXCURSION.

1935	5th	A study of the Lucas County, Ohio-Monroe County, Michigan monocline and stratigraphy of northwestern Ohio and southeastern Michigan. (165)
1937	7th	[No title. Celebrating the centennial anniversary of the founding of the Michigan Geological Survey]. (165)
1938	8th	[No title available] (165)
1939	9th	Marquette and Menominee districts. (165)
1940	10th	To Afton-Onaway district. (165)
1941	11th	St. Ignace and Mackinac Island. (165)
1947		See Michigan Basin Geological Society. (165)
1948		See Michigan Basin Geological Society. (165)

DI-GS	1937-41, 47, 48
IU	1935, 37-39, 41
InU	1940
PPiGulf	1937

OU	1938-40
OkU	1940
TxDaM	1947
TxU	1941

(165) MICHIGAN BASIN GEOLOGICAL SOCIETY. ANNUAL GEOLOGICAL EXCURSION.

1935	5th	See Michigan Academy of Science, Arts, and Letters. (164)
1937	7th	See Michigan Academy of Science, Arts, and Letters. (164)
1938	8th	See Michigan Academy of Science, Arts, and Letters. (164)
1939	9th	See Michigan Academy of Science, Arts, and Letters. (164)
1940	10th	See Michigan Academy of Science, Arts, and Letters. (164)
1941	11th	See Michigan Academy of Science, Arts, and Letters. (164)
1946		Ontario geological excursion to Kettle Point, Owen Sound, Waubaushene.
1947		Michigan copper country. (164)
1948		Pleistocene and early Paleozoic of eastern part of the northern peninsula of Michigan. (164)
1949		The northern part of the southern peninsula of Michigan.
1950		The Ordovician rocks of the Escanaba-Stonington area.
1951		The Devonian and Silurian rocks of parts of Ontario, Canada and western New York.
1952		Stratigraphy and structure of the Devonian rocks in southeastern Michigan and northwestern Ohio.
1953		The Ordovician stratigraphy of Cincinnati, Ohio and Richmond, Indiana areas.
1954		The stratigraphy of Manitoulin Island, Ontario, Canada.
1955		The Niagara escarpment of peninsular Ontario, Canada.
1956		The Devonian strata of the London-Sarnia area, southwestern Ontario, Canada.
1957		Silurian rocks of the northern peninsula of Michigan.
1958		Precambrian geology of parts of Dickinson and Iron counties, Michigan.
1959		Geology of Mackinac Island and Lower and Middle Devonian south of the Straits of Mackinac.
1960		Lower Paleozoic and Pleistocene stratigraphy across central Wisconsin.
1961		Geologic features of parts of Houghton, Keweenaw, Baraga, and Ontonagon counties, Michigan.
1962		Silurian rocks of the southern Lake Michigan area.
1963		Stratigraphy of the Silurian rocks in western Ohio.
1964		See American Association of Petroleum Geologists. (12)
1965		Geology of central Ontario. (Second edition of American Association of Petroleum Geologists-Society of Economic Paleontologists and Mineralogists-Geological Association of Canada guidebook for joint meeting, Toronto, 1964.) (12, 274)
1966		Cambrian stratigraphy in western Wisconsin. (346)
1967		Correlation problems of the Cambrian and Ordovician outcrop areas, northern peninsula of Michigan.
1968		Geology of Manitoulin Island.
1969		Studies of the Precambrian of the Michigan Basin.
1970		No. 1. Devonian strata of Alpena and Presque Isle counties, Michigan. (98)
		No. 2. Glacial history of the Glacial Grand valley. (98)
		No. 3. Precambrian of the Marquette area, Michigan. (98)
1971		Geology of the Lake Erie Islands and adjacent shores.
1972		Niagaran stratigraphy; Hamilton, Ontario.
1973		Geology and the environment; man, earth and nature in northwestern lower Michigan.
1974		Silurian reef-evaporite relationships.
1976		Devonian strata of Emmet and Charlevoix counties, Michigan.

AzTeS	1950, 57-59, 62, 67, 69
CLU-G/G	1947, 48, 50, 72

(165) Michigan Basin Geological Society.

CLhC	1962
CSdS	1950
CU-EART	1951, 52, 54-57, 70, 72, 73
CaAC	1956
[CaACAM]	1965, 68
CaACl	1968
[CaBVU]	1954, 57, 59, 60
CaOHM	1950-52, 56-63, 67-70, 73, 74
CaOKQ	1950-63, 65, 67-71
CaOLU	1946, 49, 50, 52-63, 65, 66, 68, 70, 73
CaOOG	1948, 50-63, 65, 66
CaOWtU	1950-52, 57-63, 65, 68-72
CoG	1948-63, 65-74
CoU	1954, 69, 70
DI-GS	1937, 46-73
ICF	1947-52, 54-63, 66, 68, 70-73
ICIU-S	1955, 56, 58-74
ICarbS	1966, 69
IEN	1947-50, 52, 54, 56-63, 65-74
[I-GS]	1959, 66, 71, 73, 74
IU	1946, 47, 49-52, 54-63, 65-74
IaU	1950, 52, 54, 57-59, 61-63, 65-74
InLP	1947, 50, 52, 55, 57-63, 66-70
InRE	1953, 55, 63
InU	1940, 47-52, 54-57, 59-64, 66, 69-74
KyU	1950-52, 57-63, 66-70, 73
MH-GS	1970
MNS	1954, 66
MiDW	1950-52, 54-63, 65, 67-69, 71-73
MiHM	1935, 37-41, 44, 46-63, 65-72
MiU	1971, 72
MnU	1948, 50-52, 54-68
MoSW	1966, 69
MoU	1950, 52, 55, 57-63, 66-74
[Ms-GS]	1954, 55
NBiSU	1969, 73
NNC	1946-57, 59-63
NOneoU	1969
NRU	1970
NSyU	1969, 73
NbU	1950-63, 65-74
NcU	1950, 52, 57-60, 62-64, 66-68
NdU	1950, 52, 57-60, 63, 66-69, 73
NhD	1950-74
NjP	1950, 52, 57, 58, 68-74
OCU	1950, 52, 57-60, 62, 63, 66-69, 71-74
OU	1946-55, 57-59, 61, 62, 65, 67-73
OkT	1956
OkU	1948-63, 66-69, 74
PBL	1966
PBm	1969
PSt	1954-56
SdRM	1962, 63, 66
TMM	1957

TxDaAR-T	1949, 50, 54, 56-61, 63, 66-70, 71, 73
TxDaDM	1948, 50-63, 65-70, 72, 74
TxDaM	1947, 48, 50-52, 54-63, 65, 66
TxDaSM	1948, 50-63, 70, 74
TxHSD	1957, 59, 62, 63, 71
TxHU	1954-60, 63, 65-70
TxLT	1956
TxMM	1955-57, 70
TxU	1946-63, 65-71
TxU-Da	1950-68
UU	1956
ViBlbV	1956
WU	1947, 57-63, 65-74, 76

(166) MICHIGAN. EASTERN MICHIGAN UNIVERSITY, YPSILANTI. EARTH SCIENCE FIELD STUDY.

1959 — No. 1. Glacial geology of central and western Washtenaw County; Field study 1, A traverse from Ypsilanti to Waterloo Recreation Area and return; Cary drifts of the Erie and Saginaw lobes, their genesis and surface expression.

InU	1959

MICHIGAN GEOLOGICAL SOCIETY. See MICHIGAN BASIN GEOLOGICAL SOCIETY. (165)

(167) MICHIGAN TECHNOLOGICAL UNIVERSITY.

1965 — Geology of the Lake Superior region.

NSyU	1965

(168) MICHIGAN. UNIVERSITY. MUSEUM OF PALEONTOLOGY. PAPERS ON PALEONTOLOGY.

1974 — No. 7 — Devonian strata of Emmett and Charlevoix counties, Michigan.

NdU	1974

(169) MICHIGAN. WESTERN MICHIGAN UNIVERSITY. DEPARTMENT OF GEOLOGY.

1970 — Studies in geology.
No. 1. Coastal sedimentation of southeastern Lake Michigan; field trip guidebook.

1972 — A field guide to the geology of southwestern Michigan (Publication ES-1).

1973 — Source book and field guide to the geology of the west-central lower peninsula of Michigan (Publication ES-2).

CaOLU	1972
CaOOG	1973
IU	1972, 73
InLP	1972
InRE	1972
InU	1972
KyU	1972
MiHM	1972
NjP	1972
OU	1970, 73
TMM	1972
TxDaSM	1970
TxU	1970

(170) MIDWESTERN GEOLOGICAL SOCIETY. WICHITA FALLS, TEXAS.

1961 See Southwestern Association of Student Geological Societies. (294)

(171) MINERALOGICAL ASSOCIATION OF CANADA.

1963 See Geological Association of Canada. (94)
1966 See Geological Association of Canada. (94)
1967 See Geological Association of Canada. (94)
1968 See British Columbia. University. (52)
1969 See Geological Association of Canada. (94)
1970 See Geological Association of Canada. (94)
1975 See Geological Society of America. North Central Section. (98)

(172) MINERALOGICAL SOCIETY OF AMERICA.

1965 See American Crystallographic Association. (19)

(173) MINERALOGICAL SOCIETY OF UTAH. FIELD TRIP.

1958 Apr. Gold Hill, Utah, Clifton district, Tooele County.
May Birds Eye marble quarry, Birds Eye, Utah.
Aug. Park City via Brighton.
DI-GS 1958

(174) MINNESOTA ACADEMY OF SCIENCE. GUIDEBOOK.

1964 Guidebook to the geology of the Duluth area.
MnU 1964

(175) MINNESOTA. GEOLOGICAL SURVEY. BULLETIN.

1925 No. 20 A guidebook to Minnesota Trunk Highway No. 1.
1964 See Friends of the Pleistocene. Midwest Group. (90)

[A-GS] 1925
CLU-G/G 1925
CU-EART 1925
CaOKQ 1925
CaOON 1925, 64
CoG 1925
CoU 1925
DI-GS 1925, 64
ICF 1925
IU 1925
IaU 1925, 64
InU 1925
KyU 1925
MNS 1925
MnU 1925, 64
MoSW 1925
MoU 1925
NSyU 1925
NhD 1925
NjP 1925

NvU	1925
OU	1925
OkT	1925
OrU	1925
PSt	1925
RPB	1925
TxDaDM	1925
TxDaM	1925
TxHU	1925
TxLT	1925
UU	1925
ViBlbV	1925
WU	1925

(176) MINNESOTA. GEOLOGICAL SURVEY. FIELD TRIP GUIDEBOOK.

1968 Geological field trip in the Rochester, Minnesota area.

1972 No. 2. Field trip guidebook for lower Precambrian volcanic-sedimentary rocks of the Vermilion district, Minnesota. (96)

No. 3. Field trip guide book for Precambrian rocks of the North Shore Volcanic Group, northeastern Minnesota. (96)

No. 4. Field trip guide book for Paleozoic and Mesozoic rocks of southeastern Minnesota.

No. 5. Field trip guide book for Precambrian migmatitic terrane of the Minnesota River valley. (96)

No. 6. Field trip guide book for Precambrian geology of northwestern Cook County, Minnesota. (96)

No. 7. Field trip guide book for geomorphology and Quaternary stratigraphy of western Minnesota and eastern South Dakota. (96)

No. 8. Field trip guide book for hydrogeology of the Twin Cities artesian basin. (96)

CLU-G/G	1972
DI-GS	1972
InRE	1972
MiHM	1972
MiKW	1968, 72
MnDuU	1972(8)
MnU	1968
TxDaAR-T	1972(2)

(177) MINNESOTA. UNIVERSITY. DULUTH BRANCH.

1959 No title but subject is the [Pleistocene glacial deposits and granitic outcrops from Duluth to Burntside Lake, Minnesota.]

OkU	1959

(178) MISSISSIPPI GEOLOGICAL SOCIETY. GUIDEBOOK FOR THE FIELD TRIPS.

1940	1st	Jackson to Recent.
	2nd	Claiborne and Wilcox.
	3rd	Upper Cretaceous of Mississippi and Alabama.
	4th	Northwest Alabama Paleozoics.
1945	5th	Eutaw-Tuscaloosa.
1948	6th	Upper Eocene, Oligocene and lower Miocene of central Mississippi.
1949	7th	Pre-Cambrian and Paleozoic rocks of northern Alabama and south-central Tennessee.

1950	8th	Cretaceous of Mississippi and south Tennessee.
1952	9th	Claiborne of western Alabama and eastern Mississippi.
1953	10th	Wilcox and Midway groups, west-central Alabama. Supplement; road log, [1957].
1954	11th	Paleozoic rocks, central Tennessee and northwest Alabama.
1956	13th	Covering outcrops of the Vicksburg, Jackson, Claiborne and Wilcox groups of central Mississippi.
1959	14th	Upper Cretaceous outcrops, northeast Mississippi and west-central Alabama.
1960	15th	Cenozoic of southeastern Mississippi and southwestern Alabama.
1962	16th	Paleozoics of northwest Arkansas: Magnet Cove, Arkansas Valley, Ouachita Mountains, Ozark Highlands.

[A-GS]	1940(2-4), 45, 48-50, 52-54, 59, 60, 62
AzTeS	1948, 49, 52, 54, 59-62
CLU-G/G	1945, 48-50, 52-54, 59, 60, 62
CLhC	1945, 48, 49, 52-54
CSdS	1948, 49, 52, 54, 59-62
CU-EART	1948, 49, 53, 54, 59, 62
CaACM	1949, 52-54
[CaBVU]	1962
CaOHM	1948, 49, 52, 54, 59-62
CaOKQ	1948, 49, 54, 59, 60, 62
CaOWtU	1940
CoG	1945, 48-50, 52-54, 59, 60, 62
DFPC	1960
DI-GS	1940, 54, 56, 59, 60, 62
ICF	1948, 49, 52, 54, 59-62
ICarbS	1940, 45, 48-50, 52-54
IEN	1945-49, 60, 62
[I-GS]	1949
IU	1945, 48, 49, 52-54, 59, 60, 62
InLP	1948, 49, 52, 54, 59-62
InU	1945, 48-50, 52-54, 59-62
KyU	1945, 48-50, 52-54, 59, 60, 62
LU	1940, 45, 48-50, 52-54, 59, 60, 62
MNS	1945
MiHM	1962
MiKW	1945
MiU	1945-49, 52, 54, 59-62
MnU	1945, 48-50, 52-54, 59, 60, 62
MoSW	1945, 48-50, 52, 53, 60, 62
MoU	1945, 48, 54, 62
[Ms-GS]	1948-52, 54-62
MtU	1948, 49, 52, 54, 59, 62
NBiSU	1948, 49, 52, 54, 59-62
NNC	1940(2), 48-50, 52-54, 59, 60, 62
NhD	1948-54, 56-62
NjP	1940, 48-62
OU	1945-54, 59-62
[OkOkCGe]	1940-48, 50, 52
OkT	1940, 45, 48, 49, 53, 56, 59, 62
OkU	1940-54, 59-62
OrU	1948, 49, 62
PSt	1952-54, 59-62

RPB	1945
TMM	1948, 49, 52, 54, 59-62
TU	1949, 54
TxDaAR-T	1940(2-4), 45, 48-50, 52-54, 60, 62
TxDaDM	1945, 48-50, 52-54, 59, 60, 62
TxDaM	1948-50, 52, 54, 59, 60, 62
TxDaSM	1948, 52-54, 56, 60, 62
TxHSD	1948, 50, 52, 54, 62
TxHU	1940(1,2,4), 45-54, 59-62
TxLT	1940(4), 45-53
TxMM	1940(1,3,4), 45, 48
TxU	1940, 45, 48-50, 52-54, 59, 60, 62
TxU-Da	1940(2-4), 53
UU	1948, 49, 54
ViBlbV	1948, 49, 52, 54, 62
WU	1945-49, 52, 54, 59-62

(179) MISSISSIPPI. UNIVERSITY. GEOLOGICAL SOCIETY.

1972 The classical Tertiary of southwest Alabama.
[Ms-GS] 1972

(180) MISSISSIPPI VALLEY FIELD CONFERENCE. GUIDEBOOK.

1949 Natchez, Mississippi to Montgomery, Louisiana.
Loess in the southern Mississippi Valley.
IaU 1949

MISSOURI. DIVISION OF GEOLOGICAL SURVEY AND WATER RESOURCES. See MISSOURI. GEOLOGICAL SURVEY. (181)

(181) MISSOURI. GEOLOGICAL SURVEY. [MISCELLANEOUS PUBLICATION].

1960 Guidebook to the geology of the Rolla area emphasizing solution phenomena. (30)

IU	1960
MoSW	1960
NSyU	1960
ViBlbV	1960

(182) MISSOURI GEOLOGICAL SURVEY. REPORT OF INVESTIGATIONS.

1952	No. 13	West-central Missouri. (147)
1954	No. 17	Southeastern and south-central Missouri. (147)
1955	No. 20	Western Missouri: Desmoinesian section, cyclic sedimentation. (41)
1958	No. 25	Pennsylvanian (Desmoinesian of Missouri). (96)
1961	No. 26	St. Francois Mountain area. (41)
	No. 27	See Kansas Geological Society. (147)
1965	No. 30	No. 4. Cryptoexplosive structures in Missouri. (96)
	No. 31	No. 5. Geology of the Kansas City Group at Kansas City. (96)
1966	No. 34	Middle Ordovician and Mississippian strata, St. Louis and St. Charles counties, Missouri. (12)
1967	No. 37	Geology between Springfield and Branson, Missouri, emphasizing stratigraphy and cavern development.
1975	No. 58	Guidebook to the geology and ore deposits of selected mines in the Viburnum Trend, Missouri.

(182) Missouri Geological Survey. Report of Investigations.

[A-GS]	1954, 61
CLU-G/G	1952, 54, 55, 58, 61, 65-67, 75
CLhC	1955, 61
CU-EART	1952-75
CaACM	1954
[CaBVU]	1961, 65
CaOLU	1954, 61
CaOKQ	1954
CaOOG	1954
CoG	1954, 61, 67
DFPC	1961
DI-GS	1939, 52, 54, 55, 58, 61, 65-67
DLC	1965
ICF	1954, 61(26), 67, 75
ICarbS	1954, 61(26)
IEN	1952-75
[I-GS]	1952, 54, 58, 61(26), 65-75
IU	1952-75
IaU	1939, 52, 54, 55, 61, 65-67
InRE	1961, 66, 67
InU	1952-65, 67
KyU	1939, 52, 54, 55, 58, 61, 65-67
LU	1954, 61, 67
MNS	1952-67
MiDW	1954, 61, 67
MiKW	1961
MnU	1952, 54, 55, 61, 65, 66
MoSW	1954, 61, 67
MoU	1961(26), 67
NBiSU	1965(31)
NNC	1966
NSyU	1952-67
NbU	1954-75
NcU	1952, 54, 58-66
NdU	1954, 61(26), 67, 75
NhD	1952-67
NjP	1954, 61(26), 67
NvU	1967
OCU	1954, 61(26), 67, 75
OU	1954
OkT	1954, 61(26), 67
OkU	1954, 61, 65(31), 67
OrU	1952-67
PBL	1961
PPiGulf	1954
PSt	1952, 54, 55, 58, 61, 65-67
RPB	1962-67
SdRM	1961(26), 67
TxDaAR-T	1954
TxDaDM	1954, 61(26,27), 67
TxDaM	1954, 61
TxDaSM	1954

TxHSD	1954, 61(26)
TxHU	1954, 61, 67
TxLT	1954, 61(26), 67
TxMM	1952, 55, 58
TxU	1954, 61, 67
TxU-Da	1952, 54, 58, 65(30)
UU	1954
ViBlbV	1954, 61(26), 67
WU	1954, 61(26), 67, 75

(183) MISSOURI. UNIVERSITY. GEOLOGY CLUB. FIELD TRIP GUIDE BOOK.

1949 See Sigma Gamma Epsilon. (263)
1950 [Ordovician, Devonian, Mississippian, and Pennsylvanian, central Missouri.]
1951 Kansas River valley, northeast Kansas, Upper Pennsylvanian and Lower Permian.
1955 A study of the Ordovician, Devonian, Mississippian and Pennsylvanian.

[I-GS]	1951
MnDuU	1950
MoU	1950, 55
NjP	1950
TxHU	1950
TxLT	1950, 55
TxU	1955

(184) MONTANA. BUREAU OF MINES AND GEOLOGY.

1937 See Rocky Mountain Association of Geologists. (250)

(185) MONTANA. BUREAU OF MINES AND GEOLOGY. SPECIAL PUBLICATION.

1976 No. 73 Guidebook; the Tobacco Root Geological Society 1976 field conference.

IU	1976

(186) MONTANA GEOLOGICAL SOCIETY. GUIDEBOOK FOR THE ANNUAL FIELD CONFERENCE.

1950 1st Trip through western Montana, covering the stratigraphic sections from the Cambrian to the Tertiary.
1951 2nd Rocks of Mississippian age (Big Snowy Group) and the overlying unconformity, central Montana.
1952 3rd Black Hills and Williston Basin.
1953 4th The Little Rocky Mountains, Montana, and southwestern Saskatchewan.
1954 5th Pryor Mountain, northern Bighorn Basin.
1955 6th Sweetgrass arch-disturbed belt, Montana.
1956 7th Judith Mountains, central Montana.
1957 8th Crazy Mountain Basin.
1958 9th Beartooth Uplift and Sunlight Basin. (354)
1959 10th Sawtooth-disturbed belt area.
1960 11th West Yellowstone earthquake area.
1961 12th Float trip; Bighorn River from Kane, Wyoming to Yellowtail Dam site.
1962 13th Three Forks-Belt Mountains area and symposium; the Devonian system of Montana and adjacent areas.
1963 14th Northern Powder River basin. (350)
1964 15th Third International Williston Basin symposium.
1965 16th Geology of Flint Creek Range, Montana. (187)

1966	17th	[Symposium] Jurassic and Cretaceous stratigraphic traps, Sweetgrass arch.
1967	18th	Centennial Basin of southwest Montana.
1968		No guidebook published.
1969	20th	Eastern Montana symposium; the economic geology of eastern Montana and adjacent areas.
1972	21st	Crazy Mountains Basin.
1975	22nd	Energy resources of Montana. No field trip.

AzTeS	1950, 52-62, 64, 66-69, 72, 75
AzU	1959, 72
CChiS	1958
CLU-G/G	1950-62, 64-69, 72
CLhC	1951-65, 69
CSdS	1950-54, 69, 72
CSfCSM	1960
CU-EART	1950-69, 72
CaAC	1952, 55, 58, 62, 63
[CaACAM]	1950-58, 60, 62-67, 69, 72, 75
CaACI	1950, 52-58, 62, 65, 66, 69
CaACM	1950-60, 62, 65-69
[CaBVU]	1950-54, 57, 59, 60, 62
CaOHM	1953-62, 65-67
CaOKQ	1952, 53, 55, 57-60, 62-67
CaOOG	1950, 52-62, 64-67, 69
CaOONM	1952, 53
CaOWtU	1962, 72
CoG	1950-67, 69
[CoPU]	1952-57, 59, 61, 62, 66
CoU	1950-62, 64-67, 69, 72
DI-GS	1950-67, 69, 72
ICF	1952-62, 66, 67
ICarbS	1953-60, 62, 64, 65
IEN	1950-60, 62, 64-67, 69, 72, 75
IU	1950-67, 69, 72, 75
IaU	1950-67, 69, 72
IdBB	1952-60, 62, 63, 66, 67
IdPI	1952-61
InLP	1950-63, 65-67, 69, 72
InRE	1950-56
InU	1950-67, 69, 72
KyU	1950-67, 69
LU	1950-62, 64-67, 69, 72, 75
MNS	1950-59
MiDW	1950-62, 66, 67, 69
MiHM	1959, 65
MiKW	1954-56, 62
MnU	1950-67, 69
MoRM	1950-62
MoSW	1950-60
MtBC	1950-67, 69, 72, 75
MtU	1950, 52-67, 69
NNC	1951-62, 65, 66
NRU	1952-62

NSyU	1952, 53, 55-57, 59-63, 65-69, 72
NbU	1950-63, 65-67, 69, 72
NcU	1950-60, 62, 65-67, 69
NdU	1950-58, 60, 62, 65-67, 69
NhD	1950-69, 72
NjP	1950-62, 65-67, 69, 72
NvU	1953-63, 65-67, 69, 72
OCU	1950-55, 57-60, 62, 66, 67, 69, 72
OU	1950-67, 69, 72
[OkOkCGe]	1950-60, 66
OkT	1950-60, 62
OkU	1950-69
OrU	1950-62, 65-67, 69, 72
PBL	1950-62, 65-69
PPiGulf	1952, 54, 55, 59, 67, 69
PSt	1950-62, 65-67, 69, 72, 75
RPB	1950-60, 62-67, 69
SdRM	1950-63, 67, 72
SdU	1950, 52-60, 62, 65-67, 69
TU	1953-60, 62, 65, 66
TxDaAR-T	1950-62, 65-67, 69, 72
TxDaDM	1950-62, 64-67, 69
TxDaM	1951-62, 65
TxDaSM	1950-66, 69
TxHSD	1951-60, 62, 65-67, 69
TxHU	1950-62, 65-67, 69, 72
TxLT	1950-60, 62
TxMM	1950-62, 64-67, 69, 72
TxU	1950-62, 64-67, 69, 72
TxU-Da	1950-66, 69
UU	1950-62
ViBlbV	1950-62
WU	1950, 52-62, 64-67, 69, 72
WyU	1950-67

(187) MONTANA. UNIVERSITY. GEOLOGY DEPARTMENT.

1965 See Montana Geological Society. (186)

(188) NATIONAL ASSOCIATION OF GEOLOGY TEACHERS. EAST CENTRAL SECTION. ANNUAL MEETING AND FIELD TRIP.

1953		Field excursion to Serpent Mound crypto-volcanic structure, Adams County, Ohio.
1957		Gravel deposits of the Ann Arbor region.
1962		No title; [bedrock and glacial geology of the Bellefontaine outlier].
1964		The geology of southeastern Indiana, mostly glacial.
1966	1st	Some geological aspects of the Carboniferous of southern Indiana.
	fall	Southeastern New York.
1967		Middle Coastal Plain, Virginia.
1974		Energy reserves, Canton-Cadiz area.

DI-GS	1966, 67, 74
IU	1964
InU	1966
OU	1953, 57, 62

(189) NATIONAL ASSOCIATION OF GEOLOGY TEACHERS. EASTERN SECTION. ANNUAL SPRING FIELD TRIP.

1966 Field Trip No. 1. Glacial geology and geomorphology between Cortland and Syracuse.
Field Trip No. 2. Paleontology and stratigraphy of the Cortland-Syracuse-Ithaca area.
1968 Field Trip A. The Silurian-Ordovician angular unconformity, southeastern New York.
Field Trip B. The Rosendale readvance in the lower Wallkill Valley, New York.
1972 Field Trip No. 1. Geology of the Ramapo fault system.
Field Trip No. 2. Geomorphology of northern New Jersey and part of eastern Pennsylvania.
Field Trip No. 3. Sedimentology and general structure of the northern portion of the Newark Basin.
Field Trip No. 4. Mineralogy-petrology trip to northwestern New Jersey.
Field Trip No. 5. Cretaceous-Tertiary greensands and their fauna, New Jersey coastal plain.
1973 Field Trip No. 1. The geology of Chestnut Ridge anticline of Laurel Caverns, Fayette County, Pennsylvania.
Field Trip No. 2. Engineering geology at two sites on Interstate 279 and Interstate 79 northwest of Pittsburgh, Pennsylvania.
Field Trip No. 3. Nuclear power.
CaOWtU 1966, 68, 72, 73
InRE 1972

(190) NATIONAL ASSOCIATION OF GEOLOGY TEACHERS. FAR WESTERN SECTION.

1966		Berkeley Hills.
1971	Oct.	Camino Cielo field trip guidebook (to southern Santa Barbara County).
1972	18th	Groundwater geology of northern Sacramento County.
	Oct.	Geologic guidebook to the northern peninsular ranges, Orange and Riverside counties, California. (288)
		Some geologic hazards and environmental impact of development in the San Diego area, California.
1973	19th	Field trip to areas of active faulting and shallow subsidence in the southern San Joaquin Valley, California.
1974	20th	Oceanographic field trip, San Francisco Bay area.
	June	Geologic sites in Ventura County (teachers guide).
	Oct.	Northern California field trip.
1975	Mar.	Three field trips in southern California.
	Oct.	The Sierran superjacent and bedrock series in southwestern Placer County.

[CDU] 1966
CLU-G/G 1971, 72(Oct.)
CLhC 1972(Oct.)
CSdS 1972(Oct.)
DI-GS 1972(Oct.)
IU 1972(Oct.)
OU 1972(Oct.)

(191) NATIONAL ASSOCIATION OF GEOLOGY TEACHERS. NORTH CENTRAL SECTION. GUIDEBOOK.

1969 Geology of northeastern North Dakota. (217)
CLU-G/G 1969
CU-EART 1969
ICF 1969
InU 1969
MiHM 1969
MoU 1969

NSyU	1969
NbU	1969
NdU	1969
TxDaAR-T	1969

(192) NATIONAL ASSOCIATION OF GEOLOGY TEACHERS. SOUTHWEST SECTION.

1970	Four Corners, Colorado Plateau, central Rocky Mountain section.
1971	Guidebook to eastern Basin and Range, Colorado Plateau, southern Rocky Mountains.

AzFU	1970
CChiS	1970
CaOLU	1971
CoDuF	1970
CoG	1971
DI-GS	1970, 71
ICarbS	1970
InLP	1970, 71
InU	1970
KyU	1970
NdU	1970
PSt	1970
TxDaAR-T	1970, 71
TxDaDM	1970
TxMM	1970, 71
WaPS	1970

(193) NATIONAL CONFERENCE ON CLAYS AND CLAY MINERALS. PROCEEDINGS. GUIDEBOOK TO THE FIELD EXCURSIONS.

1952	1st	Clays and clay-technology. (54)
1953	2nd	[Clays of east-central Missouri in the vicinity of Columbia, McCredie, Auxvasse, Mexico, and Hermann.]
1954	3rd	No guidebook.
1955	4th	Clay minerals in sedimentary rocks.
1956	5th	[Early Tazewell moraines (Illinois).]
1957	6th	Ione clay area.
1958	7th	Northeastern Maryland and northern Delaware. (194)
1959	8th	Wichita Mountain area, southwestern Oklahoma.
1960	9th	[West Lafayette to High Bridge (Indiana).]
1961	10th	Field excursion, central Texas, bentonites, uranium-bearing rocks, vermiculites. (Texas. University. Bureau of Economic Geology. Guidebook No. 3.) (308)
1962	11th	Gatineau area, Quebec, Canada.
1963	12th	Attapulgite fuller's earth localities in Georgia and Florida.
1964-67	13-15th	No field trip held.
1968		Superseded by the periodical, Clays and clay minerals, Vol. 16.
1969	18th	Field excursion: east Texas, clay, glauconite, ironstone deposits. (308)

CLU-G/G	1953, 55-60, 62, 63
CLhC	1953, 55-63
CSdS	1956-63
CU-EART	1952, 56-63
CaACU	1957-63
[CaBVU]	1953, 55-57, 59, 60, 62, 63
CaOHM	1952-63

(193) National Conference on Clays and Clay Minerals.

CaOKQ	1953, 55-63
CaOLU	1952, 53, 55-63
CaOOG	1952-66
CoU	1953-60, 62, 63
DI-GS	1953, 55-63
ICF	1952-54, 56, 59, 60
IEN	1958
[I-GS]	1953, 55-61, 63
IU	1953-63
IaU	1953, 55-63
IdBB	1960, 62
InU	1952-63, 69
KyU	1953, 55-63, 69
LU	1953, 55-66
MNS	1957
MiDW	1953, 55-60, 62, 63
MiHM	1953, 55-57, 60, 62, 63
MoSW	1953-68
MoU	1952, 53, 55-60, 62, 63, 69
NSyU	1952, 61
NbU	1952, 53, 55-63
NcU	1952, 53, 55-62
NdU	1952, 53, 55-57, 59, 60, 62, 63
NhD	1953-63
NjP	1952-69
OCU	1953-60, 62, 63
OU	1953, 55-60, 62, 63
OkT	1953, 55, 57-60, 62
OkU	1962
OrU	1953, 55-63
PBL	1952, 53, 55-66
PSt	1932, 53-63
RPB	1952-67
TMM	1955, 57-62
TxDaAR-T	1953-63
TxDaSM	1952, 53, 55, 57-63
TxHU	1953, 55-66
TxMM	1959, 62
TxU	1953, 55-63
WU	1953, 55-60, 62, 63

(194) NATIONAL RESEARCH COUNCIL. COMMITTEE ON CLAY MINERALS. GUIDEBOOK TO THE FIELD EXCURSION.

1958 See National Conference on Clays and Clay Minerals. (193)

(195) NATIONAL SPELEOLOGICAL SOCIETY. GUIDE BOOK SERIES.

1960	1st	Carlsbad Caverns National Park.
1961	2nd	Field trip. Caves in Tennessee, Alabama, Georgia.
1962	3rd	Caves of the Black Hills, North Dakota.
1963	4th	Major caves in the vicinity of Mountain Lake, Virginia.
1964	5th	Caves of Texas.

1965	6th	1965 convention, Bloomington, Indiana.
1966	7th	Caves of the Sequoia region, California.
1967	8th	Caves of Alabama.
1968		Development of a karst area.
1971		30th Anniversary Guidebook. (The Region Record, Vol. 1, No. 4.)
		Section 3. Convention special tours.
		[1] Karstlands excursion to southwest Virginia.
		[2] Geology field trip.
		[3] Biological tour of Greenbrier Caverns.
		[4] Scenic diversions in the Blacksburg area.
1972		Selected caves of the Pacific northwest; with particular reference to the volcano-speleology of the state of Washington.
1973		[Caves of Indiana.]
1974		Upper Mississippi Valley cave region.
1975		Description of caves in the Great Basin area: California-Nevada-Oregon.

CLU-G/G	1966
CU-EART	1962, 66, 67, 71-73
CaOHM	1966
DI-GS	1960-67, 72-75
IU	1960, 62, 63, 67
InLP	1965-67
InU	1965
KyU	1967
OCU	1960, 72, 73

(196) NEBRASKA ACADEMY OF SCIENCE.

1965	7th	Central and south-central Alaska; a guidebook for field conference F.

(197) NEBRASKA GEOLOGICAL SOCIETY. FIELD CONFERENCE GUIDEBOOK.

1970	2nd	Re-exploring the Missouri.
1974		Mineral aggregate industries in southeast Nebraska.

NbU	1974

(198) NEBRASKA. GEOLOGICAL SURVEY. GUIDEBOOKS.

1966	Evidence of multiple glaciation in the glacial peri-glacial area of eastern Nebraska.
1967	Centennial guidebook to the geology of southeastern Nebraska. (38)
1969	Field guide, Sarpy County-Gretna State Fish Hatchery area.
1970	Guidebook to the geology along the Missouri River bluffs of southeastern Nebraska and adjacent areas.
	Re-exploring the Missouri.
1971	No. 1. Guidebook to selected Pleistocene paleosols in eastern Nebraska.
	No. 2. Guidebook for field trip on urban geology in eastern Nebraska.
	No. 3. Guidebook to the geology along portions of the lower Platte River valley and Weeping Water valley of eastern Nebraska.
	No. 4. Guidebook to the late Pliocene and early Pleistocene of Nebraska.

CLU-G/G	1967, 71(4)
CU-EART	1971(4)
CaOOG	1967
CoU	1966, 67, 70, 71
DI-GS	1967

(198) Nebraska. Geological Survey. Guidebooks.

[I-GS]	1967, 70, 71
IU	1967
IaU	1971
InU	1967, 70, 71(3)
KyU	1967, 71
MiKW	1966, 70, 71
MnU	1967, 70
MoSW	1967
[Ms-GS]	1971(1,2)
NdU	1967, 70, 71(2-4)
NjP	1971(4)
NvU	1966, 67, 70, 71
OU	1967, 70
OkU	1967, 70, 71(2,3)
TxU	1967, 70
UU	1970
WU	1967, 69, 70, 71(2-4)

(199) NEBRASKA. STATE MUSEUM.

1941 Guide for a field conference on the Tertiary and Pleistocene of Nebraska. (285)

NbU	1941
NjP	1941

(200) NEBRASKA. UNIVERSITY. DEPARTMENT OF GEOLOGY. ANNUAL SPRING FIELD TRIP.

n.d.	2nd	The Paleozoic of the central United States. Road log.
1951	3rd	Geology of west Texas.
1954	Apr.	West Texas.
1956	8th	(No title, no log and no date)
1959		West Texas.

NbU	n.d., 1951, 54, 56, 59

(201) NEVADA GEOLOGICAL SOCIETY.

1962 See Geological Society of Sacramento. (107)

(202) NEVADA. NEVADA BUREAU OF MINES AND GEOLOGY. REPORT.

1966 Dixie Valley-Fairview Peak (Nevada) earthquake area field trip.

1974 Guidebook to the geology of four Tertiary volcanic centers in central Nevada. (Nevada Bureau of Mines and Geology. Report 19.) (97)

Field Trip No. 4. Interbasin ground-water flow in southern Nevada. (Nevada Bureau of Mines and Geology. Report 20.) (97)

1975 Guidebook to the Quaternary geology along the western flank of the Truckee Meadows, Washoe County, Nevada. (Nevada Bureau of Mines and Geology. Report 22.) (97)

CLU-G/G	1974(20)
IU	1974
InU	1974(19), 75
MH-GS	1974(19)
MoU	1974(19)
NdU	1975
NjP	1974(19)
NvU	1966
WU	1975

(203) NEVADA. UNIVERSITY. MACKAY SCHOOL OF MINES. DEPARTMENT OF GEOLOGY AND GEOGRAPHY.

1956		Guidebook for the December 16, 1954, Dixie Valley-Fairview Peak earthquake area field trip. CU-EART 1956

NEW ENGLAND GEOLOGICAL ASSOCIATION. See NEW ENGLAND INTERCOLLEGIATE GEOLOGICAL CONFERENCE. (204)

(204) NEW ENGLAND INTERCOLLEGIATE GEOLOGICAL CONFERENCE. ANNUAL MEETING GUIDEBOOK.

1938	34th	Central Vermont marble belt.
1947		Rhode Island, glacial and shoreland features.
1948		Trip No. 1. Roxbury and Waterbury areas, Vermont.
		Trip No. 2. Bedrock geology of the Burlington area.
		Trip No. 3. Glacial geology.
1951		Purgatory Chasm in Sutton, Massachusetts.
1952		Geology of the Bennington Quadrangle [and four other trips].
1953		Triassic sedimentary rocks of central Connecticut, their petrology, petrography, stratigraphy and structure.
		Trip A. From Summit Street, Hartford...to Durham and Highway 77.
		Trip B. Hartland Formation and Nonewaug Granite trip.
		Trip C. Surficial geology of the Hartford, Connecticut area.
		Trip D. Crystallines of the eastern highlands quadrangles, Manchester and Rockville.
		Trip E. Problems of the crystalline rocks west of New Haven.
1954	46th	Glacial geology of the Hanover region [and five other trips].
1957	49th	Geology of northern part; Connecticut Valley.
1959	51st	Stratigraphy and structure of west-central Vermont and adjacent New York.
1960	52nd	West-central Maine.
1961	53rd	Vermont geologic map centennial, Montpelier.
1962	54th	Area around Montreal.
1963	55th	Geology of Rhode Island.
1964	56th	Boston area and vicinity.
1965	57th	Field trips in southern Maine.
1966	58th	Mt. Katahdin region, Maine.
1967	59th	Connecticut Valley of Massachusetts.
1968	60th	Guidebook for field trips in Connecticut. (70)
1969	61st	New York, Massachusetts and Vermont.
1970	62nd	Guidebook for field trips in the Rangeley Lakes-Dead River basin, western Maine.
1971	63rd	Guidebook for field trips in central New Hampshire and contiguous areas.
		Trip A-1. Glacial features of the Winnipesaukee Wolfeboro area.
		Trip A-2. Peterborough Quadrangle.
		Trip A-3. The Cardigan pluton of the Kinsman quartz monzonite.
		Trip A-4. Geology of the Macoma mantled gneiss dome near Hanover, New Hampshire.
		Trip A-5. Southwest side of the Ossipee Mountains, New Hampshire.
		Trip A-6. Recumbent and reclined folds of the Mt. Cube area, New Hampshire-Vermont.
		Trip A-7. The Hillsboro plutonic series in southeastern New Hampshire; field criteria in support of a partial melting petrogenetic model.
		Trip A-8. Bedrock geology of the Ossipee Lake area.
		Trip B-1. Jackson estuarine laboratory; sedimentation on Great Bay estuarine system; solid waste disposal in Gulf of Maine.
		Guidebook Supplement. Origin and distribution of gravel on Broad Cave beach, Appledore Island, Maine.
		Trip B-2. Geology of the Holderness Quadrangle.

Trip B-3. Geologic review of the Belknap Mountain complex.
Trip B-4. Surficial geology of the Merrimack River valley between Manchester and Nashua, New Hampshire.
Trip B-5. Igneous rocks of the Seabrook, New Hampshire-Newbury, Massachusetts area.
Trip B-6. Geology of the Concord Quadrangle.

1972 64th Guidebook for field trips in Vermont.
Bedrock geology trips.
Trip B-1. Stratigraphy of the east flank of the Green Mountain anticlinorium, southern Vermont.
Trip B-2. Major structural features of the taconic allochthon in the Hoosick Falls area, New York-Vermont.
Trip B-3. Excursions at the north end of the taconic allochthon and the Middlebury synclinorium, west-central Vermont, with emphasis on the structure of the Sudbury nappe and associated parautochthonous elements.
Trip B-4. The Champlain thrust and related features near Middlebury, Vermont.
Trip B-5. Analysis and chronology of structures along the Champlain thrust west of the Hinesburg synclinorium.
Trip B-6. Sedimentary characteristics and tectonic deformation of Middle and Upper Ordovician shales of northwestern Vermont north of Mallets Bay.
Trip B-7. Rotated garnets and tectonism in southeast Vermont.
Trip B-8. Stratigraphic and structural relationships across the Green Mountain anticlinorium in north-central Vermont.
Trip B-9. Superposed folds and structural chronology along the southeastern part of the Hinesburg synclinorium.
Trip B-10. Lower Paleozoic rocks flanking the Green Mountain anticlinorium.
Trip B-11. Geology of the Guilford dome area, southeastern Vermont.
Trip B-12. Stratigraphic and structural problems of the southern part of the Green Mountain anticlinorium, Bennington-Wilmington, Vermont.
Trip B-13. Polymetamorphism in the Richmond area, Vermont.
Environmental geology trips.
Trip EG-1. Mount Mansfield trail erosion.
Trip EG-2. Feasibility and design studies; Champlain Valley sanitary landfill.
Glacial geology trips.
Trip G-1. Glacial history of central Vermont.
Trip G-2. Ice margins and water levels in northwestern Vermont.
Proglacial lakes in the Lamoille Valley, Vermont.
Trip G-3. Strandline features and late Pleistocene chronology of northwest Vermont.
Trip G-5. Till studies, Shelburne, Vermont.
Trip G-6. Woodfordian glacial history of the Champlain lowland, Burlington to Brandon, Vermont.
Lake studies trips.
Trip LS-1. The sludge bed at Fort Ticonderoga, New York.
Trip LS-2,LS-3. Sedimentological and limnological studies of Lake Champlain.
Paleontology trips.
Trip P-1. Ordovician paleontology and stratigraphy of the Champlain Islands.
Paleontology and stratigraphy of the Chazy Group (Middle Ordovician), Champlain Islands, Vermont.
Paleoecology of Chazy reef-mounds.
Trip P-2. Cambrian fossil localities in northwestern Vermont.

1973 Geology of New Brunswick, field guide to excursions.
Trip A-1. Zeolite mineral assemblage, Grand Manan Island, New Brunswick.
Trip A-2. The Variscan front in southern New Brunswick.
Trip A-3,B-6. The granitic rocks of southwestern New Brunswick.
Trip A-4. Carboniferous stratigraphy and sedimentology of the Chignecto Bay area, southern

New Brunswick.
Trip A-5. Structural geology of the Bathurst-Newcastle district.
Trip A-6. The Bathurst mining camp.
Trip A-7. Pointe Verte to tide head, Chaleur Bay area, New Brunswick.
Trip A-8,B-7. Acadian orogeny in coastal southern New Brunswick.
Trip A-9. Tectonic evolution and mineral deposits of the northern Appalachians in southern New Brunswick.
Trip A-12. Molybdenum, tungsten, and bismuth mineralization at Brunswick Tin Mines, Ltd.
Trip A-10,B-8. Post-Carboniferous and post-Triassic structures in southern New Brunswick.
Trip A-11. Minto coal fields.
Trip A-13. Saint John area.
Trip A-14,B-11. The Harvey volcanic area.
Trip B-1. Tungsten mineralization at Burnt Hill tungsten mine.
Trip B-2. Silurian rocks of the Fredericton area.
Trip B-4. Vertebrate sites of northern New Brunswick and the Gaspe.

1974 66th Geology of east-central and north-central Maine.
Trip A-1. Metamorphism in the Belfast area, Maine.
Trip A-2. Recession of the late Wisconsin Laurentide ice sheet in eastern Maine.
Trip A-3. Sedimentary and slump structures of central Maine.
Trip A-4. The geology of the Camden-Rockland area.
Trip A-5. General bedrock geology of northeastern Maine.
Trip A-6. Precambrian rocks of Seven Hundred Acre Island and development of cleavage in the Islesboro Formation.
Trip A-7. Igneous petrology of some plutons in the northern part of the Penobscott Bay area.
Trip A-8. The paleontology of the present; littoral environments on a submerged crystalline coast, Gouldsboro, Maine.
Trip B-1. Late Wisconsin and Holocene geological, botanical, and archaeological history of the Orono, Maine region.
Trip B-2. Bedrock geology of Mount Desert Island.
Trip B-3. Stratigraphy and structure of central Maine.
Trip B-4. Economic deposits at Blue Hill.
Trip B-5. The concentrically zoned Tunk Lake pluton; Devonian melting-anomaly activity?
Trip B-6. Buchan-type metamorphism of the Waterville pelite, south-central Maine.
Trip B-7. Bedrock geology of northern Penobscott Bay area.
Trip B-8. The paleontology of the present: littoral environments on a submerged crystalline coast, Gouldsboro, Maine.

1975 67th Guidebook for field trips in western Massachusetts, northern Connecticut and adjacent areas of New York.
Trip A-1. Some basement rocks from Bear Mountain to the Housatonic highlands.
Trip A-2. The Hudson estuary.
Trip A-3. Structural and stratigraphic chronology of the Taconide and Acadian polydeformational belt of the central Taconics of New York State and Massachusetts.
Trip B-1. Selected localities in the Taconics and the implications for the plate tectonic origin of the Taconic region.
Trip B-2. Fold-thrust tectonism in the southern Berkshire Massif, Connecticut and Massachusetts.
Trip B-3. Proposed Silurian-Devonian correlations east of the Berkshire Massif in western Massachusetts and Connecticut.
Trip B-4. Stratigraphic and structural relationships along the east side of the Berkshire Massif, Massachusetts.
Trip B-5. The Cambrian-Precambrian contact in northwestern Connecticut and west-central Massachusetts.
Trip B-6. Cross section of the Berkshire Massif at 42°N; profile of a basement reactivation zone.

Trip B-7. The late Quaternary geology of the Housatonic River basin in southwestern Massachusetts and adjacent Connecticut.
Trip B-8. The glacial geology of the Housatonic River region in northwestern Connecticut.
Trip B-9. Basement-cover rock relationships in the Pittsfield East Quadrangle, Massachusetts.
Trip B-10. General geology of the Stockbridge Valley marble belt.
Trip C-1. Repeat of B-1.
Trip C-2. Repeat of B-2.
Trip C-4. Repeat of B-4.
Trip C-5. Repeat of B-5.
Trip C-6. Repeat of B-6.
Trip C-7. Repeat of B-7.
Trip C-8. Boulder trains in western Massachusetts.
Trip C-9. Repeat of A-1.
Trip C-10. Stratigraphy and structural geology in the Amenia-Pawling Valley, Dutchess County, New York.
Trip C-11. Polyphase deformation in the metamorphosed Paleozoic rocks east of the Berkshire Massif.

[CDU]	1962
CLU-G/G	1957, 59, 61-75
CU-EART	1938, 57, 62-64, 66-69, 72
CaOHM	1963
CaOKQ	1965, 66, 68, 69
CaOLU	1962, 72
CaOOG	1959, 61, 62, 67, 70, 71, 74
CaOWtU	1972, 74
CoG	1964, 69
CoU	1967, 69
DI-GS	1938, 47, 48, 51-54, 59-69
ICIU-S	1967
ICarbS	1968
IEN	1938, 63, 68, 72
IU	1938, 57, 59, 61-75
IaU	1957, 63, 67, 68
InLP	1963
InRE	1967
InU	1938, 60, 62, 66, 68, 72
KyU	1937, 63, 66-68, 73
MH-GS	1938, 54, 57, 59-61, 63-75
MNS	1957, 62, 67, 68, 71
MiDW	1963, 68
MiHM	1968
MiKW	1968
MnU	1938, 57, 59-69
MoRM	1968
MoSW	1938, 57, 62, 68
MoU	1963
NBiSU	1959, 61, 63-66, 68-73
NNC	1938, 52, 57, 59, 62, 63
NOneoU	1967
NRU	1938, 59, 61, 71
NSyU	1938, 57, 59, 62, 65, 66, 68, 70, 73

NbU	1959, 60, 68
NcU	1938, 57, 59-70, 72, 75
NdU	1962, 63, 68, 69
NhD	1954, 57, 59-70, 72, 74, 75
NjP	1938, 52, 57, 59, 61-70, 75
OCU	1961, 62, 70, 72
OkOkU	1967
OkU	1938, 59, 62, 67, 69, 71
PBL	1959
PBm	1967
PSt	1963, 68-74
RPB	1938, 57, 63, 68
TxDaAR-T	1967, 68, 70, 71, 73
TxDaDM	1957, 59-65, 68
TxDaM	1959, 62
TxHU	1962, 63, 72
TxLT	1938
TxU	1938, 57, 59-66, 68
TxU-Da	1963-66
UU	1968
[VtPuW]	1954, 59, 61, 63-74
WU	1938, 67-69, 72

NEW ENGLAND PLEISTOCENE GEOLOGISTS. See FRIENDS OF THE PLEISTOCENE. EASTERN GROUP. (89)

(205) NEW MEXICO. BUREAU OF MINES AND MINERAL RESOURCES. GUIDEBOOK.

1940	Sierra and Socorro counties, New Mexico.
1941	Near Socorro, New Mexico.
1945	Los Pinos Mountains, Chupadera Mesa, Manzano Mountains.
1946	San Juan Basin. (In conjunction with New Mexico. School of Mines.)

InU	1946
OkU	1945
TxDaAR-T	1940, 41, 46
TxLT	1945, 46
TxMM	1945, 46
TxU	1946
TxU-Da	1945

(206) NEW MEXICO. BUREAU OF MINES AND MINERAL RESOURCES. SCENIC TRIPS TO THE GEOLOGIC PAST.

1955	No. 1	Santa Fe, New Mexico.
1956	No. 2	Taos-Red River-Eagle Nest, New Mexico.
1958	No. 3	Roswell-Capitan-Ruidoso and Bottomless Lakes State Park, New Mexico.
	No. 4	Southern Zuni Mountains.
1959	No. 5	Silver City-Santa Rita-Hurley, New Mexico.
1960	No. 6	Trail guide to the Upper Pecos.
1961	No. 7	High Plains, northeastern New Mexico-Raton-Capulin Mountain-Clayton.
1964	No. 8	Mosaic of New Mexico's scenery, rocks and history, a brief guide for visitors.
1965	No. 7	High Plains, northeastern New Mexico, Raton-Capulin Mountain-Clayton. 2nd edition.
1967	No. 3	Roswell-Capitan-Ruidoso and Bottomless Lakes State Park, New Mexico. 2nd edition.
	No. 5	Silver City-Santa Rita-Hurley, New Mexico. 2nd edition.

	No. 6	Trail guide to the Upper Pecos. 2nd edition.
	No. 7	High Plains, northeastern New Mexico-Raton-Capulin Mountain-Clayton. 3rd edition.
	No. 8	Mosaic of New Mexico's scenery, rocks, and history, a brief guide. 2nd edition.
1968	No. 1	Santa Fe, New Mexico. 2nd edition.
	No. 2	Taos-Red River-Eagle Nest, New Mexico. 4th edition.
	No. 4	Southern Zuni Mountains. 2nd edition.
1971	No. 4	Southern Zuni Mountains. Zuni-Cibola Trail. Revised 1971.
	No. 10	Southwestern New Mexico: Lordsburg, Silver City, Deming, Las Cruces.
1972	No. 11	Cumbres and Toltec scenic railroad.
1974	No. 9	Albuquerque: its mountains, valley, water, and volcanoes. Revised 1974.
	No. 12	The story of mining in New Mexico.
1975	No. 6	Trail guide to the geology of the Upper Pecos. 3rd edition, revised.

[CDU]	1955-61
CLU-G/G	1955-61, 64-68, 72, 73, 74(9)
CU-EART	1955-61, 64-68, 70-72
CoG	1955-61 64-68
[CoPU]	1959
CoU	1955, 56, 58-61, 64-68 71-74
DI-GS	1955-74
ICarbS	1955, 56, 58-61, 64, 71
IdBB	1968(1)
IdPI	1955-57, 58(3), 59-61, 64, 71-74
InU	1955, 56, 58, 71, 72
KyU	1967(4-8), 68(2)
MH-GS	1960
MNS	1955, 56, 58-61, 71
MiHM	1955-58, 60, 61, 64-68, 72
MoSW	1955-61, 64-68, 70-75
MoU	1955-58, 60, 61, 64
NbU	1955-61, 64-68, 71, 72
NcU	1955-61, 71
NdU	1955-61, 64-68, 70-72
NhD	1972
NjP	1967(3), 68(1,2,4), 71, 72, 74(9)
NmPE	1956-62, 64-68, 70-74
NvLN	1971-74
OCU	1955-61, 64-68, 70-74
OU	1955-61, 64-68, 70-74
OkT	1955-61
OkU	1955-61, 64-68, 70-74
PSt	1955-61, 64-68, 70-72
SdRM	1955-61
TxDaAR-T	1955, 58(2,3,4), 59, 61, 64, 71, 72
TxHU	1955-61, 64-68, 70-72
TxLT	1955-61, 64-67
TxU	1955-61, 64-68, 70-74
TxU-Da	1955
ViBlbV	1955-61, 64-68, 70-74

(207) NEW MEXICO GEOLOGICAL SOCIETY. GUIDEBOOK FOR THE ANNUAL FIELD CONFERENCE. (TITLE VARIES)

1932		Sierra Blanca region.
1949		No. 2. See West Texas Geological Society. (338)
1950	1st	San Juan Basin, New Mexico and Colorado.
1951	2nd	South and west sides of the San Juan Basin, New Mexico and Arizona.
1952	3rd	Rio Grande country, central New Mexico.
1953	4th	Southwestern New Mexico.
1954	5th	Southeastern New Mexico. Road logs: Alamogordo to Alamo Canyon. Alamogordo to Cloudcroft. Cloudcroft to Carlsbad. Guadalupe Mountains area, New Mexico and Texas. Carlsbad to International Minerals and Chemical Corporation Potash Mine. Carlsbad to Carlsbad Caverns. Northern part of West Side Road, Sacramento Mountains. Road log from Cloudcroft to Pinon. Road log from Dunken to Pinon. Road log from Pinon to Texas Hill. Road log from Texas Hill anticline to Hope, New Mexico. Road log from Junction Highway 83 and State Road 24 to Bluewater anticline. Road log from Carlsbad to mouth of Dark Canyon. Road log from Highway 62-180 to mouth of Slaughter Canyon. Road log from Highway 62-180 to mouth of McKittrick Canyon.
1955	6th	South-central New Mexico.
1956	7th	Southeastern Sangre de Cristo Mountains.
1957	8th	Southwestern San Juan Mountains, Colorado.
1958	9th	Black Mesa Basin, northeastern Arizona. (34)
1959	10th	West-central New Mexico.
1960	11th	Rio Chama country, northern New Mexico.
1961	12th	Albuquerque country, New Mexico.
	spring	Last Chance Canyon, Guadalupe Mountains, road log, Roswell Sitting Bull Falls.
1962	13th	Mogollon Rim region, east-central Arizona.
1963	14th	Socorro region, New Mexico.
1964	15th	Ruidoso country.
1965	16th	Southwestern New Mexico, II.
1966	17th	Taos-Raton-Spanish Peaks country, New Mexico and Colorado.
1967	18th	Defiance-Zuni-Mt. Taylor region, Arizona and New Mexico.
1968	19th	San Juan-San Miguel-La Plata region, New Mexico and Colorado.
1969	20th	Guidebook of the border region (northern Chihuahua, Mexico and the United States).
1970	21st	Tyrone-Big Hatchet Mountains-Florida Mountains region, New Mexico.
1971	22nd	Guidebook of the San Luis Basin, Colorado. 1st day; Alamosa to the eastern San Juan Mountains, via Alamosa River, Jasper, Summitville, South Fork, and return. 2nd day; Alamosa to the Great Sand Dunes National Monument, Poncha Pass, Salida, Howard and return via Saguache and Monte Vista. 3rd day; Rail log from Antonito, Colorado to Chama, New Mexico. Supplemental logs: 1. Villa Grove to Bonanza. 2. Del Norte to Summer Coon volcanic area and return. 3. Fort Garland to Romeo via San Luis, San Acacio and Manassa. 4. Chama, New Mexico to Antonito, Colorado.

(207) New Mexico Geological Society.

1972	23rd	East-central New Mexico. Road logs: 1st day; Tucumcari, Mosquero and San Juan country. 2nd day; Tucumcari, Canadian escarpment, and Santa Rosa country. 3rd day; Santa Rosa, Clines Corners, Encino, Duran, and Vaughn country. Subsurface geology of east-central New Mexico. [supplement] (New Mexico Geological Society. Special publication No. 4.)
1973	24th	Monument Valley and vicinity, Arizona and Utah. Road logs: 1st day Farmington, New Mexico to Kayenta, Arizona, via Shiprock, Four Corners, Aneth, Bluff, Cedar Mesa, Goosenecks and Mexican Hat. 2nd day; Kayenta, Arizona to Black Mesa and Navajo National Monument. 3rd day; Kayenta, Arizona to Gallup, New Mexico, via Dinnehotso, Rock Point, Round Rock, Many Farms, Chinle, Canyon de Chelly, Granado, St. Michaels, Hunters Point and Lupton.
1974	25th	Ghost Ranch, central-northern New Mexico. Road logs: 1st day; Ghost Ranch to Cuba and Nacimiento Mine and return. 2nd day; Coyote Junction to U. S. 84 and New Mexico 96 to Abiquiu, El Rito, Petaca, Tres Piedras, Hopewell Lake, Chama Basin, and return to Ghost Ranch. 3rd day; Junction of U. S. 84 and El Rito Turnoff to Espanola, Valle Grande, San Ysidro and Bernalillo; with optional trip beginning at mile 99.6 to examine Mississippian and Pennsylvanian rocks at Guadalupe Box. 3rd day; Optional trip; beginning at mile 111.6 to examine Cretaceous and Tertiary at south end of Nacimiento uplift.
1975	26th	Guidebook of the Las Cruces country (central-southern New Mexico). Road logs. 1st day; Las Cruces to southern San Andres Mountains and return. 2nd day; Las Cruces to the Sierra de las Uvas and Aden volcanic area and return. 3rd day; Las Cruces to North Mesilla Valley, Cedar Hills, San Diego Mountain, and Rincon area. Exit A(North); Rincon area to Derry Hills via Interstate 25 North. Exit B(West); Hatch and Deming via New Mexico 26. Exit C(South); Upham Interchange to Anthony, New Mexico-Texas via Interstates 25 South and 10 East. Exit D(East); Mesilla Valley to Tularosa Basin via U. S. 70 East.
1976	27th	Guidebook of Vermejo Park, northeastern New Mexico. Road logs. 1st day; Las Vegas to Raton via Montezuma, Sapello, La Cueva (and vicinity), Ocate, Wagon Mound and Springer. 2nd day; Raton to Underwood Lakes, through the Raton coal field via the York Canyon mine, Vermejo Park and Gold Creek, with a discussion of timber types and site factors. 3rd day; Raton to Adams and Bartlett Lakes, Vermejo Park, New Mexico, through Trinidad coal field and Tercio anticline, Colorado; return via Van Bremmer Canyon and Colfax, New Mexico.
1977	28th	San Juan Basin III.

AzFU	1950-54, 56-73
AzTeS	1952-54, 56-75
AzU	1968-74
CChiS	1950, 51, 53, 54, 56-72
CLU-G/G	1950-74
CLhC	1952-60, 61(12), 62-64, 67, 69, 72-74
CaACU	1951, 52, 60
[CaBVU]	1956, 60, 65, 67, 69
CaOKQ	1953, 54, 56-59, 62, 63, 65
CaOOG	1964, 69, 72(23)
CaOWtU	1950-74
CoDuF	1950-62, 67, 68, 71, 73

CoFS	1959, 60, 61(12), 63
CoG	1950-60, 61(12), 62-75
[CoPU]	1950-73
CoU	1950-75
DFPC	1953-58
DI-GS	1950-60, 61(12), 62-71, 72(23), 73, 74
ICF	1952-54, 56-59, 62-64, 67
ICIU-S	1953, 54, 56-60, 61(12), 62-73
[I-GS]	1952, 69
IU	1950-60, 61(12), 62-76
IaU	1950-60, 61(12), 62-73
IdBB	1958, 73
IdPI	1973
InLP	1950-71, 72(23), 73, 74
InU	1949-60, 61(12), 62-71, 72(23), 73-75
KyU	1949-74
LU	1950-60, 61(12), 62-73
MH-GS	1951, 52, 58, 69, 71, 72, 74
MNS	1951, 58
MiDW	1951-64
MiHM	1953
MiKW	1950, 51, 57-59, 61(12), 66, 70, 73
MiU	1951, 53-67
[MnSSM]	1969
MnU	1950-60, 61(12), 62-66
MoSW	1950, 57
MoU	1951, 53, 54, 56-67
MtU	1957
NNC	1950-60, 61(12), 62-64
NOneoU	1950-75
NRU	1953, 54, 59, 60, 62, 65, 66, 69, 72, 73
NSyU	1959
NbU	1952-60, 61(12), 62-73, 75
NcU	1950-56
NdU	1950-54, 56-60, 61(12), 63-71, 72(23), 73
NhD	1950-60, 61(12), 62-71, 72(23), 73-75
NjP	1950-71, 72(23), 73, 74
NmU	1950-56, 59-61, 63-68, 70
NvLN	1971, 74
NvU	1953, 54, 56-62
OCU	1950-60, 61(12), 62-71, 72(23), 73-75
OU	1950-75
[OkOkCGe]	1950, 54
OkT	1950-60, 61(12), 64, 65
OkU	1950-73
OrCS	1951-60, 61(12), 62-71, 72(23), 73-75
OrU	1953-60, 61(12), 62-73
PBm	1950-74
PPiGulf	1950, 51, 54, 58, 69
PSt	1950-60, 61(12), 62-71, 72(23), 73
TxDaAR-T	1932, 51-60, 61(12), 62-74
TxDaDM	1951-60, 61(12), 62-71, 72(23), 73, 74
TxDaM	1950-60, 61(12), 62-65
TxDaSM	1950-60, 61(12), 62-71, 72(23), 73, 74

TxHSD	1950-60, 61(12), 62, 64-66, 68, 69, 71-73
TxHU	1950-54, 56-71, 73
TxLT	1950-65
TxMM	1950-71, 72(23), 73, 74
TxU	1950-71, 72(23)
TxU-Da	1949-74
UU	1951-56, 59-66, 68, 73
ViBlbV	1950-60, 61(12), 62-71, 72(23), 73, 74
WU	1953-71, 72(23), 73-75
WyU	1953, 54, 56-62, 68

(208) NEW ORLEANS GEOLOGICAL SOCIETY. GUIDEBOOK.

1961		Jefferson Island salt dome.
1962		Peninsula of Yucatan.
1965		Oil and gas fields of southeast Louisiana.
1966		Field trip to southeast pass of Mississippi River. (No guidebook issued.)
1967		Yucatan field trip (2nd ed. 1967). No. 7. See Geological Society of America. (96)
1968		Depositional environments; a comparison of Eocene and Recent sedimentary deposits of the northern Gulf Coast.
1970		A study of the lower Mississippi River delta, its processes, sediments, and structures.
1971		The Lafourche delta and the Grand Isle Barrier Island; destruction of an ancient delta of the Mississippi River.
		Part 1. Flight over Bayou Lafourche, an ancient delta of the Mississippi.
		Part 2. Grand Isle-Barrier Island in the Gulf of Mexico.
1972		Guidebook, Louisiana salt domes and the Mississippi deltaic plain, with a visit to Morton Salt Company Mine, "Weeks Island," Louisiana.
1973		Geology of the Mississippi-Alabama coastal area and nearshore zone.
1974	fall	West-central Louisiana field trip.
		See Geological Society of America. (96)
1975		Modern carbonate environments of the upper Florida Keys.
1976		Carbonate rocks and hydrogeology of the Yucatan peninsula, Mexico. (12, 274)

CChiS	1968
CLU-G/G	1961, 62, 67, 68, 71-73
CLhC	1961, 73
CU-EART	1961-65, 68, 71-73
[CaACAM]	1961, 71, 73
CaOHM	1967, 68
CaOKQ	1967
CaOWtU	1973
CoG	1961, 62, 67, 68, 70-72
CoU	1962
DI-GS	1961, 62, 67, 68, 71-73, 74(Fall)
DLC	1968
IU	1961-73, 74(Fall), 75, 76
IaU	1967
InRE	1973
InU	1962, 67, 68, 70, 71, 73, 74(Fall), 75
KyU	1967, 68, 71
LU	1961, 62
MiKW	1967
MnU	1961, 62, 67, 68
MoU	1961, 65

[Ms-GS]	1973
NBiSU	1973
NNC	1961
NSyU	1968, 73
NbU	1961, 62
NcU	1962, 65, 71-73
NdU	1968, 71-74
NhD	1961, 67, 68, 70-73
NjP	1967, 68, 73
OCU	1962
OU	1968, 71, 72
OkT	1962
PPiGulf	1961, 62
PSt	1974
RPB	1967
TMM	1973
TxDaAR-T	1962, 68, 71-73
TxDaDM	1961, 68, 70-73
TxDaM	1961, 62
TxDaSM	1961, 62, 67, 73
TxHSD	1961, 62, 70, 71
TxHU	1962
TxMM	1961, 62
TxU	1961, 62, 66, 70, 71
WU	1973

(209) NEW YORK ACADEMY OF SCIENCE.

1965 See Oregon. State Department of Geology and Mineral Industries. (236)

(210) NEW YORK STATE GEOLOGICAL ASSOCIATION. ANNUAL MEETING. FIELD TRIP GUIDEBOOK. (TITLE VARIES)

1933		Excursion of the New York State Geological Association in the New York City region.
1940	16th	Catskill, New York.
1949		Geology of the Cayuga Lake region.
1950		[Geology around the Syracuse region.]
1951	26th	Northeastern Adirondack Mountains and Plattsburg area.
		Chazyan stratigraphy, Plattsburg.
		Supplementary guidebook to Chazyan stratigraphy.
1955	27th	[No title available].
1956	28th	Western New York.
1957	29th	Geology of the southwestern tier oil and gas fields, oil refining field trips.
		Trip A. Geological outcrops in the Wellsville area.
		Trip B. Harrison Valley-Oriskany gas storage field.
		Trip C. Sinclair oil refinery (no log).
		Trip D. Oil fields and well shooting.
		Trip E. Stratigraphy of southwestern New York.
1958	30th	Peekskill, New York.
1959	31st	Geology of the Cayuga Lake basin. (71)
1960	32nd	Clinton, New York (region around Utica and southern Adirondack Mountains).
1961	33rd	Troy, New York-southern Taconics.
1962	34th	Port Jervis.

		Trip A. The Onondaga Limestone and Schoharie Formation.
		Trip B. Geology of the...southern part of the Monroe Quadrangle.
		Trip C. Structure and stratigraphy of the Port Jervis-South Otisville quadrangles.
1963	35th	Geology of south-central New York.
1964	36th	South-central Adirondack highlands.
1965	37th	The Schenectady area.
		Trip A. Mohawk Valley strata and structure, Saratoga to Canajoharie.
		Trip B. Geologic excursion from Albany to the Glen via Lake George.
		Trip C. Glacial lake sequences in the eastern Mohawk-northern Hudson region.
		Trip D. Geologic phenomena in the Schenectady area.
1966	38th	Geology of western New York: Silurian, Devonian, and Pleistocene of western New York and adjacent Ontario.
1967	39th	Field trips; mid-Hudson Valley region.
		Trip A. Pleistocene geology of the Wallkill Valley.
		Trip B. The economic geology of the mid-Hudson Valley region.
		Trip C. Middle and Upper Devonian clastics of the Catskill front, New York.
		Trip D. Upper Silurian-Lower Devonian stratigraphic sequence, western mid-Hudson Valley region, Kingston vicinity to Accord, Ulster County, New York.
		Trip E. Geologic structure of the Kingston Arc of the Appalachian fold belt.
		Trip F. Structure and petrology of the Pre-Cambrian allochthon and Paleozoic sediments of the Monroe area, New York.
		Trip G. [No title available.]
		Trip H. [No title available.]
1968	40th	Trip A. Bedrock geology in the vicinity of White Plains, New York.
		Trip B. Cretaceous deltas in the northern New Jersey coastal plain.
		Trip C. The Triassic rocks of the northern Newark Basin. Road log.
		Trip D. Sterling and Franklin area in the highlands of New Jersey.
		Trip E. Taconian islands and the shores of Appalachia.
		Trip F. Pleistocene geology of the Montauk peninsula.
		Trip G. Structure and petrology of Pelham Bay Park.
		Trip H. Stratigraphic and structural relations along the western border of the Cortlandt intrusives.
		Trip I. Deep-well injection of treated waste water; an experiment in re-use of groundwater in western Long Island.
		Trip J. Geology, geomorphology and late-glacial environments of western Long Island, New York.
1969	41st	Trip A. Sedimentary characteristics and tectonic deformation of Middle Ordovician shales in northwestern Vermont north of Malletts Bay.
		Trip B. Recent sedimentation and water properties of Lake Champlain.
		Trip C. Bedrock geology of the southern portion of the Winesburg synclinorium.
		Trip D. Surficial geology of the Champlain Valley, Vermont.
		Trip E. Stratigraphy of the Chazy Group (Middle Ordovician).
		Trip F. The paleoecology of Chazyan (Lower-Middle Ordovician) reefs or mounds.
		Trip G. Evidence of late Pleistocene local glaciation in the high peaks region, Adirondack Mountains, I.
		Trip H. Adirondack meta-anorthosite.
		Trip J. Evidence of late Pleistocene local glaciation in the high peaks region, Adirondack Mountains, II.
1970	42nd	Trip A. Benthic communities of the Genesee Group (Upper Devonian).
		Trip B. Upper Devonian deltaic environments.
		Trip C. Transitional sedimentary facies of the Catskill deltaic system in eastern New York.
		Trip D,H. Stratigraphy, paleontology and paleoecology of the Ludlowville and Moscow formations (upper Hamilton group), central New York.
		Trip E,I. Mineral industries in parts of Onondaga, Cortland and Tompkins counties.

		Trip F. Deglaciation of the eastern Finger Lakes region.
		Trip G. Paleontology of the Cortland area.
		Trip H. See Trip D.
		Trip I. See Trip E.
		Trip J. Proglacial lake sequence in the Tully Valley, Onondaga County.
		Trip K. Glacial history of the Fall Creek Valley at Ithaca, New York.
1971	43rd	Trip A. Some aspects of Grenville geology and the Precambrian/Paleozoic unconformity, northwest Adirondacks, New York.
		Trip B. Precambrian and lower Paleozoic stratigraphy, northwest St. Lawrence and north Jefferson counties.
		Trip C. Some aspects of engineering geology in the St. Lawrence Valley and northwest Adirondack lowlands.
		Trip D. Economic geology of International Talc and Benson Iron Mines.
		Trip E. Some Pleistocene features of St. Lawrence County, New York.
		Trip F. Mineral collecting in St. Lawrence County.
1972	44th	The Clinton Group of east-central New York.
		Sedimentation and stratigraphy of the Salina Group (Upper Silurian) in east-central New York.
		Stratigraphy of the marine limestones and shales of the Ordovician Trenton Group in central New York.
		Glacial geology of the northern Chenango River valley.
		Stratigraphy and structure of the Canada Lake nappe, southernmost Adirondacks.
		Paleontological problems of the Hamilton Group (Middle Devonian).
		Paleoecology of a black limestone, Cherry Valley Limestone; Devonian of central New York.
		Sedimentary environments of biostratigraphy of the transgressive early Trentonian Sea (Middle Ordovician) in central and northwestern New York.
		Syracuse channels; evidence for a catastrophic flood.
		Half-day trip to Herkimer diamond grounds in Middleville, New York.
1973	45th	Rochester, New York area.
		Trip A. Glacial geology of the western Finger Lakes region.
		Trip B. A comparison of environments, the Middle Devonian Hamilton Group in the Genesee Valley.
		Trip C. Lower Upper Devonian stratigraphy from the Batavia-Warsaw meridian to the Genesee Valley; goniatite sequence and correlations.
		Trip D. Eurypterid horizons and the stratigraphy of the Upper Silurian and Lower Devonian of western New York State.
		Trip E. Late glacial and postglacial geology of the Genesee Valley in Livingston County, New York; a preliminary report.
		Trip F. The Pinnacle Hills and the Mendon Kame area; contrasting morainal deposits.
		Trip G. Pleistocene and Holocene sediments at Hamlin Beach State Park, New York.
		Trip H. Mineral collecting at Penfield Quarry.
		Trip I. Stratigraphy of the Genesee Gorge at Rochester.
1974	46th	Geology of western New York State.
		Trip A. Lockport (Middle Silurian) and Onondaga (Middle Devonian) patch reefs in western New York.
		Trip B. Upper Devonian stratigraphy of Chautauqua County, New York.
		Trip C. Late Middle and early Upper Devonian disconformities and paleoecology of the Moscow Formation in western Erie County, New York.
		Trip D. From Lake Erie to the glacial limits and beyond.
		Trip E. Environmental geology of the Fredonia-Dunkirk area.
		Trip F. Glacial geology and buried topography in the vicinity of Fredonia, Gowanda and Zoar Valley, New York.
1975	47th	Trip A-1. Stratigraphy, structure and petrology of the New York City Group.
		Trip A-2. Structure and form of the Triassic basalts in north-central New Jersey.

Trip A-3. Placer mining and concentration processes of ilmenite sand deposits near Lakehurst, New Jersey.
Trip A-4. Shinnecock Inlet tidal flood delta and problems of coastal stabilization.
Trip A-5(AM). Barrier island accretion features, Democrat Point, Fire Island.
Trip A-5(PM). Environmental geology of the Jones Beach barrier island.
Trip A-6(AM). Geological oceanography of a segment of Long Island Sound.
Trip A-6(PM). Sedimentary dynamics of a coastal pond; Flax Pond, Old Field, Long Island.
Trip A-7. Quaternary geology of the Montauk peninsula.
Trip A-8(AM). Environmental engineering aspects and tour at Shoreham of Long Island Lighting Company Nuclear Reactor Site at Shoreham, Long Island.
Trip A-8(PM). Foreshore and backshore natural environments of a barrier island, Fire Island.
Trip B-1. Lower Paleozoic metamorphic stratigraphy of Mamaroneck area, New York.
Trip B-2. Geological aspects of Staten Island, New York.
Trip B-3(AM). Natural and man-made erosional and depositional features associated with stabilization of migrating barrier islands, Fire Island inlet, New York.
Trip B-3(PM) A major beach erosional cycle at Robert Moses State Park, Fire Island, during the storm of December 1-2, 1974.
Trip B-4. Jamaica Bay, Borough of Queens, New York City; a case study of geo-environmental stress.
Trip B-5. Wisconsinan glacial stratigraphy and structure of northwestern Long Island.
Trip B-6. Geological oceanography of a segment of Long Island Sound. (See Trip A-6(AM).)

CLU-G/G	1957-71
CU-EART	1933, 57-71
CaAC	1968
CaAEU	1965
CaOLU	1961
CaOOG	1957-68
[CaOTOM]	1967
CaOWtU	1958-66
CoU	1958-68, 71
DI-GS	1940, 57-69, 72-74
[I-GS]	1958
IU	1955-75
IaU	1962, 65(A,B), 68
InLP	1958-63, 69-71
InU	1958-60, 62, 64, 65, 68
KyU	1957-71
MH-GS	1957, 59, 61, 63-74
MiHM	1957-69
MiU	1957, 59-67
MnU	1955, 57-68
MoSW	1965, 71
MtBC	1968
NBiSU	1957-72, 74
NNC	1949-51, 55, 57, 61-66
NOneoU	1965
NRU	1956-63, 66-74
NSyU	1957-75
NbU	1959
NcU	1957-73
NdU	1971
NhD	1958-74

NjP	1955-74
OCU	1956, 60
OU	1958-68
OkU	1958-64, 68
TMM	1957, 65, 67
TxDaAR-T	1957, 67-69, 71
TxDaDM	1957-66
TxDaM	1957-62
TxDaSM	1959, 62, 63
TxHSD	1933, 51, 52
TxMM	1956
TxU	1957-71
TxU-Da	1958
ViBlbV	1957-71
WU	1966-75

(211) NEW YORK STATE MUSEUM. HANDBOOK.

1927 A popular guide to the geology and physiography of Allegany State Park.
1933 Guide to the geology of John Boyd Thacher Park (Indian Ladder region) and vicinity.
1942 No. 19 Guide to the geology of the Lake George region, New York.

CLU-G/G	1927, 33, 42
ICF	1942
IEN	1927
IaU	1942
MNS	1942
MiU	1927
MoU	1942
NBiSU	1927, 33, 42
NOneoU	1942
NdU	1927, 33, 42
OU	1942
PBL	1942
PSt	1942

(212) NEW YORK STATE MUSEUM AND SCIENCE SERVICE. EDUCATIONAL LEAFLET.

1962 No. 12. Field guide to the central portion of the southern Adirondacks.
1965 No. 18. Guidebook field trips. Mohawk Valley strata and structure, from Albany to Glen via Lake George.

CaAEU	1962
CaOHM	1962
CaOLU	1962
[CaOTOM]	1962, 65
CoFS	1962
CoG	1962, 65
ICF	1962, 65
[I-GS]	1962, 65
InU	1962, 65
LU	1962
MH-GS	1962, 65
MNS	1962
MiHM	1965

(212) New York State Museum and Science Service.

MoSW	1965
NOneoU	1962
NdU	1962, 65
NvU	1965
OU	1962, 65
OkU	1962, 65
PBL	1962, 65
PBm	1962
TMM	1962
TxU	1962, 65
ViBlbV	1962, 65

(213) NORTH CAROLINA ACADEMY OF SCIENCE. SCIENCE EDUCATION PROJECT COMMITTEE.

1967 Guide for geologic field trip in Wayne County for earth science.

InU	1967
NjP	1967
OU	1967

(214) NORTH DAKOTA GEOLOGICAL SOCIETY. GUIDE BOOK FOR THE ANNUAL FIELD CONFERENCE.

1952	1st	Southern Manitoba and the Interlake area, Province of Manitoba.
1954	2nd	Upper Cretaceous and Tertiary beds in western North Dakota.
1955	3rd	South Dakota. Central and southern Black Hills.
1966	4th	Black Hills field conference including an informal study of adjacent areas in southwest North Dakota and northwest South Dakota.

AzTeS	1952-66
CLU-G/G	1952, 54, 55
CU-EART	1952, 54, 55
CaAC	1952, 54, 55
[CaACAM]	1954, 56, 58, 67
CaACI.	1952, 54, 55
CaOHM	1955
CaOOG	1952, 54, 55
CaOWtU	1954
CoG	1952, 54, 55
CoU	1952, 54, 55
DI-GS	1952, 54, 55, 67
ICF	1952, 54, 55
ICIU-S	1955
IEN	1954
IU	1952, 54, 55, 66
IaU	1952, 54, 55, 66, 67
IdPI	1955
InU	1952, 54, 55, 67
KyU	1952, 54, 55, 66
LU	1952, 54, 55
MiDW	1954
MiU	1952, 54, 55
MnU	1952, 54, 55, 67
MoSW	1954
MoU	1954
MtU	1952, 54, 55

NSyU	1967
NbU	1952, 54, 55
NcU	1952, 54, 55, 67
NdU	1952, 54, 55, 66
NhD	1967
NjP	1954, 55
NmU	1952, 54
OU	1952, 54, 57
[OkOkCGe]	1952, 55
OkT	1952, 54, 55
OkU	1952, 54, 55
PBL	1954
PPiGulf	1952
PSt	1952, 54, 55
SdRM	1955
SdU	1952, 54, 55, 66
TxDaAR-T	1952, 54, 55, 66
TxDaDM	1952, 54, 55, 66
TxDaM	1952, 54, 55
TxDaSM	1952, 54, 55
TxHSD	1955
TxMM	1954, 55
TxU	1952, 54, 55, 66, 67
TxU-Da	1952, 54, 55
UU	1955
ViBlbV	1952, 55
WU	1954

(215) NORTH DAKOTA. GEOLOGICAL SURVEY. BULLETIN.

1956 No. 30 Guide for geologic field trip in northeastern North Dakota.

CaOLU	1956
IU	1956
MnDuU	1956
NdU	1956

(216) NORTH DAKOTA. GEOLOGICAL SURVEY. EDUCATIONAL SERIES.

n.d. No. 1. Geology along North Dakota Interstate Highway 94.

1972 No. 2. Guide to the geology of northeastern North Dakota, including Cavalier, Grand Forks, Nelson, Pembina, and Walsh counties.

No. 3. Guide to the geology of southeastern North Dakota, including Barnes, Cass, Griggs, Ransom, Richland, Sargent, Steele, and Traill counties.

1973 No. 4. Geology along the South Loop Road, Theodore Roosevelt National Memorial Park.

No. 6. Guide to the geology of south-central North Dakota, including Burleigh, Dickey, Emmons, Kidder, LaMoure, Logan, McIntosh and Stutsman counties.

1974 No. 7. Guide to the geology of north-central North Dakota, including Benson, Bottineau, Eddy, Foster, McHenry, Pierce, Ramsey, Rolette, Sheridan, Towner, and Wells counties.

1975 No. 8. Guide to the geology of northwest North Dakota, including Burke, Divide, McLean, Mountrail, Renville, Ward, and Williams counties.

No. 9. Guide to the geology of southwestern North Dakota, including Adams, Billings, Bowman, Dunn, Golden Valley, Grant, Hettinger, McKenzie, Mercer, Morton, Oliver, Sioux, Slope, and Stark counties.

CoU	1972-75
DI-GS	1972-75
ICarbS	1972-74, 75(8)
ICF	1972-74
IEN	n.d., 1972-74, 75(8)
[I-GS]	1973(6)
IU	n.d., 1972-75
IaU	1972-74
InRE	1972(3), 73, 74, 75(8)
InU	1973(6), 74, 75
KyU	1972
MH-GS	1975(8)
MiHM	1972, 73(4,6), 74
MiU	1972(3)
NSyU	1972-74
NdU	n.d., 1972-74
OCU	n.d., 1972-74
OU	n.d., 1972-75
OkT	1972(3), 73, 74
OkU	1972, 73
PSt	1972(3,6), 74
TxLT	1972(2), 74
ViBlbV	1972
WU	1975

(217) NORTH DAKOTA. GEOLOGICAL SURVEY. MISCELLANEOUS SERIES.

1957 No. 1. Valley City area.
No. 2. Minot area.
No. 3. Devils Lake area.
No. 4. Bismarck-Mandan area.
No. 5. Dickinson area.
No. 6. Williston area.
No. 7. Jamestown area.
No. 8. Fargo to Valley City.
No. 9. Grand Forks to Park River.
1958 No. 10. East-central North Dakota. (90)
1967 No. 30. Glacial geology of the Missouri Coteau and adjacent areas. (90)
1968 No. 40. Geological field trip from Grand Forks, North Dakota to Kenora, Ontario.
No. 42. Guide to the geology of Burleigh County, North Dakota.
1969 No. 39. Geology of northeastern North Dakota. (191)
1972 No. 50. Depositional environments of the lignite-bearing strata in western North Dakota. (96, 218)
1975 Guide to the geology of northwest North Dakota including Burke, Divide, McLean, Mountrail, Renville, Ward and William counties.

[A-GS]	1957
CLU-G/G	1957(2,3,5-9), 58, 67-69, 72
CU-EART	1957, 58, 67
CaOLU	1957, 58, 68, 69
CaOOG	1958
CoFS	1958
CoG	1958
CoU	1957

DI-GS	1957, 58, 68, 69, 72
ICF	1958, 68, 69
IEN	1957, 58, 67-69, 72
[I-GS]	1957, 58
IU	1947, 57, 58, 69, 72
IaU	1956-58, 67-69, 72
InU	1958, 67, 69, 72
KyU	1956-58, 67, 69
LU	1957, 58
MNS	1957, 67
MiDW	1957, 58, 67-69
MiHM	1957, 58, 67-69
MiU	1967, 69, 72
MnDuU	1957(1,2,4-7), 68, 69, 75
MnU	1957, 58, 67
MoSW	1957, 67-69, 72
MoU	1958, 69
NBiSU	1967-69
NSyU	1957, 58, 67-69
NbU	1957, 58, 67, 69
NcU	1957, 58, 67, 68
NdU	1957, 58, 68, 69, 72
NjP	1957, 58, 67-69, 72
OCU	1968, 69
OU	1958, 68, 69
OkU	1957, 58, 67-69
OrU	1957, 58, 67-69
PBL	1957, 58, 67-69
PSt	1957, 58, 69(39 or 42)
RPB	1958
TMM	1972
TxDaAR-T	1957(2,3,5,7-9), 58, 68, 72
TxDaDM	1957, 58
TxDaM	1957, 58
TxHU	1957, 58
TxLT	1957, 58, 67, 69, 72
TxMM	1957
TxU	1957, 58, 67, 68
ViBlbV	1957(1-7), 69
WU	1957, 67-69, 72

(218) NORTH DAKOTA. UNIVERSITY. GEOLOGY DEPARTMENT. GUIDEBOOK.

1960		Geology of the Black Hills and route between Grand Forks and Rapid City.
1961	2nd	The geology of southeastern Minnesota and northwestern Iowa and routes between Grand Forks, North Dakota and Dubuque, Iowa.
1972	3rd	Depositional environments of the lignite-bearing strata in western North Dakota. (96, 217)

CU-EART	1960, 61, 72
IU	1972
IaU	1972
InU	1972
MH-GS	1972
MiDW	1972

MnU	1960, 61
MoU	1972
NdU	1960, 61
NjP	1972
OrU	1972
TxDaSM	1960, 61, 72

(219) NORTH TEXAS GEM AND MINERAL SOCIETY.

1957 Mid-winter field trip to Wichita Mountain area.

TxU	1957

(220) NORTH TEXAS GEOLOGICAL SOCIETY. ANNUAL FIELD TRIP.

1923 Symposium of north Texas oil field.
1939 Pease River Group and Custer in north Texas, Texas Panhandle and southwestern Oklahoma.
1940 Strawn and Canyon series of the Brazos and Trinity River valleys.
1947 Cambrian and Ordovician rocks of the Wichita Mountains.
1956 Facies study of the Canyon-Cisco series in the Brazos River area, north-central Texas.
1958 Guide to the Strawn and Canyon series of the Pennsylvanian system in Palo Pinto County, Texas. (13)
1959 Guide to the Upper Permian and Quaternary of north-central Texas.

CLU-G/G	1939
CaOKQ	1959
CoG	1956, 59
CoU	1959
DI-GS	1940, 47, 56, 59
ICF	1959
MnU	1956
NNC	1956, 59
NbU	1959
NcU	1956, 59
OU	1959
OkU	1947
TxDaDM	1959
TxDaM	1959
TxDaSM	1956
TxHU	1956, 59
TxLT	1947, 56
TxMM	1940, 47, 56, 59
TxU	1947, 56, 59
TxU-Da	1923, 56
ViBlbV	1959

(221) NORTHERN CALIFORNIA GEOLOGICAL SOCIETY.

1954 Capay-Wilbur Springs and west side Sacramento Valley. (16, 256)
1968 Field trip to the Geysers, Sonoma County, California.
1969 Mount Diablo-Camp Parks (northern California).
1970 San Andreas Fault and Point Reyes peninsula.

[CDU]	1954
CLU-G/G	1954

CSdS	1954
CSfCSM	1954, 68
CU-EART	1954, 70
CoG	1954
DI-GS	1954
ICF	1954
IU	1954
InU	1954, 68
MnU	1954
TxDaAR-T	1968
TxDaDM	1968
TxDaM	1954
TxDaSM	1954
TxHSD	1954
TxHU	1954
TxU	1954, 68
ViBlbV	1954

(222) NORTHERN OHIO GEOLOGICAL SOCIETY.

1970 Guide to the geology of northeastern Ohio.

IU	1970
InRE	1970
MiU	1970
TxDaAR-T	1970

(223) NOVA SCOTIA. DEPARTMENT OF MINES.

1948 The mineral province of eastern Canada; mineral and geological guidebook.
1954 Mineral and geological guide book.

TxHU	1954

(224) OHIO ACADEMY OF SCIENCE. SECTION OF GEOLOGY. GUIDE TO THE ANNUAL FIELD CONFERENCE.

1948	23rd	A study of the geology of Lucas County and the lime-dolomite belt.
1949	24th	A study of the geology of Perry County.
1950	25th	Glacial geology of west-central Ohio.
		Study of stratigraphy and sedimentation of Sharon Conglomerate northeastern Ohio.
1951	26th	No title available; [southwestern Ohio].
1952	27th	Glacial deposits of northeastern Ohio.
1953	28th	No title available; [Columbus, Ohio area].
1954	29th	Some geologic features of Athens County.
1955	30th	Geology of the Bellefontaine outlier.
1956	31st	The natural environment of the Springfield area.
1957	32nd	Geology of the central lake plains area.
1958	33rd	Geology of the Akron-Cleveland area.
1959	34th	Geology of the Columbus-Galena-Gahanna area.
1960	35th	Geology of the Yellow Springs region.
1961	36th	Geology of the Cincinnati region.
1962	37th	Geology of the Toledo area.
1963	38th	Geology of the Highland-Adams County area.
1964	39th	Upper Paleozoic stratigraphy of Lake and Geauga counties.
1965	40th	Drainage history of a part of the Hocking River valley.

(224) Ohio Academy of Science.

1966	41st	Industrial minerals in northeastern Perry and southwestern Muskingum counties [Development, Utilization and Stratigraphy of].
1967		Silurian geology of western Ohio, Dayton.
1968	43rd	Structures and fabrics in some Middle and Upper Silurian dolostones, northwestern Ohio.
1970	45th	Cincinnatian strata from Oregonia to the Ohio River with notes on Pleistocene geology along the route (Warren and Clermont counties).
1971	46th	Geology and suburban-urban land use in portions of Summit, Portage and Stark counties, Ohio.

CLU-G/G	1949, 54-66, 71
DI-GS	1949, 54, 55, 57-66
[I-GS]	1955
IU	1961-63, 65-67, 74
InU	1967
KyU	1967, 69
MH-GS	1958
MnU	1961
NNC	1961
OCU	1952, 55, 57, 60, 63, 65, 67, 70
OU	1948-67, 69, 70
TxDaAR-T	1959
TxDaDM	1949, 54-57, 68
TxU	1959, 60, 62, 68, 70

(225) OHIO. DIVISION OF GEOLOGICAL SURVEY. GUIDEBOOK.

1973	No. 1	Natural and man-made features affecting the Ohio shore of Lake Erie.
1974	No. 2	Selected field trips in northeastern Ohio. (98)
		Field Trip No. 1. General geology of the International Salt Company Cleveland Mine, Cleveland, Ohio. (Kent State University. Dept. of Geology. Contribution No. 96.)
		Field Trip No. 2. Sedimentary environments of the Lower Pennsylvanian Sharon Conglomerate. (Kent State University. Dept. of Geology. Contribution No. 97.)
		Field Trip No. 3. Engineering and Pleistocene geology of the lower Cuyahoga River valley. (Kent State University. Dept. of Geology. Contribution No. 98.)
	No. 3	Pennsylvanian conodont localities in northeastern Ohio. (98, 240)
1975	No. 4	Geology of the Hocking Hills State Park region.

CLU-G/G	1973, 74
CU-EART	1973-75
CaOHM	1973-75
CaOKQ	1973, 74
CaOOG	1973
DI-GS	1973, 74
[I-GS]	1973, 74
IU	1973, 74
IaU	1973, 74
InRE	1973, 74
KyU	1973, 74
MiKW	1973, 74
MoSW	1973-75
NvU	1973, 74
OU	1973-75
PSt	1973, 74
ViBlbV	1973, 74
WU	1973-75

(226) OHIO GEOLOGICAL SOCIETY. [GUIDEBOOK] FIELD TRIP.

1965		Cambrian and Ordovician formations in the vicinity of the Cumberland overthrust block of Tennessee and Virginia.
1967		Guide to the annual field conference, northeastern Ohio.
1968		Geological aspects of the Maysville-Portsmouth region, southern Ohio and northeastern Kentucky. (104)
1969	spring	A field guide to Allegheny deltaic deposits in the upper Ohio Valley with a commentary on deltaic aspects of Carboniferous rocks in the northern Appalachian Plateau. (245)
1970		Guidebook to the Middle Devonian rocks of north-central Ohio.
1972		See American Association of Petroleum Geologists. Eastern Section. Field Trip Guidebook. (14)

CLU-G/G	1965, 69
CaOKQ	1965, 70
CaOOG	1969
CaOWtU	1969(spring)
CoU	1969, 70
DI-GS	1965, 68, 70
ICF	1972
[I-GS]	1969(spring), 70
IU	1969(spring), 70
InLP	1969
InU	1969(spring), 70
KyU	1965, 67-70
MH-GS	1970
MnU	1965, 68, 69
MoSW	1970
NBiSU	1969
NcU	1970
NjP	1969
OCU	1967, 69, 70
OU	1965, 67, 69
OkOkU	1969
OkU	1969
PSt	1969
TxDaAR-T	1965, 67, 69, 70
TxDaDM	1965, 69, 70
TxHSD	1969(spring)
TxU	1965, 68-70
ViBlbV	1970

(227) OHIO INTERCOLLEGIATE GEOLOGY. FIELD TRIP.

1950-51	1st	Cuyahoga Gorge and Cheppewa Creek sections, Northeastern, Ohio.
1951-52	2nd	Not held.
1952-53	3rd	[Van Buren Lake.]
1953-54	4th	[Bedford Glens.]
1954-55	5th	Southeastern Stark County.
1955-56	6th	[Delaware County.]
1956-57	7th	Geologic setting of Granville and Newark in Licking County, Ohio.
1957-58	8th	Some Pennsylvania cyclothems in Athens County, Ohio.
1958-59	9th	[Oxford area.]
1959-60	10th	Judy Gap trip. (See 16th.)

1960-61	11th	[Northwestern Ohio.]
1961-62	12th	[Delaware County.]
1962-63	13th	Fairport Mine, Painesville, Ohio. (Also Kent State Geological Society Professional Paper 2).
1963-64	14th	Pennsylvanian in Muskingum and Coshocton (Ohio).
1964-65	15th	[Holmesville, Wooster] (Ohio).
1965-66	16th	Judy Gap trip. (same as 10th)
1966-67	17th	[Southwestern Ohio].
1967-68	18th	[Vicinity Alliance, Ohio].
1968-69	19th	[Granville-Newark area].
1969-70	20th	Type localities of selected Mississippian and Pennsylvanian strata in northwestern Pennsylvania and northeastern Ohio.
1970-73		No guidebooks.
1974	25th	Some geological features in Pendleton County, West Virginia and Highland County, Virginia.
1975-76		No guidebooks.

CLU-G/G	1950-70
CaOKQ	1950-70
CaOOG	1950-70
DI-GS	1950-70
IaU	1950-70
InLP	1950-70
InRE	1950-70
InU	1950-70
KyU	1950, 51, 53-70
NcU	1969, 70
NdU	1950-70
OCU	1950-70
OU	1950, 51, 56, 61, 66, 67, 74
PSt	1950-70
TMM	1950-70
TxDaDM	1950-70
TxU	1950-70
ViBlbV	1950, 52-70

(228) OHIO. STATE UNIVERSITY, COLUMBUS. DEPARTMENT OF GEOLOGY. GEOLOGY CLUB.

1958	No title available; [Appalachian region].
1960	The southern Appalachians and the Great Smoky Mountains.
1962	Field trip to Missouri.
1963	Central Appalachian seminar and field trip.
1965	Great Smoky Mountain. Columbus, Ohio to Gatlinburg, Tennessee.
1966	Appalachians highlands of Pennsylvania.
1968	Appalachian spring field trip.
1969	Southern Illinois fluorspar and southeast Missouri lead-zinc districts.

OU	1958, 60, 62, 63, 65, 66, 68, 69
TxDaDM	1965

(229) OKLAHOMA ACADEMY OF SCIENCE.

1947	May	Braggs Mountain section. Muskogee to Prague, Oklahoma; a geological road guide.
1952		Road log, geological field trip in eastern part of the Ouachita Mountains in Oklahoma. (266)
1953		Boiling Springs State Park, Woodward, Oklahoma.
1955		Road log, field trip from Dwight Mission to Tahlequah.
1959		Camp Egan area.

DI-GS	1952
OkU	1947, 52, 53, 55, 59
TxLT	1947, 52, 53

(230) OKLAHOMA CITY GEOLOGICAL SOCIETY. GUIDEBOOK FOR THE FIELD CONFERENCE.

1930		Stratigraphic section from Neva Ls thru Elgin Ss.
1932		See American Association of Petroleum Geologists. (12)
1936		Field trip, study of the Simpson Formation, Sections 5, 8 and 17-T, 2S-R1W.
		Study of the Simpson Formation, Sections 24 and 25-T, 2S-R1E.
1937		Simpson Formation, Section 2 and 12-T1N-R6E.
1939		See American Association of Petroleum Geologists. (12)
1940		Field trip; structural and stratigraphic features of Wichita Mountains.
1941		Mesozoic rocks of the Oklahoma Panhandle, including an area in northeastern New Mexico.
1946		Lower Permian and Upper Pennsylvanian, north-central Oklahoma.
1949		Precambrian, Cambrian and Ordovician rocks of the Wichita Mountain area.
1950		Eastern part of the Ouachita Mountains in Oklahoma; with special reference to the pre-Pennsylvanian and Lower Pennsylvanian rocks.
1953		See Oklahoma. Geological Survey. (232)
1954		See Oklahoma. Geological Survey. (232)
1955		[1] See Panhandle Geological Society. (241)
		[2] Highway geology of Oklahoma; road logs of the major highways of the State, with notations on Oklahoma's historic sites. (232)
1956	Apr.	See Oklahoma. Geological Survey. (232)
	Sept.	Panhandle of Oklahoma, northeastern New Mexico, south-central Colorado.
1964		Variations in limestone deposits, Desmoinesian and Missourian rocks in northeast Oklahoma.
1968		See American Association of Petroleum Geologists. (12)
		[2] A guidebook to the geology of the western Arkhoma Basin and Ouachita Mountains, Oklahoma. (12, 274)
1970		The Bahamas and southern Florida. (Shale Shaker, Vol. 21, No. 1, Sept. 1970.)

[A-GS]	1940
AzFU	1955
CLU-G/G	1932, 49, 50, 68
CLhC	1953, 54, 56(Apr.)
CU-EART	1932, 55(2), 56(Sept.), 68
CaACM	1950, 55(2)
CaOHM	1955(2), 64, 68
CaOKQ	1932, 64
CaOLU	1968, 72
CaOOG	1968(1)
CoG	1932, 56(Sept.), 64, 68
[CoPU]	1968
CoU	1955, 56, 64, 68(1,2)
DI-GS	1946, 49, 50, 56, 68
ICF	1932, 64
ICIU-S	1968(2)
ICarbS	1955(2), 68(1), 72
IEN	1949, 50, 55(2), 68(2)
[I-GS]	1932, 39, 41, 68(2)
IU	1946, 50, 53, 54, 64, 68
IaU	1932, 54, 55, 64, 68
InU	1949, 54, 56, 68
KyU	1953, 54, 56, 68

MNS	1953, 54, 55(2), 56
MiKW	1968(2)
MiU	1955, 68
MnU	1953, 54-56, 64, 68
MoRM	1946
MoSW	1949, 50, 55(2)
MoU	1932, 64, 68
NBiSU	1968(2)
NNC	1949, 56
NRU	1968
NSyU	1953, 54, 56
NbU	1950, 68
NcU	1932, 53, 54, 56(Apr.), 64, 68
NdU	1932, 68(1,2)
NhD	1953, 54, 56(Apr.), 68
NjP	1932, 50, 68
NmPE	1955, 68
NmU	1956
OCU	1968
OU	1932, 49, 56(Sept.), 64, 68
[OkOkCGe]	1946, 50, 64, 68(1)
OkT	1950, 56, 64
OkU	1930, 32, 36, 37, 40, 41, 46, 49, 50, 55(2), 56(Sept.), 64, 68, 70
PBL	1968
PPiGulf	1956
RPB	1956
TxDaAR-T	1932, 49, 50, 56, 68(2), 70
TxDaDM	1932, 36, 40, 50, 55, 56, 64, 68(1,2)
TxDaM	1940, 49, 50, 54, 56, 64
TxDaSM	1956, 64, 68(1,2), 70
TxHSD	1932, 50, 56(Sept.), 68
TxHU	1940, 46, 50, 55, 56, 68(2)
TxLT	1932, 36, 37, 40, 41, 49, 50, 55(2)
TxMM	1932, 40, 41, 46, 49, 50, 56, 64, 68(1,2)
TxU	1941, 50, 56, 64, 68
TxU-Da	1932, 53, 54, 56
ViBlbV	1955(2), 56, 64, 68
WU	1968(2)

(231) OKLAHOMA. GEOLOGICAL SURVEY. EDUCATIONAL PUBLICATION.

1972 No. 3 Guidebook for geologic field trips in Oklahoma.

[I-GS]	1972
IU	1972
IaU	1972
InU	1972
NdU	1972
OkU	1972

(232) OKLAHOMA. GEOLOGICAL SURVEY. GUIDEBOOK.

1946		Mineral resources field trip, Wichita Mountains district.
1953	1st	Pre-Atoka rock in western part of the Ozark uplift, northeastern Oklahoma. (230)
1954	2nd	Desmoinesian rocks of northeastern Oklahoma. (230)
1955	3rd	Field conference on the geology of the Arbuckle Mountain region. (32)
		Part 1. Geology of the Arbuckle and Timbered Hills groups.
		Part 2. Regional stratigraphy and structure of the Arbuckle region.
1956	4th	Geology of the Turner Turnpike; road log, geologic profile, route map. (233, 230, 314)
1957	5th	Geology of the Wichita Mountain region. (233, 241)
	6th	Subsurface stratigraphic names of Oklahoma.
1958	7th	Guide to Robbers Cave State Park and Camp Tom Hale.
1959	8th	Logging drill cuttings.
	9th	Guide to Roman Nose State Park.
1960	10th	Common minerals, rocks and fossils of Oklahoma.
1963	11th	Guide to Beavers Bend State Park.
	12th	Parks and scenic areas in the Oklahoma Ozarks.
	13th	Well-sample descriptions Anadarko Basin.
1964		Northeastern Oklahoma. (147)
	14th	Logging drill cuttings, 2nd edition.
1966	16th	Late Paleozoic conodonts from the Ouachita and Arbuckle Mountains of Oklahoma.
1969	15th	Alabaster Cavern and Woodward County.
	17th	Regional geology of the Arbuckle Mountains.

[A-GS]	1953, 54, 56
AzFU	1955
CLU-G/G	1953-69
CLhC	1953-57, 59(8), 66, 69(17)
CU-EART	1954
CaACU	1959, 68(17)
[CaBVU]	1955, 68
CaOHM	1954, 56, 57(6), 58, 59(9), 69
CaOKQ	1956, 57, 59(9), 60-69
CaOLU	1954, 56, 57(6), 59(9), 60-69
CaOOG	1953-63, 65-69
CoFS	1956, 57(6), 58, 59(9), 60-64, 69(15), 69(17)
CoG	1953-60, 63, 64, 66, 68, 69
[CoPU]	1954, 58, 59(9), 60, 63(11,12), 66, 69
CoU	1953-56, 57(6), 58, 59-69
DI-GS	1953-57, 68, 69
DLC	1969(17)
ICF	1953-55
ICIU-S	1955(3), 56, 57(6), 58, 59(9), 60-69
ICarbS	1953-56, 57(6), 58, 59(9), 60, 69
IEN	1953-69
[I-GS]	1956, 57(6), 58, 59(9), 63(13)
IU	1953-69
IaU	1954, 59(9), 60, 63(13), 66, 69
IdBB	1969
InLP	1953-56, 58-64, 66, 69
InRE	1971
InU	1953-59, 64, 69
KyU	1953-57, 58(7), 59-64, 66, 68, 69(15), 71
LU	1953-64, 66, 69

MH-GS	1955
MNS	1953-69
MiDW	1953-57, 69(17)
MiHM	1969
MiU	1953-69
MnDuU	1953, 54
MnU	1953-69
MoSW	1953-69
MoU	1953-56, 57(6), 58, 59(9), 60-69
NBiSU	1969(17)
NNC	1953-57
NSyU	1954-63, 69
NcU	1953-59, 69(17)
NdU	1953-56, 58-60, 63(13), 66, 69(15)
NhD	1953-57
NjP	1953-63, 66-69
NmPE	1954, 69
OCU	1953, 54
OU	1953-69
[OkOkCGe]	1953-55, 63, 69(17)
OkOkU	1953-55, 57(6), 60, 69
OkT	1953-59, 63-69
OkU	1927, 53-69
OrU	1953-60, 63, 64, 66, 68, 69(17)
PBm	1954-56, 57(6), 58, 59(9), 60-62, 63(12), 69(17)
PSt	1953-57, 68
RPB	1953-57
TMM	1956, 57(6), 58(7), 59(9), 60-69
TU	1953-57
TxDaAR-T	1953-57, 68
TxDaDM	1953-57, 69(17)
TxDaM	1946, 53-57
TxHSD	1953-55
TxHU	1953-57, 68, 69
TxLT	1953-55, 56(4)
TxMM	1952-57, 68
TxU	1953-57, 59, 60, 63-69
TxU-Da	1953, 56, 69(17)
UU	1953-54, 56-60, 63(11,12), 66, 69
ViBlbV	1953-55, 58, 59(9), 63(13), 66, 69
WU	1953-56, 69(17)

(233) OKLAHOMA. UNIVERSITY. SCHOOL OF GEOLOGY.

1956	See Oklahoma. Geological Survey. (232)
1957	See Oklahoma. Geological Survey. (232)

(234) ONTARIO. DEPARTMENT OF MINES. GEOLOGICAL GUIDEBOOK SERIES.

1968	No. 1	Geology and scenery of Rainy Lake and east to Lake Superior.
1969	No. 2	Geology and scenery of north shore of Lake Superior.
	No. 3	Geology and scenery of Peterborough, Bancroft and Madoc area.
1972	No. 4	Geology and scenery, north shore of Lake Huron region.

CLU-G/G	1968-72
CU-EART	1968-72
CaOHM	1968-72
CaOKQ	1968, 69
CaOLU	1969(3)
CaOOG	1968, 69
CaOONM	1968-72
CoG	1972
CoU	1972
DI-GS	1968, 69(2)
ICF	1968, 69
ICIU-S	1968-72
IEN	1972
IU	1968-72
MH-GS	1968-72
MnU	1968, 69(3)
MoSW	1968-72
NhD	1972
NjP	1968-72
OkU	1968, 69(3), 72
TxU	1968, 69(3)

(235) ONTARIO. DEPARTMENT OF MINES. MISCELLANEOUS PAPER.

1969 No. 29 A geological guide to Highway 60, Algonquin Provincial Park.

KyU	1969
NdU	1969
OkU	1969

(236) OREGON. STATE DEPARTMENT OF GEOLOGY AND MINERAL INDUSTRIES. BULLETIN.

1959 No. 50 College teachers conference in geology. Field guidebook; geologic trips along Oregon highways.

1965 No. 57 State of Oregon lunar geological field conference guidebook. (209)
[1] Devils Hill-Broken Top area and Lava Butte area field trip.
[2] Newberry Volcano area field trip.
[3] Hole-in-the-ground - Fort Rock - Devils Garden area field trip.
[4] Belknap Crater-Yapoah Crater-Collier Cone area field trip.
[5] Crater Lake area field trip.

1968 No. 62 Andesite conference guidebook. (International Upper Mantle Project Scientific report 16-S) Includes:
1. McKenzie Pass area.
2. Crater Lake area.
3. Newberry Caldera area.
4. Mount Hood area.
5. Andesite petrochemistry.

1973 No. 77 Geologic field trips in northern Oregon and southern Washington. (97, 294)
Trip 1. Cretaceous and Cenozoic stratigraphy of north-central Oregon.
Trip 2. Volcanics and intrusive rocks of the central part of the Oregon Coast Range.
Trip 3. Cenozoic stratigraphy of northwestern Oregon and adjacent southwestern Washington.
Trip 4. The Columbia River Gorge; basalt stratigraphy, ancient lava dams, and landslide dams.

Trip 5. Urban environmental geology and planning, Portland, Oregon.
Trip 6. Stratigraphy and structure of Yakima basalt in Pasco Basin, Washington.
Trip 7. Geological field trip guide, Mount St. Helens lava tubes, Washington.

CLU-G/G	1959, 65, 68, 73
CU-EART	1959, 65, 73
[CaBVU]	1965
CaOKQ	1968
CaOOG	1959, 68
[CaOTOM]	1959, 68
CoG	1968
CoU	1965, 68
DI-GS	1959, 65, 68, 69, 73
IEN	1959, 65, 68
[I-GS]	1959, 65, 73
IU	1959, 65, 68, 73
IaU	1965, 68
IdBB	1965, 73
InU	1959, 65, 68
KyU	1965
MH-GS	1959, 65, 68
MiHM	1965
MnU	1965, 69
MoSW	1959, 65, 68, 73
NRU	1965
NSyU	1950
NdU	1959, 65, 68
NhD	1965, 68, 73
NjP	1959, 65, 68, 73
NvU	1968
OU	1959, 65
OkU	1965, 68
OrU	1959, 65, 69
PBL	1959, 65, 68
PSt	1965
RPB	1965
TxDaM	1965
TxLT	1965
TxMM	1959
TxU	1968
WU	1965, 68

(237) OREGON. STATE DEPARTMENT OF GEOLOGY AND MINERAL INDUSTRIES. THE ORE BIN.

1974 The Columbia River Gorge; the story of the river and the rocks: Vol. 36, No. 12.

CoU	1974
IU	1974

(238) OREGON. UNIVERSITY. MUSEUM OF NATURAL HISTORY. BULLETIN.

1973 No. 21 Guide to the geology of the Owyhee region of Oregon.

DLC	1973
IU	1973
IdBB	1973

NvLN 1973
TxLT 1973
UU 1973

(239) PALEONTOLOGICAL SOCIETY.

1966 Precambrian-Cambrian succession; White-Inyo Mountains, California.
1969 North American Paleontological Convention.
No. 1. Minnesota and Wisconsin. Shallow-water Precambrian and Paleozoic communities.
No. 2. The middle Paleozoic paleontology and biostratigraphy of eastern Iowa.

CLU-G/G	1966
CU-EART	1966
CaOOG	1966
ICF	1969
IaU	1969
MnU	1969
MoU	1969
TxU	1969(1)

PAN AMERICAN GEOLOGICAL SOCIETY. See SOUTHWESTERN ASSOCIATION OF STUDENT GEOLOGICAL SOCIETIES. (294)

(240) PANDER SOCIETY. ANNUAL MEETING. GUIDEBOOK.

1972 See Illinois. State Geological Survey. (126)
1974 Pennsylvanian conodont localities in northeastern Ohio. (98, 225)

[I-GS]	1972, 74
TxDaDM	1974

(241) PANHANDLE GEOLOGICAL SOCIETY. FIELD TRIP GUIDEBOOK. (TITLE VARIES)

1938 Southern Colorado and northern New Mexico.
1946 Dry Cimarron River valley, Panhandle of Oklahoma and adjoining area; Front Range of Rocky Mountains in southeastern Colorado.
1949 Fossil and early man sites in the Texas Panhandle.
1951 May 5 Antelope Creek Pueblo and Triassic fossil site, Hutchinson and Potter counties, Texas.
May 17 Dry Cimarron River valley, Panhandle of Oklahoma and adjoining area.
Lower front range of the Rocky Mountains in southeastern Colorado.
1953 Raton Basin region and the Sangre de Cristo Mountains of New Mexico.
1954 Fossil and early man sites in the Texas Panhandle.
1955 Dry Cimarron River valley, the Panhandle of Oklahoma, northeastern New Mexico; lower front range of the Rocky Mountains and southeastern Colorado. (230)
1957 See Oklahoma. Geological Survey. (232)
1958 Saddleback Pueblo and Rotten Hill Triassic fossil site, Oldham County, Texas.
1959 Southern Sangre de Cristo Mountains, New Mexico.
1963 Alibates flint quarries, Alibates Indian ruin, Santa Fe Trail, Sanford dam.
1965 Field trip of the Rocky Dell site.
1969 Pre-Pennsylvanian geology of the Western Anadarko Basin.

AzFU	1957
CLU-G/G	1951, 53-55, 57-59, 63, 65
CLhC	1957
CU-EART	1951, 54, 55, 57
CaOOG	1969

(241) Panhandle Geological Society.

CoDuF	1957
CoG	1938, 51(May 17-19), 54, 55, 57, 59, 63
CoU	1951(May 5), 55, 57, 59
DI-GS	1946, 49, 51, 53-55, 57-59, 63, 65
ICF	1954, 55, 57-59, 63
IEN	1959
IU	1946, 49, 54, 55, 57-59, 63
IaU	1969
InU	1949, 57, 59
KyU	1954, 57, 63, 65, 69
LU	1949, 51(May 17), 53-55, 57, 59, 61, 63, 65
MNS	1957
MiDW	1969
MiU	1954, 55, 57, 59, 63
MnU	1951, 53-55, 57-59, 63
MoSW	1949
MoU	1969
NBiSU	1969
NNC	1951(May 17), 53-55, 58, 59, 63
NSyU	1957
NbU	1953, 55, 57, 59
NcU	1957
NmU	1955
OU	1949, 51(May 17-19), 53-63, 69
OkOkU	1957
OkT	1953-55, 59, 69
OkU	1946-57, 59-69
TxDaAR-T	1951(May 17), 53, 55, 59
TxDaDM	1951, 54, 55, 57-59, 63, 65, 69, 73
TxDaM	1954, 55, 58, 59, 63, 65
TxDaSM	1951, 53, 57, 59
TxHSD	1946, 51, 53, 55(May 17-19), 59, 63
TxHU	1946, 53-55, 57-59, 63, 65
TxLT	1951(May 17), 53
TxMM	1946, 51(May 17), 53-55, 57, 59
TxU	1949, 51, 53-55, 57-59, 63, 69
UU	1957, 59
ViBlbV	1954, 55, 57, 63
WU	1951(May 17-19), 53, 55

(242) PENNSYLVANIA COUNCIL FOR GEOGRAPHY EDUCATION. SPRING CONFERENCE.

1967	14th	Geology and geography of the South Mountain and environs.
1969	April	Field trip guide to Fayette County, Pennsylvania.

DI-GS	1969
InU	1967

PENNSYLVANIA. TOPOGRAPHIC AND GEOLOGIC SURVEY. See FIELD CONFERENCE OF PENNSYLVANIA GEOLOGISTS. (83)

(243) PENNSYLVANIA. TOPOGRAPHIC AND GEOLOGIC SURVEY. 4TH SERIES. BULLETIN. G SERIES.

1938	G-8	Guidebook: A Paleozoic section in south-central Pennsylvania.
	G-11	Guidebook: A Paleozoic section at Delaware Water Gap.
1939	G-12	Guidebook: Highway geology from Philadelphia to Pittsburgh.
	G-13	Guide to the geology from Dauphin to Sunbury.
	G-14	Guide to the geology of the upper Schuylkill Valley.
	G-15	Guidebook to the geology near Reading, Pennsylvania.
	G-16	Guidebook to places of geologic interest in the Lehigh Valley, Pennsylvania.
	G-17	Guidebook to the geology about Pittsburgh.
1942	G-20	Guidebook to the geology of the Pennsylvania Turnpike. (replaced by G-24)
1949	G-24	Guidebook to the geology of the Pennsylvania Turnpike from Carlisle to Irwin.
1958	G-29	Guide to the highway geology from Harrisburg to Bald Eagle Mountain.
1961	G-35	Guide to the geology of Cornwall, Pennsylvania.
1964	G-41	Guidebook to the geology of the Philadelphia area.
1965	G-50	Guide to the Horse Shoe Curve section between Altoona and Gullitzin, central Pennsylvania.

CLU-G/G	1939, 42, 49, 58, 61, 65
CU-EART	1942, 49, 57, 58, 61, 64, 65
CaOHM	1947, 49, 64
CaOKQ	1939(G-17), 49, 64
CaOLU	1949, 64
CoG	1938(G-11), 39, 42, 49, 58, 64, 65
DFPC	1939(G-15,G-17)
ICF	1939(G-12 thru G-14), 42, 58, 64
IEN	1939(G-15 thru G-17), 49, 64, 70
IU	1932-65
IaU	1939, 42, 58, 64, 65
InU	1939(G-15 thru G-17), 49, 58, 64, 65
KyU	1949, 63, 64
MiHM	1939, 49, 61, 64, 65
MoSW	1949
MoU	1939(G-15 thru G-17), 49, 64
NNC	1964
NOneoU	1964
NSyU	1938-49, 64
NdU	1939, 42, 49, 58, 64, 65
NhD	1938, 39, 64
NjP	1939(G-15 thru G-17), 49, 58, 64, 65
NvU	1938(G-11), 42, 49, 58, 64
OCU	1939, 42, 49-65
OU	1938, 39, 42, 49, 61, 64, 65
OkT	1939(G-15 thru G-17), 49, 64, 65
OrU	1939(G-13 thru G-17), 65
PBL	1939, 64
PSt	1939, 49, 64
TMM	1964
TxU	1964
UU	1949, 58, 61, 64, 65
ViBlbV	1939, 49, 64

(244) PETROLEUM EXPLORATION SOCIETY OF NEW YORK.

1974 Guidebook to field trip in Rockland County, New York.

(245) PITTSBURGH GEOLOGICAL SOCIETY. GUIDEBOOK FOR THE FIELD TRIP.

1948		Geology of the northern portion of the Appalachian Basin. (13)
1955		Appalachian geology; guidebook from Pittsburgh to New York City, New York. (12)
1959		See Appalachian Geological Society. (31)
1961		See Appalachian Geological Society. (31)
1963		See Appalachian Geological Society. (31)
1964		See Appalachian Geological Society. (31)
1969	spring	See Ohio Geological Society. (226)

AzFU	1955
CLU-G/G	1948, 55
CSdS	1955
CU-EART	1955, 63
[CaACAM]	1948
[CaBVU]	1948
CaOKQ	1955
CaOLU	1955
CaOOG	1955, 63
CoG	1948, 55
CoU	1955
DI-GS	1948, 55, 59, 63
ICF	1948, 55
ICarbS	1955
IEN	1948, 55
[I-GS]	1948, 55
IU	1948, 55
IaU	1955, 69
InU	1948, 55, 63
KyU	1955, 69
LU	1948, 55
MH-GS	1948
MNS	1948, 55
MiDW	1948, 55
MnU	1948, 55, 57, 59, 61, 63, 64, 69
MoRM	1955
MoSW	1955
NBiSU	1948, 55
NNC	1948, 55
NbU	1955
NcU	1955, 63
NhD	1955
NjP	1948, 55
OCU	1948
OU	1948
OkT	1948, 55
OkU	1955
OrU	1955
PBL	1948, 55
PBm	1948, 55

PSt	1955, 63
RPB	1948
TU	1948
TxDaAR-T	1948
TxDaDM	1955, 69
TxDaSM	1955
TxHU	1948
TxLT	1955
TxU	1948, 55, 69, 70
UU	1955
ViBlbV	1955
WU	1948

(246) PLEISTOCENE FIELD CONFERENCE. GUIDEBOOK.

1947 1st State geologist's conference on the loess deposits, Illinois, Iowa, South Dakota, Nebraska.
1949 2nd Late Cenozoic geology of the Mississippi Valley; southeastern Iowa to central Louisiana.
1951 3rd Middle to late Pleistocene stratigraphy of the central Great Plains.
Part 1. Road log, post-Kansan Pleistocene deposits of central Great Plains.
Part 2. Road log, northeastern Kansas, southwestern Nebraska, western Kansas.
1953 4th Basis of subdivisions of Wisconsin glacial stage in northeastern Illinois...and Wisconsin stratigraphy of the Wabash Valley and west-central Indiana.
1955 5th Wisconsin stratigraphy of northern and eastern Indiana.
Pleistocene chronology of southwestern Ohio.

CLU-G/G	1955
DI-GS	1947, 49, 51, 53, 55
ICarbS	1953
I-GS	1947, 49, 51, 53, 55
IU	1949, 51, 55
IaU	1949, 51, 53
InU	1949, 51, 53, 55
MH-GS	1949, 55
OCU	1955
OU	1955

(247) QUATERNARY STRATIGRAPHY SYMPOSIUM.

1975 Notes on Pleistocene stratigraphy of the Toronto area.

(248) QUEBEC. GEOLOGICAL EXPLORATION SERVICE. FIELD GUIDE.

1969 Oka area; description and itinerary.

CLU-G/G	1969
CaOKQ	1969
CaOOG	1969
ICarbS	1969
InU	1969
KyU	1969
MH-GS	1969
MiHM	1969
NhD	1969
NjP	1969
OU	1969
OkU	1969
WU	1969

(249) **RIO GRANDE VALLEY INTERNATIONAL GEOLOGICAL SOCIETY.**

1965 Cerraivo. McAllen, Rio Grande City, Roma, Miel, Cerraivo. [with road log]

IU	1965
OkU	1965
TxU	1965

(250) **ROCKY MOUNTAIN ASSOCIATION OF GEOLOGISTS. GUIDEBOOK FOR THE FIELD CONFERENCE.**

1937 Bighorn Basin-Yellowstone Valley tectonics. (184, 315, 351, 354)
1938 See Kansas Geological Society. (147)
1947 Central Colorado.
1948 See American Association of Petroleum Geologists. (12)
1953 Northwestern Colorado.
1954 Oil and gas fields of Colorado.
Trip 1. Denver to Colorado Springs and return.
Trip 2. Denver to Canon City and return.
1955 See Intermountain Association of (Petroleum) Geologists. (133)
Geology of the Front Range foothills west of Denver; Deer Creek to Ralston Creek, Jefferson County, Colorado.
1956 Geology of the Raton Basin, Colorado.
1957 Geology of north and middle Parks Basin, Colorado.
1958 Symposium on Pennsylvanian rocks of Colorado and adjacent areas.
1959 11th Washakie, Sand Wash, and Piceance basins. Symposium on Cretaceous rocks of Colorado and adjacent areas.
1960 See Geological Society of America. (96)
Geological road logs of Colorado.
Roag Log No. S1. Trinidad to Colorado-Kansas line.
Road Log No. S2. Trinidad to Colorado-New Mexico line.
Road Log No. S3. Pagosa Springs to Colorado-New Mexico State line.
Road Log No. S4. Mineral-Archuleta county line to Durango.
Road Log No. S5. Bayfield to Durango.
Road Log No. S6. Intersection of U. S. 550 and U. S. 160 near Durango to Colorado-New Mexico line.
Road Log No. S7. Durango to Colorado-Utah state line.
Road Log No. S8. Cortez to Colorado-New Mexico state line.
Road Log No. S9. Cortez to Whitewater.
Road Log No. S10. Durango to Montrose.
Road Log No. S11. Montrose to Grand Junction.
Road Log No. S12. Newcastle to Meeker.
Road Log No. S13. Rifle to Craig.
Road Log No. S14. Junction U. S. 40 and Colorado 387 to Rio Blanco.
Road Log No. S15. Craig to Utah state line.
Road Log No. S16. Craig to Maybell.
Road Log No. S17. Steamboat Springs to Craig.
Road Log No. S18. Steamboat Springs to Hayden.
Road Log No. S19. Granby to the Wyoming line.
Road Log No. S20. Junction Colorado 125 and 127 to Wyoming line.
Road Log No. S21. From Junction 0.2 mile east of Rand to Walden.
Road Log No. S22. Kremmling to Dillon.
Road Log No. S23. Glenwood Springs to Intersection of Colorado 82 and U. S. 24
Road Log No. S24. Rangely to Grand Junction, Colorado.
Road Log No. S25. Poncha Springs to Montrose.

		Road Log No. S26. Trinidad to Walsenburg.
1961	12th	South-central Colorado. Symposium on lower and middle Paleozoic rocks of Colorado.
1962		[1] Geology of foothills and Front Range in the vicinity of Morrison, Colorado.
	13th	Exploration for oil and gas in northwestern Colorado.
1963		Geology of North Denver Basin and adjacent uplift.
1964	16th	[Central Rockies, Colorado; tectonics and associated sedimentation] (Mountain Geologist, Vol. 1, No. 3, July 1964.)
1965		Piceance and eastern Uinta basins, Colorado and northeast Utah. (Mountain Geologist, Vol. 2, No. 3, July, 1965.)
1966		No field trip.
1967		No field trip.
1968		Southeastern Colorado (Mountain Geologist, Vol. 5, No. 3, July, 1968.)
1969		Raton Basin, Colorado and New Mexico (Mountain Geologist, Vol. 6, No. 3, July, 1969.)
1970		Dakota and related rocks of the Front Range (Mountain Geologist, Vol. 7, No. 3, July, 1970.)
1971		No field trip.
1973		Cretaceous stratigraphy, central Front Range. (Mountain Geologist, Vol. 10, No. 3, July, 1973.)
1974	25th	Energy resources of the Piceance Creek Basin, Colorado.
1975		Symposium (seminar and field trip) on the deep drilling frontiers in the central Rocky Mountains.

AzFU	1956, 58-63, 65, 68, 70
AzTeS	1954, 55, 57, 58, 60, 61, 62(13), 65, 68-70, 74
[CDU]	1957, 58, 61, 63-73
CLU-G/G	1937, 47, 54-63, 65, 68-70, 73-75
CLhC	1937, 47, 54-61, 62(13), 63-65, 68-70, 73, 74
CSdS	1953, 55-59, 60(a?), 63, 64
CSfCSM	1955, 58
CU-EART	1954-59, 60(b?), 61-65, 68-70, 73, 74
[CaACAM]	1937
CaACI	1955, 60, 69, 70
CaACU	1947, 53-59
CaAEU	1963
[CaBVU]	1960
CaOHM	1954, 56, 57, 60(a,b?), 63, 68-70
CaOKQ	1954, 56, 58-61, 63
CaOLU	1948, 60(a,b)
CaOOG	1958-65
CoDuF	1960, 74
CoFS	1947, 62
CoG	1937, 47, 54-65, 68-70, 73, 74
[CoPU]	1959, 60, 63
CoU	1947, 54-61, 62(13), 63-65, 68-70, 72-74
DI-GS	1937, 47, 53, 55-65, 69
ICF	1954-61, 63-65, 68-70, 73
ICarbS	1959-61, 62(13), 63
IEN	1947, 54, 55(b), 56-61, 62(13), 63, 64, 74
IU	1947, 54, 56, 58-61, 62(13), 63-65, 68-75
IaU	1937, 38, 48, 54-70, 73, 74
IdBB	1955, 56, 58, 60, 62, 74
IdPI	1956-58, 59(11), 61, 68-70, 72, 73
InLP	1956-61, 62(13), 63
InU	1937, 38, 47-61, 63-65, 68-70

KyU	1938, 48, 54-65, 70, 74
LU	1947, 54-64
MH-GS	1937, 60
MNS	1938, 54-56, 60, 63
MiDW	1954, 56, 57, 60
MiKW	1947
MiU	1947, 54-59, 61-65
MnU	1937, 54-65, 68, 69
MoSW	1947, 54
MoU	1954-61, 62(13), 63
MtBC	1954-64, 74
MtU	1955
NBiSU	1954, 56, 58-63
NNC	1947, 54-61, 62(13), 63
NRU	1956, 58-60(b?)
NSyU	1955-58, 60(a), 64, 65, 68-70, 73, 74
NbU	1947, 54-61, 62(13), 63, 64
NcU	1938, 54, 56, 74
NdU	1937, 56, 57, 59, 60(b), 64, 65, 68-70, 73, 75
NhD	1937, 38, 60(b), 63-70, 73
NjP	1937, 54-60, 62(13), 64, 65, 68-71, 73-75
NmPE	1960
NvU	1956-63
OCU	1937, 60(a), 75
OU	1937, 47, 54-59, 60(a), 61, 62(13), 63-65, 68, 73
[OkOkCGe]	1952
OkT	1937, 56-59, 61, 62, 74
OkU	1937, 47, 54-59, 60(b), 61, 62(13), 63, 64, 69, 70, 73
OrCS	1947, 54, 56, 58, 59, 61, 62(13), 63-65, 68, 70, 73, 74
OrU	1957-59, 61-65, 68-70, 72, 73
PBL	1937
PPiGulf	1955
PSt	1954-57, 60
RPB	1937, 55
SdRM	1947, 54, 55,(front range?), 56, 57, 59-61, 63
SdU	1954, 55, 58-60
TxDaAR-T	1947, 54-61, 62(13), 63-65, 68-70, 74
TxDaDM	1947, 54-61, 62(13), 63-65, 68-70, 73
TxDaM	1937, 47, 54-61, 62(13), 63-65
TxDaSM	1937, 54-57, 59-61, 62(13), 63, 74
TxHSD	1956-59, 60(a?), 62, 64, 74, 75
TxHU	1947, 54-59, 61, 62(13), 63, 74
TxLT	1954, 56-61, 62(13), 63, 64
TxMM	1947, 54-61, 63, 74
TxU	1937, 47, 54-61, 62(13), 63-65, 68-70
TxU-Da	1957, 60
UU	1947, 54, 56, 58-60
ViBlbV	1954, 58, 59, 61, 74
WU	1954-75
WyU	1937, 47, 53, 55-64

(251) ROSWELL GEOLOGICAL SOCIETY. GUIDEBOOK OF THE FIELD CONFERENCE.

1950	2nd	Pre-Permian stratigraphy of the Sacramento Mountains, New Mexico.
1951	4th	Permian stratigraphy of the Capitan reef area of the southern Guadalupe Mountains, New Mexico.
	5th	Capitan-Carrizozo-Chupadera Mesa region, Lincoln and Socorro counties, New Mexico.
1952	6th	Surface structures of the foothill region of the Sacramento and Guadalupe Mountains, Chaves, Eddy, Lincoln and Otero counties, New Mexico.
	7th	The Pedernal positive element and the Estancia Basin, Torrance and northern Lincoln counties, New Mexico.
1953	8th	Stratigraphy of the West Front and Sacramento Mountains, Otero and Lincoln counties, New Mexico.
1956	9th	The Stauber Copper mine and the Santa Rosa asphalt deposit, Guadalupe County, New Mexico.
1957	10th	Slaughter Canyon, New Cave and Capitan reef exposure, Carlsbad Caverns National Park, New Mexico.
1958	11th	Hatchet Mountains and the Cooks Range-Florida Mountain areas, Grant, Hidalgo and Luna counties, southwestern New Mexico.
1959		See Society of Economic Paleontologists and Mineralogists. Permian Basin Section. (280)
1960	12th	Northern Franklin Mountains, southern San Andres Mountains with emphasis on Pennsylvanian stratigraphy.
1961		See Southwestern Federation of Geological Societies. (295)
1962	13th	See West Texas Geological Society. (338)
1964	14th	Geology of the Capitan reef complex of the Guadalupe Mountains, Culberson County, Texas, and Eddy County, New Mexico.
1968		Roswell artesian basin.
1971		Stratigraphy and structure of the Pecos County, southeastern New Mexico. (West Texas and Roswell Geological Societies. Publication No. 71-58.) (338)

AzFU	1965, 66
AzTeS	1958-60, 62-68
AzU	1971
CChiS	1958
CLU-G/G	1951, 53, 56, 57, 60, 64, 71
CLhC	1958, 59, 62
CSdS	1951
CU-EART	1957, 60, 64, 68
[CaBVU]	1959
CaOHM	1960, 64
CaOKQ	1968
CoG	1956-58, 60, 64-66, 71
[CoPU]	1964
CoU	1952(6,7), 53
DI-GS	1951(6), 52, 53, 56-62, 64, 71
ICF	1957, 58, 60, 64
ICIU-S	1960, 62, 64
IEN	1958
IU	1957-62, 71
IaU	1958, 59, 62, 64, 71
InLP	1957, 60, 64
InU	1958-60, 62, 64, 68, 71
KyU	1959, 60, 62, 64, 71
MiKW	1960
MiU	1960, 64

(251) Roswell Geological Society.

MnU	1956-60, 62, 64
MoSW	1958, 60, 64
MoU	1960, 64
MtU	1957, 58, 60, 62, 64
NNC	1951(5), 52, 57, 58, 60
NOneoU	1964
NbU	1960-62
NcU	1959, 62
NdU	1964
NhD	1962
NjP	1960, 62, 64, 68
NmPE	1957, 60, 62, 64
NmU	1956, 58, 60
OU	1951-53, 57, 58, 64
OkT	1958, 64
OkU	1956-58, 60, 64
PPiGulf	1956, 57, 60
TxDaAR-T	1951(5), 52, 53, 55-66
TxDaDM	1951(5), 52(6), 53, 56-58,,60, 64, 71
TxDaM	1956-60, 62, 64
TxDaSM	1951(5), 53, 56-58, 64
TxHSD	1950, 56, 57, 60, 64
TxHU	1956-60, 64
TxLT	1956-58, 62, 64
TxMM	1950, 51, 52(7), 53, 56-58, 60, 64-65
TxU	1950, 52, 53, 56-60, 64, 68, 71
TxU-Da	1958
UU	1957, 58
WU	1964
WyU	1964

(252) ROSWELL GEOLOGICAL SOCIETY. ONE DAY FIELD TRIP SERIES.

1965-66 Trip 1. IMC Potash Mine field trip, Carlsbad, New Mexico.

AzTeS	1965, 66
CLU-G/G	1965, 66
CU-EART	1965, 66
CaACU	1965, 66
CaOHM	1965, 66
CoG	1965, 66
IU	1965, 66
InLP	1965, 66
InU	1965, 66
KyU	1965, 66
MiU	1965, 66
MnU	1965, 66
NjP	1965, 66
OU	1965, 66
OkU	1965, 66
TxDaDM	1965, 66
TxDaM	1965, 66
TxLT	1965, 66
TxMM	1965, 66
TxU	1965, 66
TxU-Da	1965, 66

(253) SAN ANGELO DESK AND DERRICK CLUB.

1959		Geological field trip featuring plains and canyons.
		TxU 1959

(254) SAN ANGELO GEOLOGICAL SOCIETY. GUIDEBOOK TO THE BIENNIAL FIELD TRIP.

1954	1st	See West Texas Geological Society. (338)
1956	2nd	Four provinces: central mineral region, Balcones fault zone, Kerr Basin, and Rio Grande embayment.
1958		Base of the Permian; a century of controversy.
1961		See West Texas Geological Society. (338)

CChiS	1958
CLU-G/G	1954, 56, 58
CLhC	1954, 56, 58
CU-EART	1954, 56
[CaBVU]	1956, 58, 61
CaOOG	1956, 58
CoG	1954, 56, 58
CoU	1954, 56, 58
DI-GS	1954, 56, 58, 61
ICF	1956, 58
IEN	1956, 58
IU	1954, 56, 58
IaU	1958, 61
InLP	1956
InU	1954, 56, 58, 61
KyU	1954, 56, 58, 61
LU	1954, 56, 58, 61
MNS	1954, 58
MiDW	1958
MiHM	1954
MnU	1954, 56, 58, 61
MoSW	1954
MoU	1956, 58
NNC	1954, 56, 58
NSyU	1956, 58
NbU	1954, 56, 58
NcU	1956, 58, 61
NdU	1954, 56, 58
NhD	1954, 56, 58
NjP	1954, 56, 58
NvU	1954, 56, 58
OCU	1956, 58
OU	1954, 56, 58
OkT	1954, 56, 58
OkU	1954, 56, 58
OrU	1954
PBL	1956, 58
PPiGulf	1954, 56
PSt	1954, 56, 58
RPB	1958
SdRM	1956

(254) San Angelo Geological Society.

TU	1956, 58
TxDaAR-T	1954, 56, 58
TxDaDM	1954, 56, 58
TxDaM	1954, 56, 58
TxDaSM	1954, 56, 58
TxHSW	1956
TxHSD	1954, 56, 58
TxHU	1954, 56, 58, 61
TxLT	1954, 56, 58
TxMM	1954, 56, 58
TxU	1954, 56, 58
TxU-Da	1954, 56, 58
ViBlbV	1954, 56, 58
WU	1954, 56

SAN ANTONIO GEOLOGICAL SOCIETY. See SOUTH TEXAS GEOLOGICAL SOCIETY. (290)

(255) SAN DIEGO ASSOCIATION OF GEOLOGISTS. GUIDEBOOK.

1973 Studies on the geology and geologic hazards of the greater San Diego area, California.

[CDU]	1973
CSfCSM	1973
DI-GS	1973
NSyU	1973

(256) SAN JOAQUIN GEOLOGICAL SOCIETY. GUIDEBOOK FOR THE FIELD TRIP. (TITLE VARIES)

1948		See Society of Economic Paleontologists and Mineralogists. Pacific Section. (279)
1949		Hollister Ranch, El Bulito Canyon and vicinity of Refugian type section, Santa Barbara, California. (279)
1951	May	See Society of Economic Paleontologists and Mineralogists. Pacific Section. (279)
1954		See Northern California Geological Society. (221)
1955		See Society of Economic Paleontologists and Mineralogists. Pacific Section. (279)
1956	May	See Society of Economic Paleontologists and Mineralogists. Pacific Section. (279)
1957		See Society of Economic Paleontologists and Mineralogists. Pacific Section. (279)
1958		Round Mountain area, Kern County, California.
1959		Chico-Martinez Creek area, California.
1960		See Society of Economic Paleontologists and Mineralogists. Pacific Section. (279)
1961		See Society of Economic Paleontologists and Mineralogists. Pacific Section. (279)
1962		See Society of Economic Paleontologists and Mineralogists. Pacific Section. (279)
1963		See Society of Economic Paleontologists and Mineralogists. Pacific Section. (279)
1964		See Society of Economic Paleontologists and Mineralogists. Pacific Section. (279)
1965		San Joaquin Valley.
1966		Santa Susana Mountains.

CChiS	1958
[CDU]	1958, 59, 62
CLU-G/G	1958, 59, 62
CLhC	1958, 62
CSfCSM	1958, 59, 62
CU-EART	1959, 62
CoG	1958, 59, 62
DI-GS	1955-59, 61, 62, 64-66
ICF	1959, 62

IU 1958, 59, 62
IaU 1963, 64
IdBB 1962, 64
InU 1954
MnU 1949, 58-59, 62, 64
NNC 1958, 59, 62
NbU 1958, 59, 62
NcU 1962, 64
OCU 1959, 62
OU 1958, 59, 62
TxDaAR-T 1962
TxDaDM 1959, 62
TxDaM 1958, 59, 62
TxDaSM 1962
TxHSD 1962
TxMM 1959
TxU 1948, 49, 54, 56, 58, 59, 62
TxU-Da 1958, 59, 62
UU 1958
ViBlbV 1959

(257) SASKATCHEWAN GEOLOGICAL SOCIETY. FIELD TRIP.

1956 Field trip. Report of the Mississippian Names and Correlations Committee.
1958 Field trip. Report of the lower Palaeozoic Names and Correlations Committee.
1965 Geological road log of the Winnipeg and Interlake area, Manitoba.
1966 Geological road log of the Hanson Lake road, Flin-Flon area, Saskatchewan-Manitoba.
1967 Geological road logs of the Lakes Winnepegosis and Manitoba areas, Manitoba.
1969 Field trip. Geological road log of the Cypress Hills area, southwestern Saskatchewan.
1970 Geological road log of the Montreal Lake-Lac La Ronge area, Saskatchewan.
1971 Field trip. Geological road log of the Cypress Hills-Milk River area, southeastern Alberta.
1972 Field trip. Guidebook on geology and its application to engineering practice in the Qu'appelle Valley area.
1973 An excursion guide to the geology of Saskatchewan. Road logs.
Geological road log of the Winnipeg and Interlake areas.
Geological road log of the lakes Winnipegosis and Manitoba areas, Manitoba.
Geological road log of the Hanson Lake Road-Flin Flon area, Saskatchewan-Manitoba.
Geological road log of the Montreal Lake-Wapawekka Hills area.
Tour of the Estevan coalfield.
Geological road log of the Avonlea-Big Muddy Valley area.
Geological road log of the Cypress Hills-Milk River area, southeastern Alberta.
Upper Cretaceous and Tertiary stratigraphy of the Swift Current-Cypress Hills area.
Geological road log for Highway 2; La Ronge to Reindeer Lake.
Northern Saskatchewan uranium tour: La Ronge-Rabbit Lake-Beaverlodge-Cluff Lake.
Geology and ores of the Hanson Lake, Flin Flon and Snow Lake areas of Saskatchewan and Manitoba.

CLU-G/G 1966, 67, 69-73
CaAC 1973
[CaACAM] 1956, 58, 65-67, 69, 71, 72
CaACM 1967
CaOKQ 1965
CaOOG 1966, 73
CoG 1965, 66

(257) Saskatchewan Geological Society.

DI-GS	1965-67, 69-71
IU	1966, 67, 69-73
IaU	1965
InLP	1966, 67
InU	1968, 73
MiU	1966, 67
MnU	1965, 66
MtU	1966
NdU	1965
TxDaDM	1965, 69
TxDaM	1965, 66
TxDaSM	1965
TxU	1965

(258) SHAWNEE GEOLOGICAL SOCIETY. FIELD CONFERENCE (TITLE VARIES)

1938	[1]	A study of surface rocks from Calvin Sandstone to Permian through Township 6 north to Township 10 north, Hughes, Seminole, and Pottawatomie counties, Oklahoma.
	[2]	A study of surface rocks from McAlister Shale to Thurman Sandstone through Townships 4,5, and 6 north, Ranges 12-17 east, Pittsburg County, Oklahoma.

DI-GS	1938([2])
IU	1938
MoSW	1938([2])
OU	1938([2])
OkU	1938([2])
TxDaSM	1938([2])
TxLT	1938
TxMM	1938
TxU	1938([2])

(259) SHREVEPORT GEOLOGICAL SOCIETY. ANNUAL FIELD TRIP. GUIDEBOOK.

1923		Upper Cretaceous formation of south Arkansas.
1924		Hope, Arkansas: Wilcox outcrop, Arkadelphia Formation and Midway outcrop.
1925		Saratoga section, Rocky Comfort section, Cerro Gordo section, Basal section, Dequeen section, Dierks section, Basal Trinity section.
1926	4th	[Title unknown.]
1927		Wilcox and Clairborne outcrops of east Texas.
1928		Northeast Texas and southeast Oklahoma.
1929	7th	Tennessee-Muscle Shoals, Alabama-Tupelo, Mississippi.
1932	9th	Tertiary formations of Mississippi and Alabama.
1933	10th	Oligocene and Eocene Jackson formations of Caldwell and Catahoula parishes, Louisiana.
1934	11th	Stratigraphy and paleontological notes on the Eocene (Jackson Group), Oligocene and lower Miocene of Clarke and Wayne counties, Mississippi.
1939	14th	Upper and Lower Cretaceous of southwest Arkansas, supplemented by contributions to the subsurface stratigraphy of south Arkansas and north Louisiana.
1947	15th	Upper and Lower Cretaceous of southwestern Arkansas.
1948	16th	Ouachita Mountains; Cambrian through Pennsylvanian Magnet Cove.
1949	17th	Cretaceous of Austin, Texas area.
1951	18th	Guidebook to the Paleozoic rocks of northwest Arkansas. (36)
1953	19th	Upper and Lower Cretaceous of southwest Arkansas, Cambrian-Pennsylvanian of the Ouachita Mountains, and Magnet Cove.
1960	20th	Interior salt domes and Tertiary stratigraphy of north Louisiana.

1961	21st	Cretaceous of southwest Arkansas and southeast Oklahoma.
1965	22nd	Cretaceous of southwest Arkansas.
1966		Iron ore deposits and surface geology (Tertiary) of north Louisiana. (Louisiana Geological Bulletin, No. 41 used as guidebook this year.)
1967		Natchitoches Parish, Louisiana.
1969	23rd	Comanchean stratigraphy of the Fort Worth-Waco-Belton area, Texas.
1970		Southeast Oklahoma and northeast Texas.
1971		Geology of the Llano region and Austin area, Texas. (308)
1973		A study of Paleozoic rocks in Arbuckle and western Ouachita Mountains of southern Oklahoma.
1975		Paleozoic Ozark shelf of northern Arkansas. (Louisiana State University, School of Geoscience, Guidebook No. 73-1, 1973.)

[A-GS]	1934, 60, 61, 65
CLU-G/G	1939, 49, 51, 53, 60, 66, 73
CLhC	1948, 49, 53, 60
CSdS	1960
CU-EART	1949, 53, 60, 61, 67, 69, 70, 73
CaOHM	1960, 61, 65, 69
CaOKQ	1960, 65
CoG	1947, 49, 53, 60, 61, 65, 66, 69-71
CoU	1939, 66
DI-GS	1932-34, 39, 47-49, 51, 53, 60, 61, 65, 66, 70
ICF	1960
IEN	1948, 49, 60
IU	1939, 47-49, 51, 53, 60, 61, 65, 66, 70, 73
IaU	1934, 39, 49
InLP	1931, 53, 60, 65, 69, 70
InU	1948, 49, 60
KyU	1949, 51, 53, 60, 61, 65, 66, 69, 70
LU	1932-34, 39, 46, 49, 51, 53, 60, 61, 65, 66, 69 70
MNS	1939
MiDW	1960
MiU	1939, 49, 53, 60, 61, 65
MnU	1949, 51, 53, 60, 61, 65, 66, 69
MoSW	1934, 47-49, 51, 53, 60
MoU	1939, 47-60, 63
[Ms-GS]	1934
NNC	1939, 48, 49, 53, 60, 61
NSyU	1951, 66
NbU	1939, 49, 60, 61
NcU	1949-65, 70
NdU	1951, 66
NhD	1960, 66
NjP	1934, 39, 53, 61, 65, 69-71, 73
NvU	1960
OU	1939, 48-61
[OkOkCGe]	1939, 53
OkT	1939, 49, 60, 61
OkU	1923-29, 34-61, 73
OrU	1960
PPiGulf	1939, 48, 49, 53, 60, 61
PSt	1971

TMM	1960, 61, 71
TxDaAR-T	1934, 48, 49, 51, 61, 63, 69, 71, 73, 75
TxDaDM	1949, 51, 53, 60, 61, 65, 66, 69, 70
TxDaM	1934, 39, 48, 49, 51, 53, 60, 61, 65
TxDaSM	1932-34, 39, 49, 51, 53, 61, 65, 71, 73
TxHSD	1947-49, 53-61, 69, 73
TxHU	1932-49, 53, 60-70
TxLT	1934, 39, 48-51, 60
TxMM	1939, 49, 61
TxU	1929, 32-34, 47-49, 51, 53, 60, 61, 65, 66, 69-71, 73
TxU-Da	1933, 34, 39, 47, 51
UU	1960
ViBlbV	1949, 53-61, 69, 70
WU	1948, 49, 53

(260) SIERRA CLUB. MOTHER LODE CHAPTER, YAHI GROUP.

1966 A guide to the geology of the Yahi Trail, Bidwell Park, Chico, California.
CChiS 1966

(261) SIGMA GAMMA EPSILON.

n.d. SGE presents a field trip to Llano.
TxHU n.d.

(262) SIGMA GAMMA EPSILON. ALPHA CHAPTER. UNIVERSITY OF KANSAS.

1965 Cyclothems of Kansas. (Guidebook)
InU 1965

(263) SIGMA GAMMA EPSILON. ALPHA CHAPTER. UNIVERSITY OF MISSOURI.

1949 Study of Marmaton-Pleasanton, Kansas City and Lansing Pennsylvanian between Lexington, Missouri and Lawrence, Kansas. (183)
MnDuU 1949
MoU 1949
NjP 1949
OkU 1949

(264) SIGMA GAMMA EPSILON. ALPHA NU CHAPTER. KANSAS STATE UNIVERSITY. ANNUAL SPRING FIELD TRIP. GUIDEBOOK.

1969 Southeast Kansas, central Arkansas, southeast Missouri.
TxDaDM 1969

(265) SIGMA GAMMA EPSILON. GAMMA ALPHA CHAPTER. UNIVERSITY OF WISCONSIN, SUPERIOR.

1974 6th Twin Ports area.
IU 1974

(266) SIGMA GAMMA EPSILON. GAMMA CHAPTER. UNIVERSITY OF OKLAHOMA.

1936	Conference on the Pennsylvanian of Oklahoma, Kansas and north Texas.
1937	Conference on Permian of Oklahoma and southern Kansas.
1940	Conference on the Pennsylvanian of Texas, Oklahoma and Kansas.
1941	Muskogee area.
1947	Criner Hills field trip.
1952	See Oklahoma Academy of Science. (229)
1953	Pt. 1. Cambrian stratigraphy of the Wichita Mountains.
	Pt. 2. Stratigraphy and structure of the Criner Hills.
1959	Wichita Mountains field trip.

OkU	1941, 47, 53, 59
TxLT	1936, 37, 40
TxMM	1937

(267) SIGMA GAMMA EPSILON. NATIONAL CONFERENCE. (TITLE VARIES)

1937	11th	[1] Luling oil fields and San Antonio.
		[2] Points of geologic interest in the vicinity of Austin, Texas.
1947		Criner Hills field trip.
1951		Summary of Arkansas geology and field trip itineraries, Hot Springs.
		Field trip in Hot Springs-Little Rock area.
		Field trip to Magnet Cove and Potash Sulphur Springs area.
		Bus trip to Little Rock, with stop enroute to inspect nepheline syenite quarries.
1968		[Assorted trips in Cincinnati, Ohio area.]
1973		The Cretaceous of Parker and Tarrant counties, Texas

CLU-G/G	1937([2])
CoG	1951
CoU	1951
DI-GS	1951, 68
IU	1947, 51
InU	1951
MoRM	1951
OCU	1951
OU	1951
OkU	1951, 73
PSt	1951
TMM	1968
TxHU	1937([1])
TxMM	1937
TxU	1937, 51

(268) SIGMA GAMMA EPSILON. RHO CHAPTER. INDIANA UNIVERSITY.

1966	A survey of Indiana geology with road logs for two field trips. (129)

CLhC	1966
CU-EART	1966
CaOOG	1966
CoG	1966
CoU	1966
DI-GS	1966
IU	1966
IaU	1966

InU	1966
KyU	1966
LU	1966
MiHM	1966
NdU	1966
NjP	1966
OU	1966
OkU	1966
TU	1966
TxDaAR-T	1966
WU	1966

(269) SIGMA GAMMA EPSILON. XI CHAPTER. WASHINGTON STATE UNIVERSITY.

1962 Washington State University, Columbia Basin field trip guidebook.

(270) SIGMA GAMMA EPSILON. ZETA CHAPTER. THE UNIVERSITY OF TEXAS AT AUSTIN.

1966	Jan.	Northern Chihuahua field trip.
	Nov.	No. 1. Problems in Precambrian igneous and metamorphic rocks, Llano uplift, central Texas.
	Dec.	No. 2. Tertiary sediments, central Texas.
1967	Jan.	No. 3, Pt. 1. Carbonate depositional environments, central Texas.
		Pt. 2. Carbonate depositional environments, central Texas.
		Pt. 3. Carbonate depositional environments, central Texas: Marble Falls and Glen Rose.
		No. 4. Problems in engineering geology in Austin, Texas.
		No. 5. Upper Cambrian succession, southeast Llano uplift, Blanco County.
	Apr.	No. 6. West Texas field trip.
		No. 7. Problems in geomorphology, central Texas.
1968	Jan.	No. 3. Early Cretaceous depositional environments.
	Nov.	No. 1. Metamorphic rocks, Llano uplift; sedimentary rocks, Marble Falls area.
	Dec.	No. 2. [Stratigraphic units of the Jackson Group and adjacent formations, south-central Texas.]
		No. 4. Indio Lagoon system, Wilcox Group (Eocene), south Texas.
1969		Trip 1. Environmental and engineering geology, Austin area.
1970		Trip 2. Austin-San Antonio-Eagle Pass-Piedras Negras-Nuevo Rosita-Monclova-Saltillo, Mexico.

DI-GS	1966(1), 67(5,7), 68(1,2,3)
TxU	1966-70

(271) SOCIEDAD GEOLOGICA MEXICANA. CONVENCION NACIONAL. GUIA DE LA EXCURSION GEOLOGICA.

1970		Libro-guia de la excursion Mexico-Oaxaca. Itineria geologica.
		Pt. 1. Mexico, D. F.-Cuautla, Mor.-Izucar de Matamoros, Pur.-Huajuapan de Leon, Oax.
		Pt. 2. Huajuapan de Leon, Oax.-Oaxaca, Oax.
1972	2nd	Mazatlan, Sinaloa.
		Excursiones geologicas.
		Torreon-Durango.
		Cerro de Mercado, Durango, Dgo. (no text)
		Durango-Mazatlan.
		Distrito minero de Tayoltita, Dgo. (no text)
1974	3rd	Zacatecas, Zac.-Guanajuato, Gto.

TxU	1970

(272) SOCIETY FOR THE STUDY OF EVOLUTION. FIELD EXCURSION.

1955 From Austin to Palmetto State Park via Bastrop, Red Rock, and Luling. San Marcos, Wimberly, and Dripping Springs.

TxU	1955

(273) SOCIETY OF ECONOMIC GEOLOGISTS.

1963 Geology and technology of the Grants uranium region. Prepared for Uranium Field Conference. (New Mexico. Bureau of Mines and Mineral Resources. Memoir 15.)

1969
1. Papers on the stratigraphy and mine geology of the Kingsport and Mascot formations (Lower Ordovician) of east Tennessee. (300)
2. Field conference on Wyoming uranium deposits. (353)

1970
1. Lead-zinc deposits in the Kootenay Arc, northeastern Washington and adjacent British Columbia. (Washington. (State). Division of Mines and Geology. Bulletin No. 61.)
2. Foraminifera, stratigraphy and paleoecology of the Quinault Formation, Point Grenville-Raft coastal area, Washington. (Washington. (State). Division of Mines and Geology. Bulletin No. 62.)

1971
1. Field conference on Wyoming trona deposits. (353)
2. Michigan copper district.

1974 Field conference on kaolin and fuller's earth. (112)

1975 Guidebook to the Bingham mining district.

AzFU	1963
CLU-G/G	1963, 69(1)
CLhC	1969(2)
CaOKQ	1971(2)
CaOLU	1969(1), 70
CaOOG	1970
CoG	1963, 69(1), 71(2)
CoU	1970(1)
DI-GS	1971, 74, 75
ICF	1969(1)
IU	1971, 75
IaU	1963, 69(1)
InU	1963, 69(1), 71
KyU	1969(1), 71, 74
MiHM	1963, 69(1), 71(2)
MoSW	1963, 69(1)
NSyU	1969(1)
NbU	1969(1)
NcU	1969(1)
NdU	1963, 69(1)
NhD	1963, 69(1), 71(2)
NjP	1969(1), 75
OCU	1963, 69(1), 75
OU	1963, 69(1)
OkU	1963, 69(1), 70(1)
PSt	1963, 69(1)
TMM	1969(1)
TxDaAR-T	1969(2), 74
TxDaDM	1969(1,2), 71(1)
TxU	1963, 69
ViBlbV	1969(1), 71(2)

(274) SOCIETY OF ECONOMIC PALEONTOLOGISTS AND MINERALOGISTS. ANNUAL MEETING. GUIDEBOOK FOR ANNUAL FIELD TRIP.

1927	1st	Field excursion across Comanchean and Cretaceous section.
1929	3rd	Vicinity of Fort Worth, Texas. (12)
1930		Arbuckle Mountains, Oklahoma.
1944		See American Association of Petroleum Geologists. (12)
1947		See American Association of Petroleum Geologists. (12)
1950		See Illinois. State Geological Survey. (126)
1952		See American Association of Petroleum Geologists. (12)
1953		See American Association of Petroleum Geologists. (12)
1956		See Illinois. State Geological Survey. (126)
1958		See American Association of Petroleum Geologists. (12)
1959		See American Association of Petroleum Geologists. (12)
1960		Guidebooks. (12, 145)
		1. Geology of north-central part of the New Jersey coastal plain.
		2. Geology of the region between Roanoke and Winchester, Appalachian Valley of western Virginia.
		3. Lower Paleozoic carbonate rocks in Maryland and Pennsylvania.
		4. See same series, 1958, 17th.
1962		See California. Division of Mines and Geology. (54)
1963		See American Association of Petroleum Geologists. (12)
1964		See American Association of Petroleum Geologists. (12)
1968		See American Association of Petroleum Geologists. (12)
1969		Field Trip No. 1. A guidebook to the stratigraphy, sedimentary structures and origin of flysch and pre-flysch rocks of the Marathon Basin, Texas. (12)
		Field Trip No. 2. A guidebook to the depositional environments and depositional history of Lower Cretaceous shallow shell carbonates, west-central Texas. (12)
		Field Trip No. 3. A guidebook to the Late Pennsylvanian shelf sediments, north-central Texas. (12)
		Field Trip No. 4. Late Cenozoic stratigraphy of southwestern Florida. (114, 277)
		Field Trip No. 5. Geological field guide to Neogene sections in Jamaica, West Indies. (This volume of the Journal of the Geological Society of Jamaica was prepared and published separately as field guide for a field trip held in Jamaica as part of the 19th Annual Convention of the Gulf Coast Association of Geological Societies and the Society of Economic Paleontologists and Mineralogists.) (114)
1970		See American Association of Petroleum Geologists. (12)
1971		Trace fossils, a field guide to selected localities in Pennsylvanian, Permian, Cretaceous, and Tertiary rocks of Texas and related papers. (Louisiana State University. School of Geoscience. Miscellaneous Publication No. 71-1.)
1972		Environments of sandstone, carbonate and evaporite deposition. (Mountain Geologist, Vol. 9, Nos. 2-3, Part II.)
		Field Trip 1. Environments of sandstone deposition, Colorado Front Range.
		Field Trip 2. Carbonate and evaporite facies of the Paradox Basin. Road log.
1973		Field Trip No. 1. Miocene sedimentary environment and biofacies, southeastern Los Angeles Bay.
		Field Trip No. 2. Sedimentary facies changes in Tertiary rocks, California transverse and southern coast ranges.
		Field Trip No. 3. Field conference on Borden Group and overlying limestone units, south-central Indiana.
		Geology of the Llano region and Austin area, Texas, central mineral region.
1974	48th	Field Trip No. 1. Stratigraphy of the Edwards Group and equivalents, eastern Edwards Plateau, Texas.

Field Trip No. 2. A field guide: Shallow marine sediments of Early Cretaceous (Trinity) platform of central Texas. (Louisiana State University. School of Geoscience. Miscellaneous Publication No. 74-1.) (12)

Field Trip No. 3. Aspects of Trinity Division geology; a symposium on the stratigraphy, sedimentary environments, and fauna of the Comanche Cretaceous Trinity Division (Aptian and Albian) of Texas and northern Mexico.

Guatemala field trip guidebook. (114, 277)

1975 Field Trip No. 1. A guidebook to the sedimentology of Paleozoic flysch and associated deposits, Ouachita Mountains-Arkoma Basin, Oklahoma. (Published by the Dallas Geological Society for the Annual Meeting of the A.A.P.G. and the Society of Economic Paleontologists and Mineralogists, Dallas, Texas, April 1975.) (12)

Field Trip No. 2. A guidebook to the Mississippian shelf-edge and basin facies carbonates, Sacramento Mountains and southern New Mexico region. (Published by the Dallas Geological Society for the Annual Meeting of the AAPG and SEPM, Dallas, Texas, April 1975.) (12)

1976 See American Association of Petroleum Geologists. (12)

CLU-G/G	1972-74
CLhC	1952, 53, 62, 72
CSdS	1947
CSfCSM	1973(1,2)
CU-EART	1971, 72
[CaACAM]	1972
[CaBVU]	1953
CaOOG	1971, 72, 73(3)
CaOWtU	1970
DI-GS	1947, 69(see 7)
ICF	1972
[I-GS]	1953, 58, 60, 62
IU	1930, 62, 63, 68, 69(4), 74
IaU	1953, 58-60, 64, 68, 69, 71, 72
InU	1950, 56, 58-60, 68, 69
KyU	1950-60, 69(1-3), 70-72, 73(4), 74(1,2)
MNS	1956, 58, 60, 71
MnU	1950, 52, 53, 56, 58, 60, 64, 67-69
MoSW	1971, 72, 74(3)
MoU	1971
NSyU	1972
NcU	1959, 64, 68
NdU	1971, 72
NhD	1959, 60, 64, 68
NjP	1958, 68, 69(5), 72
OkU	1929, 71, 72
OrCS	1972
OrU	1972
RPB	1956
TxDaAR-T	1971, 72, 74(1-4), 75(2)
TxDaDM	1972, 73(1)
TxDaSM	1968(1,2), 69(1-3), 71
TxHSD	1974(2)
TxHU	1929
TxLT	1930
TxMM	1929, 30

TxU	1927, 29, 30, 68, 72
ViBlbV	1970, 71
WU	1972

(275) SOCIETY OF ECONOMIC PALEONTOLOGISTS AND MINERALOGISTS. EASTERN SECTION.

1969 Field trip guidebook; Coastal environments of northeastern Massachusetts and New Hampshire. (Its Contribution No. 1) (161)

1970 Sedimentology and origin of Upper Ordovician clastic rocks, central Pennsylvania.

1972 Sedimentary facies: products of sedimentary environments in Catskill Mountains, Mohawk Valley, and Taconic sequence, eastern New York State.

DI-GS	1970, 72

(276) SOCIETY OF ECONOMIC PALEONTOLOGISTS AND MINERALOGISTS. GREAT LAKES SECTION.

1973 3rd Field conference on Borden Group and overlying limestone units, south-central Indiana.

1975 5th Silurian reef and interreef environments with emphasis on interreef petrology, paleontology, stratigraphy, and sedimentation.

IEN	1973
InU	1973
KyU	1973
NRU	1973
NdU	1973
OCU	1973
OU	1973
OkU	1973
TxDaSM	1973

(277) SOCIETY OF ECONOMIC PALEONTOLOGISTS AND MINERALOGISTS. GULF COAST SECTION. GUIDEBOOK FOR THE ANNUAL FIELD TRIP.

1956 A summary of the geology of Florida with emphasis on the Miocene deposits and a guidebook to the Miocene exposures.

[No. 2] Lower Claiborne. (114)

[No. 3] Lower Cretaceous. (114)

1957 Oligocene-Eocene of western Mississippi, central Louisiana and extreme eastern Texas. (118)

1958 Upper and middle Tertiary of Brazos River valley, Texas. (118)

1959 May Lower Tertiary and Upper Cretaceous of Brazos River valley, Texas. (118)

See Gulf Coast Association of Geological Societies. (114)

1960 May Jackson Group, Catahoula and Oakville formations and associated structures of northern Grimes County, Texas. (118)

2. See Gulf Coast Association of Geological Societies. (114)

1961 May Middle Eocene Houston County, Texas.

1962 Little Stave Creek-Salt Mountain Limestone, Jackson, Alabama. (114)

1963 See American Association of Petroleum Geologists. (12)

1965 1. Salt Dome field trip: Belle Isle.

2. Recent organisms and sediments, Galveston Heald Bank area, Gulf of Mexico.

1967 Selected Cretaceous and Tertiary depositional environments.

1969 1. Field guide to some carbonate rocks environments, Florida Keys and western Bahamas.

4. See Society of Economic Paleontologists and Mineralogists. (274)

Trips in conjunction with Gulf Coast Association of Geological Societies. (114, 274)

1970 Geology of Lone Star, Texas area, specifically Lone Star Steel's open pit iron mines, and visit to Lone Star Steel's iron processing plants.

1971 The southern shelf of British Honduras. (114)

Robledo Mountains, New Mexico and Franklin Mountains, Texas.

1974 Guatemala field trip guidebook. (114, 274)

[A-GS]	1957, 61
CLU-G/G	1957-61, 67, 70, 71
CLhC	1959, 60
CSdS	1957, 61, 62
CU-EART	1957, 59, 61, 63, 65(1), 69(4), 70
CaOHM	1957, 59, 61, 63, 67, 70
CaOKQ	1957, 59(May)
CoG	1957-61, 63, 67, 71
CoU	1957-60, 67
DFPC	1961
ICarbS	1959, 60, 63
ICF	1957, 58, 59(May), 60(May), 61(May), 63
IEN	1959, 60, 61(May), 70
IU	1957-61, 63, 67(a?), 69, 70, 74
IaU	1957-62
InU	1957, 67, 69, 71
KyU	1957, 59, 61-63, 71
LU	1957-60, 67
MH-GS	1970
MNS	1958, 60(May)
MiDW	1971
MiU	1957
MnU	1957-63, 65, 67, 69
MoSW	1957, 58, 59(May), 61, 62, 67
MoU	1956
[Ms-GS]	1956, 63
MtU	1957, 61
NNC	1957-61, 63
NRU	1957
NbU	1957, 58, 59(May), 60(May), 61(May), 62
NcU	1957, 59(2), 60-62, 67, 69(4), 70
NdU	1967
NjP	1957, 67
OCU	1957, 59(May), 60(May), 61, 63, 67, 69(4), 70
OU	1958, 59(May), 60(May), 61(May), 67
OkT	1958-60, 63
OkU	1958, 59(May), 60(May), 63, 65(2), 67
PBL	1963
TMM	1957, 61(May), 62
TxDaAR-T	1957-60, 63, 67, 69
TxDaDM	1957-61, 67, 70, 71
TxDaM	1957-61
TxDaSM	1956-58, 60, 67
TxHSD	1959(May), 60(May), 63, 65, 67
TxHU	1953, 57-59, 61-62, 67
TxMM	1958, 59
TxU	1957-61, 63, 67
TxU-Da	1958-60
ViBlbV	1959(May)
WU	1957, 58

(278) **SOCIETY OF ECONOMIC PALEONTOLOGISTS AND MINERALOGISTS. NORTHEASTERN SECTION. FIELD TRIP GUIDEBOOK.**

1968 Coastal sedimentary environments, Lewes-Rehoboth Beach, Delaware. (Co-sponsor: University of Delaware. Department of Geology.)

CaOOG	1968
DI-GS	1968
InU	1968
OkU	1968
TxDaAR-T	1968
TxDaSM	1968

(279) **SOCIETY OF ECONOMIC PALEONTOLOGISTS AND MINERALOGISTS. PACIFIC SECTION. GUIDEBOOK FOR THE FIELD TRIP.**

1944		Type locality of Sycamore Canyon Formation, Whittier Hills, Los Angeles County, California. (16)
1947		Gaviota Pass-Refugio Pass areas, Santa Barbara County, California. (16)
1948		San Emigdio Creek, Kern County, California. (256)
1949		See San Joaquin Geological Society. (256)
1950		North Mt. Diablo monocline, Contra Costa County, California. (16)
1951	May	Cuyama district, California. (16, 256)
	Dec.	Road log. Death Valley to San Fernando.
1952		See Arizona Geological Society. (34)
1953		The stratigraphy and related geology of the northern Santa Ana Mountains, California.
		Ventura-Ojai-Santa Paula area. (16)
1954		San Marcos Pass to Jalama Creek. (16)
1955		Devils Den-McLure Valley area. (16, 256)
1956	Feb.	Liveoak Canyon...Tehachapi Mountains.
	May	Huasna Basin, San Luis Obispo County, California. (16, 256)
	Oct.	Ventura and San Miguelito fields.
1957		La Jolla area, California. (256)
1958		Imperial Valley, California. (16)
1959	Apr.	[1] Geology and paleontology of the southern border of San Joaquin Valley, Kern County, California.
		[2] Big Basin area, Santa Cruz Mountains, California.
1960		Type Panoche-Panoche Hills area, Fresno County, California. (16, 256)
1961		1. Geology and paleontology of the southern border of San Joaquin Valley, Kern County, California. (16, 256, 284)
1962	Mar.	See California. Division of Mines and Geology. (54)
	Oct.	Geology of Carrizo Plains and San Andreas Fault. (16, 256)
1963		1. Geology of Salinas Valley: production, stratigraphy, structure and the San Andreas Fault. (16, 256)
		2. Road log for field trip to Hathaway Ranch area.
1964		San Andreas Fault zone from the Temblor Mountains to Antelope Valley, southern California. (16, 256)
1965		See American Association of Petroleum Geologists. Pacific Section. (16)
1966		See American Association of Petroleum Geologists. Pacific Section. (16)
1967		See American Association of Petroleum Geologists. Pacific Section. (16)
1968		1. Tehachapi Mountain crossing of the California aqueduct, Kern and Los Angeles counties, southern California. (16, 284)
		2. Field trip guide to Santa Rosa Island. (16)
		See American Association of Petroleum Geologists. Pacific Section. (16)

1969 Geology of the northern Channel Islands and southern California borderlands. (AAPG/SEPM. Pacific Section. Special Publication.) (16)

Mar. Geology and oilfields of coastal areas, Ventura and Los Angeles basins, California. (16)

Oct. Geologic setting of upper Miocene gypsum and phosphate deposits upper Sespe Creek and Pine Mountain, Ventura County, California. (16)

Geology of the central part of the Fillmore Quadrangle, Ventura County, California. (16)

1970 Pacific slope geology of northern Baja California and adjacent Alta California. (16, 284)

1971 Geologic guidebook; Newport Lagoon to San Clemente, California, coastal exposures of Miocene and early Pleistocene rocks.

1972 1. Geology and oil fields, west side, central San Joaquin Valley. (16, 284)

2. Cretaceous of the Coalinga area.

Central Santa Ynez Mountains, Santa Barbara County, California.

1973 1. Miocene sedimentary environments and biofacies, southeastern Los Angeles Basin. (16, 284)

2. Sedimentary facies changes in Tertiary rocks; California transverse and southern coast ranges. (16, 284)

3. Cretaceous stratigraphy of the Santa Monica Mountains and Simi Hills, southern California.

4. Metropolitan oil fields and their environmental impact. [AAPG Guidebook No. 29] (16)

5. Imperial Valley regional geology and geothermal exploration. [AAPG-SEPM-SEG Guidebook No. 30] (16, 284)

1974 The Paleogene of the Panoche Creek-Cantua Creek area, central California.

1975 A tour of the oil fields of the Whittier fault zone, Los Angeles Basin, California. (16, 284)

[CDU]	1944, 48, 50, 51, 53-55, 56(Feb.,May), 57, 58, 60, 61, 63, 64, 69
CLU-G/G	1947, 50, 53-55, 56(May), 58, 60, 61(1), 63(2), 64, 69, 71, 72(2), 74, 75
CLhC	1960, 63, 64, 65(1), 68, 69, 72(2)
CSdS	1950, 69, 71-73
CSfCSM	1950, 52, 56(Oct.), 57, 59(2), 60, 61(2), 64, 71, 72, 74
CU-EART	1948, 49, 51, 53, 56(Feb.,May), 57, 58, 59(2), 60, 61(1), 69, 71-73
[CaBVU]	1964, 67
CaOHM	1972(2), 74
CaOLU	1963(1)
CoG	1947, 50, 56(May,Oct.), 58, 60, 61, 62(Oct.), 64
DI-GS	1948, 50-58, 60, 62, 70, 71, 72(2), 73(3), 74, 75
IU	1961, 63, 64, 71-73
IaU	1958, 63, 64, 66, 67(2), 68, 71, 72(2), 73, 74
IdBB	1971
IdPI	1963
InU	1952, 59, 62, 68-72
KyU	1965-67, 69-71, 72(2), 73(3)
MH-GS	1971
MnU	1944, 48, 50, 51, 53-58, 61, 63, 64, 67-69
MoSW	1963(1)
MoU	1969, 70, 72(3)
NBiSU	1959
NNC	1959(2), 61, 63
NSyU	1972(1), 73(3)
NbU	1959(2), 60
NcU	1952, 62(Mar.), 64, 65(2), 72(2)
NhD	1962(Mar.), 73(3)
NjP	1967, 70, 72(2), 74
OCU	1947, 56, 60, 61(1), 63(2), 64, 69, 71

OU	1947, 55-57, 60, 61(1), 63(1), 64, 69, 71, 72(2), 74
OrU	1964
TxDaAR-T	1961, 63, 64, 69, 71, 72(2), 73, 74
TxDaDM	1956, 59(2), 60, 61, 63(2), 69, 71(1,2), 72(2), 73(3)
TxDaM	1958, 61
TxDaSM	1959(2), 60, 61, 63, 64, 71, 72(2), 73(1,2), 74
TxHSD	1961(1), 64, 73(3), 74
TxHU	1964
TxMM	1960, 61(1), 64
TxU	1944, 47, 48, 51(May), 53, 55-58, 59(2), 60-63, 69, 71, 74
TxU-Da	1951(May,Dec.), 54, 60, 61, 64, 65, 71, 72(1,2), 73
ViBlbV	1972(2)
WU	1950

(280) SOCIETY OF ECONOMIC PALEONTOLOGISTS AND MINERALOGISTS. PERMIAN BASIN SECTION. GUIDEBOOK FOR THE FIELD TRIP.

1955	Permian field conference to the Guadalupe Mountains.
1956	Symposium of the Fort Worth Basin area and field study of the Hill Creek beds of the lower Strawn, southwestern Parker County, Texas.
1957	Wolfcamp of the Glass Mountains and the Permian Basin.
1958	Cretaceous platform and geosyncline, Culberson and Hudspeth counties, Trans-Pecos, Texas.
1959	Sacramento Mountains of Otero County, New Mexico. (251)
1960	Study of the Cisco facies near Breckenridge, Texas. (295)
1962	Leonardian facies of the Sierra Diablo region, west Texas.
1964	Filling of the Marathon geosyncline; symposium and guidebook.
1965	Amistad Dam field trip. (Guidebook used for this trip was the West Texas Geological Society Val Verde Basin guidebook, 1959.)
1967	One day field trip; Bank to basin transition in Permian (Leonardian) carbonates, Guadalupe Mountains, Texas.
1968	Guadalupian facies, Apache Mountains area, west Texas.
1969	See El Paso Geological Society. (81)
1970	Geology of the southern Quitman Mountains area, Trans-Pecos, Texas. (338)
1971	Robledo Mountains, New Mexico, Franklin Mountains, Texas.
1972	Capitan reef, New Mexico and Texas: facts and questions to aid interpretation and group discussion.
1974	Lower Cretaceous shelf, platform, reef, and basinal deposits, southwest Texas and northern Coahuila. (338)
1975	Geology of the Eagle Mountains and vicinity, Trans-Pecos Texas. (338)

AzTeS	1959-64, 70-72
AzU	1970, 71
CChiS	1964, 68
[CDU]	1956-60, 62, 64, 67, 68
CLU-G/G	1955, 57-59, 62, 64, 68, 70-72, 74, 75
CSdS	1960, 62, 68
CU-EART	1956-60, 62, 64, 68, 70, 71
CaACU	1955-60, 62, 68
[CaBVU]	1959, 64, 68
CaOLU	1964
CaOOG	1957, 60, 62, 64
CoG	1956-60, 62, 64, 65, 68, 70, 71
[CoPU]	1959, 62, 64, 68, 70, 71

CoU	1956-60, 62, 64, 65, 68, 70, 71
DI-GS	155-60, 62, 64, 68, 69, 71, 72, 75
ICF	1959, 71
ICarbS	1972
IU	1955-60, 62, 64, 71, 72, 74, 75
IaU	1957, 59, 60, 62, 64, 65, 68, 70-72, 74
IdPI	1972
InLP	1957-59, 61, 62, 68, 70, 71
InU	1959, 60, 64, 71, 72
KyU	1956-60, 62, 64, 68, 70-72, 74, 75
LU	1964
MH-GS	1964, 68
MdU	1955-60, 62, 64
MiDW	1971
MiHM	1955-60, 62
MiKW	1957
MiU	1956-60, 62, 64
MnU	1956-60, 62, 64, 65, 68-70
MoRM	1959, 62
MoSW	1970
MoU	1970-72, 75
MtU	1955-62
NBiSU	1959, 60, 62, 68, 70, 71
NNC	1958-60, 62, 64
NOneoU	1972
NRU	1967
NbU	1957, 59, 60, 62, 64, 67, 68, 70-72
NcU	1957-64, 68, 70, 71
NdU	1955-57, 59, 60, 62, 64, 68
NhD	1965
NmPE	1955, 57-60, 62, 64, 68, 70, 71
NmU	1959
OCU	1959, 62, 64, 70-72
OU	1955-60, 62, 64, 68, 70
OkT	1958
OkU	1956, 59, 60, 62, 64, 67, 68, 70-72
PBL	1967, 70
PPiGulf	1959, 68
RPB	1964, 68
SdRM	1959
TMM	1959, 60, 62, 68, 70-72
TxDaAR-T	1956-60, 62, 64
TxDaSM	1955-60, 64, 68, 70, 71
TxHU	1955-60, 62, 64, 67, 68, 70, 71
TxLT	1955-60, 62, 64
TxMM	1955-60, 62, 64, 68, 70-72
TxU	1955-60, 62, 64, 65, 67-71
TxU-Da	1960
WU	1956-60, 62, 64, 68, 70-72, 75
WyU	1955, 59

(281) Society of Exploration Geophysicists.

(281) SOCIETY OF EXPLORATION GEOPHYSICISTS. ANNUAL MEETING.

1944	See American Association of Petroleum Geologists. (12)
1947	See American Association of Petroleum Geologists. (12)
1952	See American Association of Petroleum Geologists. (12)
1953	See American Association of Petroleum Geologists. (12)

(282) SOCIETY OF EXPLORATION GEOPHYSICISTS. REGIONAL MEETING.

1950	See Canadian Society of Petroleum Geologists. (61)

(283) SOCIETY OF EXPLORATION GEOPHYSICISTS. MIDWESTERN SECTION.

1963	See American Association of Petroleum Geologists. (12)

(284) SOCIETY OF EXPLORATION GEOPHYSICISTS. PACIFIC SECTION.

1961	See American Association of Petroleum Geologists. Pacific Section. (16)
1962	See California. Division of Mines and Geology. (54)
1965	See Society of Economic Paleontologists and Mineralogists. Pacific Section. (279)
1966	See Society of Economic Paleontologists and Mineralogists. Pacific Section. (279)
1968	See Society of Economic Paleontologists and Mineralogists. Pacific Section. (279)
1970	See Society of Economic Paleontologists and Mineralogists. Pacific Section. (279)
1972	See Society of Economic Paleontologists and Mineralogists. Pacific Section. (279)
1973	See Society of Economic Paleontologists and Mineralogists. Pacific Section. (279)
	A profile of southern California geology and seismicity of Los Angeles basin.
1975	See Society of Economic Paleontologists and Mineralogists. Pacific Section. (279)

CLU-G/G	1973
CSfCSM	1973
CU-EART	1973
CSdS	1973
IU	1973
IaU	1973
TxDaAR-T	1973
TxDaDM	1973
TxDaSM	1973

(285) SOCIETY OF VERTEBRATE PALEONTOLOGY. GUIDEBOOK.

1941	1st	Tertiary and Pleistocene of Nebraska. (Reprinted in Plateau, Vol. 20, No. 1, July, 1947.) (199)
1947	2nd	Continental Triassic of northern Arizona. (Reprinted in Plateau, Vol. 20, No. 1, July, 1947.)
1948	3rd	Southeastern Wyoming.
1950	4th	Northwestern New Mexico.
1951	5th	Western South Dakota.
1953	6th	Northeastern Utah.
1954		The late Eocene beds of the Sespe Formation on Pearson Ranch, Simi Valley (now known as the Wharton Ranch) and the Tick and Mint Canyon faunas in the Soledad Basin.
1956	7th	Miocene Texas Gulf Coastal Plain.
1958	8th	Western Montana.
1961	9th	Tertiary and Pleistocene of western Nebraska.
1964		Central Florida.
1966		[1] Southern California field trip, Anza-Borrego desert and Barstow areas.
	Nov.	Trip No. 1. Fort Funston...Thornton Beach Pliocene and Pleistocene.
		Trip No. 2. The beginning of continental deposition in the Mt. Diablo area.
1972		Field conference on Tertiary biostratigraphy of southern and western Wyoming.

CLU-G/G	1958
CU-EART	1941, 47, 50-61, 66(Nov.)
[CaBVU]	1958
CoG	1948, 50, 51
CcU	1950, 51
DI-GS	1941, 47, 48, 50, 51, 53, 58, 61
IEN	1958
[I-GS]	1941
IU	1948, 50, 51, 61
IaU	1941, 58
InLP	1958
InU	1948, 50, 51, 53, 58, 61
KyU	1941, 47, 48, 50, 51, 53, 58
LU	1941, 47, 48, 50, 51, 53, 58, 61
MNS	1958
MiDW	1958, 61
MiU	1950, 58
MnU	1948, 50, 51, 53, 58
MoRM	1958
MoSW	1958
MoU	1941, 58, 64
NNC	1941, 50, 51, 53, 58, 61, 64
NRU	1958
NbU	1941, 47, 61
NcU	1958
NdU	1951, 58
NjP	1950, 58, 64
NmU	1950
OU	1948, 50, 58, 64
OkU	1941-64
OrCS	1941, 48-51, 58, 61
OrU	1958
PBL	1958
PSt	1958
SdRM	1941, 51
TxDaAR-T	1950
TxDaDM	1951
TXDaM	1941, 47
TxMM	1950
TxU	1947, 48, 50, 51, 53, 58, 64, 66, 72
WU	1958, 64
WyU	1941, 48, 59, 64

(286) SOIL SCIENCE SOCIETY OF AMERICA.

1970 Guidebook, Soil-geomorphology Field Conference. Distribution and genesis of soils and geomorphic surfaces in a desert region of southern New Mexico.

CLU-G/G	1970
NdU	1970
TxU	1970

(287) SOUTH CAROLINA. DIVISION OF GEOLOGY. BULLETIN.

1957 Guidebook for the South Carolina coastal plain field trip. (63)

CLU-G/G	1957
DI-GS	1957
IEN	1957
[I-GS]	1957
IU	1957

(288) SOUTH COAST GEOLOGICAL SOCIETY. FIELD TRIP GUIDEBOOK.

1971 San Fernando earthquake field trip. Road log.

1972 Geologic guidebook to the northern Peninsular Ranges, Orange and Riverside counties, California. (190)

1973 Guidebook to the Tertiary geology of eastern Orange and Los Angeles counties, California.

CLU-G/G	1972, 73
TxDaDM	1971

(289) SOUTH DAKOTA. GEOLOGICAL SURVEY. GUIDEBOOK.

1965 1st Upper Mississippi Valley. (Reprint of South Dakota part of International Association for Quaternary Research, 7th Congress, with supplemental data.)

1969 2nd Major Cenozoic deposits of southwestern South Dakota.

AzU	1969
CLU-G/G	1969
CU-EART	1969
CoG	1965, 69
DI-GS	1965, 69
IEN	1965, 69
[I-GS]	1965
IaU	1965, 69
IdBB	1965, 69
InLP	1965, 69
InRE	1965, 69
InU	1965, 69
KyU	1965, 69
MiDW	1965, 69
MiHM	1969
MiKW	1969
MiU	1965
MoSW	1965, 69
MtU	1969
NBiSU	1965, 69
NSyU	1969
NdU	1969
NhD	1969
NjP	1969
NvLN	1965, 69
NvU	1965, 69
OkU	1965, 69
OrU	1969
RPB	1969
TxDaAR-T	1965, 69

TxLT	1965, 69
TxU	1965, 69
ViBlbV	1969

(290) SOUTH TEXAS GEOLOGICAL SOCIETY. GUIDEBOOK FOR THE FIELD TRIP.

1930	1st	Southern Uvalde and northern Zavala counties.
1931	2nd	Darst Creek, Salt Flat and Luling oil fields, data on Edward Lime oil fields, paleontological field trip, Bexar and Medina counties, road log, San Antonio to Laredo.
		Field Trip No. 2. Laredo to Corpus Christi.
		Field Trip No. 2A. San Antonio to Laredo.
1932	3rd	San Antonio to Corpus Christi.
	4th	Laredo to Roma, Texas; Miel, General Trevino, Agualeguas, Sabinas Hidalgo, Monterrey, and Saltillo, Mexico; Monterrey to Laredo; Laredo to Corpus Christi; Laredo to San Antonio.
1933	5th	Victoria to Corpus Christi and George West to Casa Blanca.
1934	6th	San Antonio to Laredo via Campbellton and Government Wells. Road log in Tamaulipas and Nuevo Leon, Mexico portion of trip.
1935	7th	Laredo to Mexico City. Geologic map.
1936	8th	Oct. 16-18. No. 1. Pleasanton to Pearsall (Texas).
		No. 2. Pearsall to Loma Vista (Texas).
		Nov. 18. No. 3. Loma Vista to Eagle Pass (Texas).
		No. 4. Carrizo Springs to north of Eagle Pass (Texas).
1937	June	Rock asphalt deposits, Uvalde County.
	July	Bee and Live Oak counties.
	Nov.	Cretaceous of Bexar and Medina counties.
1938		Gasoline extraction plants; McCampbell, Plymouth and Saxet fields.
1939	11th	No. 1. Rio Grande Valley; Laredo to Mission and Brownsville. (296)
		No. 2. [Rio Grande delta and Quaternary formations.]
	Nov.	See Texas. University. Department of Geology. (309)
1940	12th	Lower Tertiary: Austin-Manor-Elgin-McDade-Page-Bastrop-Smithville.
1941	13th	Road log from Monterrey, Mexico to Laredo, Texas.
1947	14th	San Antonio-George West-Beeville-Falls City. (13)
1948	15th	A spectacular circle tour: Mexico-Tuxpan-Mexico.
1949	16th	San Antonio-Uvalde-Bracketville-Del Rio-Langtry.
1950	17th	Monterrey to Huasteca Canyon.
1951	18th	Paleozoic and Cretaceous of eastern Llano uplift. (13)
1953	19th	Geological section; Taylor to Glen Rose.
1954	20th	Fault line: Seguin, Darst Creek, and Luling fields.
	21st	Cook Mountain to Jurassic.
1958	24th	Eocene-Miocene-oil-uranium: Falls City, Fordilla Hill and Fashing areas, Wiison, Karnes, Atascosa counties, Texas.
1959	25th	Mesozoic stratigraphy and structure, Saltillo-Galeana areas, Coahuila and Nuevo Leon, Mexico.
1960	26th	Geological section; Taylor to Glen Rose.
1961		See Gulf Coast Association of Geological Societies. (114)
1962		Contributions to the geology of south Texas.
1964		Mesozoic stratigraphy and structure, Monterrey-Saltillo-Monclava areas, Coahuila and Nuevo Leon, Mexico.
1967		San Antonio, Hondo, Eagle Pass, Laredo.

[CDU]	1930-36, 37(July)
CLhC	1959
CU-EART	1947, 53-56, 58, 59

(290) South Texas Geological Society.

CaOHM	1947, 53, 54, 56, 58, 59
CoG	1930-41, 47, 50-54, 58, 59
DI-GS	1930-38, 39(11), 40, 41, 47-51, 53, 54, 56, 58-60
ICF	1959
[I-GS]	1951
IU	1947, 53, 54, 58, 59
IaU	1961
InU	1956, 60
KyU	1947, 53, 58, 59, 61
LU	1930-38, 39(11[1]), 40, 41, 47, 49, 51, 53, 54, 58, 59
MH-GS	1935
MNS	1941, 53, 54, 56
MnU	1930-34, 39(11), 40, 41, 47, 49-51, 53, 54, 58-60
MoSW	1958
MoU	1947, 51-56, 58, 59
NNC	1930, 31, 32(4), 33-38, 39(11), 40, 58, 59
NbU	1940, 41, 47-51, 53, 54(20,21), 56
NcU	1947, 51-54, 58, 59, 61
NmPE	1953, 58, 59, 62
OCU	1947, 53
OU	1958, 59
OkT	1962
OkU	1930-34, 36(Oct.), 37-47, 49, 51-54, 58, 59
OrCS	1954, 59
TxDaAR-T	1940, 51, 53, 58, 59
TxDaDM	1930, 32(4), 36-38, 41, 47, 48, 51, 53, 54(May), 58, 59
TxDaM	1930, 31, 32(4), 33-38, 39(11), 40, 41, 47, 50, 51, 53, 54(May), 58
TxDaSM	1930-34, 36-41, 47, 49, 51, 53, 54(May), 56, 58
TxHSD	1931, 32, 34, 36-38, 40-48, 54, 59, 60
TxHU	1931, 39(11), 40, 41, 47, 51, 53, 54(Dec.), 59, 60
TxLT	1931, 47, 58
TxMM	1939(11[2]), 40, 41, 47, 51, 53, 54(May?), 58-60
TxU	1930-41, 47-51, 53, 54, 56(1,2), 58-60, 62, 64, 67

(291) SOUTHEASTERN GEOLOGICAL SOCIETY. FIELD TRIP.

1944	June	Trip 1. Southwestern Alabama.
	Nov.	Trip 2. Southwestern Georgia.
1945	3rd	Western Florida.
1946	4th	Southeastern Alabama.
1947	5th	Portion of central Florida; Gulf Coast.
1948	6th	Cretaceous of east-central Alabama.
1951	7th	Geology of the crystalline rocks and of the Paleozoic area of northwest Georgia.
1954	8th	Carbonate deposits in south Florida.
1960	9th	Late Cenozoic stratigraphy and sedimentation of central Florida.
1963	10th	Summary of Paleocene and Eocene stratigraphy and economic geology of southeastern Alabama.
1965	11th	Some highlights of the Cretaceous and crystalline terranes of Georgia.
1966	12th	Geology of the Miocene and Pliocene series in the north Florida-south Georgia area. (112)
1967	13th	Miocene-Pliocene problems of peninsular Florida.
1970	14th	Geology and geohydrology of the Cross-Florida Barge Canal area, Ocala, Florida.
1971	15th	Geological review of some north Florida mineral resources.
1972	16th	Space age geology; terrestrial applications, techniques and training.
1973		Carbonate rock environments, Florida Keys and western Bahamas.
1975	19th	Hydrogeology of west-central Florida.

[A-GS]	1946-48, 51, 54, 60, 63
AzU	1970-72
CLU-G/G	1946, 47, 51, 54, 60, 63, 65-67
CLhC	1946-48
CU-EART	1946, 47, 51, 60, 65-67, 70
CaOHM	1970
CaOKQ	1951, 60, 63
CoG	1945-48, 51, 54, 60, 63, 65-67, 70
CoU	1951, 54, 60, 63, 65-67
DI-GS	1944-48, 51, 54, 60, 63, 65-67, 70-72
ICF	1951, 54, 60, 63, 66
ICIU-S	1966, 70
ICarbS	1951, 54, 60, 63, 65-67
IEN	1951, 54, 60
[I-GS]	1970
IU	1944-48, 51, 54, 60, 63, 65-67, 70
IaU	1946, 47, 51, 54, 60, 63, 65-67, 70-72
InLP	1951-67
InRE	1951, 54, 60
InU	1944-46, 51, 54, 60, 63, 65-67
KyU	1944-47, 51, 54, 60, 63, 65-67, 70
LU	1944(Nov.), 45-48, 51, 54, 60, 63, 65-67
MNS	1946, 48
MiDW	1966, 70
MnU	1946, 47, 51, 54, 60, 63, 65-67
MoSW	1946, 47, 51, 54, 60, 63, 65-67, 70
MoU	1944(Nov.), 45-70, 72
[Ms-GS]	1945, 48-65, 67
MtU	1951-63
NBiSU	1951, 60-65, 67-72
NNC	1946, 48, 51, 54, 60, 63, 66
NSyU	1944-46
NbU	1947-63, 70
NcU	1946, 51, 54, 65-72
NdU	1951, 60, 63, 65-67
NhD	1951, 54-72, 75
NjP	1944-48, 51, 54, 60, 63, 65-67, 70-72
NvU	1951-63, 66
OCU	1944(June), 46-70
OU	1945-72, 75
OrU	1970
PPiGulf	1946-48, 54
PSt	1951-63, 66
RPB	1944(June)
TU	1951
TxDaAR-T	1944(Nov.), 46-48, 51, 54, 60, 63, 65, 66, 73
TxDaDM	1946-48, 51, 54, 60, 63, 65-67, 70, 71
TxDaM	1946-48, 51, 54, 60, 63
TxDaSM	1944, 46, 51, 54
TxHSD	1946-48, 60, 64
TxHU	1944-60, 65, 67, 70
TxLT	1951, 60-67

TxMM	1944, 54
TxU	1944-48, 51, 54, 60, 63, 65-67
TxU-Da	1944, 46, 48, 54
UU	1970
ViBlbV	1951, 54, 60
WU	1944(Nov.), 45, 46, 48-72, 75

(292) SOUTHERN ILLINOIS UNIVERSITY. GEOLOGY DEPARTMENT.

1965 Devonian of Jackson and Union counties, Illinois.
ICarbS 1965

(293) SOUTHERN ILLINOIS UNIVERSITY AT EDWARDSVILLE. DEPARTMENT OF GEOLOGY.

1970 Guidebook to engineering geologic features and land use relationships in the St. Louis metropolitan area.
ICarbS 1970

(294) SOUTHWESTERN ASSOCIATION OF STUDENT GEOLOGICAL SOCIETIES. FIELD CONFERENCE GUIDEBOOK.

1960	1st	See Baylor University, Waco, Texas. Baylor Geological Society. (46)
1961	2nd	Structure and stratigraphy of the Arbuckle anticline and the Criner Hills area, Oklahoma. (170)
1962	3rd	Field conference on the Llano uplift, Llano and Burnet counties, Texas. (310)
1963	4th	Geology of west-central Texas [Pennsylvanian-Permian-Cretaceous sequences of west-central Texas]. (115)
1964	5th	Monterrey, Mexico. (Partial translation of Guidebook C-5, 20th International Geological Congress, 1956.) (305)
1965	6th	Recent and Pleistocene sediments and geomorphology of southwestern Louisiana and southeastern Texas. (304)
1966	7th	Geology of Palo Duro Canyon and the Panhandle of Texas. (311)
1967	8th	Geology of south-central Texas. (297)
1968	9th	Geology of the Claiborne Group of central Texas. (303)
1969	10th	Geology of the Pennsylvanian-Permian Quaternary sequences of west-central Texas.
1970	11th	Geology of northeastern Mexico, prepared by Pan American Geological Society for Southwestern Association of Student Geological Societies.
	fall	First fall field trip. Field trip through the classic type lower Comanchean section of North America, vicinity of Glen Rose, Texas. Host Baylor Geological Society.
1971		Tertiary of central Louisiana and Mississippi.
1972	13th	Paleozoic geology of the Arbuckle Mountains, Oklahoma.
	[fall]	Urban geology.
1973		Geologic field trips in northern Oregon and southern Washington. (97, 236)
	fall	Eocene of central Louisiana and east Texas.
1974	spring	Economic geology of the central mineral region of Texas.
		Geology of Huizachal-Peregrina anticlinorium.
1975	spring	Geologic field guide to Mariscal Canyon.
	fall	Structural geology of central Texas.

CLU-G/G	1965, 70, 72(fall)
CLhC	1970
CU-EART	1962, 63, 69, 70(11), 71, 73, 74(spring), 75(spring,fall)
ICF	1970(11)
IU	1961-66, 70(fall), 71, 73, 74

IaU	1970
InU	1960, 70(11), 71, 72
KyU	1970(11), 72
MH-GS	1970
MiU	1961
MnU	1966
MoU	1972(13)
NNC	1961-64
NdU	1968, 72
NjP	1970
OU	1970(11), 72(13)
OkU	1963, 64, 68
PBm	1972(13)
PPiGulf	1961, 62
TMM	1972(13)
TxDaAR-T	1963, 65, 70(11), 72(13)
TxDaDM	1961
TxDaM	1961, 63
TxDaSM	1970, 72(13)
TxHSD	1972(13)
TxHU	1961, 63-65, 67, 70(11)
TxLT	1963
TxU	1961-70, 72(13)

(295) SOUTHWESTERN FEDERATION OF GEOLOGICAL SOCIETIES. GUIDEBOOK FOR REGIONAL MEETING FIELD TRIP.

1958	1st	Guide to the Strawn and Canyon series of the Pennsylvanian system in Palo Pinto County, Texas. (13)
1960	2nd	See Society of Economic Paleontologists and Mineralogists. Permian Basin Section. (280)
	3rd	Natural gas in the southwest. (1, 13)
1961	4th	Guidebook for the southern Franklin Mountains. (37, 251)
1962	5th	Geology of the type area, Canyon Group, north-central Texas. (Journal of the Graduate Research Center, Vol. 30, No. 3, 1962.)
1965	7th	Fredericksburg facies, Austin area.

CLU-G/G	1961
CU-EART	1960(3)
CoG	1960-62
DI-GS	1961, 62
IaU	1958, 60(3)
InU	1958
KyU	1960(2,3)
MNS	1958
MnU	1958, 60, 61
NNC	1961
NbU	1962
NcU	1960
OU	1960(3)
PSt	1958
TxDaDM	1960
TxDaM	1960, 62
TxHU	1961
TxMM	1960
TxU	1960(3), 61, 62, 65

(296) **SOUTHWESTERN GEOLOGICAL SOCIETY. FIELD TRIP.**

1937		[1] Lower Cretaceous.
		[2] Lower Tertiary.
		[3] Llano uplift.
1939		See South Texas Geological Society. (290)

TxHSD	1937
TxMM	1937
TxU	1937, 39

(297) **ST. MARY'S GEOLOGICAL SOCIETY. SAN ANTONIO, TEXAS.**

1967		See Southwestern Association of Student Geological Societies. (294)

STANFORD UNIVERSITY, CALIFORNIA. CONFERENCE ON GEOLOGIC PROBLEMS OF THE SAN ANDREAS FAULT SYSTEM. See CONFERENCE ON GEOLOGIC PROBLEMS OF THE SAN ANDREAS FAULT SYSTEM, STANFORD UNIVERSITY. (68)

STATE GEOLOGISTS FIELD TRIP. See PLEISTOCENE FIELD CONFERENCE. (246)

(298) **TENNESSEE ACADEMY OF SCIENCE. FIELD TRIP.**

1954		Cumberland plateau.
1960		Mississippian stratigraphy of the northwestern highland rim.
1972	spring	Mineral industry in Scott County, northern Cumberland plateau.

[A-GS]	1954, 60
IU	1972
TMM	1972

(299) **TENNESSEE. DIVISION OF GEOLOGY. BULLETIN.**

1973	No. 70	Geology of Knox County, Tennessee. (102)
		No. 1,2. Stratigraphy and depositional environments in the Valley and Ridge at Knoxville.
		No. 3. Mineral resources of Knox County, Tennessee.

CU-EART	1973
CaOOG	1973
CoU	1973
[I-GS]	1973
IU	1973
NSyU	1973
NdU	1973
OCU	1973
TMM	1973
TxDaDM	1973

(300) **TENNESSEE. DIVISION OF GEOLOGY. REPORT OF INVESTIGATIONS.**

1958	No. 5	Guidebook to geology along Tennessee highways.
1961	No. 12	Geology of the Mascot-Jefferson City zinc district, Tennessee. (102)
	No. 13	Structural geology along the eastern Cumberland escarpment, Tennessee. (102)
1969	No. 23	Papers on the stratigraphy and mine geology of the Kingsport and Mascot formations (Lower Ordovician) of east Tennessee. (273)
1972	No. 33	Carboniferous depositional environments in the Cumberland plateau of southern Tennessee and northern Alabama. (102)

Guidebook for field trips. (102)
Trip 1. Meta-Paleozoic rocks, Chilton County, Alabama.
Trip 2. Upper Cretaceous series in central Alabama.
Trip 3. Southern Appalachian Valley and Ridge province; structure and stratigraphy.
Trip 4. Limestone hydrology and environmental geology.

1975 No. 36 Field trips in west Tennessee; a guidebook to field trips of the 1975 Southeastern Section Meeting of the Geological Society of America. (102)

CLU-G/G	1958, 61, 69
CU-EART	1958, 61, 69
CaOLU	1969, 72
CoG	1958
DI-GS	1961(12,13), 72
ICF	1958, 72, 75
[I-GS]	1972, 75
IU	1958, 61, 69, 72, 75
IaU	1961(12,13), 75
InU	1958, 61, 69, 75
KyU	1958, 61(13), 75
MNS	1972
MnU	1961(12,13)
MoSW	1958, 61, 69, 75
MoU	1958
NRU	1975
NSyU	1958, 61, 69, 72
NbU	1958, 61, 69
NcU	1958, 61, 69
NdU	1958, 72, 75
NhD	1961, 72
NjP	1961(12,13), 72
NvU	1958
OCU	1958
OU	1958
OkU	1975
OrU	1972, 75
PSt	1958, 61, 69
RPB	1961
TMM	1958, 61, 69
TxDaAR-T	1972, 75
TxLT	1958, 61, 72
TxU	1969
UU	1958
[VtPuW]	1958

TENNESSEE. GEOLOGICAL SURVEY. REPORT OF INVESTIGATIONS. **See TENNESSEE. DIVISION OF GEOLOGY. REPORT OF INVESTIGATIONS. (300)**

(301) TENNESSEE. UNIVERSITY. DEPARTMENT OF GEOLOGY AND GEOGRAPHY. REGIONAL STUDIES IN ECONOMIC GEOLOGY. FIELD TRIP.

1949	2nd	Arkansas, Oklahoma, and Missouri.
1950	3rd	Southeastern states.
1964		Georgia-Florida.
1965		Tennessee, Virginia, Pennsylvania, New Jersey.
1966		Alabama, Mississippi, Tennessee, Arkansas, Oklahoma, Missouri.
1967		North Carolina, South Carolina, Georgia and north Florida.

TU 1949, 50, 64-67

TENNESSEE. UNIVERSITY. DEPARTMENT OF GEOLOGY AND GEOGRAPHY. GUIDEBOOK FOR...ANNUAL SPRING FIELD TRIP. See TENNESSEE. UNIVERSITY. (301)

(302) TEXAS ACADEMY OF SCIENCE.

1939 See West Texas Geological Society. (338)
1957 The Fredericksburg Group in the valley of the Trinity River, Texas.
1968 See Texas. Lamar State College of Technology, Beaumont. (304)
TxU 1957
TxU-Da 1957

(303) TEXAS. AGRICULTURAL AND MECHANICAL UNIVERSITY. DEPARTMENT OF GEOLOGY. GEOLOGICAL SOCIETY.

1940 Road log of a field trip from Hempstead to College Station over Highway 6.
1962 Upper Cretaceous and lower Tertiary rocks in east-central Texas.
1968 See Southwestern Association of Student Geological Societies. (294)
TxU 1940

(304) TEXAS. LAMAR STATE COLLEGE OF TECHNOLOGY, BEAUMONT. DEPARTMENT OF GEOLOGY.

1965 See Southwestern Association of Student Geological Societies. (294)
1968 Recent and Pleistocene in the Beaumont-High Island-Anahuac area (Jefferson and Chambers counties) of the eastern Gulf Coast of Texas. (302)
TxDaM 1968

(305) TEXAS. PAN AMERICAN UNIVERSITY, EDINBURG. GEOLOGICAL SOCIETY.

1964 See Southwestern Association of Student Geological Societies. (294)

(306) TEXAS. SUL ROSS STATE UNIVERSITY. ALPINE, TEXAS. GEOLOGICAL SOCIETY.

1969 A field guide to Permian, Cretaceous, and Tertiary rocks in the Pinto Canyon, Presidio County, Texas, with auxiliary field guides to Paleozoic rocks of the Marathon Basin and Tertiary volcanics in the vicinity of Alpine, Texas.
IaU 1969
TxU 1969

(307) TEXAS. TECH UNIVERSITY.

1970 Ogallala aquifer symposium; field trip guidebook, Lubbock-Lake Ransom Canyon.
IEN 1970
TxU 1970

(308) TEXAS. UNIVERSITY. BUREAU OF ECONOMIC GEOLOGY. GUIDEBOOK SERIES.

1920 On the underground position of the Ellenburger Formation in north-central Texas, with a preliminary contour map. (University of Texas Bulletin 1849.)
1945 Instructions and road logs for a field conference on the Ellenburger Group of the Llano region, Texas.
1958 No. 1. Eastern Llano region. (38)
1960 No. 2. Texas fossils; an amateur collector's handbook.
1961 No. 3. Central Texas; bentonites, uranium-bearing rocks and vermiculites. (193)

1963	No. 4. The geologic story of Longhorn Cavern.
	No. 5. Geology of Llano region and Austin area. (Same as Houston Geological Society, 1962, Field Trip No. 1.) (For supplement see: Corpus Christi Geological Society, 1966.) (96)
1964	No. 6. Texas rocks and minerals; an amateur's guide.
1968	No. 7. The Big Bend of the Rio Grande, a guide to the rocks, geologic history and settlers of the area of Big Bend National Park.
	Burnet County. (87)
1969	No. 8. The geologic story of Palo Duro Canyon.
	No. 9. Field excursion east Texas: clay, glauconite, ironstone deposits. (193)
1970	No. 10. Geologic and historic guide to the state parks of Texas.
	No. 11. Recent sediments of southeast Texas; Brazos alluvial and deltaic plains and Galveston Barrier Island complex.
1971	No. 12. Uranium geology and mines, south Texas. (12, 118)
1972	No. 13. Geology of the Llano region and Austin area, field excursion. (Bureau of Economic Geology Guidebook No. 5, 1963, updated and combined with Shreveport Geological Society's Geology of the Llano region and Austin area, Texas, 1971.) (259)
1973	No. 14. Pennsylvanian depositional systems in north-central Texas, a guide for interpreting terrigenous clastic facies in a cratonic basin. (96)
	No. 15. The Edwards Reef Complex and associated sedimentation in central Texas. (96)

[CDU]	1969(8)
CLU-G/G	1958-73
CLhC	1958, 61, 63(4), 70(11), 71-73
CSdS	1970(11), 73(15)
CSfCSM	1958
CU-EART	1958-73
[CaBVU]	1968(7)
CaOHM	1969(9), 70-72, 73(14)
CaOKQ	1970
CaOLU	1920, 70-73
CaOOG	1968, 72
CoG	1958, 61, 63, 68, 69(8), 70(11)
CoU	1958, 61, 63, 64, 68-72, 73(14)
DI-GS	1958, 61, 63, 64, 68, 69, 73
ICF	1958-68, 69(8), 70
ICarbS	1968-72, 73(14)
IEN	1958-73
[I-GS]	1958(1), 61, 63(4), 64, 68, 69(8), 70(11), 71-73
IU	1958-73
IaU	1958, 61, 64(4), 68-71
IdBB	1970
IdPI	1958, 70
InLP	1958-73
InRE	1968, 71, 72
InU	1958-61, 63(4), 64-71
KyU	1958, 61, 63, 64, 68-73
LU	1958, 61, 63
MNS	1958-69, 73(14)
MiDW	1958, 61, 63-73
MiHM	1958, 61, 64-73
MiU	1958-68, 69(8), 70, 71(12)
MnU	1958, 61, 63, 64, 68, 69

MoSW	1958-73
MoU	1958-62, 63(4), 64-72
NBiSU	1958-73
NNC	1951, 61
NSyU	1958-70, 73
NbU	1958, 61, 63
NcU	1945, 58-70, 73(15)
NdU	1958(1), 63(4), 64, 68, 69(8), 70
NhD	1970(10)
NjP	1958, 60, 61, 63, 64
NvLN	1972
NvU	1958, 60, 63-70
OCU	1958-62, 63(4), 64-70, 72, 73
OU	1958-70
OkT	1961, 68, 69(8), 70(10)
OkU	1958-73
OrU	1958-73
PBL	1958, 70(11), 71(12)
PSt	1958-64, 68-70, 72, 73
RPB	1958(2), 61, 63
TMM	1958-69, 70(11), 72(13)
TxDaAR-T	1960, 61, 63, 68(7), 69(8), 70-73
TxDaM	1958, 61, 63, 68
TxDaSM	1958-68, 69(8), 70(11), 72(13), 73
TxHSD	1958
TxHU	1958-73
TxLT	1958, 61, 63, 69, 70(11), 71-73(14)
TxMM	1958(1), 61(3), 63(5), 69(9), 70(11)
TxU	1945, 58-71
TxU-Da	1958-71
UU	1961
ViBlbV	1958-73
WU	1958-61, 63(5), 69(9), 71-73

(309) TEXAS. UNIVERSITY. DEPARTMENT OF GEOLOGY.

1937		No. 1. Lower Tertiary. Route: Austin, Manor, Elgin, McDade, Paige, Bastrop, Smithville, Bastrop, Austin.
		No. 2. Lower Cretaceous. Route: Austin, Cedar Park, Leander, Travis Peak, Marshall Ford Dam, Austin, Buda, San Marcos, Austin.
		No. 3. Llano uplift. Route: Austin, Fredericksburg, Llano, Burnet, Austin.
1939		No. 1. Points of geologic interest in the vicinity of Austin, Texas. (290, 310)
	Nov.	No. 2. Marshall Ford Dam. (290, 310)
1967		Cooperative soils; geology field study [by] University of Texas, Department of Geology, USDA Soil Conservation Service and Texas A & M University Soil and Crop Sciences Department.

TxU 1937, 39, 67

(310) TEXAS. UNIVERSITY. GEOLOGICAL SOCIETY. GUIDEBOOK.

1939	See Texas. University. Department of Geology. (309)
1949	Cretaceous Comanche field trip. (82)
1950	Cretaceous field trip.

1951	Mar.	Tertiary field trip.
	Apr.	Geology of Pilot Knob.
1952		Igneous metamorphic field trip. [central Texas]
1953		Tertiary field trip. [Bastrop and Fayette counties]
1954		Tertiary field trip.
1955		Tertiary field trip: structural geology, sedimentary structures, petrographic stratigraphy of the Texas Gulf Coast Tertiary, soils, vegetation. Contains road log of trip. [Bastrop and Fayette counties]
1956	[1]	Paleozoic field trip; Cambrian stratigraphy, central Texas.
	Nov.	Pre-Cambrian field trip; igneous and metamorphic rocks of central Texas.
1957		[Carboniferous strata of San Saba County]
1958	Apr.	Pre-Cambrian field trip; igneous and metamorphic rocks of central Texas.
	Dec.	Cretaceous field trip. [Travis County]
1959		Tertiary field trip; petrographic stratigraphy of the Texas Gulf Coast Tertiary. [Bastrop and Fayette counties]
1960	Feb.	Igneous and metamorphic rocks of the southeastern part of the Llano uplift, central Texas.
	Dec.	Tertiary field trip. Same as field trip of Oct. 1955, except no conventional road log is included.
1961	May 13	Llano uplift field trip.
1962		See Southwestern Association of Student Geological Societies. (294)
1963		Interpretation of Eocene depositional environments, Little Brazos River valley, Texas. (46)

CLU-G/G	1949, 51-53, 55-60, 63
DI-GS	1949, 54, 55, 56(Nov.), 58, 60(Dec.), 62, 63
IU	1955
TxDaAR-T	1963
TxMM	1953
TxU	1949-61, 63

(311) TEXAS. WEST TEXAS STATE UNIVERSITY, CANYON. GEOLOGICAL SOCIETY. FIELD TRIP GUIDEBOOK.

1959		Claude-Silverton field trip.
1960	2nd	Palo Duro.
1961	3rd	Palo Duro. (held in April)
	Nov.	Claude-Silverton. (Sames as 1959, except has 6 stops instead of 8.)
1962		Palo Duro, 4th edition.
1964		Palo Duro, 5th edition.
1966		See Southwestern Association of Student Geological Societies. (294)
1967?		Palo Duro.
1971?		Palo Duro.
1972		Palo Duro.
1973		Sedimentology of the upper Triassic sandstones of the Texas high plains.
[1975]		Palo Duro Canyon.

IU	1960, 61
TxCaW	1959-67, 71, 72, 75
TxDaAR-T	1973
TxDaSM	1973
TxHSD	1973
TxU	1959-62, 72

(312) TRI-STATE GEOLOGICAL FIELD CONFERENCE. GUIDEBOOK FOR THE ANNUAL FIELD CONFERENCE.

1933	1st	Upper Mississippi Valley.
1934	2nd	Southern Wisconsin.
1935	3rd	Clinton, Jackson and Dubuque counties, Iowa.
1936	4th	Calhoun and Jersey counties, Illinois.
1937	5th	Southeastern Wisconsin.
1938	6th	Madison, Dallas, Guthrie, and Polk counties, Iowa.
1939	7th	Western Illinois.
1940	8th	North-central Wisconsin, igneous rocks.
1941	9th	Southeast Iowa: Montpelier, Muscatine County, Iowa, Burlington-Keokum area.
1946	10th	Northeastern Illinois and adjacent Indiana.
1947	11th	Eastern Wisconsin.
1948	12th	Northeast Iowa.
1949	13th	LaSalle anticline, northeast Illinois.
1950	14th	Central plain of Wisconsin.
1951	15th	Devonian of north-central Iowa.
1952	16th	Central northern Illinois. (126)
1953	17th	Northern Wisconsin.
1954	18th	Northeastern Iowa.
1955	19th	West-central Illinois.
1956		Upper Mississippi zinc-lead district.
1957	21st	Southeast Iowa.
1958	22nd	Southern Illinois fluorspar district.
1959	23rd	Southwestern Wisconsin.
1960	24th	Stratigraphic sequence of north-central Iowa.
1961	25th	Southern Illinois; Marion to Dongola, Illinois on Interstate 57.
1962	26th	Northeastern Wisconsin, McCaslin syncline-Tigerton anorthosite.
1963	May	See Geological Society of Iowa. (103)
	27th	See Geological Society of Iowa. (103)
1964	28th	Western Illinois. (126)
1965	29th	Cambro-Ordovician stratigraphy of southwest Wisconsin. (346)
1966	30th	Devonian of northern Iowa Cedar Valley, Shell Rock and Lime Creek.
1967	31st	The Mississippi River arch.
1968	32nd	A greenstone belt in central Wisconsin.
1969	33rd	The many faces of geology.
1970	34th	Trip 1. Cambro-Ordovician stratigraphy and structure of north-central Illinois, plus underground gas storage.
		Trip 2. Stratigraphy of Pleistocene deposits in northeastern Illinois.
1971	35th	Geology of the Twin Ports area, Superior-Duluth.
1972	36th	General geology in the vicinity of northern Iowa.
1973	37th	Depositional environments of selected Lower Pennsylvanian and Upper Mississippian sequences of southern Illinois.
1974	38th	Field Trip No. 1. Precambrian rocks of the Chippewa region.
		Field Trip No. 2. Paleozoic rocks of the Eau Claire area.
		Field Trip No. 3. Quaternary.
1975	39th	Field Trip No. 1. Devonian limestone facies; Cedar Valley and State Quarry limestones in the Iowa City region.
		Field Trip No. 2. Strip mine reclamation in south-central Iowa.
		Field Trip No. 3. Ordovician structure and mineralization in northeastern Iowa.

CLU-G/G	1968, 69
[CaBVU]	1969
CaOKQ	1966, 70

CaOOG	1968, 71
CoG	1960, 65, 69
CoU	1965, 69
DI-GS	1933-41, 46-55, 57-69, 71
DLC	1969
ICF	1965, 67
ICarbS	1952, 61, 64, 65, 73
IEN	1948, 49, 52, 64, 69, 70
[I-GS]	1933-75
IU	1934-75
IaU	1933-70, 72, 73
InLP	1948, 49, 53, 62-67, 69, 70
InU	1951, 55, 60, 64, 65, 68-70
KyU	1955, 65, 70, 71, 73, 74
MH-GS	1969
MNS	1964, 65
MiHM	1965, 68, 71
MnDuU	1938, 40, 41, 62, 68, 75(1)
MnU	1948, 49, 51, 52, 54, 59, 60, 62, 65, 68, 69
MoSW	1951, 55, 64, 65, 69
MoU	1938, 66, 69
MtU	1969
NBiSU	1966, 69
NNC	1948-55
NRU	1973
NSyU	1964
NdU	1965, 69, 70
NjP	1938, 48, 49, 65, 67-69
OCU	1965, 73
OU	1949, 51, 52, 67, 69
OkU	1940, 41, 49, 55, 61, 65, 69, 70
PBL	1965
PSt	1969
TxDaAR-T	1951, 54, 65, 68, 70-74
TxDaDM	1948, 58, 60, 61, 64-68
TxDaM	1965
TxDaSM	1954, 55, 60, 73
TxHSD	1973
TxHU	1965
TxLT	1969
TxU	1938, 41, 52, 54, 55, 57, 59-68, 70
UU	1969
WU	1937, 38, 52, 57, 59, 61, 62, 64, 65, 68-70, 74, 75

TRI-STATE GEOLOGICAL SOCIETY. **See TRI-STATE GEOLOGICAL FIELD CONFERENCE. (312)**

(313) TRIARTHRUS CLUB, AUSTIN, TEXAS.

1940 Feb. 4 Field trip through the Cretaceous section near Austin, Texas.

TxU	1940

(314) TULSA GEOLOGICAL SOCIETY. GUIDEBOOK FOR THE FIELD CONFERENCE.

1941	Oct.	Tulsa to Choteau and Grand River area and return.
	Nov.	Pennsylvanian stratigraphy of Tulsa County.
1946		Pennsylvanian and Mississippian rocks of eastern Oklahoma.
1947		Western part of the Ouachita Mountains in Oklahoma.
1950	Oct.	To the mines and mill of the Eagle-Picher Mining and Smelting Company.
	Dec.	Coody's Bluff to Burbank, Oklahoma.
1951	Apr.	Tulsa to Spavinaw, Oklahoma.
	May	Kansas, Oklahoma to Marble City, Oklahoma.
1954		Tulsa-Woolaroc-Bartlesville.
1956		See Oklahoma. Geological Survey. (232)
1957		Eastern Oklahoma. (15)
1961		Arkoma Basin and north-central Ouachita Mountains of Oklahoma. (85)
1968	Oct.	Guidebook and roadlog; geology of the Tulsa metropolitan area.
1972	Apr.	Sandstone environments, Keystone reservoir area.
1973	Apr.	Guide to sandstone environments, Keystone Reservoir area, Oklahoma.
	Oct.	"The big lime" southern margin of the Oologah Limestone banks.
1975	May	Basinward facies changes in the Wapanuck Limestone (Lower Pennsylvanian) Indian Nations Turnpike, Ouachita Mountains, Oklahoma.
1976	Apr.	Coal and oil potential of the Tri-State area.

CLU-G/G	1950, 51, 54, 57, 61, 68
CaACl	1961
CU-EART	1961
CaOHM	1957, 68
CaOWtU	1957
CoG	1950, 51
CoU	1954, 57, 68
DFPC	1957, 61
DI-GS	1941(Oct.), 46, 47, 50, 51, 54, 56, 57, 61, 68, 73(Oct.), 75
ICF	1961
ICIU-S	1957, 68
IEN	1947, 57
[I-GS]	1954, 72
IU	1947, 50, 51, 54, 57, 61, 68, 73(Oct.)
IaU	1961
InLP	1957, 61
InU	1947, 50, 51, 54, 56, 61, 68
KyU	1947, 50, 51, 56, 68
LU	1947, 50, 51, 54, 57, 61
MH-GS	1947
MNS	1947, 50, 51, 54
MiHM	1950, 51
MnU	1950, 51, 54, 56, 57, 61, 68
MoRM	1947, 50
MoSW	1947, 50, 51
NNC	1947, 54, 61
NSyU	1956
NbU	1947, 57, 61
NcU	1956
NdU	1950, 51, 54
NhD	1947
NjP	1950, 51, 54, 61

NmPE	1957, 68
OCU	1947, 54
OU	1947, 50-54, 57, 68
[OkOkCGe]	1947, 50, 51
OkT	1954, 68, 73(Oct.)
OkU	1941-54, 57-68, 73, 76
PPiGulf	1947, 61
RPB	1947, 56
TMM	1957
TxDaAR-T	1947, 50, 51, 54, 57, 61
TxDaDM	1957, 61, 68
TxDaM	1947, 50, 51, 54, 57, 61
TxDaSM	1950, 51, 54, 61
TxHSD	1947, 61
TxHU	1941, 46, 47, 57, 61
TxLT	1941(Oct.), 46, 47, 50, 51
TxMM	1941(Oct.), 46, 47, 50, 51, 54, 61
TxU	1941, 46, 47, 50, 51, 54, 61, 68
TxU-Da	1947, 50, 51, 54, 56
UU	1950, 51, 54
ViBlbV	1957
WU	1950, 51

(315) U. S. NATIONAL PARK SERVICE.

1937 See Rocky Mountain Association of Geologists. (250)

(316) UNITED STATES GEOLOGICAL SURVEY. BULLETIN.

1915

No. 611. Guidebook of the western U. S. Part A. The Northern Pacific Route.

No. 612. Guidebook of the western U. S. Part B. The Overland Route with a side trip to Yellowstone Park.

No. 613. Guidebook of the western U. S. Part C. The Santa Fe Route with a trip to the Grand Canyon of the Colorado.

No. 614. Guidebook of the western U. S. Part D. The Shasta Route and Coast Line.

No. 707. Guidebook of the western U. S. Part E. The Denver and Rio Grande Western Route.

No. 845. Guidebook of the western U. S. Part F. The Southern Pacific lines, New Orleans to Los Angeles.

AzFU	1915
CLU-G/G	1915
CLhC	1915(611-614)
CSdS	1915
CU-EART	1915
CaOHM	1915(611-614,845)
CaOKQ	1915
CaOLU	1915(611-614,707)
CoG	1915
CoU	1915
DFPC	1915(707)
DI-GS	1915
ICF	1915
IEN	1915

IU	1915
IaU	1915(611-614)
IdBB	1915(613,614)
InU	1915
KyU	1915
MNS	1915
MiHM	1915
MoU	1915
NBiSU	1915
NSyU	1915
NbU	1915
NcU	1915
NdU	1915
NhD	1915
NjP	1915
NmPE	1915
NvLN	1915
NvU	1915
OCU	1915
OU	1915
OkU	1915
OrU	1915
PBL	1915
PSt	1915
SdRM	1915(611)
TMM	1915
TxDaSM	1915
ViBlbV	1915

(317) UNITED STATES-JAPAN CONFERENCE ON RESEARCH RELATED TO EARTHQUAKE PREDICTION.

1966 2nd Guidebook for Nevada earthquake sites.

(318) UNIVERSIDAD NACIONAL AUTONOMA DE MEXICO. INSTITUTO DE GEOLOGIA.

1946 Guia geologica de Oaxaca, Mexico.

CLU-G/G	1946
InU	1946

(319) UNIVERSITY OF COLORADO, MUSEUM.

1968 Guidebook to the high altitude and mountain deposits of Miocene age in Wyoming and Colorado.

CoDuF	1968
CoU	1968

(320) UTAH FIELD HOUSE OF NATURAL HISTORY.

1948 No. 1 The Uinta Mountains and vicinity, a field guide to the geology. (322, 323)

CLU-G/G	1948

(321) UTAH. GEOLOGICAL AND MINERALOGICAL SURVEY. BULLETIN.

1966 No. 80. Central Utah coals. (96)

1969 No. 82. Guidebook of northern Utah. (100)

AzFU	1966, 69
CLU-G/G	1966, 69
CU-EART	1966, 69
CaOLU	1969
CoG	1966, 69
CoU	1966
ICF	1966, 69
IEN	1966, 69
IU	1966,,69
IaU	1966, 69
IdBB	1966
InU	1966, 69
KyU	1966, 69
LU	1966
MiDW	1966
MnU	1966, 69
MoSW	1966, 69
MoU	1966, 69
NBiSU	1966
NSyU	1966, 69
NbU	1966, 69
NdU	1966, 69
NhD	1966
NjP	1966
NvLN	1966, 69
OU	1966, 69
OkU	1966, 69
OrU	1966, 69
PBL	1966
PSt	1966, 69
TxDaAR-T	1966, 69
TxDaDM	1966
TxHU	1966, 69
TxMM	1966, 69
TxU	1966, 69
UU	1969

(322) UTAH. GEOLOGICAL AND MINERALOGICAL SURVEY. EARTH SCIENCE EDUCATION SERIES.

1966? No. 1 Field guide to the geology of the Uinta Mountains and adjacent synclinal basins. (320, 323)

ICIU-S	1966?
IaU	1966?
InLP	1966?
OU	1966?

(323) **UTAH. GEOLOGICAL AND MINERALOGICAL SURVEY. REPRINT.**

1954 The Uinta Mountains and vicinity; a field guide to the geology. Reprint 43 from Paper No. 1 of the Utah Field House of Natural History. (320, 322)
[CaBVU] 1954

(324) **UTAH GEOLOGICAL ASSOCIATION. PUBLICATION.**

1971	No. 1	Environmental geology of the Wasatch Front. See also 1975. (96) Field Trip No. 1. Farmington to Draper. Field Trip No. 2. Nephi to Draper. Field Trip No. 3. Brigham City to Farmington.
1972	No. 2	Plateau-Basin and Range transition zone, central Utah.
1973	No. 3	Geology of the Milford area.
1974	No. 4	Energy resources of the Uinta Basin, Utah. Road logs, reference data, bibliography.
1976	No. 6	Geology of the Oquirrh Mountains and regional setting of the Bingham mining district, Utah.

CU-EART	1971-74
IU	1971-74, 76
KyU	1971-74
NdU	1972
OCU	1971-74
OU	1971
OkU	1972-74
PSt	1973
TxDaAR-T	1971-73
TxDaSM	1972
TxHSD	1972
WU	1972-74

(325) **UTAH GEOLOGICAL SOCIETY. FIELD CONFERENCE. ROAD LOG.**

1955 Utah Geological Survey field trip; Tertiary and Quaternary stratigraphic features of the Ogden Valley area, Utah. Supplemental road log.

CLU-G/G	1955
DI-GS	1955

(326) **UTAH GEOLOGICAL SOCIETY. GUIDEBOOK TO THE GEOLOGY OF UTAH.**

1946	1st	The geology and geography of the Henry Mountain region.
1947	2nd	Some structural features of the intrusions in the Iron Springs district.
1948	3rd	Geology of the Utah-Colorado salt dome region with emphasis on Gypsum Valley, Colorado.
1949	4th	The transition between the Colorado Plateau and the Great Basin in central Utah.
1950	5th	Petroleum geology of Uinta Basin. (133)
1951	6th	Geology of the Canyon, House and Confusion ranges, Millard County, Utah. (133)
1952	7th	Cedar City, Utah to Las Vegas, Nevada. (133)
	8th	Geology of the central Wasatch Mountains.
1954	9th	Uranium deposits and general geology of southeastern Utah.
1955	10th	Tertiary and Quaternary geology of the eastern Bonneville Basin.
1957	12th	Geology of the East Tintic Mountains and ore deposits of the Tintic mining districts.
1958	13th	Geology of the Standbury Mountains, Tooele County, Utah.
1959	14th	Geology of the southern Oquirrh Mountains and Fivemille Pass, northern Boulder Mountain area, Tooele and Utah counties, Utah.
1960	15th	Geology of the Silver Island Mountains; Box Elder and Tooele Counties, Utah and Elko County, Nevada.

1961	16th	Geology of the Bingham mining district and northern Oquirrh Mountains.
1965	19th	Geology and resources of south-central Utah; resources for power. (133)
1967	21st	Uranium districts of southeastern Utah.
1968	22nd	Geology of the Park City mining district.
1969		See Intermountain Association of (Petroleum) Geologists. (133)
1970	23rd	Western Grand Canyon district.

AzFU	1951, 52(8), 54, 58, 61, 63, 66, 68, 70
AzTeS	1948, 49, 51-70
AzU	1968, 70
CLU-G/G	1946-70
CLhC	1948-52, 54-61, 63-68, 70
CSdS	1946, 48, 49, 51, 52(8), 54-56, 58, 70
CU-EART	1946-70
[CaACAM]	1951-61, 65-68
CaACU	1946-52, 54
[CaBVU]	1948-52, 54-61, 63-66
CaOHM	1952, 55
CaOKQ	1952, 54-61, 63-68, 70
CaOLU	1954, 57, 61, 63, 70
CaOOG	1946-50, 52(8)
CoFS	1948, 61, 65
CoG	1946-68, 70
[CoPU]	1948, 49, 52-70
CoU	1946-52, 54-68, 70
DFPC	1965
DI-GS	1946-52, 54-61, 63-68
ICF	1948-52, 54-61, 63, 64, 67
ICIU-S	1952(8), 55-70
ICarbS	1948, 49, 51, 52, 54-61, 63-68, 70
IEN	1946-70
IU	1946-52, 54-61, 63-66, 68
IaU	1946-52, 54-70
IdBB	1950-59, 63, 65-67
IdPI	1956, 57, 60
InLP	1948, 49, 51, 52(8), 54-70
InRE	1946-56, 66, 70
InU	1946-70
KyU	1946-52, 54-61, 63-69, 70
LU	1948, 49, 51, 52, 54-68, 70
MH-GS	1946-48, 51, 54, 57, 66
MNS	1949, 52, 54, 58, 64, 65
MiDW	1946, 48-52, 54-61, 63-70
MiHM	1946-48, 61, 67
MiKW	1952(8), 54-70
MiU	1948-70
MnU	1946-51, 63-68
MoRM	1946-59, 61-70
MoSW	1947-51, 52(7), 54-61, 63-70
MoU	1946-70
NBiSU	1952(8), 54-61
NNC	1946-70
NOneoU	1970

NRU	1951, 65
NSyU	1948-68
NbU	1946-52, 54-68, 70
NcU	1946, 48, 49, 51-66
NdU	1946-48, 52, 54-61, 63-68, 70
NhD	1946-69
NjP	1946-52, 54-61, 63-68, 70
NvLN	1967
NvU	1948-70
OCU	1946-48, 52(8), 54-70
OU	1946-70
OkT	1946, 48-60, 64, 65
OkU	1946-70
OrCS	1948-70
OrU	1946-61, 63-68, 70
PBL	1946-51
PBm	1946, 47, 50, 61, 70
PSt	1946-49, 51-70
RPB	1946-67
SdRM	1946-66
TMM	1970
TU	1965, 66
TxDaAR-T	1946, 48-52, 54-61, 63-65, 67, 68, 70
TxDaDM	1946, 48-52, 54-61, 63-67, 69, 70
TxDaM	1946-52, 54-61, 63-67
TxDaSM	1948-52, 54-57, 59, 61, 65, 67, 70
TxHU	1946-49, 51-70
TxMM	1948, 49, 51, 54, 65, 69
TxU	1946-52, 54-61, 63-70
TxU-Da	1952
UPB	1946-68
UU	1946-68
ViBlbV	1946-70
WU	1946-70
WyU	1946-68

(327) VIRGINIA ACADEMY OF SCIENCE. GEOLOGY SECTION. GUIDEBOOK; FIELD TRIP.

1953		[Log only]
1956		Pleistocene terraces south of the James River, Virginia.
1958		[Log only]
1959		[Log only]
1960		[Log only]
1962	40th	Norfolk meeting.
		Trip A. Tour of the Langeley Research Center of the National Aeronautics and Space Administration.
		Trip B. Tour of the U. S. Naval Station, Norfolk, Virginia.
		Trip C. Tour of the Norfolk Botanical Gardens.
		Trip D. Tour of the Chesapeake Bay Bridge-Tunnel Project.
		Part 1. Field trip log.
		Part 2. Pleistocene record in the subsurface of the Norfolk area, Virginia.
		Part 3. Fact file on the Chesapeake Bay Bridge Tunnel.
		Trip E. Excursion to Seashore State Park.

		Trip F. Excursion to the Back Bay National Wildlife Refuge.
1965		[Log only]
1968		Structure and Paleozoic history of the Salem synclinorium, southwestern Virginia.
1972		Geologic features of the Bristol and Wallace quadrangles, Washington County, Virginia and anatomy of the Lower Mississippian Delta in southwestern Virginia. [Emory & Henry College. Department of Geology. Field Guide. No. 1.]

DI-GS	1953, 56, 58-60, 62, 65, 68
[I-GS]	1962
IU	1962, 72
MH-GS	1962
NjP	1968
OCU	1972
ViBlbV	1962

(328) VIRGINIA. DIVISION OF MINERAL RESOURCES.

1974	No. 35	Geology of Woodstock Wolf Gap, Conicville and Edinburg quadrangles, Virginia.
1975	No. 40	Geology of the Front Royal Quadrangle, Virginia.

ICarbS	1974, 75
IU	1974, 75

(329) VIRGINIA. DIVISION OF MINERAL RESOURCES. BULLETIN.

1976	No. 86. Geology of the Shenandoah National Park, Virginia. Contains roadlog of Skyline Drive.

IU	1976

(330) VIRGINIA. DIVISION OF MINERAL RESOURCES. INFORMATION CIRCULAR.

1962	No. 6	Guidebook to the coastal plain of Virginia north of the James River. (43)
1971	No. 16	Field trip to the igneous rocks of Augusta, Rockingham, Highland, and Bath counties, Virginia.

CU-EART	1971
IU	1962, 71
MoU	1971
NdU	1971

(331) VIRGINIA. DIVISION OF MINERAL RESOURCES. VIRGINIA MINERALS. ROAD LOGS. (TITLE VARIES)

1969	Road logs: Staunton, Churchville, Greenville, and Stuarts Draft quadrangles.
1970	Road log of storm-damaged areas in central Virginia.
1971	Road log of the geology of Frederick County, Virginia.
1973	Field trip across the Blue Ridge anticlinorium, Smith River allochthon, and Sauratown Mountains anticlinorium near Martinsville, Virginia.
1975	Road log to some abandoned gold mines of the gold-pyrite belt, northeastern Virginia.
	Road log of the geology from Madison to Cumberland counties in the Piedmont, central Virginia.
1976	Road log of the geology in the northern Appalachian Valley of Virginia.

IU	1969-76
KyU	1973
NdU	1975
WU	1975

(332) VIRGINIA GEOLOGICAL FIELD CONFERENCE. ANNUAL.

1969		See College of William and Mary. (65)
1970		Central Valley and Ridge.
1971		Triassic Basin-Culpeper.
1972		Southwestern Valley and Ridge.
1973	5th	Blue Ridge anticlinorium, Smith River allochthon, and Sauratown Mountains anticlinorium near Martinsville, Virginia.
1974	6th	Environmental geology and stratigraphy of the Richmond, Virginia area. (43)
1975		Appalachian plateau area.
1976		North-central Valley and Ridge.

ICIU-S	1974
TxDaAR-T	1971, 73, 74

VIRGINIA. GEOLOGICAL SURVEY. See VIRGINIA. DIVISION OF MINERAL RESOURCES. (330)

(333) VIRGINIA. GEOLOGICAL SURVEY. GUIDE LEAFLET.

1938	No. 1. See Field Conference of Pennsylvania Geologists. (83)

(334) VIRGINIA POLYTECHNIC INSTITUTE AND STATE UNIVERSITY. DEPARTMENT OF GEOLOGICAL SCIENCES. GEOLOGICAL GUIDEBOOK.

1961	No. 1	Grand Appalachian field excursion. (96)
1963	No. 2	Geological excursions in southwest Virginia. (102)
1968	No. 3	Structure and Paleozoic history of the Salem synclinorium, southwestern Virginia.
1969	No. 4	Appalachian field trip (unpublished).
1971	No. 5	Guidebook to Appalachian tectonics and sulfide mineralization of southwestern Virginia. (102)
	No. 6	Guidebook to contrast in style in deformation of the southern and central Appalachians of Virginia. (96)

CU-EART	1971(6)
IEN	1961, 63, 68, 71
InLP	1961, 68, 71
InU	1971(6)
MNS	1961
MoRM	1971(6)
MoSW	1971(6)
NBiSU	1971(6)
NhD	1971(5)
NjP	1961, 63
OkU	1961, 63, 71(6)
PBm	1971(6)
PSt	1971(6)
TMM	1971
ViBlbV	1968, 69, 71
WaPS	1971(5)

VIRGINIA POLYTECHNIC INSTITUTE, BLACKSBURG. ENGINEERING EXTENSION DIVISION. ENGINEERING EXTENSION SERIES. See VIRGINIA POLYTECHNIC INSTITUTE AND STATE UNIVERSITY. (334)

(335) WASHINGTON. DEPARTMENT OF NATURAL RESOURCES. DIVISION OF GEOLOGY AND EARTH RESOURCES. INFORMATION CIRCULAR. (TITLE VARIES)

1975 No. 54 A geologic road log over Chinook, White Pass, and Ellensburg to Yakima highways.

CoU	1975
DI-GS	1975
IU	1975
InU	1975
MoSW	1975
NdU	1975
WU	1975

(336) WASHINGTON. UNIVERSITY. GEOLOGY DEPARTMENT.

1963 A geologic trip along Snoqualmie, Swauk, and Stevens Pass highways. (Washington. Division of Mines and Geology Information Circular No. 38.).

ICF	1963
IEN	1963
MoSW	1963
MoU	1963
NcU	1963
NdU	1963
TxU	1963

(337) WAYNE STATE UNIVERSITY.

1963 Guidebook; Structures and origin of volcanic rocks, Montana-Wyoming-Idaho; a summer conference sponsored by Wayne State University through a grant from the National Science Foundation.

1968 Guidebook; Structures and origin of volcanic rocks, Montana-Wyoming-Idaho; a summer conference sponsored by Wayne State University through a grant from the National Science Foundation.

1970 Guidebook; Structures and origin of volcanic rocks, Montana-Wyoming-Idaho.

CoU	1963
DI-GS	1968
IEN	1963
IdBB	1963, 68
InU	1963, 65, 70
MoSW	1968
NdU	1963
NjP	1968
NvU	1968
OkU	1968
TxU	1963

(338) WEST TEXAS GEOLOGICAL SOCIETY. GUIDEBOOK FOR THE FIELD TRIP.

1927	Feb.	Glass Mountains.
	May	Delaware and Guadalupe Mountains of Texas and New Mexico.
1933		San Saba to Mason, central Texas mineral region; road log. Contains composite section showing formations of Ellenberger Group.
1936		Marathon Basin area.
1937		Hueco and Franklin Mountains.
1938	spring	East side outcrops (of Permian Basin).

(338) West Texas Geological Society.

		See American Association of Petroleum Geologists. (13)
1939	spring	Van Horn area, Culberson and Hudspeth counties, Texas; road log.
	fall	Geologic excursion; Paleozoic section of the Llano uplift. (86, 302)
1940	spring	Sacramento Mountains, New Mexico.
	fall	Eddy County, New Mexico.
1941	spring	Fort Worth to Midland, Texas on Highway 80 along the Texas and Pacific. Additional notes on El Reno and Whitehorse Group.
	fall	Big Bend Park area, Brewster County, Texas.
1942		El Paso to Carlsbad along U. S. Highway 62.
1946	spring	Stratigraphy of the Hueco and Franklin Mountains.
	fall	Glass Mountain-Marathon Basin.
1947		Guadalupe Mountains of New Mexico and Texas.
1948		Green Valley and Paradise Valley; Wire Gap and Solitario; Limpia Canyon and Barrilla Mountains.
1949		No. 1. Marathon region, Big Bend region, Green Valley-Paradise Valley region, Sierra Blanca region, Texas. (96)
		No. 2. Cenozoic geology of the Llano Estacado and Rio Grande Valley. (96, 207)
		No. 3. Geology and ore deposits of Silver City region, New Mexico. (22)
		No. 4. Permian rocks of the Trans-Pecos region. (96)
		No. 5. Pre-Permian rocks of the Trans-Pecos area and southern New Mexico. (96)
1950		Sierra Blanca region, Franklin Mountains, Texas.
1951	Jan.	Introduction to the petroleum geology of the Permian Basin.
	spring	Pennsylvanian of Brazos River and Colorado River valleys, north-central Texas.
	fall	Apache Mountains of Trans-Pecos Texas.
1952		Marathon Basin, Brewster and Pecos counties, Trans-Pecos Texas.
1953	spring	Chinati Mountains, Presidio County, Texas.
	fall	Sierra Diablo, Guadalupe and Hueco areas of Trans-Pecos Texas.
1954		Cambrian-Llano area. (254)
1955		Big Bend National Park, Texas.
1956		Eastern Llano Estacado and adjoining Osage plains. (159)
1957		Glass Mountains.
1958	fall	Franklin and Hueco Mountains.
		[1] Road log, Del Rio-El Paso.
1959		Geology of the Val Verde Basin.
1960		Geology of the Delaware Basin.
1961		Upper Permian to Pliocene; San Angelo area. (254)
1962		Permian of the central Guadalupe Mountains, Eddy County, New Mexico. (117, 251)
1964		Geology of Mina Plomosas-Placer de Guadalupe area, Chihuahua, Mexico.
1965		Geology of Big Bend area, Texas; with road log and papers on natural history of the area.
1966		Geology of the Val Verde Basin. (Note: 1959 guidebook used, with supplement.)
1967		No field trip.
1968		Delaware Basin exploration: Guadalupe Mountains, Hueco Mountains, Franklin Mountains, geology of the Carlsbad Caverns.
		Basins of the southwest. (Publication No. 70-68-SWS.)
1969		Same as 1968.
1970		See Society of Economic Paleontologists and Mineralogists. Permian Basin Section. (280)
1971		Field trip guidebook and Memoir 24; Stratigraphy and structure of Pecos country, southeastern New Mexico. (Memoir published by State Bureau of Mines and Mineral Resources, New Mexico Institute of Mining and Technology, Socorro, New Mexico.) (251)
1972		Geology of the Big Bend area, Texas. Field trip guidebook with road log and papers on natural history of the area. (Publication No. 72-59 which is a reprint with additions of Publication 65-51.)
1974		No. 1. Guidebook through the states of Chihuahua and Sinaloa, Mexico. (Publication No. 74-63.)

No. 2. Lower Cretaceous, shelf, platform, reef and basinal deposits, southwest Texas and northern Coahuila. (Publication No. 74-64.) (280)

1975 Permian exploration, boundaries, and stratigraphy. (Publication No. 75-65.) (280)

[A-GS]	1941, 46(fall), 47, 49, 50, 52, 53, 56
AzFU	1955, 56, 58(fall), 59-62, 64, 68, 71, 72
AzTeS	1949(3), 51, 52, 55-57, 58(fall), 59-65, 67, 68, 71, 74(2)
AzU	1968, 71
[CDU]	1968
CLU-G/G	1936, 39(spring), 49(3,5), 50-53, 55-57, 58(fall), 59-62, 64, 65, 69, 71-75
CSdS	1949, 51, 52, 53(spring), 55, 64
CU-EART	1949(2,4,5), 51-53, 55-65, 68, 69, 71-75
CLhC	1946(spring), 47, 48, 49(1,2,4,5), 50-53, 55-57, 58(fall), 60-62, 64, 68
CaAC	1957, 59
CaACM	1949(5), 58(1), 68
CaACU	1952, 54, 56-61
[CaBVU]	1945, 57, 60-62, 64, 65, 68
CaOHM	1956-59, 61-64, 66, 68, 69, 71, 72
CaOKQ	1952, 56-62, 64, 65, 68
CaOLU	1955, 57, 60, 62, 64, 68
CaOOG	1959-62, 64, 65, 68, 69
CoFS	1956-59, 61, 62, 64, 65, 68
CoG	1940(fall), 41, 47-65, 68, 71
[CoPU]	1962, 68, 71
CoU	1949, 50, 52-62, 64-66, 68, 69, 71, 72
DI-GS	1939(fall), 40(fall), 41, 46-62, 64, 65, 68, 75
ICF	1952, 55-57, 58(fall), 59-62, 64
ICIU-S	1956, 58(fall), 59-64, 68, 69, 71, 74
ICarbS	1940(fall), 52, 53(fall), 57
IEN	1949-53, 56, 57, 58(fall), 59, 61-65, 68, 71-74
[I-GS]	1949(2,5), 50, 52-57, 59
IU	1946(spring), 47, 49-62, 64-66, 69-72, 74(2)
IaU	1941(fall), 49(4,5), 52, 53, 56-62, 64, 65, 68, 71, 74
IdPI	1958(1), 72
InLP	1955-59, 61, 64, 65, 68, 72
InRE	1952
InU	1949, 50, 51(fall), 52-62
KyU	1941(spring), 49(2,4), 51-62, 64, 65, 68, 69, 71, 72, 74(2)
LU	1939, 49-53, 55-57, 58(fall), 59-65, 68, 71
MH-GS	1949
MNS	1941, 53, 54, 58
MiDW	1956, 57, 58(fall), 59-66, 68, 71, 72
MiHM	1952, 55-65, 68, 71, 72, 74
MiKW	1956, 57
MiU	1949, 56-65, 68, 71, 72, 74
MnU	1948, 49(2,4,5), 50, 51, 53-62, 64-69
MoRM	1948, 49, 52, 53, 56, 57, 58(fall)
MoSW	1946(spring), 47-49, 52, 53, 55-57, 58(fall), 59, 61, 62, 64, 65, 68
MoU	1949(2,4,5), 50-64, 68
MtU	1949-52, 54, 56-62, 64
NBiSU	1956, 58-64, 68
NNC	1958(fall), 59-62, 64-66
NOneoU	1965

(338) West Texas Geological Society.

NRU	1949, 56-58, 61, 62
NSyU	1968
NbU	1939(fall), 41(spring), 47, 49-57, 58(fall), 59-65, 68, 71, 72, 74(2), 75
NcU	1952, 56-64, 68, 69, 71, 74
NdU	1952, 56-62, 64, 65, 68
NhD	1949, 52, 54, 56, 57, 58(1), 59, 60, 62, 64, 68, 69, 71, 72, 74
NjP	1949, 51-53, 55, 56, 58(fall), 59, 61-65, 68, 69, 71, 72
NmPE	1956, 58, 60, 62, 65, 68, 71
NmU	1949(5), 62, 71
NvU	1941, 49, 53, 55-65, 69-72, 74(2)
OCU	1949(3), 56, 58, 60-64, 68, 71, 72, 74, 75
OU	1949-53, 55-65, 68, 69, 71, 72, 74(1)
OkT	1940(fall), 46, 47, 49(1-5), 50, 51(spring), 52, 53, 56, 59, 61, 62, 64
OkU	1941, 46-53, 55-69, 71, 72, 74
OrCS	1949(4), 52, 53(fall), 54, 56-58, 60-65, 69, 71, 72, 74(1), 75
OrU	1949(2,4), 52-57, 58(fall), 59-65, 68, 69, 71, 72
PBL	1958, 61, 68
PPiGulf	1939, 49(2,5), 50-52, 56, 57, 58(fall), 60-64
PSt	1956, 57, 58(fall), 59-62, 64-66, 68, 71, 72, 74
SdRM	1961, 62, 64, 68
TMM	1949(1)
TU	1949(2-4), 52, 53, 55-57, 58(fall), 59, 60, 62, 64, 65
TxCaW	1952, 56-58, 60, 61, 65
TxDaAR-T	1937, 40(fall), 41(spring), 48, 49, 52, 53(spring), 55-62, 64, 65, 68, 70-72, 74(2)
TxDaDM	1948, 49(4,5), 52, 53, 55-62, 64, 65, 68, 69, 72
TxDaM	1948, 49(4,5), 52, 53, 55-62, 64, 65, 68
TxDaSM	1941(spring), 47, 48, 49(2,4,5), 50-53, 55-57, 59-62, 65, 68, 71, 74(2)
TxHSD	1941, 46, 47, 49(1-5), 51-53, 55-65, 71, 72
TxHU	1939(fall), 40(fall), 41, 48, 49(1), 52, 53(fall), 54-65, 68, 69, 71, 72, 74(2)
TxLT	1938, 39(fall), 48, 49(2-5), 50-53, 56-61, 64, 65, 68, 69, 71, 72, 74
TxMM	1936, 37, 38(spring), 39-42, 46-53, 55-57, 58(fall), 59-62, 64, 68, 71, 72
TxU	1927, 33, 36, 37, 38(spring), 39-42, 46-62, 64-72
TxU-Da	1939(fall), 46(spring), 47, 48, 49(1,2,4,5), 50, 54, 55, 57, 58
UU	1949(4), 53(spring), 56-65
ViBlbV	1949(2,5), 50, 51, 56, 57, 58(fall), 59-65, 68, 69, 71, 74, 75
WU	1949(1,2,4,5), 50-53, 56-65, 68, 69, 71, 72, 74(2), 75
WyU	1941, 46-50, 52-53, 55-62, 64, 65, 68

WEST TEXAS STATE COLLEGE. GEOLOGICAL SOCIETY. See TEXAS. WEST TEXAS STATE UNIVERSITY, CANYON. (311)

(339) WEST VIRGINIA. GEOLOGICAL AND ECONOMIC SURVEY.

1950	Field guide for the special field conference on the stratigraphy, sedimentation and nomenclature of the Upper Pennsylvanian and Lower Permian strata (Monongahela, Washington, and Green series) in the northern portion of the Dunkard Basin of Ohio, West Virginia, and Pennsylvania.
1953	See Appalachian Geological Society. (31)
1955	See Appalachian Geological Society. (31)
1957	See Appalachian Geological Society. (31)
1958	Conservation of non-renewable resources, log of field trip.
1961	See Appalachian Geological Society. (31)

1963 See Association of American State Geologists. (38)
1964 See Appalachian Geological Society. (31)
1969 Some Appalachian coals and carbonates; models of ancient shallow-water deposition. (Preconvention Geological Society of America field trip, Nov. 1969).
1972 I. C. White memorial symposium field trip.

CU-EART 1972
CaOKQ 1972
DI-GS 1950, 58
ICF 1972
[i-GS] 1950, 72
IU 1950, 72
IaU 1950, 72
InLP 1972
InU 1950, 53
KyU 1955, 59, 72
MnU 1952, 53, 55, 57, 63, 64
NBiSU 1972
NSyU 1972
NbU 1972
NcU 1955
NhD 1969
NjP 1969
OU 1950, 72
OkU 1950, 72
PBm 1972
RPB 1953
WU 1972
WaPS 1972

(340) WEST VIRGINIA. GEOLOGICAL SURVEY. STATE PARK SERIES BULLETIN.

1958 No. 6 Blackwater Falls State Park and Canaan Valley State Park; resources, geology and recreation. Includes road log of "Little Switzerland Tour". Revised 1971.

IU 1958
OCU 1958

(341) WEST VIRGINIA. UNIVERSITY. DEPARTMENT OF GEOLOGY.

1957 See Geological Society of America. Southeastern Section. (102)
1969 See Geological Society of America. (96)

(342) WESTERN RESERVE UNIVERSITY. WESTERN RESERVE GEOLOGICAL SOCIETY. ANNUAL FIELD TRIP. GUIDEBOOK.

1953 Euclid Creek reservation, Bedford Glens.

DI-GS 1953

(343) WICHITA FALLS GEOLOGICAL SOCIETY. FIELD TRIP.

1946 Wichita Group-Red Bed phase, southeast Baylor County, southwest Archer County; non-red phase, Throckmorton County, Shackelford County.

DI-GS 1946
TxU 1946

(344) WISCONSIN CLAY MINERALS COMMITTEE.

1964 Guidebook; field trips in southern Wisconsin.
Field Trip No. 1. South-central Wisconsin.
Field Trip No. 2. East-central Wisconsin.
OkU 1964

(345) WISCONSIN. GEOLOGICAL AND NATURAL HISTORY SURVEY.

1935 See Kansas Geological Society. (147)

(346) WISCONSIN. GEOLOGICAL AND NATURAL HISTORY SURVEY. INFORMATION CIRCULAR.

1965 No. 6. Cambro-Ordovician stratigraphy of southwest Wisconsin. (312)
1966 No. 7. Cambrian stratigraphy of western Wisconsin. (165)
1970 No. 11. Cambrian-Ordovician geology of western Wisconsin. (96)
No. 13. Glacial geology of Two Creeks Forest Bed, Valderan type locality, and northern Kettle Moraine State Forest. (96)
No. 14. Geology of the Baraboo district, Wisconsin; a description and field guide incorporating structural analysis of the Precambrian rocks and sedimentologic studies of the Paleozoic strata. (96)
No. 15. Pleistocene geology of southern Wisconsin; a field trip guide with special papers. (96)
No. 16. Guidebook to the upper Mississippi Valley base-metal district. (96)
No. 17. Field trip guidebook to the hydrogeology of the Rock-Fox River basin of southeastern Wisconsin. (96)

CLU-G/G	1965, 66, 70
CU-EART	1970
CoU	1970(16)
DLC	1970(14,16)
IEN	1965, 66, 70
[I-GS]	1965, 70(17)
IU	1965, 66, 70
InRE	1970(11)
MNS	1965, 66, 70
NcU	1965, 66, 70
NjP	1970
NvU	1970(16)

(347) WISCONSIN STATE UNIVERSITY GEOLOGICAL FIELD CONFERENCE. (TITLE VARIES)

1971 3rd Geology of the Eau Claire region.
WU 1971

(348) WISCONSIN. UNIVERSITY. DEPARTMENT OF GEOLOGY. GUIDEBOOK FOR ANNUAL SPRING FIELD TRIP.

1946 1st Southern Missouri, Arkansas, and eastern Oklahoma.
1947 2nd Rocky Mountain Front Range.
1948 3rd Southern Appalachians.
1951 Field trip to the Lake Superior region.
WU 1946-51

(349) **WISCONSIN. UNIVERSITY. DEPARTMENT OF GEOLOGY AND GEOPHYSICS. GUIDEBOOK: FIELD TRIP IN ECONOMIC GEOLOGY.**

1970	Southern Illinois and southeastern Missouri.
1971	Central and eastern Tennessee; western North Carolina.
1972	The Colorado mineral belt.
1973	Mineral deposits of northern Ontario and northwestern Quebec.
1974	Mineral deposits of the central Mississippi Valley.

WU 1970-74

(350) **WYOMING GEOLOGICAL ASSOCIATION. GUIDEBOOK FOR THE ANNUAL FIELD CONFERENCE.**

1946	1st	Central and southeastern Wyoming.
1947	2nd	Bighorn Basin. (354)
1948	3rd	Wind River basin, Wyoming.
1949	4th	Powder River basin.
1950	5th	Southwest Wyoming.
1951	6th	South-central Wyoming.
1952	7th	Southern Bighorn Basin, Wyoming.
1953	8th	Laramie Basin, Wyoming, and North Park, Colorado.
1954	9th	Casper area.
1955	10th	Green River basin.
1956	11th	Jackson Hole.
1957	12th	Southwest Wind River basin.
1958	13th	Powder River basin.
1959	14th	Bighorn Basin.
1960	15th	Overthrust belt of southwestern Wyoming and adjacent areas.
1961	16th	Symposium on Late Cretaceous rocks, Wyoming and adjacent areas.
1962	17th	Symposium on Early Cretaceous rocks of Wyoming and adjacent areas.
1963	18th	Northern Powder River basin. (186)
1964		Highway geology of Wyoming; road logs of the highways, including points of geologic, economic, historic and scenic interest. [Unnumbered guidebook].
1965	19th	Sedimentation of Late Cretaceous and Tertiary outcrops, Rock Springs uplift.
1966		One half-day field trip to Casper Mountain; held at same time of symposium on Permo-Pennsylvanian environments of deposition of Wyoming and contiguous area. (20th Annual Conference not 20th Annual Field Conference.)
1967		No guidebook published (Petroleum Information).
1968	20th	Black Hills area, South Dakota, Montana, Wyoming.
1969	21st	Symposium on Tertiary rocks of Wyoming.
1970	22nd	Symposium on Wyoming sandstones.
1971	23rd	Symposium on Wyoming tectonics and their economic significance.
1972	24th	South-central Wyoming; stratigraphic, tectonics and economics.
1973	25th	Symposium and Core Seminar on the geology and mineral resources of the greater Green River basin, Casper, Wyoming.
1974	26th	Muddy Sandstone-Wind River basin. [in Wyoming Geological Association. Earth Science Bulletin, Vol. 7, No. 1.]
1975		Geology and mineral resources of the Bighorn Basin, Cody, Wyoming.

AzFU	1956-58, 60-63, 66, 68-70
AzTeS	1956-58, 60-65, 68-71
AzU	1969-71
CChiS	1953, 55-58, 60-66, 68-72, 73(1)
CLU-G/G	1946-66, 68-71, 73(1)
CLhC	1947-73

(350) Wyoming Geological Association.

CSdS	1948-56, 58, 60-63, 65, 68-71, 73(1)
CSfCSM	1950, 52-56
CU-EART	1947-54, 56-66, 69-73
[CaACAM]	1947, 49, 58, 60, 63, 70, 71, 73(1)
CaACI	1947, 49, 57, 58, 60-62, 65, 66
CaACU	1947, 49-58, 61
[CaBVU]	1954, 56-61
CaOHM	1956-65
CaOKQ	1947, 53-58, 60, 61, 69, 70
CaOLU	1954, 56-58, 60-62, 68
CaOOG	1957, 60, 61, 63, 65, 66, 69.
CoDuF	1963
CoFS	1960
CoG	1946-66, 68, 69, 71, 73
CoU	1947-66, 68-72, 73(1), 74, 75
DI-GS	1946-63, 65, 68-72, 73(1), 74
ICF	1947, 50, 51, 54-58, 60-64, 69
ICIU-S	1948, 49, 56-58, 61, 68-72, 73(1)
ICarbS	1954, 56-58, 60-66, 68-70
IEN	1946, 47, 49-65, 68-73
[I-GS]	1947, 48
IU	1947-63, 65, 66, 68, 71, 73-75
IaU	1947-58, 60-66, 68-70, 74
IdBB	1956, 58, 60, 61, 68, 69
IdPI	1953-62, 73
InLP	1949, 50-54, 56-58, 60-63, 65, 66, 68-71
InRE	1954, 56, 58-61
InU	1946-63
KyU	1946-63, 65, 66, 68-71, 73, 74
LU	1948-63, 65, 68-71
MH-GS	1947, 48, 50, 56
MNS	1951, 53-58
MiDW	1949, 50, 53-64, 68, 70
MiKW	1968
MiU	1947, 49, 50, 60-66, 68-70
MnU	1948-63, 65, 66, 68, 69
MoRM	1947, 48, 53-58, 60, 61, 66
MoSW	1948-50, 53-58, 60-62, 65
MoU	1947, 48, 52-58, 61-63, 68, 70
MtBC	1947, 52, 54-62, 65, 66, 68, 69, 71, 73
MtU	1948-54, 56-71, 73
NBiSU	1956, 57, 60-63
NNC	1948-58, 60-65
NOneoU	1956, 61, 68-70
NRU	1947, 54, 56-58, 63, 68, 69, 71, 73
NSyU	1954, 56, 57, 59, 63, 68
NbU	1947-58, 60-63
NcU	1948, 50-54, 64, 65, 68, 72
NdU	1949-51, 53-58, 60-66, 68-70, 74
NhD	1949-52, 55, 57-70
NjP	1947-66, 68-74
NmPE	1958, 63, 68, 71, 73
NvLN	1956, 57, 60
NvU	1949, 53-64

OCU	1947, 54, 56-58, 60-66, 68-74
OU	1947-49, 51-58, 60-66, 68-71
[OkOkCGe]	1948-50, 52, 54, 58, 62, 63, 66, 68
OkT	1947-58, 60, 61
OkU	1946-58, 60-73
OrCS	1947, 49-63, 65, 66, 68-73
OrU	1949, 51-66, 68-73
PBL	1954, 56-62, 65, 66, 68-70
PBm	1947, 54, 56-58, 60, 73
PPiGulf	1947-49, 51, 52, 54-58, 61, 71
PSt	1947, 53-65, 68-71
RPB	1953-68
SdRM	1947-70
TMM	1956, 60, 61, 65, 66, 68, 69
TU	1956, 57, 60-63, 65
TxDaAR-T	1946-58, 60-63, 65, 66, 68-73
TxDaDM	1947-50, 52-66, 68-74
TxDaM	1947-66
TxDaSM	1947, 49-58, 60-63, 65, 66, 68-71, 73
TxHSD	1947-52, 54, 56-58, 60-63, 65, 66, 68-71, 73(1)
TxHU	1948, 50-69
TxMM	1947-63, 65, 66, 68-71, 73
TxU	1947-66, 68-71
TxU-Da	1947, 49, 51-63, 65, 66, 69
UU	1948, 49, 51-54, 56-58, 60-63, 65, 66, 68-72
ViBlbV	1953-58, 60, 61, 63
WU	1950-66, 68-71, 73, 74
WyU	1946-69

(351) WYOMING. GEOLOGICAL SURVEY.

1937 See Rocky Mountain Association of Geologists. (250)

(352) WYOMING. GEOLOGICAL SURVEY. BULLETIN.

1971 No. 55 Traveler's guide to the geology of Wyoming.

CaOLU	1971
ICF	1971
IU	1971
NdU	1971
OkU	1971

(353) WYOMING. UNIVERSITY. DEPARTMENT OF GEOLOGY. CONTRIBUTIONS TO GEOLOGY. (TITLE VARIES)

1969 Wyoming uranium issue. (273)

1971 Wyoming trona issue. (273)

IU	1969, 71
OkU	1969
OrU	1971

(354) YELLOWSTONE-BIG HORN RESEARCH ASSOCIATION.

1937 See Rocky Mountain Association of Geologists. (250)
1947 See Wyoming Geological Association. (350)
1958 See Montana Geological Society. (186)

(355) MISCELLANEOUS GUIDEBOOKS

1 Adams, Virginia. Illustrated guide to Yosemite Valley, by Virginia and Ansel Adams. 1952. 128 p. OkU.

2 Allen, John Eliot. Geologic field guide to the northwest Oregon coast, by John Eliot Allen and Robert VanAtta. Portland, OR, Portland State College, 1964. 39 p. IU.

3 Alt, David D. and Donald W. Hyndman. Roadside geology of northern California. Missoula, MT, Mountain Press Publishing Co., 1975. 244 p. CLU-G/G, CU-EART, CaOOG, DLC, IU, InLP, KyU, MH-GS, OU, OkU. KyU, MH-GS, OU, OkU.

4 Alt, David D. Rocks, ice and water. The geology of Waterton-Glacier Park. Missoula, MT, Mountain Press Publishing Company, 1973. CLU-G/G.

5 Aufmuth, Ray. Four day field trip to central Kentucky, by Ray Aufmuth et al. John K. Pope, Field Trip Chairman. Oxford, OH, Miami University, Department of Geology. 1965. OU.

6 Bacon, Edwin M. Boston; MA a guidebook to the city and vicinity by Edwin M. Bacon, revised by LeRoy Phillips. Boston, MA, Ginn & Company, 1903. CaOOG.

7 Banks, P. O. Guide to the geology of northeastern Ohio. Edited by P. O. Banks and Rodney M. Feldmann. Cleveland? Northern Ohio Geological Society, 1970. 168 p. OU.

9 Bohakel, Charles A. A guidebook to: Mt. Diablo, the "Devil" Mountain of California, by Charles A. Bohakel. Revised edition, 1973. 20 p. CU-EART.

10 Brewster, Eugene B. Guidebook to the Paleozoic rocks of northwest Arkansas, prepared by Eugene B. Brewster and Norman F. Williams. Little Rock, Arkansas Geological and Conservation Commission, 1955. OkU.

11 Camsell, Charles. Guide to the geology of the Canadian National Park on the Canadian Pacific railway between Calgary and Revelstoke. Department of the Interior, Ottawa, Ontario. (Material taken largely from the guidebooks by D. B. Dowling, J. A. Allan and R. A. Daly for the excursions of the 20th International Geological Congress and published by the Survey.) 1914. OkU.

12 Canada: Department of Northern Affairs and National Resources, National Parks Branch, Education and Interpretive Section. A guide to geology for visitors in Canada's National Parks. 1960. NOneoU.

13 Christiansen, R. L., Poole, F. G., et al. Guidebook for past field trips to the Nevada test site. U. S. Geological Survey Open File Report, 1969. NvU.

14 Coates, Donald R. Glacial geology of the Binghamton-western Catskill region. Binghamton, NY, State University of New York. (SUNY Binghamton, publications in geomorphology, Contribution No. 3.), 1973. NSyU.

15 Conkin, James Elvin and Barbara M. Conkin. Guide to the rocks and fossils of Jefferson County, Kentucky, southern Indiana and adjacent areas. [Louisville, KY, Univ. of Louisville Printing Services, 1972]. 331 p. IU

16 Davis, James F. Field guide to the central portion of the southern Adirondacks. Albany, NY. New York State University Educational Leaflet Series No. 2, 1962. PBL.

17 Denis, R. et G. Prichonnet. Colloque [sur] le Quaternaire du Quebec, 2d: Aspects du Quaternaire dans la region au nord de Joliette, Montreal, Quebec, 1973. n.p. CaOOG.

18 DeWindt, J. Thomas. Geology of the Great Smoky Mountains, Tennessee and North Carolina, with road log for field excursion, Knoxville-Clingmans Dome-Maryville, by J. Thomas DeWindt. Printed in The Compass, Sigma Gamma Epsilon, 1975. 129 p. IU.

19 Eisbacher, G. Geological Association of Canada. Cordilleran Section. Vancouver geology; a short guide, Vancouver, the Section, 1973. 56 p. CaOOG.

20 Fichter, H. Ardmore Basin-Arbuckle Mountain field trip. Prepared by H. J. Fichter [and] B. O. Prescott. Revised by B. O. Prescott and N. J. Ellis. [Oklahoma City?], 1956.

21 Finlay, George Irving. A guidebook describing the rock formations in the vicinity of Colorado Springs. Colorado Springs, CO, The Out West Company. CoDUF.

22 Gaenslen, George. A trip on glacial geology in the North Kettle moraine area. Milwaukee Public Museum, Milwaukee, Wisconsin. Lore Leaves, No. 11, 1969. WM.

23 Gander Conference. Geology along the North Atlantic; field trips. (Field trips are in Newfoundland.) Sponsored by Columbia University. [Distributed by] New York, NY, Department of Geology, Columbia University, [1967]. 36 p. DLC, MH-GS, OU, WU.

24 Gentile, Richard J. Guidebook to the field trips held in conjunction with the Symposium on the development and utilization of underground space. Kansas City, Missouri; sponsored by the Department of Geosciences, University of Missouri-Kansas City, and supported by local underground industry in Greater Kansas City and the National Science Foundation, Washington, D.C. [Kansas City, MO, Department of Geosciences, University of Missouri-Kansas City, 1975]. IU.

25 Geology, landscape, and mineral resources, Camp Naish area, Wyandotte County. Geologic Field Conference for Kansas School Teachers, No. 1. Camp Naish, Wyandotte County. Kansas. Lawrence, KS, State Geological Survey, 1956. 25 p. OU.

26 Greeley, Ronald. Hawaiian Planetology Conference, Mars Geologic Mappers Meeting, Hilo, Hawaii. Guidebook to the Hawaiian planetology conference. (comment edition) Moffet Field, CA, NASA-Ames Research Center. (Government Printing Office), 1974. 257 p. CLU-G/G, CU-EART, MH-GS, OU, OkU, PSt.

27 Greene, D. A. Geologic road log: Tulsa to Sulphur, Oklahoma. Prepared by D. A. Greene. Log from Tulsa to Stroud modified after Oklahoma Geological Society, 1936. OkU.

28 Guillet, G. R. A geological guide to Highway 60; Algonquin Provincial Park. Ontario Department of Mines, Miscellaneous Paper No. 29, [1969]. NhD.

29 Halladay, I. A. R. and D. H. Mathewson. Canadian Exploration Frontiers Symposium: A guide to the geology of the eastern Cordillera along the Trans-Canada Highway between Calgary, Alberta and Revelstoke, British Columbia. Calgary, Alberta, Society of Petroleum Geologists, 1971. CaOOG, NBiSU.

30 Hamblin, W. Kenneth. Grand Canyon perspectives, a guide to the Canyon scenery by means of interpretive panoramas, by W. Kenneth Hamblin and Joseph R. Murphy. Provo, UT, Brigham Young University Printing Services. (Brigham Young University Geology Studies, Special Publication No. 1.), 1969. 47 p. CU-EART, IU, MiHM.

31 Hamblin, W. Kenneth. Roadside geology of U. S. Interstate 80 between Salt Lake City and San Francisco, the meaning behind the landscape, by W. Kenneth Hamblin and J. Keith Rigby, John L. Snyder, William H. Matthews, III. Sponsored by the American Geological Institute. Van Nuys, CA, Varna Enterprises, 1974. 51 p. CLU-G/G, CU-EART, CaOOG, IU, MoSW, NcU, NdU, OU, OkU.

32 Harbaugh, John Warvelle. Geology field guide to northern California [by] John W. Harbaugh. Dubuque, IA, W. C. Brown Co. (The Regional geology series), [1974]. 123 p. CSdU, DLC, ICIU-S, IU, InRE, NBiSU, NOneoU, NSyU, NcU, NhD, NvLN, OU, OkU, TMM.

33 Harksen, J. C. and Macdonald, J. R. Guidebook to the major Cenozoic deposits of southwestern South Dakota. South Dakota Geological Survey, 1969. InRE.

34 Haynes, Jack Ellis. Haynes guide: handbook of Yellowstone National Park, by Jack Ellis Haynes. 51st ed., 191 p. OkU.

35 Hodge, Dennis S. Field trip guide and road log to northern Laramie anorthosite complex by Dennis S. Hodge and Scott B. Smithson. 1971. n.p. CaOOG.

36 Houston Geological Society. Academic and Library Committee. Geology of Houston and vicinity, Texas; with appended guides to fossil, mineral, and rock collecting localities. 1961. OCU.

37 Hsu, K. Jinghwa. Preliminary report and geologic guide to the Franciscan melanges, of the Morro Bay-San Simeon area, California. PBm.

38 Humphrey, William E. Notes on the geology of northeast Mexico. Corpus Christi Geological

Society. "Text ...has been taken ...from the original English text written as an introduction to Excursion C-5 of the XXth International geological Congress to be held in Mexico, D.F." [1956?]. OkU.

39 Interstate Oil Compact Commission. Historical trip through Pennsylvania oil fields, Drake Well Memorial Park and Museum at Titusville, vanished city of Pithole, observing local geology. (Host: Pennsylvania Geological Survey), 1965. NdU.

40 Jenkins, Olaf Pitt. Geologic guidebook along Highway 49, Sierran Gold Belt, the Mother Lode country. (By Olaf P. Jenkins and others.) Centennial edition. San Francisco, CA, 1948. CoDuF.

41 Jillson, Willard Rouse. Geological excursions in Kentucky; a series of twelve descriptions of localities in and about the bluegrass region exhibiting earth phenomena of unusual interest. Frankfort, KY, Roberts Print Co., 1948. IU, OkU.

42 Johnson, Douglas Wilson. Blue book of the geological field excursion from New York to Gettysburg. New York, NY, Columbia University Press, 1926. OkU.

43 Jorgensen, Neil. A guide to New England's landscape. [Barre, MA, 1971]. NhD.

44 Langenheim, R. Geology along the highway route from Urbana, Illinois to San Francisco and Los Angeles, California and return via St. Joseph, Missouri, Denver, Colorado, Carson City, Nevada and Las Vegas, Nevada, Kingman, Arizona, Grand Canyon, Arizona, Albuquerque, New Mexico, Tulsa, Oklahoma and St. Louis, Missouri. Compiled from guidebooks of the Rocky Mountain Association of Petroleum Geologists, the Intermountain Association of Petroleum Geologists, the California Division of Mines, the New Mexico Geological Society, the Oklahoma City Geological Society; from State geological maps; and from other sources, by B. J. Bluck [and others] under the direction of R. L. Langenheim, Jr. 1962. NhD.

45 Lintz, Joseph Jr. International Conference on the Permian and Triassic Systems, Calgary. Guidebook; Permian and Triassic exposures of western North America; Calgary, Alberta to El Paso, Texas. Reno, NV, Mackay School of Mines, University of Nevada, 1971. CaOOG.

46 Lobeck, Armin Kohl. Airways of America; Guidebook No. 1. The United Airlines; a geological and geographical description of the route from New York to Chicago and San Francisco. New York, NY, the Geographical Press, Columbia University, 1933. MiHM, NhD, OkU.

47 Lobeck, Armin Kohl. Kentucky. Geological Survey. The Midland trail in Kentucky; a physiographic and geologic guidebook to U. S. Highway No. 60. (Published as an appendix to "Devonian Rocks of Kentucky" by T. E. Savage), 1971. NhD.

48 Lokke, Donald H. Selected guides for geologic field study in Canada and the United States. Englewood Cliffs, NJ, Prentice-Hall, n.d. CaOOG.

49 Lutzen, Edwin E. Guidebook to engineering geologic features and land use relationships in the St. Louis metropolitan area, by Edwin E. Lutzen [and] Paul B. DuMontelle. [Edwardsville, IL, Southern Illinois University, 1970]. [10] p. NNC.

50 Lyons, John B. Guidebook for field trips in central New Hampshire and contiguous areas, edited by John B. Lyons and Glenn W. Stewart. Concord, NH, 1971. CaOOG.

51 Macfarlane, James. An American geological railway guide, giving the geological formation at every railway station, with altitudes above mean tide-water, notes on interesting places on the routes and a description of each of the formations. New York, NY, D. Appleton and Company, 1890. ICIU-S, IU, NhD.

52 McQueen, H. S. Informal field conference, Mississippian stratigraphy, southwest Missouri. Wichita Stratigraphic Society. Rolla, MO, Missouri Geological Survey, 1936. IU.

53 Matthews, William Henry. Guidebook for geological field trips in southwestern British Columbia. Vancouver, British Columbia, Geological Discussion Club, 1960. CaOOG.

54 Muilenburg, Grace. Guidebook: geology and landscape of Camp Naish area, Wyandotte County; notes on counties in administrative area, Kaw Council, Boy Scouts of America. Prepared by G. Muilenburg and J. M. Jewett, Lawrence, KA, State Geological Survey, University of Kansas, for the Kaw Council of Boy Scouts of America. 1956. OU

55 Muilenburg, Grace. Land of the post rock: tour guide. Includes log for 2-day tour, Manhattan to Wilson Reservoir area. Prepared for University for Man, Kansas State University.

Coordinator: Steve Ernst, and UFM staff. Leaders: Grace Muilenburg and Ada Swineford. 1976. 30 p. IU.

56 Multer, H. Field guide to some carbonate rock environments; Florida Keys and western Bahamas, compiled by H. Gray Multer. [Madison, NJ, Fairleigh Dickinson University, 1971.] CaOOG, IU, NhD, OCU, OU, PBL.

57 Nason, Robert D. and Thomas H. Rogers. Hayward-Hollister field trip: Hayward, Calaveras and San Andreas Faults. (U. S. Environmental Science Services Administration, Earthquake Mechanism Laboratory and California Division of Mines and Geology), n.d., unpaginated. IU.

58 Oakeshott, Gordon B. California's changing landscapes; a guide to the geology of the state. New York, NY, McGraw-Hill, 1971. 388 p. IU, NhD, OU.

59 Oakeshott, Gordon B. A walker's guide to the geology of San Francisco, [by G. B. Oakeshott and C. Wahrhaftig]. San Francisco, CA, California Division of Mines and Geology. [1966]. 31 p. CaOOG, IU.

60 Parizek, Richard R. Hydrogeology and geochemistry of folded and faulted carbonate rocks of the central Appalachian type and related land use problems, by Richard R. Parizek, William B. White and Donald Langmuir. Washington, 1971. CaOOG.

61 Pennsylvania. Geological Survey. Geologic field trip guide, Interstate 81 from Harrisburg to Hazelton. Harrisburg, PA, n.d. IU.

62 Peterson, Helen. Peterson guide to mineral collecting, Bancroft area; including locations at Bancroft, Tory Hill, Wilberforce, Gooderham, Harcourt, Haliburton, Madoc, Quadville, Marmora, Norland, Kinmount [and] Minden. Compiled by Helen Peterson. Bancroft, Ontario, Parkwood Beach Ltd., 1970. CaOOG.

63 Pewe, Troy Lewis. Colorado River guidebook; a geologic and geographic guide from Lees Ferry to Phantom Ranch, Arizona. 2nd ed. Tempe, AZ, The Author, 1969. 78 p. CLU-G/G, IU, InLP, NSyU, NhD, NvLN, OU, OkU, PBm, UU.

64 Powell, Richard L. A guide to the caverns and geology of Cave River Valley Park and vicinity, Washington County, Indiana. Prepared for use by the members of the Sixth Annual Cave Man Expedition, 1962, unpaginated. InLP.

65 Price, Raye Carleson. Guidebook to Canyonlands country: Arches National Park, Moab, Colorado River, Canyonlands National Park. [Pasadena, CA] W. Ritchie Press [1974] 96 p. AzFU.

66 Raasch, Gilbert O. Illinois. State Geological Survey. Oregon area, Ogle and Lee counties. A field demonstration in conjunction with Earth Science Teacher Conference, Lorado Taft Field Campus. Leader: Gilbert O. Raasch. Urbana, IL, n.d. 20 p.

67 Rast, N. A guide to the geology of southern New Brunswick; from the city of Saint John to Passamaquaddy Bay by N. Rast and others, 1975, unpaginated. CaOOG.

68 Sabina, Ann P. Rocks and minerals for the collector: the Alaska Highway; Dawson Creek, British Columbia to Yukon/Alaska border. Ottawa, Geological Survey of Canada, Paper 72-32, 1973. CaOOG, IU.

69 Sanders, John Essington. Guidebook to field trip in Rockland County, New York. New York City, NY, Petroleum Exploration Society of New York, 1974. 87 p. NSyU, OU.

70 Schuberth, Christopher J. The geology of New York City and environs [by] Christopher J. Schuberth. [1st ed.] Garden City, NY. Published for the American Museum of Natural History [by] Natural History Press [1968]. 304 p. [OkOkcGE]

71 Sharp, Robert Phillip. Geology: field guide to southern California [by] Robert P. Sharp. Dubuque, IA, W. C. Brown Co. (The Regional geology series), 181 p. CChiS, [CDU], CLU-G/G, CU-EART, CaOLU, CaOOG, CoU, ICIU-S, ICarbS, IU, IdBB, InLP, KyU, MH-GS, MoSW, NvU, OU, OkU, TMM, WaPS.

72 Sheridan, Michael F. Superstition wilderness guidebook; an introduction to the geology and trails, including a roadlog of the Apache Trail and trails from First Water and Don's Camp, by Michael F. Sheridan. [1st ed.] Tempe, AZ, [1971], 52 p. [CDU], CoDuF, DLC, MH-GS, MoSW, OkU, UU.

73 Sheridan, Michael. Guidebook to the Quaternary geology of the east-central Sierra Nevada.

Phoenix, AZ, 1971. IU, NhD, NvU.

74 Skinner, Hubert C. Guidebook, southern Oklahoma field trip. 1958. OkU.

75 Souders, Vernon L. Guidebook to selected Pleistocene paleosols in eastern Nebraska, by Vernon L. Souders, John A. Elder [and] Vincent H. Dreeszen. Nebraska University. Conservation and Survey Division. Nebraska Geological Survey, 1971. 18 p. OkU.

76 Starr, Walter A., Jr. Guide to the John Muir Trail and the High Sierra region. San Francisco, CA, Sierra Club, 1967. CLU-G/G.

77 Stearns, Harold T. Geology of the Craters of the Moon National Monument, Idaho. Arco; Craters of the Moon National History Association, published in cooperation with the National Park Service, 1963. IdPI.

78 Stearns, Harold T. Road guide to points of geologic interest in the Hawaiian Islands by Harold T. Stearns. Palo Alto, CA, Pacific Books. CaOOG, KyU, IU.

79 Stoller, James Hough. Geological excursions; a guide to localities in the region of Schenectady and the Mohawk Valley and the vicinity of Saratoga Springs, 1930. NBiSU.

80 Stout, T. M., et al. Guidebook to the late Pliocene and early Pleistocene of Nebraska. [Lincoln, NB, University of Nebraska, Conservation and Survey Division, 1971.] NhD, OkU.

81 Strahler, Arthur Newell. Guide to outer Cape Cod and the Cape Cod national seashore. Prepared by A. N. Strahler for field trip of the Association of American Geographers, 1971. 6 p. MH-GS.

82 Strawn, Mary and Devlin L. Williams. Idaho. Parks and Recreation Department. Boise, Idaho. The geology of Massacre Rocks State Park. Boise, ID, n.d. IDPI.

83 Strong, D. F. Metallogeny and plate tectonics; a guidebook to Newfoundland mineral deposits. (Title page: Plate tectonic setting of Newfoundland mineral occurrences.) NATO Advanced Studies Institute, 1974. IU, WU.

84 Stumm, Erwin C., et al. Devonian strata of the London-Sarnia area, southwestern Ontario, Canada. 1956. InRE.

85 Terasmae, J. Quaternary stratigraphy symposium; abstracts with program. Toronto, Canada, York University [1975]. IU.

86 Untermann, G. E. and B. R. Untermann. A popular guide to the geology of Dinosaur National Monument. Dinosaur Nature Association, Dinosaur National Monument, Utah-Colorado, 1969. UU.

87 Wegemann, Carroll H. A guide to the geology of Rocky Mountain National Park, Colorado. Washington, D.C., Government Printing Office, 1944. CLU-G/G.

88 West, Robert M. Field conference on Tertiary biostratigraphy of southern and western Wyoming. Garden City, NY, Adelphi University Department of Biology, 1972. 101 p. MiU, OU.

89 Wheelock, Walt. Desert Peaks guide; Part I. Glendale, CA, La Siesta Press, 1964. 40 p. CSfCSM.

90 Wyckoff, Jerome. The Adirondack landscape, its geology and landforms; a hiker's guide. Adirondack Mountain Club [1967]. NhD.

91 Zakrzewska-Borowiecki, Barbara. Landscapes of Wisconsin; a field guide. Prepared for the 1975 National Meetings of the Association of American Geographers, Milwaukee, WI. WU.

GEOGRAPHIC INDEX

Arkansas

California

Colorado

Central, South 12—1961(A-2); 96—1960(A-2); 147—1930, 58; 230—1956(Sept.); 250—1961
Central, West 12—1961(A-1); 96—1960(A-1)
North 100—1965(2)
Northwest 133—1955; 250—1953, 62(13th)
South 241—1938
Southeast 241—1951, 55; 250—1968

Big Thompson Canyon 100—1965(6)
Boulder 12—1948(1); 134—1965(K)
Canon City 12—1948(2); 96—1960(C-1); 250—1954(2)
Climax 12—1961(B-3); 96—1960(B-3)
Colorado National Monument 12—1961(A-1)
Colorado Plateau 50—1974; 136—1933(18)
Colorado Springs 12—1948(2), 60(C-1); 96—1960(C-1); 250—1954(1); 355—21
Denver 12—1948(1-3), 60(C-6); 250—1954(1,2)
Denver Basin 250—1963
Denver Mountain 12—1972(1)
Dinosaur National Monument 355—86
Durango 17—1964
Estes Park 92—1952
Fort Collins 100—1965(5)
Front Range 12—1961(B-1,B-2,C-3 thru C-5), thru C-5), 72(SEPM 1); 96—1960(B-1,B-2,C-4 thru C-6); 100—1958, 67, 73(1); 147—1929, 38; 241—1946; 250—1955, 62(1), 70, 73; 274—1972(1)
Glenwood Springs 12—1948(3)
Golden 12—1948(1)
Gypsum Valley 326—1948
Leadville 12—1948(3)
Morrison 12—1948(1)
North Park 350—1953
Orient Mine 12—1961(A-2)
Paradox Basin 12—1972(SEPM 2); 274—1972(2)
Parks Basin 250—1957
Piceance Creek Basin 250—1965, 74
Raton Basin 250—1956, 69
Raton Mesa 12—1961(A-2)
Rifle 12—1948(3)
Rocky Mountain National Park 355—87
Rocky Mountains, Central 250—1964, 75
San Juan Basin 207—1950, 77
San Juan Mountains 113—1961; 207—1957
San Luis Basin 207—1971
Sangre de Cristo Mountains 12—1961(A-2)
Silverton 17—1964
South Park 12—1948(3)
Twin Lakes 92—1953
Uinta Basin 250—1965

Connecticut

General 70—1968(2nd,B-4); 204—1975(B-7)
Central 70—1968(C-2,F-6); 204—1953
Central, South 70—1968(C-4,D-1), 70
East 70—1968(F-4)
North 204—1975
Northeast 70—1968(F-5)
Northwest 204—1975(B-5,B-8)
South 70—1968(C-2)
Southeast 96—1963(2)
Southwest 70—1968(B-3,D-6)
West 70—1968(B-1,B-2,D-2); 204—1953(B)

Berkshire Massif 204—1975(B-3)
Burlington 204—1948(2)
Coastal 70—1965, 68(A-1); 96—1963(5)
Collinsville 70—1968(D-4)
Connecticut Valley 70—1968(C-1,C-5); 204—1957
Dinosaur Park 70—1968(C-3)
Glenville 70—1968(D-6)
Hartford 38—1953; 204—1953(A,C)
Honey Hill Fault 70—1968(F-1)
Killingworth Dome 70—1968(F-3)
Lake Char Fault 70—1968(F-1)
Long Island Sound 70—1968(E-1)
Manchester 204—1953(D)
Naugatuck 70—1968(B-1,D-2)
New Haven 70—1968(D-2); 204—1953(E)
Oxford 70—1968(B-2)
Rockville 204—1953(D)
Rocky Hill 70—1968(C-3)
Thomaston 70—1968(B-2,D-5)
Torrington 70—1968(B-1)
U. S. Highway 77 204—1953(A)
Waterbury 70—1968(B-2,D-5)
Westport 70—1968(D-2)

Delaware

General 43—1967; 96—1957(6)
North 193—1958

Coastal Plain 43—1961, 71, 73; 96—1971(1)
Lewes 278—1968
Rehoboth Beach 278—1968

District of Columbia

General 136—1891(A), 1933(16th); 137—1962

Florida

General 38—1952; 102—1967(3); 143—1972; 163—1969(3rd); 193—1963; 277—1956; 291—1967; 301—1964
Central 291—1947, 60
Central, West 96—1964(6); 291—1975
North 112—1967; 291—1966, 71; 301—1967
South 96—1964(1,3,7,10), 74(6); 163—1968; 230—1970; 291—1954
Southeast 96—1964(4)
Southwest 274—1969(4)
West 102—1967(2); 291—1945

Alligator Point 102—1967(1)
Barrier Islands 96—1974(5)
Everglades 29—1972(2); 96—1974(6)
Everglades National Park 163—1967
Florida Keys 96—1974(12); 163—1969, 71; 208—1975; 277—1969(1); 291—1973; 355—56
Great Bahama Bank 96—1964(2)
Key Largo 29—1972(1)

Mississippi

Missouri

Montana

Nebraska

Nevada

Oklahoma

Oregon

Pennsylvania

Utah

Vermont

Barbados
General 21—1970

Bermuda
General 48—1970

Cuba
General 21—1970; 73—1938

Dominican Republic
General 21—1970

Haiti
General 21—1970

Jamaica
General 21—1970; 96—1974(1); 274—1969(5)

Puerto Rico
General 21—1970; 40—1970(6); 96—1964(9); 106—1966
Central 62—1959; 110—1959
West 62—1959; 110—1959
Guayanes River 40—1968

Trinidad and Tobago
General 21—1970

Virgin Islands
General 62—1968
St. Croix 62—1968(2)
St. John 62—1968(1)
St. Thomas 62—1968(1)

CORRECTIONS
TO THE 3RD EDITION

In order to make the 4th edition of the *Union List of Geologic Field Trip Guidebooks of North America* as current, complete, and accurate as possible, we welcome corrections to this edition. Please fill in all the information requested below, including the 3rd edition page number on which it appears.

____
Society no. Society name page no.
____
Year Series or ID no. (if any) Full title page no.
____
Check one: We do hold ☐ We do *not* hold ☐

____
Society no. Society name page no.
____
Year Series or ID no. (if any) Full title page no.
____
Check one: We do hold ☐ We do *not* hold ☐

____
Society no. Society name page no.
____
Year Series or ID no. (if any) Full title page no.
____
Check one: We do hold ☐ We do *not* hold ☐

Library symbol: _______________

Library: _______________

____

____

____

Respondent: _______________

Date: _______________

Return to:

UNION LIST UPDATE
American Geological Institute
5205 Leesburg Pike
Falls Church, VA 22041

YOU MAY PHOTOCOPY THIS PAGE